Professionals in
Western Film and Fiction

ALSO BY KENNETH E. HALL

John Woo: The Films, 2d ed. (McFarland, 2012)

*Stonewall Jackson and Religious Faith
in Military Command* (McFarland, 2005)

Professionals in Western Film and Fiction

The Portrayal of Doctors, Lawyers, Journalists, Clergymen and Others

Kenneth E. Hall

Foreword by
Peter Noçon *and* Peter Bischoff

McFarland & Company, Inc., Publishers
Jefferson, North Carolina

ISBN (print) 978-0-7864-9729-4
ISBN (ebook) 978-1-4766-3599-6

LIBRARY OF CONGRESS AND BRITISH LIBRARY
CATALOGUING DATA ARE AVAILABLE

© 2019 Kenneth E. Hall. All rights reserved

No part of this book may be reproduced or transmitted in any form or by any means, electronic or mechanical, including photocopying or recording, or by any information storage and retrieval system, without permission in writing from the publisher.

Front cover: Kirk Douglas as Doc Holliday in the 1957 film *Gunfight at the O.K. Corral* (Paramount Pictures/Photofest)

Printed in the United States of America

McFarland & Company, Inc., Publishers
Box 611, Jefferson, North Carolina 28640
www.mcfarlandpub.com

For Carla

Acknowledgments

Among those with whom I have consulted in preparing this study, I wish to single out my friend and colleague Christian Krug, who suggested to me the term "civil professionals," which has been of great assistance in focusing my work. I would also like to thank professors Peter Bischoff and Peter Noçon for contributing the foreword. Professor Junko Tezuka-Arnold, of East Tennessee State University, graciously provided me with Japanese-language assistance. Professor Joshua Reid, also of East Tennessee State University, and Professor Emeritus Gene Dubois, of the University of North Dakota, assisted me with references on medieval chivalry. Professor Stephen L. Tanner assisted me with the sequencing of the Toole novels by Richard S. Wheeler. I have also been greatly assisted by consulting the website https://pro.imdb.com for film information.

Table of Contents

Acknowledgments	vi
Foreword by Peter Noçon and Peter Bischoff	1
Introduction	5
1. Professional Case Studies: Doctors on the Frontier	7
2. Professional Allies: Lawyers, Gunsmiths and Other Fixers	30
3. Masquerades: Civil Professionals in Disguise	66
4. Encroachments of Culture: The Frontier in History and Fiction	108
5. Professionals as Civilization Meets Barbarism	115
6. Professionals Across the Border: Mexican Revolution Fiction and "Professional Westerns"	131
Chapter Notes	169
Works Cited	180
Index	211

Foreword
by Peter Noçon and Peter Bischoff

It is a pleasure for us to provide the foreword to a book written by our good friend and stalwart member of The German Association for the Study of the Western. This is an all-inclusive thesaurus-like study of Western film and fiction aimed at both the aficionado and the general reader interested in the subject. Ken Hall not only places the films and fictions in their historical context, he establishes a political and ideological link to the period of their origin, thereby attracting his readers' curiosity and sustaining their involvement throughout. He evidently draws from an abundance of scholarly expertise and acumen enabling him to detect connections between even disparate phenomena.

Hall chooses an unusual approach to the Western. Rather than focusing on overworked and thus exhausted law-enforcing officers, gunfighters, ranchers, and dancehall girls, he opts for less frequently treated character types such as doctors, lawyers, and journalists. Even though one might not agree with Hall's understanding of the term "civil professionals," there can be no doubt that he exhaustively treats those he regards as such. According to a personal notice by the author, he wanted to "include a gamut of people in the West with either education or special training; [he] needed to limit the scope to exclude lawmen, who often were not specially trained or regular workers, who of course learned skills but didn't set up shop like a blacksmith or an assayer."

Apropos of the approach applied, Hall relies on a tried and tested method of analyzing the presence and function of a character type in a variety of movies. His catholic approach is put to good use when he establishes links to other genres such as science fiction and *film noir*. He succeeds in making

Foreword by Peter Noçon and Peter Bischoff

connections between movie contents and audience reception. Typically, he draws parallels between professionals in a Western ambience and World War II and Vietnam veterans, his prime example being *Bad Day at Black Rock*.

Hall exhibits a stupendous wealth of materials ranging from both well-established and minor Westerns via North American writers from O. Henry to Latin American authors of great repute such as Carlos Fuentes.

Selected examples of Hall's approach provide an acute insight into plot construction and character analysis. Of course, he refers to a great number of movies in several of his six chapters. We single out the most often referred-to specimens: *The Man Who Shot Liberty Valance, Bad Day at Black Rock,* and *Five-Card Stud.*

Hall is keen on asserting the outstanding position of *The Man Who Shot Liberty Valance* in any study of the Western, since the movie features all the character types that go into the making of a frontier society and thus provide a cross section of civil professionals who act interconnectedly in the establishment of order and civilization on the American frontier.

Of the many characters peopling the frontier it is probably the ubiquitous newspaperman who is most in the limelight. Gary McCarthy's "Derby Man" novels, for instance, revolve around a journalist who has arrived in the West to report to his readers the "truth" of frontier life; a tinhorn in the beginning, he is initiated into Western life to which he then contributes his Eastern knowledge and civilization thus tying East and West inextricably.

As for frontier newspapers, Hall emphasizes the political role played by frontier newspapers referenced by the "Knight thesis" arguing for "the frontier newpaper as a catalyst in social change" and the countervailing "Lyon thesis," according to which "the editor [was] bound and hemmed in by the norms of his frontier community." As an example of adopted opposing positions in the conflict between the Earps and the Clantons mounting to the gunfight at the O.K. Corral on October 26, 1881, Hall mentions John P. Clum's Republican and business-oriented *Epitaph* (supporting the Earps) and Richard Rule's *Nugget* (siding with the cowboy factions of the Clantons). It becomes obvious from Hall's discussions that the linking of ideas and characters is the ultimate benchmark to which all Westerns aspire: East vs. West, civilization vs. barbarism, order vs. lawlessness, fixed social norms vs. freedom. Again, *The Man Who Shot Liberty Valance* can be adduced as proof, centering on the enmity between the two titular characters, the lawyer and the outlaw. John Ford sophisticates

Foreword by Peter Noçon and Peter Bischoff

the formula in that he introduces a character who belongs to the Liberty Valance world of unruliness but is open to a new world of order and civic conventions. It is through the mutual interactions of the different character types that the plot gains momentum and conflicting ideas are debated and, finally, resolved.

Bad Day at Black Rock is perhaps the prime example of the interrelatedness between the foundation of a civic society in the West and the destiny of soldiers returning from war. At the time the movie was made, America was in the grip of this question which was still waiting for an answer. What could the many returning civil professionals do to reestablish a community that had been disrupted by the war? How could a backslide into disorderliness be counteracted? The community still has to reaccommodate itself to a changing view of friend and foe and, in a state of transition, is in need of an outsider to become aware of and find a solution to its problems. The community's dirty linen includes the murder of a Japanese American as the result of greed and prejudice; it threatens to be continued in an attempt on the outsider's life, which, however, is unsuccessful and ironically prepares for a return of civilization.

Hall is at his best when he turns to those civil professionals who put on a masquerade to conceal their real agenda. This is best exemplified by the preacher who exploits the traditional associations with his avocation to further his very specific aims. A case in point is *Five-Card Stud*, in which a dissembling man of the frock is in reality the avenger of his lynched brother.

Hall is at home in both the world of film and that of literature. This is attested to by his voluminous bibliography and the critical apparatus he appends. We wholeheartedly commend his valuable book to a wide readership not least because it opens up new vistas of the frontier while, at the same time, reinforcing, albeit with a slightly different slant, timehallowed ideas of the West.

—The German Association for the Study of the Western

Dr. Peter Noçon, president of the German Association for the Study of the Western, is a former professor of English and American literature and media studies, and the author of numerous articles.

Dr. Peter Bischoff (1942–2019) was crucial as leader of the above Association, taught at the University of Münster and wrote articles on a broad range of Western film topics.

Introduction

Genre film and fiction such as the American Western feature recurring character types, including the gunfighter,[1] the lawman, the rancher, and the dancehall girl. Many examples of these types have been discussed in criticism and have entered the public consciousness as part of the Western genre. Less attention has been paid to the role of civil professionals like the journalist, physician, and clergyman in Westerns, whether in printed fiction or in film. In the case of Westerns, it is often very useful to study both novel or short story and film, as both fields are rich in samples for research and because they frequently interact, as Western films have frequently been adaptations of novels, short stories, or magazine articles.

These character types are also significant to fiction and film about the Mexican Revolution of 1910. Such narratives sometimes have connections to American Westerns through Hollywood examples, such as *The Wild Bunch* and *The Professionals*. Among the important fictions about the Mexican Revolution are the novel *Los de abajo* by medical doctor-turned-writer Mariano Azuela, which features a fellow traveler of the Revolution who had been an aspiring physician, and the works of journalist and politician Martín Luis Guzmán, who integrated reportage in his novel *La sombra del caudillo*. Professional characters, as representatives of a growing urban middle class, appear in Mexican Revolution fiction (as well as in regionalist fiction from other Latin-American countries), in which they represent both civilizing and corrupting forces. These dual functions also appear commonly in Westerns, where on occasion members of the two professions (law enforcement and civil) work together, or against each other, depending upon their relative places along the spectrum between reform and corruption.

Besides the socializing importance of professional figures like journalists and doctors in Westerns and in Mexican Revolution fiction and

Introduction

film, such characters often appear at the service of, or occasionally as a counter to, mythmaking. The most readily remembered example of this is newspaper editor Dutton Peabody in Ford's *The Man Who Shot Liberty Valance*, with his familiar "Print the legend" line.[2] Both this film and Eastwood's *Unforgiven* employ the journalist character to debunk or to question received legend; both films can also be discussed in terms of their treatment of the law and (especially in the Ford film) of the lawyer character. Many of the professional characters in Westerns are also disguised versions of pastoral stock characters and their permutations are often indicative of the contextual environment of the narratives in which they appear. *The Man Who Shot Liberty Valance* is also particularly useful in illustrating one of the essential myths of the Western, the pastoral, which often presents itself in terms of an Easterner coming West to encounter untamed, vicious adversaries. Such Easterners are likely to be professional types—lawyer, engineer, teacher, doctor—and their civilized values are tested and molded when confronted with lawless savagery like that of Liberty Valance. Ian Marshall provides a nice summary of "the images that embody the idea of the Easterner ... [which] grow out of the western literary tradition":

> Where the East is intellectual, the West is physical; if the East is renowned for culture, the West celebrates nature. The Easterner is bookish, the Westerner full of *real* life [original italics]. The East is mannered and genteel, the West forthright and bold. The East is establishment, the West non-conformist [Marshall, I. 230].

Sometimes the professional must leave the accustomed environs of the town and confront the unbridled limits of the wilderness; more rarely, the professional has adapted thoroughly to the wild environment or is, in fact, a central part of it, as in Brooks's *The Professionals*; or, the professional character, like Wyatt Earp in Ford's *My Darling Clementine*, may re-enter a civilized environment after a sojourn in the wilderness and confront threats to the integrity of that civilization. In other cases, the professional is town-bound, like the veterinarian/doctor in *No Name on the Bullet*, and must confront a threat to the stability of the town, usually from outside, or perhaps try to resolve a problem from within the community. Of course, this kind of situation is normally the purview of the sheriff or marshal, both professionals and so endemic to the Western that we will only discuss their roles in unusual cases; but in films like *No Name on the Bullet*, another professional must lead the town after the failure of the sheriff to do so.

1

Professional Case Studies
Doctors on the Frontier

Professionals are generally a mark of urban civilization,[1] and in the Western the contrast between the township model from the East and the wildness of the frontier is often expressed within the pastoral complex, in which the professional character is a signal of distortion heralding an era of change.[2] This heralding of change applies particularly to the civil professional, a person not directly connected to law enforcement duties: the doctor, the clergyman, the teacher, and so forth. Citing John G. Cawelti (Cawelti, *The Six-Gun Mystique* 100) and Pam Cook (Cook 65), David Pierson notes that in Westerns "audiences can contemplate the passing of the frontier and the transition to social and cultural structures linked to the present," and can experience "a rich cross section of character types (e.g., farmer, banker, schoolmarm, prostitute) ... within modern stories that represent ongoing social and ideological struggles ... in contemporary American society" (Pierson 286). Tom Engelhardt provides a more cynical, or perhaps more realistic, view of the types presented in Westerns: "The whites portrayed in westerns or adventure films were the romanticized flotsam and jetsam of Western society—mercenaries, prostitutes, con artists, opportunists, thieves, and killers" (Engelhardt 40). R. Philip Loy observes that in Westerns until the mid–1950s "small businessmen and entrepreneurs" are the most commonly presented civil professionals, although other kinds of "professionals such as lawyers, medical doctors, veterinarians and teachers" also "show up as both good and bad guys" (Loy, *Westerns and American Culture, 1930–1955* 166–67).

In this connection, the classification of "types" by Peter Homans is helpful. Concerned primarily with the Western as a form of popular culture, Homans defines "type" as "an important figure recurring again and again, whose basic actions and patterns of relationship are relatively enduring from one version of the story to another" (Homans 76). Two of the Western types delineated by Homans are "the 'derelict-professional'" and "the 'non-violent Easterner.'" He defines the derelict-professional as "one who was originally trained in one of the traditional eastern professions ... but who has ... become corrupted," citing Doc Holliday as a famous example. The second type includes businessmen and pastors (Homans 76). In either case, the (civil) professional character often displays "Eastern" qualities on the frontier.

Thus, the familiar collision between Eastern civility and Western roughness may be highlighted by an emphasis on professions. Such is the case in Ford's *The Man Who Shot Liberty Valance*, in which the Eastern lawyer Ranse Stoddard comes to the isolated town of Shinbone to practice his legal profession but in fact must exercise a series of roles:

> Ranse ... is virtually defined by his professional adaptability. During his brief stay in Shinbone, he is shown or referred to as lawyer, dishwasher, waiter, reporter, schoolteacher, election official, gunman and convention delegate [Coursen 240].

Unlike Tom Doniphon (John Wayne) and Liberty Valance (Lee Marvin), who "alike find themselves trapped in obsolescent careers, each incapable of changing," Ranse is the new organization man, eventually becoming U.S. senator for the new state (Coursen 240). Douglas Pye classifies Valance as a "bad Westerner," Doniphon as a "good Westerner," and Stoddard as an "Easterner" but qualifies the Easterner observation with a brief summary of the type in Westerns:

> The Easterner who arrives in a Western town untutored in Western mores and values is present in the earliest film Westerns.... As he develops [as a type], the Easterner is characteristically weak, misguided and powerless.... But by 1912, and perhaps earlier, there were films ... in which the Easterner, initially humiliated, deliberately takes on Western characteristics ... to revenge himself.... He becomes ... a Westerner [Pye, "Genre and History" 119–20].

A. Carl Bredahl, Jr., groups Doniphon and Valance together; they "are part of the same world that has yielded its energy to the law books of Ransom Stoddard.... Ranse, in the restaurant scene, even yells that Tom is no different from Liberty" (Bredahl 288). As Matthew J. Costello observes, regarding another seminal Western of the period, when its titular hero, Shane, leaves the valley after dispatching the threat to the homesteaders, "The independent male [Shane, but also the Rykers] is gone, replaced by the organizational man [like Joe Starrett, leader of the farmers]—applying scientific

1. Professional Case Studies

methods to his work, building the community and the family, but never demonstrating the brutal and wonderful elements that paved the way for the bureaucratized suburban community of today" (Costello, "'I Didn't Expect'" 267; see also J.E. Smyth, "The Organization Woman Behind *The Man in the Gray Flannel Suit*," *Camera Obscura* 27.2 [2012]: 61–91).

Sometimes the newer brand of professional is highlighted as a contrast to the older ways of the wilder or more pastoral characters, but without the older type of character losing social value, as in *El Dorado* (Howard Hawks, 1966), in which the rough ex-sheriff Cole Thornton (John Wayne), who carries a bullet near his spine after an encounter with Joey (Michele Carey), the sharpshooting daughter of a landowner (R.G. Armstrong), reluctantly consults a young doctor (Anthony Rogers), who is clearly Eastern-educated, expert, and professionally precise (in the Homans schema, a "'non-violent Easterner'"). (The young Dr. Charles Donovan is recommended to Thornton by the older Dr. Miller [Paul Fix], who frankly admits to lacking the expertise for the delicate procedure required.) The Hawks film lands on the side of Eastern expertise, as Cole agrees to have the young surgeon perform the recommended procedure after the immediate threat to him and his friends is resolved.

This ready acceptance of Eastern professionalism does not extend to Wayne's rough and ready Union Cavalry Colonel John Marlowe in *The Horse Soldiers* (John Ford, 1959), as the colonel spitefully rejects the military doctor's advice and assistance, refusing even to accept him as a fellow officer. His resentment is revealed to stem from the failure of doctors to save his ailing wife. By film's end, the colonel has become able to accept the doctor, Major Henry Kendall (William Holden), as a fellow professional and even as a newfound friend. As in many other American films of the 1950s, the level of cooperation between sectors of society may indicate the political stance of the film, as Peter Biskind argues in his *Seeing Is Believing*; thus, because of the eventual truce between doctor and military man, *The Horse Soldiers* would qualify in Biskind's schema as a "corporate liberal" film. J.A. Place believes that the importance accorded a doctor such as Kendall demonstrates "that Ford is changing his earlier faith in the ability of a military organization to provide its members with a meaning and a rationale greater than any individual," because "Kendall is an individual, isolated from the camaraderie of his profession by being in the army and from the camaraderie of the army by being a doctor" (Place 176–77).

Professionals in Western Film and Fiction

Still, the confluence of social roles in Westerns has a particular poignancy not present in a "corporate liberal" film like *Panic in the Streets* (Elia Kazan, 1950): the doctor in Ford's film stands out for us not only because of his relevance to contemporary politics but even more so because he represents a civilizing, Eastern force being brought to bear upon the rough frontier (in this case, of course, not the West but Confederate Mississippi, coded in this film as a kind of Wild West, frontier-like area, outside Union control and thus subject to harsh measures of wartime). At film's end, Holden's doctor offers himself as a putative bridge between the warring sides by volunteering to stay with the wounded of both sides. He knows that the Confederate forces will soon arrive and that he will become a prisoner of war, although perhaps not subject to the harsh treatment made notorious by the history of Andersonville prison camp in southern Georgia.

An innovative variation on the doctor in the military formula employed in films like *The Horse Soldiers* appears in a 1954 film from Warner Bros., *The Command* (David Butler). Based on a James Warner Bellah novel and adapted by screenwriter Samuel Fuller, the film unusually, and often realistically, portrays a conflict within a cavalry troop on the far Northwestern frontier as well as its less-than-friendly rivalry with an infantry command. When the troop commander is fatally wounded by Arapahoes,[3] he orders the troop doctor, Captain Robert MacClaw (Guy Madison), to take over command of the troop despite the presence of the very experienced Sergeant Elliott (James Whitmore). Not only do the troopers show skepticism about the leadership qualities of the doctor, they are openly reluctant—an opinion expressed forcefully for them by Elliott— to enter the settlement of Cashman, guarded by an infantry regiment, because of their fear of ridicule as "nurses" working for the doctor.

Unlike many military-themed Westerns where the divide between cavalry and infantry is glossed over, this film clearly displays the often bitter fissures between types of military men on the frontier. Such fissures are embodied here in the acerbic, dyspeptic Colonel Janeway (Carl Benton Reid), an infantry commander with scant patience for the cavalry's supposed tendency to glory hound. In turn, the doctor is reluctant to reveal his true position as medical officer (he wears the dead captain's slashes over his medical insignia) due to his concern about being taken seriously by the colonel. Despite serious health problems with the wagon train he and his men have been detailed to protect—smallpox is suspected—and

1. Professional Case Studies

with the colonel, who is a prime candidate for a stroke,[4] MacClaw reveals himself only to Martha Cutting (Joan Weldon), whose late father was a doctor.

In a role reminiscent of the historical Joshua Lawrence Chamberlain, a professor at Bowdoin College who put his intelligence and native guile to great use in the Civil War, distinguishing himself in battle on several occasions but most famously at Little Round Top at Gettysburg, where he employed a classical maneuver to frustrate furious Confederate charges, MacClaw proves to be a resourceful and courageous commander who employs innovative techniques to bring the wagon train and many of his men to safety.[5] In the process, he wins Martha and gains the respect of his men and of the colonel. Nevertheless he scolds Martha for not following his instructions to burn all items in contact with the smallpox-infected Pellegrini boy. The pursuing Indians actually catch chicken pox from the items, in a sanitized reference to an actual incident of deliberate contamination of Indian tribes by giving them smallpox-infected blankets. MacClaw all but accuses Martha of intentionally using smallpox as a biological weapon against the Indians, but the less severe nature of the disease actually spread allows him to "forgive" her indiscretion. MacClaw is contrasted during the film with the rougher, presumably less educated, army doctor played by the always dependable Ray Teal.

Another doctor with military ties appears in *The Great Sioux Uprising* (Lloyd Bacon, 1953). The film is set during the Civil War, with the interesting twist of presenting differing perspectives among Indian tribes. The historical figures of Stand Watie (1806–1871), a Cherokee who became a commander for the Confederacy, reaching the rank of brigadier general and not surrendering until June 23, 1865 (Boatner 894–95), and Red Cloud (1822–1909), an Oglala Sioux chief who was to make peace with the United States some years later, are put to fictional use here.[6] The conflict revolves around horses, needed by both sides in the war and belonging to Red Cloud's band, who consider them sacred. A perfidious group of white rustlers led by Stephen Cook (Lyle Bettger) are the catalysts of violence as they repeatedly try to steal the horses. In characteristic Western tale fashion, a mysterious stranger interjects himself into the conflict: Doctor Jonathan Westgate (Jeff Chandler), who turns out to be a former Union Army surgeon trying to make a new start. Given the needs of the area in Wyoming to which he has come, Westgate serves more as veterinarian for horses than as physician for people. In fact, an injury to Red Cloud's paint horse, given to the doctor by Red Cloud himself (John War Eagle) in gratitude for his veterinary services, is an important clue to the identity of the rustlers, and the horse is later cruelly destroyed as potential evidence in a fire set by Cook's psychopathic henchman Uriah (Stacy S. Harris). Chandler plays a rather complex role which combines doctor of animals and people: detective, diplomat, and soldier, neatly switching from his role as Cochise in *Broken Arrow* (Delmer Daves, 1950) to a role paralleling James Stewart's peacemaking Tom Jeffords in the Daves film. After the resolution of the conflict, Westgate decides to re-enlist in the Union Army as a surgeon.

The Great Sioux Uprising also features a rather unusual, even a somewhat cartoonish, blacksmith character, solidly played by skilled character actor Peter Whitney.[7] Ahab Jones is a physically formidable civil professional who becomes an ally of Westgate, after persuading him to stay in his town as a veterinarian, against corrupt local forces. Later he assists Westgate in hiding the paint horse at the ranch of Joan Britton (Faith Domergue), but unfortunately the intimidating blacksmith suffers from a tendency to loose lips when intoxicated, and he lets slip the secret location of the horse, which is to serve as evidence against Cook (Lyle Bettger) and his gang. When Westgate, Joan, and Ahab go to Red Cloud's war council to try to explain about the horse and avert an attack on the nearby fort, Ahab allows himself to be captured, and presumably killed, by the Indians in order to allow Westgate and Joan to escape.

The town doctor serves in many Westerns as a pivot point between the forces of savagery and civilization, or between lawlessness and law enforcement. Other professionals may function similarly, for instance the newspaperman or editor, but the medical profession seems more often represented in the context of town progress. A good example of the civilizing influence of the doctor can be found in *The Tin Star* (Anthony Mann, 1957), the story of bounty hunter Morg Hickman (Henry Fonda), conflicted over his role in society. Morg, a disillusioned professional who has changed his line of work (he was a sheriff), lives on the fringes of society, afraid to try to settle into a more normal life. In this film he serves as the teacher of young, untried Sheriff Ben Owens (Anthony Perkins) but also as a catalyst for the remaking of the town. His reluctant ally is the old town doctor, Doc McCord, who reserves judgment on the bounty hunter's motives and character. This doctor is played by the formidable John McIntire, an actor who could convey a wide range of character tones, from vil-

1. Professional Case Studies

lainy (as in *The Far Country*) to chicanery (*Winchester '73*) to sage, noble steadiness, as in this film and in non–Westerns like *The Phenix City Story* (Phil Karlson, 1955). Here, the doctor serves as the unofficial town historian, recalling his many childbirth visits; but he is also the conscience of a town whose survival as a civilized concern is threatened by tyranny, criminality, and mob violence. Serving as a Homeric Nestor in Mann's little epic, he cautions headstrong Sheriff Owens against rash actions and counsels taking a long view of the bounty hunter. Significantly, the events which will resolve the town conflicts take place after his murder at the hands of the McGaffey brothers (Lee Van Cleef and Peter Baldwin), who fear that he may reveal their whereabouts. His death will also result in the coming of age, or competence, of Ben as sheriff and the healing of Morg, who decides to marry Nona Mayfield (Betsy Palmer), to become a father to her son Kip, and to migrate to a new town as sheriff. Thus the doctor's life cycle in this film is the cement of the civilizing process in the town. Paralleling my statement, Matthew J. Costello observes that "Doc is represented throughout the film as the moral center of the town: he delivers the babies that people the families that give the town identity and purpose; his diaries, in which he records all these births, serve as the only history of the town" (Costello, "Rewriting" 182). Costello cites Jim Kitses in a note, only to differ from his position about the moral source of the murder of McCord (Costello, "Rewriting" 195–96n4) (Kitses, *Horizons* 60).

A doctor of a rather different stamp helps to civilize a frontier town in *Legion of the Lawless* (David Howard, 1940). A man fitting the drunken doctor type, Doctor Denton (Herbert Heywood), first appears as a figure of ridicule, unfit to carry out his duties, but as the narrative progresses, he acquires added stature due to his basic good nature and general decency. Unable to assist a man beaten by one of the town "vigilantes," Doc Denton cedes authority over the health of the town, or at least its well-being, to a new arrival, young lawyer Jeff Toland (George O'Brien). Like other young lawyers arriving in rough frontier towns like Ivestown (Ranse Stoddard as the epitome of the type), Toland is more or less ignored by the existing power structure. He discovers that Ivestown has a twin, East Ivestown, whose impoverished inhabitants are considered criminals and wastrels by the citizens of Ivestown. The towns are divided by a bridge which Toland crosses to visit East Ivestown, where he learns of the ill treatment of citizens like shopkeeper Lafe Barton (Eddy Waller), the man who had been beaten by a vigilante thug, Les Harper (Norman Willis).

Professionals in Western Film and Fiction

The "vigilantes" are a band of men who exert a proto-legal influence on Ivestown by enforcing their own ad hoc justice, often quite summary, and like corrupt cop Ray Donlan (Harvey Keitel) in *Cop Land* (James Mangold, 1997), the enforcer for the group boasts that no crime is permitted in the town. In the Mangold film, Ray tells Freddie Heflin (Sylvester Stallone), the idealistic, conflicted, and underestimated sheriff of the "cop town" Garrison, New Jersey, "We made a place where things make sense and you can walk across the street without fear" (Mangold, *Cop Land* Ch. 19). Director James Mangold, who also scripted, envisioned the film as an "urban Western" (Mangold, "Making of an Urban Western") (see also Pizzello). Like the cops in the Mangold film, who have financed their homes with mob money, the vigilantes are themselves an organized crime group, simply the biggest and toughest game in town, permitting only their own criminal activities to flourish. As Francis M. Nevins notes, Ellen (Virginia Vale), the daughter of respectable but woefully deceived vigilante leader Henry Ives (Hugh Sothern), tells Toland, "This is the best-run town in the territory" (Nevins 61). Nevins refers (64) to Richard Slotkin's "town-tamer" category. Slotkin frames questions concerning "'social justice'" and asserts that "The 'town-tamer' Western, of which *Dodge City* and *My Darling Clementine* are classic examples, offered a 'progressive' answer [to such questions]: social injustice is imposed by powerful criminals; the hero must defeat them and thus empower the 'decent folks' who bring progress to the Frontier" (Slotkin, *Gunfighter Nation* 379).

Doc Denton assists Toland and his new ally, the shopkeeper Lafe Barton, in opposing the machinations of the vigilante concern, but along the way Doc succumbs once again to drinking and reveals crucial information about the actual route of the new railroad. According to the railroad surveyors, the tracks will not go through Ivestown but instead will be laid through East Ivestown, making that property very valuable. The vigilantes organize attacks on the landowners there, forcing them to sign over their property for pittances. Doc Denton is certainly a stereotyped character, but the script lends him some individuality, adding another dimension to this B-Western sample.

Unlike ill-fated Doc McCord, Dr. John Storrow in *Decision at Sundown* (Budd Boetticher, 1957) survives the mayhem in the town of Sundown. Like McCord, he provides an importantly rational perspective for the protagonist, Bart Allison (Randolph Scott), in this town-based film, unusual among the Ranown Budd Boetticher Westerns. Bart, a Civil War

1. Professional Case Studies

veteran, and his friend Sam (Noah Beery, Jr., as the loyal sidekick) arrive in Sundown from Texas, searching for a man named Tate Kimbrough (John Carroll), whom Bart wants to kill for unexplained reasons. The Civil War veteran character appears rather frequently in Westerns of the 1950s, and he often displays the negative effects of the war:

> ... the Western hero in postwar years was noticeably a more vulnerable, flawed character than had been the case with previous films. A common motif at this time of national concern about the peacetime adjustment and rehabilitation of World War II veterans was the traumatized or uprooted Civil War veteran [Lenihan, "Classics and Social Commentary: Postwar Westerns, 1946–1960" 37].

The narrative gradually reveals that Bart hates Kimbrough for taking his wife, Mary, from him—she eventually committed suicide. Although Kimbrough has the town under his thumb, relying on the corrupt Sheriff Swede (Andrew Duggan) to maintain order, Dr. Storrow (John Archer) soon makes his position as "no friend of Tate Kimbrough" quite clear, and he begins from early in the events in Sundown to stake out a position as an ethical outsider, skeptical of Allison's intentions toward Kimbrough but still clearly opposed to Kimbrough's malign influence. After the Texas men disrupt Kimbrough's wedding to Lucy Summerton (Karen Steele, familiar to Ranown followers), the two friends take refuge in the stable, barricading themselves and trading shots with the sheriff and his henchmen until Sam is lured out under false pretenses and murdered by Spanish (H.M. Wynant). Since Dr. Storrow has been floating in and out of the story (let into the stable, for instance, to treat the wounded Spanish, who had tried to ambush the two men), he had heard from Sam just prior to his death that Mary was serially unfaithful to Bart, who either does not know this or does not want to admit it, and he tells John Storrow to promise to tell Bart the truth about her. Despite his best efforts, however, Bart will not listen to him until the situation in town results in further violence.

Soon the doctor functions as a catalyst to civic action by a crew of ranch hands led by reluctant Morley Chase (Ray Teal). Rather like the isolationist United States before entering World War I, Morley and his men have stayed on the sidelines while Tate and Swede ran the town by cowing its inhabitants. Only the drunken barber Mr. Baldwin (Vaughn Taylor) dares to talk back to Tate, who does not take him seriously enough to act against him. This balance of terror changes when Storrow begins to harangue the townspeople and the ranchers about their passivity. As a professional member of the community who refuses to take sides in an openly partisan manner, his appeal to the civic pride and the social conscience of the townspeople stirs the ranchers into belated action, and they "just even them odds up a little" (Boetticher, *Decision at Sundown* Ch. 10), as Morley says, so that Bart and Tate may fight on even terms. (Despite the ranchers' evening of the odds by disarming Tate's well-placed henchmen, Ruby [Valerie French] has to intervene by wounding Tate to keep him from killing Bart, partially disabled from a prior injury.) After Tate and Ruby leave town, the doctor and Lucy watch Bart preparing to ride out. Lucy is troubled by Bart's despondency and wants to help him, but the doctor remarks sententiously that "he changed things for everybody in town. But unfortunately there's nothing we can do for him" (Boetticher, *Decision at Sundown* Ch. 12).

A similarly wise doctor appears in *The Violent Men* (Rudolph Maté, 1954). A less important character for the narrative than the doctor in *The Tin Star*, Dr. Henry Crowell (Raymond Greenleaf) nonetheless functions as an adviser to the film's protagonist, John Parrish (Glenn Ford). Parrish is a Union Cavalry veteran (with Col. Kirkpatrick [probably based on Gen. Judson Kilpatrick] in Georgia) who owns a ranch bordering the huge holdings of Lew Wilkison (Edward G. Robinson), an expansionist who wants to buy him out. Parrish wants only to sell his land and stock and to marry his fiancée before moving East. Early in the film he is shown at an office visit with his doctor as he recovers from an undisclosed illness, apparently connected to his wounding in the recent Civil War. The avuncular Dr. Crowell tries to advise Parrish about his situation in the valley, where landowners are being forced out by Wilkison: "You'll either have to run like they did or stand and fight." The doctor tries to convince the stubborn Parrish that he is indebted to the valley: "You came out here to die, Mr. Parrish. This country gave you back your life, and you still owe it nothin'?" (Maté Ch. 1).

A similarly avuncular, or perhaps fatherly, physician appears in the intriguing *The Man from Colorado* (Henry Levin, 1948), a film about the tragic effects of the Civil War on Owen Devereaux (Glenn Ford), a cavalry commander who becomes psychotic after the war. His downturn begins to manifest itself during the last battle in the war in Colorado, when he viciously orders an attack on a Confederate unit trying to surrender. This act, and others after he is appointed federal judge in the town of Glory Hill, will lead to a break with his friend (and romantic rival) Del Stewart (William Holden). Owen's wife, Caroline (Ellen Drew), is the friend of

1. Professional Case Studies

fatherly Dr. Merriam (Edgar Buchanan), who fills his usual homey role as the voice of caution and wisdom in the town. Doc's role in the narrative, which includes advice about the effects war has on the psyche of veterans, is of a piece with that of characters like Police Captain Finley (Robert Young) in *Crossfire* (Edward Dmytryk, 1947), who represents the voice of unprejudiced reason after a murder driven by anti–Semitism. The murder is perpetrated by a World War II veteran whose racism was probably exacerbated by war trauma; in any case, characters like the anti–Semitic Montgomery (Robert Ryan) and the psychotic Devereaux, both war veterans, find their positive counterparts in stalwarts such as Finley and Doc. Doc Merriam advises Del that Owen may recover with "time" and that he needs help from his friends, but this advice soon becomes fruitless as Owen becomes more and more tyrannical. Eventually Doc takes an active role in assisting Del and the townspeople, and some veterans of Owen's troop turned bandits, in wresting control of the town from the crazed Owen.

Another disturbed character, in *The Cariboo Trail* (Edwin L. Marin, 1950), is assisted by a caring physician in a Canadian mining town. Mike Evans (Bill Williams) loses an arm in a stampede during a cattle drive. His business partner and friend Jim Redfern (Randolph Scott) tries to console and to help him, but Mike becomes embittered and blames Jim for the accident, because Jim had insisted on trying to sell cattle instead of trying to mine gold. Mike is left in the care of the town doctor, Dr. John S. Rhodes (Tony Hughes), a typically avuncular, or perhaps grandfatherly, figure who exudes good will and compassion. Although Dr. Rhodes does not have a large role in the film, he does stand out as a positive professional force in a town which is essentially the property of the villainous and grasping Frank Walsh (Victor Jory). The narrative bears some similarities to *The Far Country* (Anthony Mann, 1954), also set in the Far Northwest and featuring James Stewart and Walter Brennan as a pair of entrepreneurs who try to confront the monopoly of sinister Gannon (John McIntire). They are assisted by Renee Vallon (Corinne Calvet), the daughter of a kind surgeon. The Brennan character Ben Tatum, like Mike Evans in the Marin film, dies by the end of the film. Ben dies because of a foolish error that results in his murder, while Mike eventually recovers his sanity and his friendly disposition towards Jim. He eventually dies during an attempt to save Jim's life.

In a lower key, the narrative of *Strange Lady in Town* (Mervyn LeRoy, 1955) features not one but two doctors in a retelling of *The Taming of the*

Professionals in Western Film and Fiction

Shrew. Set in Santa Fe, New Mexico, in the latter decades of the 19th century (but obviously filmed in and around the Old Tucson movie location), this Greer Garson vehicle features Garson as Julia Winslow Garth, M.D., the "strange lady in town" who is running from her past, having left her position in Boston because of the intolerance of the male-dominated profession. Pam Cook observes that "when it comes to movies, ... the impoverished range of female stereotypes on offer (mother, schoolteacher, prostitute, saloon girl, rancher, Indian squaw, bandit) never matches up to reality ... the heroines who fought to change the course of history (the suffragettes, farmers, professional women) fare badly" (Cook 240–41).

An Easterner, educated in Philadelphia and in Europe, where she studied the advanced theories of Dr. Lister,[8] Dr. Garth arrives in Santa Fe only to discover that the town has an established doctor, Rourke O'Brien (Dana Andrews), a voluble man with strong anti-feminist views which, however, are somewhat belied by his tolerance of his strong-willed, spunky daughter Spurs (Lois Smith). An interesting feature of the battle between the two doctors is its concentration in a rather provisional hospital run by the parish priest Father Gabriel (Walter Hampden) and the Catholic sisters and medically supervised by O'Brien. Garth's intrusion into O'Brien's fiefdom leads to predictable fireworks, although clearly the two are becoming emotionally entangled. A marriage proposal from O'Brien is firmly refused by Garth, who believes that the two are incompatible.

The film clearly reflects the tensions between men and women in the postwar years, after men returning from World War II (and then Korea) found their wives or other female companions in the workforce or desiring to join it. Increased professional roles for women, as in this film, were a feature of this evolution, and here the woman doctor is shown to be more progressive (e.g., Lister's theories about the danger of infection in medical procedures)[9] than the more traditional, and defensive, Dr. O'Brien. Additionally O'Brien's conservatism in medicine is linked to a macho bluster that lends him an unattractive quality. O'Brien even mocks the courtly pursuit of Juliet by Romeo as too tentative, not aggressive enough, and then proceeds to force himself, or nearly so, on Dr. Garth.

Dr. Garth's advanced medical knowledge is particularly useful—and irritating to O'Brien—when she is able to cure a case of blindness: a young Mexican who sings in the parish choir turns out to have a case of curable glaucoma. Later in the film, after she refuses Rourke's marriage proposal but still accompanies him to the Governor's Ball, she meets the territorial

1. Professional Case Studies

governor, General Lew Wallace (Ralph Moody),[10] dances with him, and attends to him when he suffers an apparent heart attack. Wallace tells her that Dr. O'Brien had diagnosed heart problems, but Dr. Garth notices that he wears a very tight collar, and recommends that he not do so because the collar is cutting off his air flow. Although she tries to be diplomatic, O'Brien rightly perceives that she is contradicting his diagnosis, and he expresses his heated outrage.

The face-off between the two doctors is eventually resolved, of course, as this film fits the usual Hollywood paradigm despite its emphasis on a woman professional—or perhaps, precisely because of its focus on a female professional who must be "tamed" into a conventional marriage. Julia's "bad" brother, Army Lieutenant David Garth (Cameron Mitchell), a suitor for Spurs but also a gambler and a cattle thief, leads a bank robbery crew during a town festival. Father Gabriel is killed accidentally, and the robbers are besieged by the sheriff's men and by an angry mob. David is killed, and the town blames Julia for the incident through association of guilt with David. The ostracized Julia prepares to move to another town to hang out her shingle but is "rescued" by Rourke, who speaks defiantly to the mob gathered near her house, vowing that she will stay in town and will become his wife. Presumably the two will work together as doctors, and perhaps Rourke will learn the newest praxis from Julia. Perhaps one is stating the obvious by noting that endings with a potential or actual wedding are common in Westerns. Still, Raymond Bellour summarized the trope effectively in an interview with Janet Bergstrom:

> ... the western is subtended from one end to the other by what one can call the problematic of marriage. If you think about it, you notice that after a certain situation posed at the start as a problem [with our film, two doctors in a town] or as an enigma, the film gradually leads to a final solution which allows the more or less conflicting terms posed at the beginning to be resolved, and which in the majority of cases takes the form of a marriage [Bergstrom 88].

An offbeat civilizer is to be found in the series of four novels by the celebrated Richard S. Wheeler, set in 1880s Montana and featuring Irish doctor-sheriff Santiago Toole. The novels are: *Incident at Fort Keogh, The Final Tally, Deuces and Ladies Wild,* and *The Fate* (Tanner 61). The Santiago Toole character is an Irish immigrant, descendant of an aristocratic family (a baronet), and a graduate of the University of Edinburgh, who has come West to ply his trade. As the first novel opens, he has assumed the job of sheriff in rough Milestown (the future Miles City) because no one occupies the position. He views this as a short-term situation, but of course the reader suspects that he will be both doctor and sheriff for some time to come. As Toole muses in the last novel in the series, his doctor job is widely defined: "Frontier physicians doctored teeth, people, dogs and cats and livestock" (Wheeler, *The Fate* 93). Toole is a good and conscientious doctor, well-educated and current with the best science of his time, familiar with Lister (as is Dr. Julia Garth of *Strange Lady in Town*) and Pasteur (Wheeler, *Incident* 61),[11] but he is also a proficient marksman: "The dexterity that made him a deft surgeon made him a swift man with a gun, and more importantly, an accurate one" (Wheeler, *Incident* 9). His father had named him Santiago as a caprice (Wheeler, *Incident* 27) but perhaps the name fits: Santiago (St. James), the patron saint of Spain, was the Christian warrior's patron in the fight against the Moorish invaders of their peninsula.[12]

Toole's mixed-heritage name (though not his genealogy) mirrors the mixed-blood heritage of his beloved wife, Mimi, a French-Assiniboin[13] woman fiercely devoted to Toole. Her rationalistic French cultural inheritance combined with her Assiniboin ferocity make of her an intriguing mix of stereotypes. As she explains to Santiago, "'When I shoot I aim and squeeze and my spirit is cold. My mother is an expert torturer.... I'm worse than my mother. It's the French in me. I can do it smiling'" (Wheeler, *Incident* 164). The narrator observes of Mimi that "her father, old Marceau, had once said that the French have mad passions and cold minds, while the Assiniboin have cold passions and mad minds" (Wheeler, *Incident* 58). Appropriately for the frontier, then, the two combine in their names and backgrounds the original *conquistadores* (Spanish), the Irish immigrants who peopled the cavalry in the West, the French fur-traders, and the Native inhabitants of the region. In this novel, other important groups make appearances: the Germans, represented particularly by the post doctor Hoffmeister at Fort Keogh, and especially the Norwegians, who have moved into land near Fort Keogh (named for Lt. Myles Keogh of Ireland, killed at Little Big Horn) and present a stubborn obstacle to the nefarious designs and rough tactics of the villain Sergeant-Major Wiltz, who leads a homicidal raid on the local sin city, Hogtown (Wheeler, *Incident* 16).

Moreover, Toole neatly encapsulates the figure of myth identified as germane to the American West by Harold H. Kolb, Jr., in his article "Mark Twain and the Myth of the West." Identifying figures like Charles Lindbergh, Daniel Boone, Abraham Lincoln, and John F. Kennedy as particu-

1. Professional Case Studies

larly American myths, he explains that "the myth of America itself complexly intertwines culture and institutions carried from Europe with those created in the New World." Rather like the Irishman Toole in our context, the Irish-American "John F. Kennedy seemed to symbolize the best of both democracy and aristocracy" (Kolb 126–27).

In another sign of his polarized situation, Toole faces the strange dilemma of serving both as a healer and as a lawman who must sometimes take a life. He meditates at times on this predicament but finds a way to make peace with his unusual situation:

> At first, when they'd pinned the star on him, he'd wrestled with it. Shoot a felon and then doctor him? What of his Hippocratic Oath? He'd finally concluded it would be a matter of offices. In the office of sheriff, he'd shoot if he had to.... As doctor, he patched up the ones he shot. Very handy [Wheeler, *Incident* 9].

In a rather whimsical and presumably an unintended fashion, the Toole character embodies within himself the two poles, doctor and cop, identified by Peter Biskind as essential to comprehension of the political stance of 1950s films. Thus, in a film like *Panic in the Streets*, Dr. Reed (Richard Widmark) and Detective Warren (Paul Douglas) learn to work together despite an initial antipathy, so that the film shows consensus. Other films leaned, according to Biskind's analysis, left or right depending on the authority accorded the doctor (or similar character) or the cop (or military officer). (For the Kazan film, see Biskind 21–33.)

The second novel in the Toole series, *The Final Tally*, places him at the center of a mystery involving a hard-driving cattleman, Hermes Bragg, who is suffering from late-stage consumption and three of his Mexican hands apparently wounded by Sioux raiders. Toole is called to doctor the men but soon finds himself acting more prominently, as the character's configuration demands, as sheriff because of the injuries to the Mexicans. Two of them soon expire, and Toole is left with one as a patient along with the recalcitrant, cantankerous, and sometimes venomous Bragg. He also must contend with, or try to care for, Bragg's two difficult children, Apollo and Athena. He tries to become a surrogate father to Apollo, who as the younger of the two siblings is less indoctrinated with Bragg's harsh, unforgiving rhetoric. Athena proves intractable, even after Toole arrests her for shooting at him. Meanwhile the novel focuses on Toole's efforts to determine how the shooting of the Mexicans took place and presents his difficulties with treating Bragg's advanced tuberculosis. As in the first novel, Toole is shown to be advanced for his time in his awareness of bacteria. He tries to explain to Bragg that his tuberculosis is not the result of bad air, as his physicians in Texas had told him, but of exposure to the bacillus that causes it. But Toole laments to himself that "in North America.... No one—not even doctors—knew about germs, bacteria, Pasteur, Lister, and Koch, who'd recently isolated the tuberculosis bacillus" (Wheeler, *The Final Tally* 73). Often Toole wrestles with himself about the doctor-sheriff conflict within him. Having viewed the sheriff job as temporary, he usually sees doctoring as his primary calling, and on one occasion in this novel he considers going back to Europe for further study (Wheeler, *The Final Tally* 138). In fact, however, Toole is drawn as much, perhaps by duty more than preference, to his lawman function, as the indirect reporting of his thoughts makes clear on another difficult occasion:

> Whenever doctor and sheriff clashed in him, he hated it, hated the hard decisions. Sheriff won this time. Almost always, in hard corners, sheriff won over doctor [Wheeler, *The Final Tally* 89].

Nevertheless, he faces dilemmas that are difficult to resolve, given the conflict between his medical oath and his responsibilities or inclinations as lawman, for example when he mulls over his course of action regarding the two Bragg children:

> Let 'em taste life behind bars and accept the consequences. Let 'em live under the brutal thumb of a wild father, unable to bend.... That was the sheriff in him. The doctor in him wasn't so sure [Wheeler, *The Final Tally* 95].

Ultimately Toole is forced to act more as a sheriff, even to the extent of arresting and charging an overly aggressive U.S. marshal. The unrepentant and nearly psychotic Athena is sentenced to hang along with some of the other Bragg men who had committed capital crimes. Toole must carry out the hangings, and the only remaining medical duty for him is a forlorn one: caring for the now terminal Apollo Bragg, who has contracted his father's tuberculosis.

Deuces and Ladies Wild opens with Toole attempting to find a tuberculosis cure and attending the funeral of Jubal Peach, the gambling king of Miles City, whom he had previously treated for "ague" (malaria). The funeral turns out to be a veiled threat placed into motion by Peach's rival, Kate Dubois, who owns the Stockman bar, his major competitor in Miles City. Toole soon becomes embroiled in the fight between Jubal and Kate for control of the lucrative trade in the city, and as doctor he is concerned

1. Professional Case Studies

with the opiate addiction of Jubal and his companion Anna, who betrays Jubal, stealing money and his bottles of opiated syrup. This novel and the previous one (*The Final Tally*) increasingly place Toole into a corrective position as he tries to palliate or prevent diseases and ailments of which he has knowledge through his superior training. Additionally a running motif has been established in which the evildoers he combats underestimate his determination and skills as sheriff, misinterpreting his medical dedication as weakness (somewhat of a turn on the Destry type made famous by James Stewart in *Destry Rides Again*—the pacifist tenderfoot who is actually an expert gunman and will fight if necessary). In *Deuces and Ladies Wild*, Toole is stymied in his attempts to protect Kate Dubois from disfigurement at Peach's hands, and she dies a suicide. Peach is eventually lynched by some of the cowhands and some army men because of his treatment of their beloved Kate, an extrajudicial proceeding that Toole is also unable to prevent. But Toole elects not to try to arrest the lynchers: the incident ends with Toole's response to Sergeant Major Gavin, one of the leaders of the lynch mob: "'Call me Dr. Toole, Sergeant'" (Wheeler, *Deuces* 194).

The Fate contains two major professional characters, Toole and Elwood Attabury III, a geologist and mining engineer. Attabury and his associates, wronged by mining magnate Ingmar Drogovich, who had illegitimately wrested the Fate mine away from Attabury, robbed the train carrying some of the magnate's profits, kidnapping Drogovich's daughter Filomena as hostage. Drogovich goes after them, and when Toole arrests him for obstructing justice, has his men kidnap Mrs. Toole to hold as hostage against Toole's pursuing him in his own chase after Attabury and his men. The tale becomes a twin chase narrative. One group of fugitives consists of the unlikely robbers—not hardened criminals—led by the determined but confused Attabury, described in a rumination by Drogovich as "the patrician Bostonian geologist and engineer who'd discovered and built the Fate" (Wheeler, *The Fate* 15). Like other Easterners moving West to seek their fortune, Attabury runs into obstacles, but the "tenderfoot" trope is given a curious twist in his interaction with Filomena, who tells him that she was headed back East "'before this detour'" because she does not like men of the West. As she says cuttingly, "'Western men are pansies,'" undercutting the normal stereotype in which men of the West are manly while men of the East are overcivilized and feminized (Wheeler, *The Fate* 65). Despite her initial distaste for her kidnappers,

23

she eventually comes around to their point of view and openly criticizes her father, especially when Toole comes to their camp to arrest them (Wheeler, *The Fate* 170).

A fugitive medical man is the lead character in the Dakota Lawman series by Bill Brooks, with three novels. The character is Jake Horn, a name adopted by the falsely accused Tristan Shade as an alias and taken from his uncle (Brooks, B., *Last Stand* 44–45). "Jake" comes to Dakota Territory hoping to stay ahead of his pursuers and is very reluctant even to reveal that he has medical training. He soon becomes ensnared in local controversies and conflicts, meeting along the way a collection of colorful denizens of the town of Sweet Sorrow and its surrounding areas. These include a fictionalized version of Judge Roy Bean, an eccentric and predictably drunk town doctor, Doc Woodrow Willis, a Mandan-French man, very educated and linguistically accomplished, named Toussaint Trueblood, and an embittered storeowner named Otis Dollar, as well as an assortment of other town types, including a Swiss man named Zimmerman, who runs the Fat Duck Café and who speaks with a heavy German accent (Brooks, B., *Last Stand* 62–63). Apart from the introduction of characters, the narrative revolves around a seemingly inexplicable outbreak of insanity in the fictional little Dakota prairie town, which is situated around Bismarck. The "law" in the town consists of two ruffians, Bob Olive and Teacup Smith, who will in due course be replaced by Jake Horn (the "Dakota Lawman"), who, somewhat like Toole in the Wheeler novels, will assume the dual role of healer (even if covert) and enforcer. He will also replace the late Dr. Willis, who turns out to have poisoned several people in the town with "seeds" "of the jimson plant, what some called Devil's Trumpet or Mad Apple" (Brooks, B., *Last Stand* 292) because of his own insane hatred. Willis had lost his wife, become lost himself in alcohol, and then become obsessed with a younger woman who married him and then ran off with her former "headmaster," an Italian named Umberto Vincenti (Brooks, B., *Last Stand* 85–90). As Jake considers settling in the town, he muses:

> And those who would come looking for him, would be looking for a man named Tristan Shade, a physician, not a lawman named Jake Horn. And as long as he didn't practice medicine for a number of years... [Brooks, B., *Last Stand* 283].

His uncle, the actual Jake Horn, dies at the end of the novel trying to save Tristan's life in a confrontation with a detective (or bounty hunter) named Prince Puckett. Now Tristan Shade will disappear behind the mask

1. Professional Case Studies

of Jake Horn. Unlike Sheriff Toole, however, Jake is notably reticent about using lethal violence against lawbreakers because of his concern for the Hippocratic Oath.

Dakota Lawman: Killing Mr. Sunday is clearly inspired by *The Shootist*, with its portrait of the last act of a dying gunman's life, but it deviates from the model in making the gunman a fugitive with bounty hunters pursuing him instead of former enemies and rivals being summoned by him to fight, and by providing him with an estranged daughter whom he has come to visit and who understandably does not wish to see him, given her ambivalent feelings for him. Jake assists Toussaint in searching for Martha, Otis's wife, who was kidnapped by a crazed Swede who had murdered his family. Following his usual script, Jake is evasive about his past, trying to sidestep questions about his medical training. He answers Toussaint's musing remark, "'Seems to me doctoring has a whole lot more going for it than having that tin target pinned to your coat'" with a nearly dismissive rejoinder: "'It was another lifetime ago.... I don't doctor anymore'" (Brooks, B., *Killing* 124). Nevertheless, he does provide some medical care during the novel, and when Mr. Sunday is near death Jake explains that although not officially a doctor, "'I had some training in the war'" (Brooks, B., *Killing* 205).

Eventually all is put right, with Sunday setting up a gunfight with the bounty hunters (three brothers) so that he can die fighting rather than suffering with the cancer, much like the model for this character, J.B. Books, the shootist of the eponymous novel. Unlike Books, though, who leaves nothing to relatives, despite the good memories of him left with Bond Rogers (in the Siegel film, Lauren Bacall) and her son Gillom (Ron Howard), Sunday buys a house (Doc Willis's former home) for his daughter Clara and her children and leaves her some money. Clara is the town schoolteacher, and at the end of the novel a romance between her and Jake, sometime doctor and town lawman, is foreshadowed. Minor appearances in the novel by town professionals include the newspaper editor Emeritus Fly, who tries to interview Clara at Tall John's funeral parlor. She refuses, so Fly interviews the undertaker Tall John for a sensationalized article typical of the period which runs in his paper, the *Grasslands Democrat* (Brooks, B., *Killing* 290–91).

A more traditional role is played in town business by Dr. Irving (Henry Travers) in *Dodge City* (Michael Curtiz, 1939). Here, the doctor, a stable figure with wife and daughter, leads the city fathers in trying to clean up the town by hiring Wade Hatton (Errol Flynn) as sheriff. A brighter vision than Mann's, Curtiz's film has the doctor suffer no bad consequences for his actions, as Hatton cleans up the town, marries the daughter (Olivia de Havilland), and goes off with his friends and wife to perform a similar service in wild Virginia City. Travers, who specialized in small-town or old-fashioned American characters, sometimes with an element of myopia (as in *The Bells of St. Mary's*), here provides a stability and a foresight lacking in the crabbed viewpoint of some of the other city fathers. He takes Wade aside early in the film for a little father-son bonding as he apologizes for his wife's intolerance about gunfighters or other outside influences.

A similar example of medical intervention in a political or legal crisis appears in *Riding Shotgun* (André de Toth, 1954). Here the doctor (James Bell) serves more as an interface between the angry townspeople, who want to kill Larry Delong (Randolph Scott), having convicted him in public opinion of murder and robbery, and the seemingly passive and easygoing deputy sheriff Tub Murphy (Wayne Morris), who adopts a more prudent course of waiting on events. The doctor scolds Tub for inaction while restraining the hotter heads in the town from rash actions; earlier the doctor was shown to be a cordial acquaintance of Larry's.

In this film the doctor does not have a close connection with the hero as did the Travers character in *Dodge City*; the professional character associated with Larry in family terms is instead the Colonel, who owns the town casino. A minor but recognizable character actor, James Bell plays Doc Winkler with the type of double-edged demeanor which he often brought to his roles: he shifts easily from agreeable to abrasive, showing a hard-edged core that qualifies his folksy veneer.[14] Like Doc McCord, Dr. Irving and Doc Winkler are not leading protagonists of their films. These characters are facilitators for the main action of their respective films.

A medical facilitator in a different context is the surgeon on the Army post in *Only the Valiant* (Gordon Douglas, 1950), who fulfills a small but important function at the end of the film. The ailing commander at the fort, Col. Drumm (Herbert Heyes), is retiring under orders of the surgeon, and Capt. Richard Lance (Gregory Peck) is to succeed him. The succession could be a little rough, since Lance had led a difficult mission against the Apache in which several men had died, and more controversy had preceded the mission, with unfounded but damaging accusations of negligence against Lance. In a conversation with Lance after his return from the latest mission, Doc helps to ease the transition to the new command, and he also advises Lance to mend fences with the woman he loves, Cathy Eversham (played by the tragic Barbara Payton),[15] who had mistakenly blamed him for the death of her suitor. Thus the most important civil professional at the fort (still a doctor, even if a military one) allies himself with, mentors, the young, energetic new commander (Douglas Ch. 12).

A rather sinister doctor as a would-be facilitator is Doc Talmadge in "The Killing at Triple Tree" by Evan Hunter. Reminiscent of *The Ox-Bow Incident* and the Randolph Scott–Budd Boetticher collaboration *Ride Lonesome*, as well as the Kirk Douglas turn in *Last Train from Gun Hill*, the story concerns the rape-murder of the wife of a town sheriff. As in the other cases mentioned, the perpetrator is the target of vengeance. As in *The Ox-Bow Incident*, the townspeople threaten lynching; unlike in the Clark novel and Wellman film, though, they are unsuccessful. During the lynch mob threat, Doc Talmadge, the town doctor, actually sides with the lynchers, egging them on, perhaps from loyalty to the sheriff or, more likely, affection for his wife. Certainly this is a strange course of action for a physician, whose character is not developed much in the story, but who seems to be a rather decent sort overall. We see him in his role as physician and coroner, trying to save the sheriff from undue shock by treating his wife's remains circumspectly. Having waited for the sheriff (named Johnny, the narrator of the story) to return, the doctor is somewhat surprised that Johnny is very impatient to leave his wife's side and pursue the killer or killers. In fact, the doctor is asked to help round up a posse—another unusual role for the doctor character in most Westerns.

Doc Talmadge does more than try to round up a posse. When Johnny returns to town with a possible suspect, he discovers that the real perpetrator has already been caught, and Doc is leading the charge to hang him. In fact, Johnny has to tell Doc to drop the rope which he is about to tighten around a tree trunk for the hanging (Hunter, E. 265). As events escalate, the sheriff even has to strike the doctor's wrist with his gun barrel to stop him from hitting the horse on which Dodd, the killer, is tied waiting to hang, and Talmadge stays the longest of any in the mob before leaving the sheriff with the criminal (Hunter, E. 267–68). Added to this unusual twist is the final disposition of the criminal, whom the sheriff shoots after freeing him from the mob—no one but the widower will take his revenge.

Like many other professionals in Western films other than sheriffs or peace officers, doctors are rarely the focus of the narrative. In fact, as

Professionals in Western Film and Fiction

in the Western TV movie *Lone Rider*, the doctor may not even appear onscreen; we see only his shingle and hear references to his work patching up injuries from the violence in the town. Sometimes, as in *The Shootist* (Don Siegel, 1976), the doctor may serve as a sage advisor or a bearer of news but has no direct influence on future events (other than the effects his prognosis may have, as in this case, when he diagnoses terminal cancer for the protagonist J.B. Books [John Wayne].) In this film, the doctor character (played by James Stewart) also functions intertextually, as do some other characters in the film, specifically the enemies of J.B. Books (see Hall, K., "*Gringo Viejo*"). Since Wayne and Stewart had played against each other most especially in *The Man Who Shot Liberty Valance*, the casting of Stewart has intertextual resonance here. In the Ford film, the professional, very Eastern lawyer Ranse Stoddard (Stewart) was the instrument of the destitution and death of Westerner Tom Doniphon (Wayne).[16] In the Siegel film, the doctor's professional role is to pronounce the inevitable demise of the Western legend J.B. Books due to stomach cancer. Thus Stewart's role as Dr. Hostetler echoes his role as lawyer and politician in the Ford film. (In parallel fashion, the "villains" of the film are played by actors who had played Wayne counterparts or heroic analogues in Westerns: Richard Boone, who had played Paladin, a gunman with his own heroic narrative, in *Have Gun, Will Travel*, as well as ruthless villain John Fain, dispatched by Jake [Wayne] in *Big Jake* [1971]; and Hugh O'Brian, the Wyatt Earp of TV fame.)

Like Doc Winkler in *Riding Shotgun*, Dr. John Brighton (Joel McCrea) in *The Oklahoman* (Francis D. Lyon, 1957) intercedes in a murky dispute, acting as peacemaker between feuding parties. Unlike Winkler, though, Brighton is the protagonist of this film, which also includes a central focus on Native American (Cherokee) characters and on the discrimination facing them. Like the Cherokees who settled in Indian Territory, now chiefly Oklahoma, following the terrible Trail of Tears episode, Brighton settles after a personal tragedy in the small town of Cherokee Wells. The script thus links Brighton to the Western band of Cherokees as settlers in a land strange to them after undergoing travails.

Brighton had intended to go to California with his wife and baby, but his wife dies in childbirth, leaving him with a baby to care for and little motivation to continue westward. After moving in with the grandmotherly Mrs. Fitzgerald, he becomes a respected professional in the community as the town doctor. After a few years pass, he finds himself embroiled in

1. Professional Case Studies

a lethal dispute over land between Cass Dobie (played by the underrated Brad Dexter), a big rancher, and Charlie Smith (Michael Pate), a Cherokee farmer, whose daughter Maria (Gloria Talbott) becomes a big sister to Louise, Dr. Brighton's young daughter. The aptly named Cherokee Wells is in fact the site of much hidden oil, which motivates Cass to try to buy or to take Smith's land, as his farm sits on a rich oil deposit. The town includes numerous Cherokee inhabitants, such as the blacksmith Jim Hawk (Anthony Caruso), who line up alongside the Smiths in the dispute.

The land argument soon escalates, as Smith kills Mel Dobie (Douglas Dick) after Mel trespasses on his land and attacks him. The land clash takes on the familiar hue of a racially motivated lynching threat, and the doctor, already offended at Cass's provocative language towards Maria and concerned about his land encroachment, sides decisively with Smith. Thus the future of the settlement, as a multiracial town with diversified economies, lies not with the reactionary rancher Cass but with the progressive doctor and his allies, including not only the Cherokees but also the more enlightened ranch family housing his future wife Anne Barnes (Barbara Hale).

Significantly for the narrative's progressive leanings, this ranch family, although natives of Atlanta, seem to be without the prejudice expressed by many town inhabitants, accepting Maria and her family as friends on the strength of their ties to the doctor. Although Maria is of marriageable age, the screenplay includes the Anne character in order to allow the doctor to marry not only someone closer to his age but also, importantly for the period of the film, to avoid a cross-racial match. The focus falls on the doctor as the leader of a multiracial—but Anglo-led—town progressing into a new future, rather than on the consequences of a principled stand against racism as portrayed in roughly contemporaneous and more left-leaning films such as Huston's *The Unforgiven* (1960). Additionally, the professional man (the town) is linked with the traditional ranch community (the country) in the match between Brighton and Anne Barnes. Both have symbolic surnames: the future of the town is "bright" in the hands of the doctor, and the ranching and farming "barns" of the past join the progress of Cherokee Wells. As one would expect given the period of the film, the Cherokee characters quietly exit in the final scenes, leaving the future to the white Americans; but somewhat unusually for the period, a clear signal is sent that Smith and his family will be wealthy because of the oil on their land.

2

Professional Allies
Lawyers, Gunsmiths and Other Fixers

Like frontier doctors, journalists were important in the formation of civil society in the West. Historian William H. Lyon observed in 1980, however, that not much had really been published about newspapers in the West, despite their ubiquity and consequent importance (Lyon, W.H. 3). At the end of his article, Lyon summarized some prevalent perspectives on frontier newspapers and proposed some avenues of investigation. In the present context, his summaries of two perspectives on frontier newspapers are relevant, even as he laments the relatively low visibility of the discussions themselves. The first is "the Knight thesis," from the article by Oliver Knight which advanced it (Knight, O.), arguing for "the frontier newspaper as a catalyst in social change," important to town-building (Lyon, W.H. 9). The countervailing "Lyon thesis" understands "the pioneer editor ... as a mirror of his society, bound and hemmed in by the norms of his frontier community.... The editor could not become too eccentric" for his community (Lyon, W.H. 9). Lyon also notes the importance of politics, and political alliances, to the fortunes of newspapers and to the community interests they represented and advanced (9).

An instructive example of the political role played by frontier newspapers is to be found in the history of the famous mining town of Tombstone, Arizona, site of the Earp-Clanton gunfight on October 26, 1881. The newspapers and their editors adopted opposing positions in the conflict between the Earps and the Clantons. The *Epitaph*, edited by John P. Clum,[1] was solidly Republican and business-oriented, supporting the Earps. The *Nugget* and its editor Richard Rule were Democratic and sided with the Clantons as representatives of the "cowboy" faction (Tefertiller

2. Professional Allies

81). (This town-country polarization is eerily reminiscent of the highly destructive, pernicious bitterness between *unitario* [town] and *federalista* [country] in mid–19th century Argentina.) A fictional instance of a newspaper editor supporting town-building, in fact state-building, without the press rivalry of the Tombstone example is to be found in Ford's *The Man Who Shot Liberty Valance*, in which *Shinbone Star* editor Dutton Peabody (Edmond O'Brien, in one of his most floridly effective performances) engages in a combination of muckraking broadsides and boosterism despite vicious treatment at the hands of the villain, Liberty Valance (Lee Marvin). The epitome of the crusading Western newspaperman (perhaps epitomized to the point of parody), Peabody prints truth, or exposes lies, while his latter-day, post-statehood successor, Maxwell Scott (Carleton Young) acquiesces in "the false myth" about Stoddard and his rise to fame (Cubillos and Brenes 21).[2] As Bandy and Stoehr note, in Ford's Westerns, "It is the inebriated who are the most highly educated professionals," and two standout examples are Thomas Mitchell's Doc Boone from *Stagecoach* and Dutton Peabody from *The Man Who Shot Liberty Valance*. Both characters are truth-tellers, perhaps following the ancient motif of the blind prophet, or the disabled prophet, who is tolerated (up to a point) because of his infirmity. Bandy and Stoehr state that these two characters "are, together with heroes played by John Wayne, the most perceptive observers and speakers of truth in Westerns" (Bandy and Stoehr 64). (See also their comments on Peabody as "the quintessential Fordian philosopher" [207], as well as Jeanne Heffernan's commentary on the *Stagecoach* characters, where she observes that "Boone, drunk though he is, perceives the deceptive face of conventional categories" [Heffernan 150].)

Lee Clark Mitchell discusses the inebriated character in connection with his concept of characters who present the "silhouette of masculinity" in Westerns, noting

> the frequency with which the town drunk stumbles through the Western, and the stakes seem significantly higher when the drunkard is, as so often, a figure of education or expertise—a doctor, say, or newspaper editor, or even a former sheriff [or a serving sheriff as drunk, as in *Lawman* (Michael Winner, 1971) and *Bad Day at Black Rock* (John Sturges, 1954)]. It is as if the rationale behind such figures of complex talents and skills were that, unlike the hero, they fail to control their desires [Mitchell 166].

According to Joseph McBride, O'Brien "draws on his background as a Shakespearean actor" for his role as Peabody, "the grandiloquent champion of the freedom of the press," who "uses Shakespearean locutions and quotes from Henry V's St. Crispin's Day speech to bolster his own courage" (McBride 628). (See also the article by Sidney A. Pearson Jr., who comments ironically on the attack on the *Star* and its editor by Valance, that words alone will not guarantee a civilized outcome: "Freedom of the press, it turns out, is also dependent on someone wielding a gun" [Pearson 26].)

The normal configuration in Westerns is for the elements of civil society to cooperate in the taming of the town or in its initial construction as a civil concern. But the process by which such solidarity is achieved may vary widely. The 1949 film *Canadian Pacific* (Edwin L. Marin) is an instructive example. An attempt to capitalize on the great success of the 1939 *Union Pacific* (Cecil B. DeMille) (see Mankiewicz), the film did well at the box office, though it falls short of the rather giddy panache of the 1939 railroad epic. Still, it features several professional characters: railroad surveyor Tom Andrews (Randolph Scott), physician Edith Cabot (Jane Wyatt), and priest Père Lacomb (John Hamilton), as well as an interesting focus on western Canada and on the *Métis* (mixed-race) population of that area. ("The Métis were mixed-blood French-Indian plainsmen, mostly French-Cree and French-Assiniboin; under the mystical Louis Riel they made a noble effort [in 1870, with an epilogue in 1885] to set up an independent semi-Indian state in Canada's great plains, and lost" [Brandon 339].)

As in *Union Pacific*, the hero is tasked with completing a difficult rail line. Here, as in *Kansas Pacific*, the troubleshooter has more problems with external opposition than with internal corruption or resistance—with one important exception. Dr. Edith Cabot (her name perhaps echoing the famous 19th century nurse Edith Cavell), played by Jane Wyatt, who was about to find her niche in Hollywood with her television role in *Father Knows Best*, is the railroad doctor and resident pacifist, strenuously opposing Tom's use of force to discipline his men and to resist the corrupt cabal, led by Dirk Rourke (Victor Jory, in one of his standard villain roles), which exploits the Indians and *Métis* to fight the railroad. Edith supplants Cecille Gautier (Nancy Olson), a beautiful and fiery *Métis*, as Tom's love-interest for a brief time, until her insistence on not allowing him to use force threatens to "emasculate" him. Resisting the feminizing influence feared by the classic Westerner, Tom finally picks up his guns and goes back to enforcing law on the rough rail workers and to fighting the cabal. Edith leaves on the train as Tom is reunited with Cecille, who is nearly as aggres-

2. Professional Allies

sive as Tom in opposing Rourke and his men. (Interestingly, the cross-racial liaison is never really a point of contention in this film as it is in other Westerns, such as *Duel in the Sun* and *The Unforgiven*.)[3]

So, in this instance, the representative of the medical profession is well to the left of the political center of the film, and she actually stands as an obstacle in eliminating the threat to the railroad, much like the pacifistic Dr. Carrington (Robert Cornthwaite) in the nearly contemporary Howard Hawks film *The Thing from Another World* (1951). She is unsuited, as the film would have it, to the tough tasks of setting up a civilized community; only the man of force and the woman in nature (Cecille) can accomplish this task—in this instance, the woman is the figure who understands the wilderness and its inhabitants because of her ethnicity. Like Cooper's Hawkeye, who seems native because he can bridge two worlds, Cecille can succeed where the Eastern-like, overcivilized Edith cannot. As Richard Slotkin observes of Hawkeye, "In a situation of cultural conflict he is ... the most effective of civilization's soldiers, since he knows how to think and fight like an Indian, to turn their methods against them" (Slotkin, "Continuity" 11). Warren S. Walker characterizes Hawkeye (or Natty) as "a white man committed to white ethics by rejecting white society; a white man, furthermore, devoid of all the traditional prejudices, pro and con, about Indians, and hence left free to form his own opinions about them" (Walker, W.S. 112).

Less contentious is the relationship between the fatherly Père Lacomb (also a historical figure) and his *Métis* charges. Although as a priest he cannot openly condone violence, he actively assists Cecille and Tom, with whom he has a good understanding, in their battle against Rourke and his allies. His position as intermediary and even activist is enhanced by his location within the indigenous community, not outside it (and the railroad world) as in the case of Dr. Cabot, who spends most of her time, significantly, inside the railroad car where she lives and works.

Contrasting to the negative view of railroading in *Canadian Pacific* is the neatly written little tale "Tough *Hombre*" by Noel M. Loomis. The titular protagonist, Big Blue Buckley, is a railroad foreman who does not mince words or fists. He is asked to head a railroad team laying a line in Mexico, from Guaymas, Sonora (south of Hermosillo, on the coast of the Gulf of California) to Nogales, Arizona, approximately a distance of three hundred miles. His job begins in 1880 with a deadline at end of year, 1882.[4] He is under contract to the government of Porfirio Díaz, president of Mexico for more than three decades until his 1911 resignation, early in the Mexican Revolution. Despite its obvious defects, the Porfirian period in Mexico contributed materially to modernization of the country, for example in railroads: "railway mileage increased from virtually none to 15,000 miles" (Knight, A., *Mexican* 12). For Díaz's resignation, see Knight, A., *Mexican* 31.

So, Buckley will have a crew of Mexicans and men from north of the border. Early in the story a group of men sail into Guaymas to join the crew. One of the toughest of this rough lot is a man named Wade Gholson, who confronts the professional foreman because Buckley had killed his brother Vince on another job. After Buckley wins his first fight with Wade, he puts Wade and his men to work. After the fight, one of Buckley's Irish workers, a man named O'Connell, comments that Gholson and the "'bunch off the boat is the cut-throatingest bunch I ever laid eyes on.'" Buckley responds gleefully that "'Every last one of them is running from the law.... They figure they'll raise a lot of hell, and I'll fire them, then nobody will go looking for them. But they're going to get a surprise.... They're going to learn how to build railroads'" (Loomis 59). Eventually Gholson and Buckley engage in a deadly fight with spike mauls. Both are injured but Gholson is subdued and finally makes his peace with Buckley, who receives an accolade about his toughness from Diego, one of the Mexicans whom he had had to discipline during the job (Loomis 67–69).

Railroads receive positive attention in *Carson City* (André de Toth, 1952) with Randolph Scott as rough-and-tumble railroad engineer Jeff Kincaid laying track through desolate and hilly terrain between Carson City and Virginia City, Nevada, mainly to transport gold bullion from the mines to assayers and bankers in Virginia City. The project is spearheaded by William Sharon (Larry Keating), manager of the Golden State Bank, and is supported by Charles Crocker (Thurston Hall), chief operating officer of the railroad. Kincaid is enlisted because of his toughness and his experience in working innovatively in difficult conditions in Panama. His work soon pits him against local interests who do not want the tracks laid. Among them are newspaperman Zeke Mitchell (Don Beddoe), who fears an increase in crime because of the types of commerce brought elsewhere by railroads: "We have a peaceful town here, and I'd like to see it kept that way. Open it up and you'll have another Dodge City, where a decent woman can't step outdoors after sundown"; and Jack Davis (Raymond Massey), a mine owner who tells Sharon, "Afraid I'll have to stay with my

2. Professional Allies

friends" (De Toth, *Carson City* Ch. 2) in opposing the railroad, but who actually wants to continue robbing the stagecoach line as the secret head of the Champagne Bandits, so called because they offer champagne and food to the passengers as they steal the bullion being transported in the stagecoaches. As one might expect in melodramatic plotting, the conflict is exacerbated and the intrigue heightened by the jealousy of Jeff's half-brother Alan (Richard Webb), the stiff and self-righteous assistant to Mitchell, who carries a torch for Mitchell's daughter Susan (Lucille Norman), who, in turn, is interested in Jeff. Alan also appears to resent Jeff's success at his work and to envy Jeff's courage and singlemindedness.

This film is rather unusual among Westerns in that it concentrates on three professional categories, or possibly even on four, if the railroad executive is included. The narrative focuses particularly on the railroad engineer and the newspaper editor, with the big banker and the railroad executive supporting the engineer. The newspaper editor, played by Don Beddoe, an actor who was accomplished at conveying both congeniality and nervous uncertainty,[5] is more concerned with maintaining an idealized status quo than with buying into the future of the territory, and so one of his functions in the narrative is to die at the hand of Davis so that the plot of the nefarious Bandits can be revealed. Like Peabody in *The Man Who Shot Liberty Valance*, who was beaten by Valance and his thugs but who survived to push for statehood, Zeke Mitchell suffers for the progress of the town. His querulously vehement objections to progress, based on fear of change, do not fit well with the ideology of the 1950s period of the making of the film, with its boosterism and managerial ethos.[6]

The newspaper itself (the *Carson City Clarion*) is divided in its leadership and thus in its focus, with Zeke as editor and Alan Kincaid as apprentice or assistant. The compassionate and cautious Zeke contrasts sharply with the impulsive and hot-tempered Alan, whose jealousy of his brother causes him to act selfishly and irrationally. His emotional opposition to the railroad adds a disruptive dimension to the newspaper's editorial stance which is based, at least officially, on the principled stand of its editor Zeke. When Zeke is killed, Alan continues to oppose any moves by his brother, even refusing to go to the aid of Jeff and some miners who are trapped in a cave-in. Finally Alan has a change of heart and saves Jeff's life (in pursuit of Davis), in a rather unconvincing, melodramatic reversal of his long-standing rancor towards his brother.

The third set of professionals in the film, the banker William Sharon and the railroad executive Crocker (whose name clearly echoes the famous Charles Crocker of the Central Pacific),[7] are not presented as controversial. Their main concern is the bottom line, although Sharon is the more developed character of the two, and he does play a prominent role in the laying of the railroad and, as we have seen, in the presentation of the idea to the miners' association in town. He becomes an ally and then a friend to Jeff, and when Jeff and some of his crew are trapped in a cave-in, Sharon works in shirtsleeves alongside the miners and Susan to free them, implying a solidarity between the financial angels of the railroad and the workers on the railroad, as well as the interests of the press, represented by Susan, that may seem exaggerated.

The stagecoach owner Henry Dodson (George Cleveland) is another professional affected by the new railroad. His ramshackle company could collapse after the railroad is opened up, an example of technological obsolescence. During part of the film he expresses repeated concerns about the fate of his company, but as a good-natured sort he seems to accept the future, observing, "I've started over before. Guess I ain't too old again to start someplace else" (De Toth, *Carson City* Ch. 3). After the railroad begins to become a reality, Henry understands that he will be able to stay in business hauling equipment for construction and other operations. This corporatist Western appears to reassure all honest participants in society that they will not be left behind in the changing circumstances of the rail, or by analogy, of the post–World War II, era.

Another failed professional figure is to be found in *Ten Wanted Men* (H. Bruce Humberstone, 1955). Overall a standard Randolph Scott vehicle, the film does contain a lawyer character of some profile. Adam Stewart (Lester Matthews), the lawyer brother of rancher John Stewart (Randolph Scott), has come out West at his brother's request to help him bring some "law" to the town. John conflates law enforcement with legal pleadings, contributing materially to the failure of his project, at least initially, and to the death of his brother precisely because of the extralegal quality of the area. Adam is coded as hopelessly Eastern from the start—British accent, overdressed, well-mannered. In a plot with some echoes of the Billy the Kid stories, he is waylaid and assassinated by spiteful Wick Campbell (Richard Boone), and the somewhat unbalanced younger Stewart brother Howie (Skip Homeier) vows revenge (as did, in legend, Billy the Kid when his British mentor John H. Tunstall was murdered [see Utley 97, 99]).

2. Professional Allies

A strangely comic medical figure appears in "After Blackjack Dropped," a story by Karl Lassiter about the bizarre aftermath of a hanging. Blackjack Ketchum is duly hanged for his crimes, but the hanging has a grotesque outcome: the rope is too slick and decapitates Blackjack. This incident affords the picaresque phrenologist Dr. George Otis his opportunity of stealing the head of the criminal during the confusion after the hanging. Employed by the Army Medical Museum, the medical doctor is a devotee of phrenology, the study of skulls to determine character or psychological makeup. This now-debunked "science" was in vogue about the time of the heyday of Wild West outlaws, and Otis is determined to prove its efficacy.[8] Having failed to negotiate with the oddly named Sheriff Salome Garcia (whose given name is an obvious reference to the woman who demanded the head of John the Baptist and whose surname recalls the Peckinpah film *Bring Me the Head of Alfredo Garcia*) for receipt of the head of Blackjack Ketchum, he resolves to purloin it. But the sheriff pursues him and retrieves the head for burial. The penalty for the doctor appears to be the loss of his opportunity for research.

More mysterious than these figures is the medical man played by Gary Cooper in *The Hanging Tree* (1959), the Delmer Daves adaptation of the Dorothy M. Johnson novel. Set in 1873 during the Montana gold days, the film centers on the enigmatic Dr. Frail (Cooper) who moves into town with little explanation or fanfare—in fact he is quite secretive, living in an old shack and isolating himself from the townspeople except for professional services. This situation changes somewhat when he rescues Rune (Ben Piazza), who has been shot by Frenchy Plante (Karl Malden) after trying to jump his claim. Frail displays a less-than-attractive side of his character as he makes Rune an "indentured servant" after treating him, threatening to reveal the source of his injury to the miners by showing them the bullet he extracted. Although he promptly throws the evidence away (secretly), revealing to the audience a wryness or even flippancy not immediately evoked by his stern exterior, he proves a tough taskmaster to Rune, even humbling him in public.[9]

Eventually the little doctor's office acquires a larger responsibility, and another lodger, after Elisabeth Mahler (Maria Schell), a Swiss traveler, is found nearly dead after her father is killed in a stage holdup. Blinded for a time by the sun, Elisabeth undergoes a long convalescence, housed in a back room off the store run by the generous Tom Flaunce (Karl Swenson). Tom becomes the liaison between Frail and the townspeople and his only real supporter in the town, and Tom evidently knows something of the doctor's background, or at least the story of a doctor named Temple who appears to fit his biography. The film displays significant *noir* qualities, without perhaps the usual signifiers of *noir*—flashbacks, for example—but including a mysterious and perhaps dangerous protagonist whose biography is only gradually pieced together, a twisted pair of villains with psychological defects (Frenchy and Grubbs [George C. Scott]), and a potentially disruptive female character (Elisabeth). The first of these characteristics, the enigmatic protagonist, recalls such *noir* Westerns as *Pursued* (Raoul Walsh) and *Blood on the Moon* (Robert Wise); and Cooper, playing against his "aw, shucks" image from earlier in his career (much as James Stewart did in his renowned Anthony Mann–directed Westerns), plants real doubt in the viewer as to his character's real intentions and even his psychic stability. The film also provides an odd twist on the "lone stranger" motif of the "classical western" as delineated by Will Wright: (*Sixguns* 1975, 32; qtd. in Baker 130): "the story of the lone stranger who rides into a troubled town and cleans it up, winning the respect of the townsfolk and the love of the schoolmarm." Not only does Frail fall short of favorable opinion in the town, but he fails to "clean it up" and must be saved by the orphaned woman Elisabeth, his former patient. At film's end, Frail and his new family leave the rough town to its own devices, riding off to a presumably more peaceful future.

Frail (the name is ironically symbolic)[10] hides his vulnerability by attempting to control first Rune and then Elisabeth, until he becomes frustrated at their resistance and suspicious of his own motives and tells them both to leave (another domination attempt). Only when Frail becomes truly vulnerable, nearly being lynched by a mob led by the vengeful and psychotic "preacher" Grubbs and other town lowlifes, does he become a healthy member of society. In fact Frail is saved by the psychically potent character Elisabeth: "Unlike the traditional woman's film, Elisabeth becomes empowered.... Elisabeth fulfills the role of charging like the cavalry to save the appropriately named Frail's life from the irrational lynch mob" (Metz 215). Metz also observes that in the Johnson story upon which the Ford film *The Man Who Shot Liberty Valance* is based and in *The Hanging Tree*, "The central female protagonist is responsible for the introduction of a school into the Western town. In 'Liberty Valence [*sic*],' the illiterate Hallie convinces Ranse to teach her to read and start a school" (Metz 217). He is able to accept Elisabeth's love, and presumably Rune's friendship (or

2. Professional Allies

adoptive son status?). As in *Ride Lonesome,* a symbolic tree signals the transition from a former life of emotional incompleteness to a future life of fulfillment.

A similar though less complex character is portrayed by Edmond O'Brien in the excellent *Silver City* (Byron Haskin, 1951). A mining engineer rather than a doctor, Larkin Moffatt (O'Brien) cannot find employment because, in a move allusive to the blacklisting atmosphere of the times in Hollywood, he has been publicized as "a crook" by his former employer Charles Storrs (Richard Arlen). Fleeing his past, he lands in the mining community of Silver City, where he opens an assay office, hiding his superior training as an engineer as he performs routine tasks examining ore. After assaying a mine as rich in silver, he becomes the foreman for a family (father and daughter) who have a lease to develop the mine. The mine is owned by R.R. Jarboe (Barry Fitzgerald), a grasping, selfish capitalist common in Western melodrama but given unique flavor by the flamboyant Irish actor, and soon Storrs re-enters the picture as another interest in the mine.

Aside from the romantic details of the film, which are important to its plot, the script by Frank Gruber[11] concentrates the pivot point of the narrative on the qualifications and the determination of the engineer character. This 1951 film fits neatly into the Cold War emphasis on managerial and technocratic professions. In the ideology of the period, "The scientist and the engineer became the war hero, not the grunt or the army officer" (Markusen 40). A professional with integrity and drive, Moffatt allies himself with family-oriented mine developers Dutch (Edgar Buchanan in a standard role for this solid actor) and Candace Surrency (Yvonne De Carlo, playing against her *noir* performance alongside Burt Lancaster and Dan Duryea in Robert Siodmak's superb *Criss Cross*). Although Larkin Moffatt is not a gunfighter, he can handle himself in a fight; like veterans of World War II, who may have received special training in fields such as engineering, Moffatt is a highly qualified, capable professional. But like Dr. Frail, his background holds a secret "mistake," which (unlike Frail's) is never specified. Finally Larkin's past is overcome by his ethical and courageous conduct in the Silver City mine.

An important model for such "fallen professional" characters (Studlar's term) is Doc Boone in Ford's *Stagecoach* (1939) (Studlar 139–40). In the opening scenes of Ford's landmark film, the Overland Stage[12] is preparing to leave the town of Tonto, and "drunken Doc Boone (Thomas Mitchell) and the prostitute Dallas (Claire Trevor) have been driven out of town by the self-righteous women of the Law and Order League" (Erisman 250). These characters, and others in the coach, will undergo a mythic "'journey into hell'" (Place 32) (qtd. Erisman 250). Leonard Engel observes that by using contrastive space (between the stagecoach and Monument Valley), "Ford suggests the gradual regeneration of the prostitute Dallas and the escaped convict the Ringo Kid [John Wayne]" (Engel 175). By employing the journey trope, Ford and his writers tap into a long tradition of storytelling based in journeys and in self-discovery, a tradition which includes not only the *Odyssey* but also the 14th century *Canterbury Tales* by Geoffrey Chaucer, and *Don Quixote* (1605, 1615) by Miguel de Cervantes. Matthew Bernstein observes that the film has "a premise critics have compared to von Sternberg's *Shanghai Express* and which [screenwriter Dudley] Nichols himself compared to *Grand Hotel*" (Bernstein 148). Erisman draws convincing parallels (with direct evidence from the series creator Joss Whedon) between the Ford film and the cult TV science fiction/Western hybrid *Firefly* (2002), including a comparison of their respective passengers (Erisman 250–51). Both the 1939 Ford film and the recent TV series as well as its sequel, the theatrical release *Serenity* (2005) feature among their travelers professional or quasi-professional characters, and both emphasize anagnorisis and often abrupt peripeteia in their plot development.

Only a limited selection of the passengers in the two films fits the civil professional template, although of course one might consider nearly the entire crew of *Serenity* (the spaceship in *Firefly*) as a sort of professional, if banditry is a profession. The two groups of passengers feature a doctor (Doc Boone, Dr. Simon Tam) and a professional driver (Buck, the pilot Wash). *Serenity* additionally includes an engineer savant, Kaylee (Jewel Staite), probably modeled to some extent on Scotty (James Doohan) from *Star Trek*. Michael W. Marek, who comments of *Firefly* that "each [major character] is a fresh take on a standard archetype of Old West myth," speculates that "Kaylee ... could be a reincarnation of the Old West blacksmith" (Marek 106–07). Robert L. Lively also notes her formally untutored status and sees her as an "intriguing character" who represents a twist on "the stereotypical pioneer woman" (Lively 191–3). Unlike Scotty, though, Kaylee is almost uneducated. She displays an innate and extraordinary talent for engineering, as Erisman notes (251) (rather like the character Happy [Jadyn Wong] on the TV series *Scorpion*).

2. Professional Allies

The two doctor characters are intriguingly contrastive yet similar in significant ways. Both are outcasts, Boone due to his drinking and unreliability, Simon due to his unwillingness to ignore the ill treatment of his sister River (Summer Glau) at the hands of Alliance scientists. Besides these evident reasons for their pariah status—Boone is shunned by the townspeople of Tonto, while Tam is a fugitive after he rescues River—both professionals object fundamentally to the values of the dominant culture. As J.A. Place explains, the negative aspects of a character such as Doc Boone are necessary to bring an exalted type down to earth: "Doctors in films and in our society take on larger-than-life dimensions because of their powers of life and death. To be human as well, their weaknesses must be similarly exaggerated" (Place 34). The drunken doctor in Westerns is a familiar fixture. The article "Doctors" in *The BFI Companion to the Western* acknowledges the figure's frequency and notes that "so persistent is the stereotype of the drunken doctor in Westerns that its origins surely predate the genre." After mentioning Mitchell's Doc Boone as "the definitive portrayal," the article concludes by identifying some "more worthy medics," including doctors such as John McIntire's Doc McCord, Gary Cooper's Dr. Frail, William Holden's Captain Marlowe, all addressed in the present study (Buscombe 111). Tonto's civilized people (especially the church women) are not to Doc's liking, due chiefly to their blinkered moralizing. Boone is also a "marginal" character, according to Charles Ramírez Berg, because of his Irish ethnicity, so that Boone's uproarious manner and his objections to the moralizing of the elites of Tonto can also be understood in Bakhtinian terms: "From the Margin's perspective, these actions [drinking, in Boone's case] are an oppositional carnival of ethnicity meant to disrupt Mainstream sensibilities." In this connection Berg cites an exchange between Boone and "the bombastic banker Gatewood," from which Boone emerges the comic victor (Berg 83). Edward Buscombe (cited in Lehman 146) comments on the viewpoint of many Westerns concerning bankers:

> Bankers are rarely accorded much respect in the Western. They are viewed through the lens of a vague but persistent populism which originated in the nineteenth century and which held eastern capitalists responsible for the hardship which seemed the invariable lot of the small farmer in the western states [Buscombe, *Stagecoach* 29].

Lehman adds that "not just bankers but railroad tycoons and businessmen are frequently portrayed in a negative light as greedy, immoral people lacking decent human values such as compassion, honesty, and loyalty" (Lehman 146). Simon Tam of *Firefly* does not necessarily object to his father's wealth and his sophisticated connections in the Alliance, but he does object to the excessive emphasis placed on these things by his parents, who cannot understand why he would discard a very promising career as a brilliant young doctor for a crusade to rescue his sister, whom they do not believe to be under threat in any event.

In other respects, the two doctors are quite different. The effusive and garrulous (and often inebriated) Doc Boone contrasts sharply with the rather epicene, abstemious, and awkward Simon Tam, who seems incapable due to shyness and general social ineptitude of responding—until the 2005 film *Serenity*—to the emphatic advances of the very attractive and outgoing Kaylee. Nevertheless, the moral similarity between Boone and Simon is even more important. Despite his drunkenness, Boone is shown to be a generous and even principled man who believes in empathy towards unfortunates like Dallas and who perceives the kindness beneath the rough exterior of Ringo and the decency beneath the diffidence of another passenger, the whiskey drummer (seller) Peacock (Donald Meek).[13] Joseph McBride links Doc Boone directly to Ford himself: "Doc is Ford's surrogate figure, a liberal-minded, fatalistic, priestlike drunk who even bears a strong physical resemblance to the director" (McBride 287). Discussing the characters in Ford's films, Stuart Kaminsky observes that "at the heart of Ford's films ... is a drinking, disillusioned professional.... This character has participated fully in the conventions of society—he can quote from Shakespeare or the Bible—but has rejected society.... He is a paternal type who reflects a weak but enlightened old guard" (Kaminsky 210). J.A. Place observes that Doc Boone "is father figure to both of them [Dallas and Ringo] without being an authority figure like Curly" (Place 34).

In her article comparing the Maupassant story "*Boule de Suif*" and *Stagecoach* and discussing the possible origins of some of the characters, including Boone, in the Maupassant tale, Elisabeth-Christine Muelsch observes that "although Doc Boone and Dallas are expelled from Tonto because of their immoral behavior ... they emerge as the morally superior human beings who take a genuine interest in the well-being of others" (Muelsch 65). Tag Gallagher offers a contrasting view on the applicability of the Maupassant story as a source; see Gallagher, *John Ford: The Man and His Films* 146. (For a comparison of the film and its frequently cited

2. Professional Allies

source, "A Stage to Lordsburg" by Ernest Haycox, see Etulain 88–92.) Etulain notes that Ford credited the Haycox story as the source for the film, and also points out important "changes in characterization" between story and film "when Haycox's lusting cattleman and wooden English sportsman are replaced ... with superb roles for a crooked banker ... and a drunken doctor" (Etulain 88–89). Erisman observes of the Joss Whedon work that "in an especially telling reversal, the prostitute Dallas becomes Inara Serra (Morena Baccarin), a licensed and respected Companion" (Erisman 251).

On the *Serenity* crew, the seemingly weak and ingenuous Simon is in fact a man of solid and even rigid beliefs, among them the need for loyalty, particularly to his sister, and for preserving life wherever possible. Despite his apparent diffidence, Simon is coded by his costuming as a man not to be underestimated. Barbara Maio notes the Western coding of his appearance: "Simon is dressed in the tradition of many doctors in Western movies, a sort of futuristic Doc Holliday or Doc Boone (with less alcohol) ... with a three-piece suit that denotes the class typical of this profession but also with some Victorian shadings" (Maio 206). The mention of Doc Holliday, whose genteel outward appearance masked a violent, mercurial interior, and of Doc Boone, whose drunkenness obscured his essential decency and courage,[14] illuminates the duality in the deceptively meek Simon.

Neither character is completely withdrawn from civilization, since Doc Boone, morally reinvested, returns to it, or a narrow cross-section of it, at the end of the film, and Simon joins a renegade "family" aboard the spaceship. As Heffernan asserts about *Stagecoach*, "It is in fact the outcasts [like Boone] who do the most to uphold the values of civilized life on the stagecoach journey" (Heffernan 150). The fact remains that both characters reside outside narrowly defined "civilization": as J.P. Telotte notes, the Alliance slogan touting "the blessings of civilization" at the opening of the 2005 film directly alludes to Doc Boone's famous remark that, when Ringo and Dallas leave for his ranch, "at least they're free from the blessings of civilization" (Telotte 139*n*4). The opposition of Doc Boone, and of Ringo and Dallas, to "society" should not be overstated, as William C. Siska asserts: "Ford's heroes, even the outlaws, although individualists and loners, are tied to society, unlike, say, the independent, asocial heroes in the Boetticher/Scott Ranown series" (Siska 11). (For a brief presentation of Ford's treatment of the East across his films, but more particularly in *Stagecoach*, see Sickels 144.) The reference to the Scott films is easily illustrated through two of their titles: *Buchanan Rides Alone* (1958) and *Ride Lone-*

some (1959). Like Ringo and Dallas, Simon and his sister River try to leave behind the constricting "blessings" of the Alliance.

Like Frail, the Steve McQueen character Max Sand in *Nevada Smith* (Henry Hathaway, 1966) is an outcast figure. Unlike Frail, he is not a professional; in fact, he is illiterate and unskilled at the outset of the narrative. He is assisted in his training and his quest by professionals, both rather unusual: a gunsmith or gun seller and a Catholic priest. Sand is a "half-breed" whose parents are murdered by some strangers led by Tom Fitch (Karl Malden), supposedly former war comrades of Sand's father (Gene Evans). In a scene allusive to *The Searchers*, Max discovers the two bodies inside the house, looking at them grief-stricken from the doorway, like Ethan Edwards at his brother's house. Also like Ethan, or like Martin Pawley, Max swears to find the killers. Unlike *The Searchers*, this film does not concern the search for a kidnapped relative but rather the revenge quest of the untutored Max. Along the way Max learns skills which will assist him.

This odd *Bildungsroman* features, first, a gunsmith-gun dealer who becomes a father-figure to Max.[15] Played by the redoubtable Brian Keith, the traveling gunsmith Jonas Cord not only teaches Max to shoot, but also how to use his intuition to survive tricky situations. Eventually, he begins the process of teaching Max to read. He also tries without much success to instruct Max morally, warning him that revenge will solve nothing. Brian Fairlamb asserts that the "gun salesman" is "a character normally portrayed ... as devious or villainous" (Fairlamb 21), perhaps because he is often associated with, or actually is, a trader with Indians, trafficking illegally in liquor and weapons. Certainly in this case, as in *Colt .45*, discussed by Fairlamb, the gun dealer is a positive figure. After they part ways, Max begins to use his new strategic and tactical knowledge to carry out a complex plan of vengeance.

After provoking one of the killers, Jesse Coe (Martin Landau), into a deadly knife fight and killing him, Max learns the whereabouts of another, Bill Bowdre (Arthur Kennedy). In the film's most extensive sequence, Max commits an armed robbery in Louisiana so that he will be sentenced to the prison gang where Bowdre is also held. Exploiting the affections of a local woman, Pilar (Suzanne Pleshette), Max engineers an escape through the bayou and is successful. Pilar dies of snakebite, cursing Max as worse than Bowdre, and Bowdre is killed by Max. Max proceeds to finish his revenge after learning that Fitch is head of a gang in California gold coun-

2. Professional Allies

try. Mistreated by some of Fitch's allies, he is rescued by the intervention of a courageous parish priest (Raf Vallone, later to play the ill-fated Pope in *Godfather III*) who tries, like the gunsmith, to warn him away from the path of vengeance. Max works his way into Fitch's gang and takes his vengeance, leaving Fitch wounded and alone but not killing him. Riding away, Max seems to leave behind "civilized" society for the wilderness which is his home. In this film, even the civil professionals—Cord and the priest—appear chiefly on the margins of organized society. Cord is a traveling salesman, and the priest lives in an isolated parish.

A much less morally attractive gunsmith is a central character in the Tom Selleck Western *Last Stand at Saber River*. In this well-mounted Turner Entertainment offering, based on an Elmore Leonard novel, Selleck plays Paul Cable, a Confederate war veteran who deserts the cavalry unit led by Gen. Nathan Bedford Forrest and returns to his ranch in Texas only to find that it has been confiscated by Union men led by Duane Kidston (David Carradine) and his brother Vern (Keith Carradine) As a returning war veteran tale, the film is easily compared to other such narratives: "The character's [Cable's] personal journey from patriot-warrior to alienated veteran reflects the similar experiences of the Vietnam War portrayed in Hollywood films such as *The Deer Hunter* (1978)" (Pierson 294).

Cable moves his family back into his old ranch after retaking it from Kidston's men, and a violent feud ensues. The wild card in this land feud is the unrepentant gunsmith Austin Dodd (Patrick Kilpatrick), who, unlike Cable, has not soured on the goals of men like Forrest. Dodd runs guns over the Mexican border to bandits, hoping to use the proceeds to fund insurrection against the Union now that the war is nearly over. Cable had left his unit because he was sickened by the massacre at Fort Pillow, which was a Union stronghold "on the Mississippi in Tennessee some forty miles above Memphis." On April 12, 1864, it was "stormed" by Forrest's forces. The capture resulted not only in numerous casualties among the defenders (both white and black) but in accusations of massacre, hotly denied by the Confederates (Catton 319). The question is still not settled. The actual casualty figures for the defenders were: "of a garrison of about 560 men, an estimated 231 were killed and approximately 100 more seriously wounded" (Castel 46); see also Gannon and Foster.

The vengeful and duplicitous Dodd exacerbates the feud between the Cables and the Kidstons by killing Duane and framing Paul Cable for the murder. Eventually, however, the truth is learned about Dodd, and in a nice plot twist, Paul and Vern unite to stop Dodd and the bandits from closing the deal on the guns. Vern had always appeared less resolute in his opposition to the Cables than had Duane, and Dodd's kidnapping of the Cables' young daughter convinces him to ally with the Cables. Of course the message of this alliance is that North and South must make common cause after a destructive war.

A town gunsmith who only wants peace appears in *Forty Guns* (Samuel Fuller, 1957), a disguised treatment of the Earp brothers' story in Tombstone, though with some significant changes. Besides the important addition of the Jessica Drummond character (Barbara Stanwyck), replacing the Clantons as the threat to law in Tombstone, the narrative highlights a father-and-daughter gunsmith pair, Shotgun Spanger (Gerald Milton) and his spunky and talented daughter Louvenia (Eve Brent). In fact the film places Shotgun rather in the background of the lively and photogenic Louvenia, who becomes engaged to Wes Bonell (Gene Barry), one of the three Bonell (Earp) brothers in Tombstone. Like Morgan Earp in history and in films about the Earps, Wes is killed by a Bonell enemy, but in this instance his death occurs at nearly the exact moment of his wedding to Louvenia. Prior to this tragedy, Louvenia assists the Bonells, who are led by Griff (Barry Sullivan, the Wyatt Earp character), with some rather modern-sounding forensics. She identifies a rifle bullet which killed one of the deputies of corrupt sheriff Dan Logan (Dean Jagger) as one of her specially made .44–40 bullets, designed for long-range accuracy. Louvenia also promises to make a custom rifle with a fine walnut stock for her future husband, who serves as the rifle backup in Bonell confrontations with criminals. Her father, Shotgun, courageously tries to intervene against Jessica's dangerous brother Brockie (John Ericson), and when Brockie eventually kills Wes in a frontier drive-by shooting, Shotgun chases him on foot, firing at him but missing. At film's end, after Brockie dies in a gunfight with Griff, Louvenia finds some solidarity with Jessica, whom she had hated for protecting Brockie.

Unlike the positive figure of the itinerant gunsmith in *Nevada Smith* or the woman gunsmith in *Forty Guns*, the character Morgan Hastings in *The Sons of Katie Elder* (Henry Hathaway, 1965) is a town-grabbing, greedy killer, a man who is not, like Kidston in *Last Stand at Saber River*, driven by any ideological imperative. Like other such characters in Westerns, Hastings (James Gregory) uses his business as an anchor to expand into owning the town, including its law officers; in this way, Hastings and his

2. Professional Allies

ilk are holdovers from the type of grasping villain popularized during the 1930s in Frank Capra films and often incarnated by Edward Arnold. The early scenes of the film show the funeral of Katie Elder, whose four sons have returned to the small town of Clearwater, Texas, for the ceremony. One, John Elder (John Wayne), has arrived later and in more secrecy than the others. Rather like *Citizen Kane*, the narrative fills in the story behind the death of the Elder parents, although neither parent is actually shown in the film. The father, Bass, is represented by his tombstone, and the mother, in an ingenious bit of visual wit, by an empty chair, recalling a favorite folk tune of the period, "The Vacant Chair," popularized during the Civil War, as a kind of dirge befitting the loss of men in the war. The father was by all accounts a drunken gambler who allegedly lost the Elder property to Hastings in a card game. The mother had to move to a different house as a nonpaying tenant. Eventually the brothers discover that their father had been cheated out of his property by Hastings and then murdered.

The narrative highlights not only the checkered background of the Elder sons (John, gunfighter; Tom [Dean Martin], gambler; Matt [Earl Holliman], wastrel; Bud [Michael Anderson, Jr.], college dropout) but also the technological skill of the villainous Hastings. In his first appearance in the film he is shown practicing marksmanship with an advanced-design sniper rifle as his hired gunman Curley (George Kennedy) and his conflicted son Dave (Dennis Hopper) observe. Later he will backshoot the very traditional and incorruptible Sheriff Billy Wilson (Paul Fix) with this rifle. His last stand against the Elders will transpire in his gun shop, in which he will die from an explosion initiated by John Elder. Hastings, whose name implies both his recklessness and his fate (like the interloper Harald Haraldson at the battle of Hastings, the gunsmith will lose his "throne"), cannot stand with all his technology against the force of the old-fashioned 'elder' gunfighter John. Other professional characters in the film include the town doctor, Doc Isdell (Karl Swenson), who is presented as totally neutral in the conflict, and the more interesting undertaker/carriage maker Hyselman (John Doucette). This character, played by the always competent and watchable Doucette, endures a beating from Curley because he will not give him information about the Elders, to whom he has remained loyal largely due to an obvious, unrequited torch carried for their late mother. Another professional in the film, a blacksmith character, is not well-rounded enough to play an important role in the conflict, but he appears to be under the thumb of Hastings and his henchmen.

Professionals in Western Film and Fiction

Trail Street (Ray Enright, 1947) presents a very different environment from the marginalized societies of *Nevada Smith*. A town Western, it concentrates, like *Abilene Town*, on the conflict between ranchers and homesteaders. Additionally, like *The Gunfight at Dodge City*, the narrative fictionalizes the story of William "Bat" Masterson in his role as town "pacifier." In this instance, Masterson (Randolph Scott), a reluctant hero as so often in Scott's portrayals, intercedes in a violent quarrel between corrupt land speculator Logan Maury (Steve Brodie) and a group of homesteaders whom he tries to dispossess. Here, as elsewhere in the consideration of heroic roles, the classifications of popular culture heroes by Orrin E. Klapp are useful. In this case, the Scott character fits the category of "delivering hero," "one who comes in time of need to save people in danger or distress" (Klapp 137).

Masterson is aided by another real estate man, a positively depicted civil professional, Allen Harper (Robert Ryan, in an early role somewhat against type). With the help of figures like the saloon singer Ruby Stone (Anne Jeffreys), who is in love with Logan but must in the end act against him, Masterson and Harper succeed in civilizing the town, making it safe for peaceful homesteaders and solid businessmen like Harper. Unusual in this story about Masterson is the emphasis on his wish to become a journalist, which in fact he did, moving to New York as he mentions at the end of the film. His trajectory in this film is from West to East, a somewhat unusual reversal of the normal direction for characters in Westerns.

Most film presentations of Bat Masterson focus on his work in Dodge City or Abilene as lawman, especially in his association with the Earps, leaving aside his much longer career as a journalist in New York. One exception is *Woman of the Town* (George Archainbaud, 1943) unremarkable in most respects other than its framing story, which begins in 1919 when Bat Masterson (Albert Dekker) is working as a journalist in New York. Approached by a collector of guns which belonged to famous Western lawmen, he explains that he no longer has his gun, telling his editor that he buried it on Boot Hill. Left alone in his office to reminisce, Bat recalls in flashback his time as marshal of Dodge City, where he was hired despite his ambition to be a newspaperman. The rest of the film reveals his triangular love affair with singer Dora Hand (Claire Trevor), who is killed accidentally by King Kennedy (Barry Sullivan), the other point in the triangle. The dying singer makes Bat promise to give up killing, and so he arrests King and then buries his gun with Dora. The framing nar-

2. Professional Allies

rative resumes, showing a pensive Bat in his office with a framed copy of the article he wrote anonymously, his first newspaper piece, for the *Dodge City Globe*, called "Woman of the Town," about the good qualities of Dora Hand.

Randolph Scott also played a journalist character, not based on an actual historical figure as in the Masterson film, in *Fort Worth* (Edwin L. Marin, 1951),[16] a civilizing and corporatist Western in which his character, former Confederate soldier and would-be newspaperman Ned Britt (Randolph Scott), is instrumental in the forward progress of the rough cowtown Fort Worth. As in other such Westerns about the making of cities and of private enterprise, a positive exemplar must defeat his dark *doppelgänger*, who often represents rapacious, unchecked greed not in line with the New Deal and Fair Deal policies of the American mid-century. Much is made in the film of the advantage of word over violent deed (or, as Churchill once remarked, "To jaw-jaw is always better than to war-war") (Bartlett 622), although from the outset the point is made that Britt is highly skilled with Colts. Of course some of the men surrounding him are skeptical of his chosen profession. One of them refers to the newspaperman as a "type-swinger" and a "quill-pusher" (Marin, *Fort Worth* Ch. 3).

Ned tries mightily to refrain from using his Colts until force becomes inevitable, first against cattleman Wade Clevenger (Ray Teal) and his henchmen, and then against Britt's "evil double" Blair Lunsford (David Brian), a speculator who schemes to profit exorbitantly from the coming of the railroad to Fort Worth. Erstwhile friends, and rivals for the hand of ranch owner Flora Talbot (Phyllis Thaxter), the two men become increasingly estranged, with the stubbornly moral Britt's loyalty to his newspaper as the focal point. Although Clevenger's rampant lawlessness, reminiscent of the street violence of the brown-shirted Storm Troopers (Sturmabteilung or SA) during the late 1920s and early 1930s in Germany, appears the larger threat to peaceful prosperity in Fort Worth, the much more sinister machinations of the manipulative and hypocritical Lunsford are eventually revealed as the true menace. Tellingly, Lunsford tries repeatedly to enlist Britt, as the representative of literate public opinion and of the rule of law, as an ally in his schemes. If Britt is encouraged at first by Lunsford's bluff assurances that his only goal is the progress of Fort Worth, he is soon disillusioned as he discovers evidence of Lunsford's machinations.

Britt never loses his early idealism about the importance of a strong newspaper in community formation. Turning from a past of gun violence, in an interesting twist on the hoary motif of the gunslinger who hangs up his guns, he arrives in Fort Worth proclaiming that "We're going to delouse this burg" (Marin, *Fort Worth* Ch. 3), using words, not guns. His friend Luther Wicks (Dick Jones) edits the town paper, the *Fort Worth Star*, and Luther mentors Britt in the methods of ethical journalism. Like the voluble Dutton Peabody (Edmond O'Brien) in *The Man Who Shot Liberty Valance*, Wicks suffers violence at the hands of lawless men, dying from a gunshot (unlike Peabody, who recovers from a savage beating). Predictably, Luther's death only spurs Ned Britt on to stronger denunciations of illegality, although he insists that "I won't use the newspaper for a personal fight" with Blair Lunsford (Marin, *Fort Worth* Ch. 5). Britt tries to combat violence and lawbreaking with journalistic tools, but he finally must turn completely to gunplay—as he warns at one point in the movie, "You don't cover that story with a pencil" (Marin, *Fort Worth* Ch. 6). Blair is conveniently killed by gunshots from Flora and Clevenger, and Ned dispatches Clevenger, leaving Ned and Flora to marry and thus to unite city and country—the town paper with the local ranch, with a progressive future for the town befitting the optimistic postwar period when the film was made.

A much more characteristic template for career building in a Western is the "Go West, young man" motif popularized by Horace Greeley[17] and exemplified in Owen Wister's *The Virginian*.[18] The much-discussed (and often lamented and lampooned) tenderfoot character illustrates the East-to-West civilizing movement so central to the Western myth. This motif is important to the Fritz Lang *Western Union* (1941), starring Robert Young as the tenderfoot Richard Blake who, like James Stewart's Destry character, turns out not to be so tender.[19] The narrative is a standard nation-building tale about the construction of the Western Union telegraph system over the opposition of Indians who, historically, fought such expansions of white technology as the railroad and the telegraph because of the threat to their food supply, the buffalo (see McDermott). In this film the Indians are actually less threatening than a gang of whites led by Jack Slade (Barton MacLane) who disguise themselves as Indians both to hide their true identity as thieves and to stir up trouble between the Indians and the whites, in a clear and topical echo of suspicions of Nazi fifth columnists and saboteurs in the then-neutral United States at the beginning of World War II. This film by celebrated German emigré director Fritz Lang[20] displays his usual attention to detail and especial interest in the opening scene as the

2. Professional Allies

stage-set for the film, as well as his tendency to present experience in stagy or theatrical terms (see Gallafent 23).[21] The camera tracks in to a herd of buffalo (the concern of the Indians) next to telegraph wires and railroad tracks (the two enterprises threatened during the film). The perspective cuts to a lone rider, whom we see to be Randolph Scott. The clear implication is that, like the buffalo, he is doomed to extinction, and this proves to be the case by film's end. Unusually for Scott, his character Vance Shaw, a former thief like Slade but now on the path to reform, will die in the final scenes.

The Easterner Richard Blake is the target of some snickers at his buckskin outfit and revolvers. Soon, though, he proves himself worthy of some respect after successfully riding a difficult horse deliberately chosen for him as a prank. Well-educated, Blake is a surveyor sent to work for district manager Edward Creighton (Dean Jagger), whom Vance had rescued from the desert at the beginning of the film. Shortly, Richard and Vance, also working for Edward as a troubleshooter, engage in some comical rivalry for the attentions of Edward's sister Sue (Virginia Gilmore).

Western Union is very much a town Western, almost an "Eastern," as the perspective of the Creightons, Blake, and the other professionals—the doctor (John Carradine) and the very accomplished cook (Slim Summerville)—governs the narrative. Slade and his band, as well as Shaw, are seen as outsiders, interfering with or otherwise hindering the progress of the civilizing project. The cook is in fact a key indicator of this. He is hired to replace the former cook, whose product was bad in the usual stereotyped way of the wagon train amateur. When asked if he can cook lamb, he spins out several options, including fricasseed. He is treated comically, because when hired he is unwilling to endanger himself; thus he is shown accidentally spilling his plate, being shot at, burning himself by falling during a chase, and so forth. Comedy aside, he is a civil professional who has replaced an untutored amateur.

The doctor for the telegraph project, played by John Carradine, also differs somewhat from the frequent stereotype of the drunken Western doctor, whose most famous incarnation was the Thomas Mitchell character in Ford's *Stagecoach* (1939). As William Indick remarks, "It is a basic truism or cliché that the western doctor is always a drunk" (Indick 145). Exceptions prove the rule: when a Western doctor is not a drunk, his character stands out in relief, usually as a wise advisor to the town lawman or leader, as in *Dodge City* or *The Tin Star*.

Professionals in Western Film and Fiction

Carradine's physician is not particularly bibulous, but he does take bets on at least one occasion—so he doubles in a sense as gambler and doctor, a melding of types to be seen to much effect in the portrayals of the historical dentist Dr. John Henry Holliday. The telegraph doctor seems competent enough, working hard off-screen to save patients injured in Indian or thief attacks. On one occasion he bets $20 that he will keep a man alive until daybreak; after an ellipsis he is shown quietly paying the money to his betting companion. This corporatist Western, complete with office manager (Edward), secretary (Sue), expert (Richard), caterer, and security (Vance), not only has a resident doctor but a germinating office betting pool. The film also highlights new technologies, of course, and in a rather demeaning scene, Blake displays his cleverness in convincing the Sioux that the telegraph lines carry divine energy or magic and that they must not be molested. At the end of the tale, Blake, the Eastern tech expert, wins Sue's hand, as his rival Vance is killed trying to eliminate the threat from Slade (revealed as Vance's brother) and his gang. Representing the wild past of the region, Vance can neither escape his criminal past nor his wilderness roots. Significantly, it is he who rescues Edward from death in the wild, thus allowing the new technological frontier to open up, with all its attendant professionals and experts. Mark Williams notes Lang's "deconstructive pulling at the seams of the genre" here, and observes that this film leaves "a disquieting aftertaste." This is in part because Richard Blake, the surveyor who had shocked the Indians with electricity, will triumph at film's end: "The casually and brutally racist easterner ... will be unencumbered in his designs to merge with both a founding industry of modernity and the New Woman [Sue] it has escorted west" (Williams, M. 265–67).

A rather late Western about the opening of the frontier is *The Oregon Trail* (Gene Fowler, Jr., 1959), a generally routine tale of the early pioneers on the famous Oregon Trail. Besides the usual formula trappings, reminiscent of B-Westerns—starkly defined villains and heroes, for example[22]—it displays a few unusual features. Among these is the presence of jaunty newspaperman Neal Harris (Fred MacMurray) on the perilous journey westward. Tasked by his New York editor[23] to cover the historic opening of the Oregon Trail, Harris is not only reluctant to undertake the journey but also critical of the effect publicity has had on the unfortunate pioneers who have died on the trail as a result of their reading of the well-known work *The Oregon Trail* by Francis Parkman. Copies of the book

2. Professional Allies

have been found at massacre sites along the way.[24] Notwithstanding his reservations, Harris accepts the charge and heads west with a wagon train led by Capt. George Wayne (William Bishop). Besides the usual hint of romantic involvement with a predictably attractive member of the wagon train (Prudence Cooper [Nina Shipman]), and the presence of an experienced "man who knows Indians" (George Seton [Henry Hull]), the caravan includes an eccentric character, Zachariah Garrison, played with enjoyable floridity by John Carradine. The Seton character is perhaps loosely based on Henry Chatillon (1808?–73), Parkman's guide on the Oregon Trail expedition (see O'Leary). James L. Stokesbury comments of Chatillon: "A man whose great reputation on the plains was belied by his modest manner.... Parkman found Chatillon to be one of those rare creatures, a natural gentleman; he might have been the prototype for the idealized frontiersman of a Zane Grey novel" (Stokesbury 7). Garrison, a tragicomic Johnny Appleseed figure, wants to plant his prized trees in Oregon but is killed before reaching his goal.

The film also features a somewhat forced subplot about the growing romance between a mixed-blood woman, Shona Hastings (Gloria Talbott) and Harris, who proves, not surprisingly, a good hand with a gun (even the Colt revolver, newly introduced at the time) and a courageous pioneer. After Harris and his sadistic Army nemesis in the wagon train are captured by a hostile Arapaho band, due to the treachery of Shona's abusive husband Gabe (John Dierkes), Shona rescues Harris. After a fierce battle at Fort Laramie, in which Gabe, Garrison, and many others are killed, Capt. Wayne, who is more or less engaged to Prudence, departs for the incipient Mexican-American War.

Political concerns are threaded through the narrative. The film shows President Polk (Addison Richards) in serial negotiations with the British Ambassador, Sir Richard Wallingham (Lumsden Hare) regarding the boundary between British possessions (Canada) and the United States. (For the diplomatic context, see Merk and McClintock. For a study of the background to the Mexican-American war, see Graebner; for discussion of Parkman's work and the war, see Lawrence.)

Following the departure of Capt. Wayne, Harris and Shona leave for the Far West. This script element may reflect an actual fact of the biography of Francis Parkman, who lived briefly with the Oglala Sioux (see Terrie 377*n*3; for a wistful evaluation of the book and its treatment of Indians, see Schramm). Harris says that he will resign forthwith from the newspaper. Presumably the two will marry, although as Jon Tuska cautions, "In the historical reality of the American West, the Oregon miscegenation law prohibiting whites from intermarrying with inferior races would have prevented such a marriage from taking place" (Tuska 231).

An early John Wayne Western, *The Lawless Nineties*, presents a rather standard version of frontier-taming, as Wayne, playing government agent John Tipton, assists the territory of Wyoming in becoming a state. In a plot oddly prophetic of the John Ford masterpiece *The Man Who Shot Liberty Valance*, the territory's fate is to be decided in an election, subjected to corrupt influence by a gang resisting incorporation. Tipton, working undercover, befriends Major Carter (George "Gabby" Hayes) and his daughter Janet (Ann Rutherford), who have moved from Virginia to run a newspaper, which supports Wyoming statehood. Janet is one of a number of women who are paired with Wayne characters in his earlier Westerns: "The virgin daughters of professional men also [in addition to ranchers' daughters, for instance] become acceptable bridal candidates for the youthful Wayne characters: judge's daughter Maxine Carter in *The Man from Utah*, doctor's daughter Barbara Forsythe in *Winds of the Wasteland*, newspaper editor's daughter Janet Carter in *The Lawless Nineties*, banker's daughter Miss Florie in *Three Godfathers*, and store owner's daughter Felece Newsome in *The Trail Beyond*" (Lewis 10–11). Lewis notes however that these pairings do not apply to women professionals, only to the daughters of male professionals (Lewis 9).

Like many other films of the 1930s, this Western emphasizes the need for a unified nation and focuses on the plight of the "little man" who is unjustly manipulated by big interests, represented here by the Tammany-like gang led by Charles K. Plummer (Harry Woods), who hides behind a law-and-order organization. Carter and his family, which includes Moses, his black "servant"—presumably free, post–Civil War—are Virginians. Peter Stanfield (Ch. 6, "Dixie Cowboys: Representing the Nation"), discusses Southerners as rehabilitated members of the Union. Stanfield observes that "by 1940, sympathetic Southern characters in Westerns had become commonplace" (212). According to J.E. Smyth, this positive appraisal was not universal even among classic Western screen artists: "[Dudley] Nichols's and [John] Ford's attitudes toward the South were highly ambivalent throughout their careers—unlike most of their colleagues, who tended to lionize southern qualities as they traveled west" (Smyth, *Reconstructing* 125).

2. Professional Allies

Carter, the former luminary of a secessionist state, makes a nice speech about the necessity for unifying the nation, and Moses is treated uniformly with respect. Unlike many other treatments of this period in Wyoming history, the film does not focus specifically on the Johnson County War, with its theme of ranchers versus homesteaders.[25] These divisions are blurred as the script presents a struggle between the upstanding newspaperman (Carter, and, after his predictable murder, his daughter Ann) and the forces of corruption. An interesting element of the film is its handling of the town telegraph, a competitor in the communication field to the newspaper. The telegraph has been co-opted, or rather hijacked, by the ingenious method of a "wiretap": the combine has a hidden telegraph which prints out the messages sent and received on the official town instrument, whose operator is unaware of the tap. Rather like a duplicate Enigma machine in World War II, the hidden telegraph allows the combine to stay one jump ahead of the authorities.

The more traditional means of communication in the town, the newspaper, is here called *The Custer Blade*: significantly the town is named after the dead hero of white expansion into the West. As will Dutton Peabody in the town of Shinbone, Major Carter uses the paper as a political weapon, fearlessly attacking the enemies of statehood as "outlaws." Unlike Peabody, who is beaten but survives, Carter is killed outside his newspaper office, which is taken over by his daughter with Moses assisting her as typesetter. Both editors, Carter and Peabody, fulfill the function of most newspaper editors in Westerns: advancing the cause of national union and "civilization" or progress.[26] The chief exception to this general rule is the propagandizing by Col. Edwards in the Jesse James films, an activity based in historical fact. Edwards was instrumental in creating the legend of the James brothers and was a well-known defender of the secessionist faction in Missouri, which remained politically divided for a number of years after the Civil War.[27]

A major coup of the two most familiar films about James and his family from the classical era of Hollywood, *Jesse James* (Henry King, 1939) and *The Return of Frank James* (Fritz Lang, 1940) is their capacity for making Major Rufus Cobb (the Edwards character, played by Henry Hull) a sympathetic, folksy, even heroic figure.[28] Especially in the Lang film, Cobb acquires a folksy wisdom and charm nearly worthy of Lincoln—and the courtroom demeanor of Cobb owes not a little to the famous interpretation of Lincoln by John Ford and Henry Fonda in *Young Mr. Lincoln*.

Unlike Cobb, Carter espouses a staunch Unionism which recalls another Virginia-born Western character, Britt Canfield (Randolph Scott) in *Santa Fe*, a member of a Confederate family who has decided to support the winning side after the Civil War, a decision which leads to violent conflict within his family (see Hall, K.E., "From *The Iron Horse* to *Hell on Wheels*" 19).

Another Joseph Kane film from the FDR period which featured Wayne in a "town-tamer" role was *King of the Pecos* (1936). Here Wayne appeared as a young lawyer, John Clayborn, who disguises his actual surname as "Clay" because of an incident from his youth which in fact motivated him to become a lawyer. His family was murdered, and he was savagely beaten, by the thugs employed by grasping cattleman Alexander Stiles (Cy Kendall), as Stiles stole his family's ranch. Stiles is accompanied by his shifty lawyer Brewster (Frank Glendon) and by his head henchman Ash (Jack Clifford) in an opening shot of the film. Francis M. Nevins comments that the shot presents the three men as symbolic figures "exceptionally evocative for audiences during the Depression": an "obese capitalist," "his tame lawyer," and "his tame killer": "the evil trinity in *King of the Pecos*" (Nevins 52). Commenting on "Hollywood westerns of the 1930s and 1940s," R. Philip Loy observes that "more than a few people were convinced that the Depression was the result of malfeasance by wealthy bankers and industrialists concerned only about profits, so it is not surprising that western outlaws were recast as victims of those same forces ... westerns reminded Americans that they were heirs to hardy pioneers [like John's family in this film] and resolute frontier sheriffs" (Loy, "The Frontier and the West" 580).

As we discover ten years after the ranch killings, John sets out to become a lawyer—and trains himself to shoot proficiently—to seek redress; he tells a prospective client that "there's one case I've got to take care of first—John Clayborn vs. Alexander Stiles" (Kane, *King of the Pecos* Ch. 2). So the narrative becomes a hybrid of a revenge Western, along the lines of *The Sons of Katie Elder*, and a "town-tamer" film, with a dash of masquerade added to the mix.

A somewhat complex example of a "non-violent Easterner" tale is a short story by Ernest Haycox, "High Wind," from 1934, which contains not one but two Eastern characters as its protagonists (for Haycox, see Gale). One of these is Buck LaGrange, who has been living in Abilene for a time and, at the beginning of the story, is awaiting the arrival of his

2. Professional Allies

fiancée Abbie from their home town in Connecticut. After they marry, Abbie becomes increasingly uneasy about the apparent changes in her husband—he is becoming tougher, seemingly more callous, more of a Westerner—and unhappy with the shabbiness and dust of Abilene, symbolized by the high winds of the title. This is the Abilene of the early boom years before it settled into placid obscurity. Buck tries to reassure Abbie that in time Abilene "will be a grown town in a settled country" (Haycox 262). Buck has come West to seek opportunity instead of remaining an Eastern store clerk. He speculates in real estate and intends to plant winter wheat. His wheat plans lead him to fence in his property, causing a violent clash with some Texas trail riders. An uneven fight ensues which is broken up by Wild Bill Hickok, previously introduced as a friend of Buck, after Abbie tries to intervene. Abbie's distaste for Hickok, whom she claims to "'hate,'" perhaps because of her own unacknowledged attraction to him—she focuses rather obsessively on his face and hair (Haycox 266)—vanishes after this incident, when Hickok approvingly calls her "'a fighter,'" and she shows herself to be a budding pioneer wife, displaying her characteristic New England spunkiness (Haycox 270).

Another instance of an Easterner moving West to work in a rather rough setting is the story "First Principal" (A.B. Guthrie, Jr., 1953). The story is partially autobiographical, according to Guthrie's biographer: "'The First Principal' is based on an actual fistfight between the father [of A.B. Guthrie, Jr.] and a cowhand who considered school teaching a sissy job." Guthrie's father was the first principal of the Teton County Free High School in Montana (Benson 162, 3–5).

In the short story, Mr. Ellenwood has moved with his family from Ohio to Montana to become the "first principal" of the new high school. So Ellenwood is a putative linchpin in the process of civilizing the town. The name of the town, Moon Dance, mentioned only once, perhaps implies secretive and perhaps sinister activity.[29] Ellenwood, his wife and son Lonnie (the "reflector-character" of the story) are greeted by Mr. Ross, who chairs the school board and, ominously enough, as the observant Lonnie notices, drinks. In this economically narrated story, the major antagonists and allies are introduced swiftly, as Lonnie also sees another man, with yellow eyes like a cat, watching the arrival of the Ellenwood family.

Soon enough this unpleasant man, named Chilters, begins to harass Mr. Ellenwood. After he causes his horse to throw mud at Ellenwood on

Professionals in Western Film and Fiction

the street, Mr. Ross comes to the Ellenwood home and offers to give Mr. Ellenwood a revolver, an offer he declines. Predictably, Chilters rides up to the Ellenwood home, finding the principal outside chopping wood—a sign of strength on the frontier that should have alerted the arrogant Chilters. As Lonnie watches in fear, Chilters strikes Ellenwood across the face with his quirt. Ellenwood pulls Chilters off his horse and beats him soundly in a fistfight. Although physically small, Ellenwood proves his courage and his skill.

The tale is a neat reversal of the lawyer Ransom Stoddard's situation in Ford's *The Man Who Shot Liberty Valance.* Stoddard, savagely beaten by Liberty Valance on his arrival in Shinbone, gradually loses his ingenuous idealism, becoming more tough-minded and finally settling for a shifty compromise to allow him to contribute to civilizing the town and the territory. David W. Livingstone neatly places the beating into the context of legality in the Ford film: "If Stoddard represents law and order coming to Shinbone, then these principles are visually represented as barely alive and in dire need of Doniphon's care and support" (Livingstone 219). As Catherine Ingrassia points out, Stoddard's slippery handling of his own history (and Tom Doniphon's) "has caused his own identity to be effectively erased," since he is identified by "a railway conductor" at the end of the film, despite his confession to Maxwell Scott, the newspaper editor, about the facts of Valance's death, as "'the man who shot Liberty Valance'" (Ingrassia 7). Unlike Stoddard, Mr. Ellenwood fights back physically and wins when provoked, significantly avoiding gunplay and reinforcing his image of quiet strength. Where Stoddard subverts or skirts the law to establish law and order, Mr. Ellenwood shows that a man of education and peace can best a rough and ignorant barbarian like Chilters. So, the story ends with a nicely laconic touch:

> Mr. Ross said: "There's one man ain't going to be thinking education is sissified."
> Father nodded at the space he was looking into. "One," he said [Guthrie 293].

Guthrie cleverly changes the narrative voice to first-person (Lonnie's) from the third-person narrative which carries the story to this point, a subtle indication that Lonnie is now on board with his father and their move to the Montana town.

Like Guthrie's story, the tale "Friends in San Rosario," one of the group of Western stories by O. Henry (William Sydney Porter, 1862–1910), is based on autobiographical material. As Trueman O'Quinn wrote in 1939,

2. Professional Allies

"It is no longer new or original to say that O. Henry ... also wrote the life of William Sidney [sic] Porter, erstwhile ranch hand, druggist, bookkeeper, draftsman, bank clerk, newspaperman, publisher and fugitive from justice" (O'Quinn 143). This well-known American author seems to have filled out his résumé with a cornucopia of civil professional roles. His fictional craft was enhanced by his varied travels: "Though a journalist by trade, O. Henry was an artist who followed the school of regional writing ... he successfully depicted every locality in which he ever lived" (Long 240). This talent for regional depiction included Nashville, Tennessee, a town visited by O. Henry and pictured in his story "A Municipal Report" (O. Henry [pseudonym for William Sydney Porter], "A Municipal Report"), which contained a character contrasting sharply with the kind of idealized Southerner portrayed in films like *The Lawless Nineties*. This character is described by E. Hudson Long: "Major Caswell, degraded and dishonest, represents the type of 'professional Southerner' that O. Henry [himself a Southerner] abhorred" (Long 230).

"Friends in Rosario" relates an incident in the Texas town of San Rosario concerning the visit of a bank examiner to that town.[30] The examiner, who bears the persnickety name J.F.C. Nettlewick, first wishes to review the books of the First National Bank and then will proceed to the other establishment, the Stockmen's Bank. O. Henry thus sets up a potentially alternating situation which will allow the tale to become both suspenseful and cleverly resolved in his trademark fashion. The story was inspired by an actual incident from Porter's career in which he was accused of bank embezzlement while working as a teller in Austin, Texas (O'Quinn 143–45). The head of the fictional First National, the redoubtable Major Thomas J. Kingman, employs serial tactics to delay the examination. He does this after receiving a note from the president of the other bank in town, a Mr. Buckley.

Using delayed revelation tactics, O. Henry gradually shows what motivates Kingman to delay the bank examination. In a metafictional move, reflecting the framing device used in *The 1001 Nights*,[31] O. Henry has Kingman tell the examiner a story about his friend Bob, who was accused of stealing money from his bank's safe but who was in fact covering for Kingman, who had taken the money out while sleepwalking. Kingman tells the examiner this tale after admitting that he has taken some securities found to be missing during the examination. He tells him also that he took the money to protect a friend. After the examiner waits patiently through the protracted tale about his friend and his own sleepwalking, he produces the securities. The examiner leaves angrily, heading for the Stockmen's bank. Only then does Kingman read the note from the other bank president, who turns out to be Bob (Buckley), asking him to delay the examiner because he had lent some money to some friends to buy cattle. Expecting some funds to be wired that same morning, he needs time to replace them. After the funds arrive, he signals Tom, who lets the examiner go. Thus the two friends are even. This unusual little tale, besides featuring a civil professional in the person of a snooty examiner (as well as two professionals of sorts, the two bank presidents), represents an exercise in wish-fulfillment by O. Henry, whose own experiences with bank examiners were not so rosy.

In some cases the Easterner participates in town activities within a relatively established community. This type of situation is exemplified by two John Wayne Westerns, both from late in his career: *Chisum* and *McLintock! Chisum* is a retelling of the major events of the Lincoln County War, placed into the frame characteristic of late Wayne Westerns, in which Wayne plays a patriarchal, crusty figure in a battle against changing times. *McLintock!*, though similar in characterization, is a rather broad comedy which echoes Ford's *Rio Grande* in its focus on the estranged marriage of the Wayne character and the Maureen O'Hara character (both actors appeared in the earlier Ford film). Both films feature "tenderfoot" characters as well as other civil professional types, including the crusty Dr. Wilkins (played by Chill Wills in *Rio Grande*).

The Easterner or civil professional character in *Chisum* is Alexander McSween (Andrew Prine), a storekeeper and former lawyer in the town near the Chisum ranch. This character is based on the historical McSween, who died in the Lincoln County War. *Chisum* differs from other films about Billy the Kid and the Lincoln County War in its increased emphasis on the McSween story; usually, he is treated as a footnote to the main storyline of Billy and his fight with the authorities, especially Billy's death at the hands of Pat Garrett. Despite its cosmeticized treatment of the major figures in the story—Billy is a lovesick young man; McSween is an upstanding lawyer and storekeeper with a beautiful wife; Pat Garrett is ruggedly upright; and Chisum is, well, John Wayne—the film is of interest in this context because it highlights one civil professional and his struggle with a group headed by another professional of sorts, Lawrence Murphy (Forrest Tucker), a ruthless entrepreneur with political aspirations. Histori-

2. Professional Allies

cally, neither side was covered in virtue, as Kathleen P. Chamberlain observes: "The battle was not between the forces of good and evil, but between merchant factions vying for economic control of southeastern New Mexico" (Chamberlain 37). The McSween-Tunstall group fought against the "Murphy-Dolan-Riley" combine (Rasch 82) (see also Utley 96).

The screenplay preserves some underlying historical fact regarding the origins of this feud, as McSween is shown first working as a lawyer for Murphy, with whose methods he disagrees, and then going to work as a manager of the Tunstall store financed by Chisum's bank. The disagreement between the historical McSween and Murphy and his business partner Dolan (also a character in the film) was in fact an insurance dispute (Chamberlain 42). In the film, the idealized McSween dies after his business is set on fire (as in fact he did); he is killed by the vengeful sheriff gunmen hired by Murphy. In other respects the film duplicates familiar Billy the Kid elements: the murder of the generous Tunstall and Billy's revenge for it, the presence of Pat Garrett, Billy's alliance with McSween.[32] Like many other figures in Western legend and history, Tunstall has been idealized. Note, however, Philip J. Rasch's corrective admonition: "It has been the fashion to present Tunstall as an English lamb fallen among Lincoln County wolves. The fact of the matter is that he was simply a fortune hunter, determined to get everything on which he could lay his hands" (Rasch 80). As Kent Steckmesser puts it, "Tunstall was an ambitious and aggressive person, quite different from the refined and sensitive idealist known to legend" (Steckmesser 350). Chisum's role and his personality are also the subject of debate (see, for example West, J.O. 33).

In a configuration reminiscent of the 19th century political division in Argentina, a country with similar economic structures at that time to those of the American Old West, ranching interests fight in this film against centralized town imperatives: Chisum and his allies are positive, or whitewashed, parallels to the *federalistas* led by Juan Manuel de Rosas who savaged the *porteño* [Buenos Aires–based] *unitarios*. As Colin M. Winston summarizes, "Rosas came to symbolize the 'authentic' Spanish hinterland ... and an authoritarian political style characterized by the 'spontaneous' allegiance of the masses to a charismatic caudillo." As Winston notes, Domingo Faustino Sarmiento became his chief ideological opponent and in his *Facundo* (1845) "established the rigid differentiation between 'civilization' represented exclusively by the liberal, European, secular cosmopolitanism of Buenos Aires and 'barbarism,' epitomized by the ignorant Hispano-Catholic inland masses and their ruthless caudillos" (Winston 308). Sarmiento was to become president of Argentina and for his critics, a caudillo of the Liberal rather than the Conservative stamp. Chisum is idealized as the ethical force of Jeffersonian tradition who overcomes the grasping power of men like Murphy and Dolan, the type of professional speculator (a term actually used approvingly about himself by Murphy in the film) who fit quite well into the American Gilded Age of the late 19th century. The parallel drawn by David B. Davis between the Old South and the frontier West is apropos:

> Like the barons and knights of Southern feudalism, the large ranch owners and itinerant cowboys knew how to have a good time.... In this respect, the cowboy West was more in the tradition of fun-loving New Orleans than of the Northeast [Davis 114].

James K. Folsom observes that "for the first time in the Gilded Age the modern imaginative theme clearly emerges that the West will redeem the East, instead of the more traditional idea that the East will reform the West in its own image" (Folsom, "Imaginative" 91).

McLintock! (1963) features the typical late-career John Wayne character, a man resisting change and, in this case, genially displaying nostalgia for a past which includes establishing a cattle ranch, helping to build a township, and fighting Comanches. Not intended very seriously, the film glosses over the real conflicts involved in much of this past, the only exception being the ill treatment afforded the Comanches at the hands of a corrupt Indian agent (an early Strother Martin role).

Of interest here is the assortment of professionals included in the population of the clearly stagy town (shot at the movie set, Old Tucson): an ineffectual governor, a feckless college student, and an avuncular Jewish storekeeper, the most intriguing of the three. The politician, bearing the W.C. Fieldsian title of Governor Cuthbert H. Humphrey (Robert Lowery), is a typical corrupt windbag who presumes to court the (not so) estranged Mrs. McLintock (Maureen O'Hara)[33] and receives his comeuppance from her as well as from the federal authorities who will investigate his crooked deals with the Indian agent. The college student, Matt Douglas, Jr. (Jerry van Dyke), is also a stock character type, the arrogant, Pecksniffian Easterner (or Westerner with Eastern airs) who prides himself on his musicianship, dancing skills, and manners, but who is totally unsuited for the still rough life of the frontier. Philip French includes "Eastern dilettantes" and "government agents" among "the butts of the movie's unconcealed

2. Professional Allies

animus and heavy-handed comedy" (French 31). In a less comic setting, his great masterwork *Stagecoach* (1939), Ford excludes Easterners, or those sympathizing with their point of view, from participating in moral growth, as William Indick observes: "All of the characters will change except Lucy and Gatewood, the representatives of Eastern society. Their snobbish codes of conduct are out of place in the West and inherently contradictory to the Western code of ethics" (Indick 147).

Although the *McLintock!* screenplay presents Matt as a featherheaded buffoon, thus appearing to adopt a totally anti-intellectual stance, its attitude towards education is rather more nuanced. Devlin Warren (Patrick Wayne), son of the McLintock cook Mrs. Warren (Yvonne De Carlo), combines both worlds, having attended Purdue for two years and worked at several "Western" jobs. In fact his college-learned skills include boxing (he was on the team), a skill which aids him in gaining the respect of McLintock's tough friends. He also learned to play chess, a capability which significantly allows him to spell McLintock in his ongoing chess match with storekeeper Jake Birnbaum (Jack Kruschen), arguably the most important professional character in the film.[34] Predictably, Devlin will be paired with McLintock's spunky, beautiful, and educated daughter Becky (Stefanie Powers), as a new generation of leaders for the town will need Eastern as well as Western skills. Becky is cut from much the same cloth as the more intriguing character played by Gene Tierney (in an early role) in *The Return of Frank James*, Eleanor Stone, the journalist who chases the story of the legendary Frank James. As Gallafent notes, "She is a female reporter (an image of American change dating back at least to the writing of Henry James)," and "the civilisation Eleanor represents is not that of the Old West but specifically modern" (Gallafent 24). A much more important character in Lang's film than is Becky in the Wayne comedy, where the modernity of the future Mrs. Devlin is part of the trope of the new generation approved by the McLintocks to succeed them in society, Eleanor fulfills the important function of discovering and propagating the story of Frank James as well as occupying a position as a civilizing force.[35]

As in the much more serious (and more pretentious) *The Hanging Tree*, a storekeeper serves here as the bridge between town and country. In *McLintock!* Jake Birnbaum provides a relatively rare example in Westerns of a Jewish, very Eastern-sounding storekeeper. Douglas Brode emphasizes the role of "Jewish businessman Birnbaum ... fair and generous to a fault, close friends with Black Irishman McLintock," in townbuilding:

"Both well-intentioned capitalists employ their hard-earned successes to allow other ethnics a fair chance to likewise reach the top of the heap in the colorblind society they are in the process of creating" (Brode 152–53). Philip French classifies the film as a "Goldwater Western" (one of French's categories tied to political figures of the era), noting that McLintock "happily embraces hard-working poor whites, bureaucrat-harassed Indians, mid–Western university graduates and a Jewish storekeeper (numbered among his close friends and admirers, and clearly reminiscent to 1964 audiences of [Barry] Goldwater's grandfather, 'Big Mike' Goldwasser) as equal partners in the free-enterprise, self-help system" (French 31).

Jack Kruschen makes Birnbaum into one of the most enjoyable characters in the film, as the storekeeper displays genial humor, compassion, intelligence, political skills, and firmness in his dealings with McLintock and the other difficult inhabitants of town and country. With respect to his firmness and equable disposition Jake runs somewhat against the grain of many examples of pusillanimous or diffident conduct among, as Wendy Chapman Peek notes, "characters in Westerns": "There are those who are consistently deferential, to the point of cowardice and humiliation. These are usually the figures of comedy—the barber, the bartender, the green immigrant" (Peek 215). Jake tries to mediate between Katherine McLintock, whom he persists in calling Katie without really angering her, a mark of the respect accorded him, and he tries to dissuade McLintock from taking rash actions like involving himself in territorial politics. Like ramrod James Pepper (Ben Johnson) in *Chisum*, Jake seems unafraid of his friend's gruffness and physicality. While other ethnic characters like the Comanche chief who likes to drink and the Chinese cook who fusses irascibly in Cantonese are clearly played only for laughs, the Jewish storekeeper is not.

If all three characters are indeed stereotypes, the storekeeper is less risible and egregious as such than the other two: Jewish businessmen, particularly shopkeepers, were a presence in the Old West but are less commonly found in fictions about it. Perhaps this is due in part to some skittishness at portraying problematized ethnics like Jews and blacks whose presence in films during the civil rights period and the postwar era might remind audiences of some very uncomfortable historical situations. Historically, however, Jewish professionals, including storeowners, sometimes played important roles in town development in the West. A good example of this activity is provided by the Summerfield family of Lawrence, Kansas. This family was rather unique because it did not occupy "a niche

2. Professional Allies

community in which most Jews were merchants or peddlers concentrated in dry goods" and other commodities (Katzman 3). "Instead," notes Katzman, "the Summerfields were deeply involved in new technologies, like railroads and mining, and engaged in professions and university teaching" (Katzman 3). While Jake in the Wayne film clearly fits the "niche" model, he does exert some political influence locally, especially in domestic matters which may change the course of such a small community.

Community-building by outsiders or newcomers is the subject of the William A. Wellman film *The Conquerors* (1932), starring Richard Dix and Ann Harding as a young Eastern couple who settle in the West and open a bank. The narrative follows the career of the young banker, who eventually succeeds with the support of his wife in establishing a thriving bank and in reinvigorating the fading town.[36] As Kathleen A. Graham observes,

> Back when the United States was primarily an agrarian society, the banker, the doctor, the preacher, the lawyer and, in a way, the bar owner, were the enduring pillars of each town. It was the town banker, however, who enabled the farm-centric communities to survive and thrive [Graham, K.A. 14].

The town progresses from a rough frontier outpost, through a period of political infighting, to a period of prosperity interrupted by the Great Depression of 1929. Like the more recent TV-movie *The Oldest Living Confederate Widow Tells All* (1994) or the Albert Dekker–Claire Trevor film *The Woman of the Town* (George Archainbaud, 1943), *The Conquerors* employs an expansive, novelistic structure to narrate its temporally longitudinal tale. So the history of the town is identified with the career of its most important civil professional, the banker, even as his active career winds down and he is supplanted by his son. The ideology underpinning the film is not difficult to identify as Roosevelt-Wister Progressivism and FDR New Dealism. As the narrative ends, the recent 1929 stock market crash is an inevitable backdrop (for the West as "myth" in the first part of the century, see Nash 221–25). The banker and his family are embedded in a setting which revalues then-recent history as John Marini asserts of Westerns more generally:

> The American Western was an artistic response to the intellectual triumph of Progressivism. By the time film arrived, the historian had ceased to celebrate the past in a way that was socially meaningful. The Western movie was intended to fill a gap created by the abandonment of the heroic understanding of the past, by those who interpreted it [Marini 267].

3

Masquerades
Civil Professionals in Disguise

An unusual example of appearances by civil professionals in Westerns is the masquerade type. A fine instance is provided by Robert Mitchum's mountebank preacher character in *5 Card Stud* (Henry Hathaway, 1968). Although the film is hardly top-drawer Hathaway, Mitchum's enjoyably hammy role, recalling—or parodying—his very sinister part in *The Night of the Hunter* (Charles Laughton, 1955), at least makes the project watchable.[1] As in the Laughton film, a malevolent man takes advantage of the reverence or at least the distance accorded clergymen in traditional societies like the West or Appalachia, carrying out an agenda difficult or impossible to achieve in transparent fashion. The preacher, Rev. Jonathan Rudd, in Hathaway's film, comes to town after an opening sequence shows the lynching of a gambler accused of cheating. The Reverend Rudd proceeds to set up a church and proselytize for members. Concomitantly the members of the lynch mob begin to turn up dead. For the viewer his ruse of adopting a preacher's job is all too transparent and harms investment in the narrative. Like Laughton's much more consequential film, *5 Card Stud* plays on the viewers' (and the other characters') suspicions of the motives of figures like preachers, salesmen, lawyers, and politicians—all people who try to sell ideas or products in their chosen venues. The film suffers as well from the inherent problem of Mitchum, with his long record of playing rebellious, sometimes violent characters—especially, of course, the preacher in *The Night of the Hunter*—convincingly appearing as a pious reformer.

A different sort of masquerade, clearly influenced by "spaghetti" Westerns, serves as a plot device in *Bandolero!* (Andrew McLaglen, 1968). Here Mace Bishop (James Stewart) waylays a traveling hangman-preacher

3. Masquerades

named Ossie Grimes (Guy Raymond) and assumes his identity in order to free his brother Dee (Dean Martin) and his accomplices from a date with the hangman in the town of Val Verde. After he frees them and the town empties out in pursuit, he calmly robs the bank, locking the teller up in a closet, the whole operation carried off in the inimitable low-key James Stewart fashion. Unlike the sinister masquerader in *5 Card Stud*, Mace is established as a sympathetic rogue, courteous, educated, and chivalrous. He apologizes for her situation to the widowed Mrs. Stone (Raquel Welch), who has been taken as hostage by Dee and his men, and makes it clear that he intends to see her released sooner rather than later. He also draws a distinction between himself and his brother when they argue their activities in the recent Civil War, in a discussion which begins at their treatment of their mother.

Here the script clearly echoes the story of the two James brothers, with Mace playing the Frank James role and Dee the Jesse James part, at least as far as their ages and temperaments are concerned. For the second time in the film—the first was in his visit to the jail as "hangman"—Mace refers cuttingly to Confederate raider Quantrill, whom Dee had joined, and his attack on Lawrence, Kansas. When Dee responds that Sherman's actions were worse (Mace had joined the Union Army), Mace fires back that "Sherman was war, Dee. Quantrill was meanness." In fact the war veteran theme is made into a secondary but significant feature of the narrative, as, according to Dee, the aggrieved sheriff of Val Verde, July Johnson (George Kennedy), a former cavalryman with Confederate General Nathan Bedford Forrest, will consider catching the gang a point of personal pride. For those familiar with Civil War military history, the mention of the tactically brilliant Forrest also signifies that Johnson will be a talented and ruthless pursuer: Dee also says that he will not hesitate to cross the Mexican border from Texas in order to chase the outlaw band. As in other late films using the James gang as a palimpsest, this narrative includes an "evil family" (taking the position formerly occupied in some James lore by the Youngers) headed by a crustily sinister Will Geer, as Pop Chaney. The preacher masquerade adopted by Mace is long forgotten, except perhaps as it resonates in his (relatively) moral attitude when contrasted with the other elder in the party, the Will Geer character. In the film's final scenes the Hays Code seems nearly resurrected, as all the criminals, including the Bishops, are killed in a shootout with invading bandits. The only two characters surviving are Mrs. Stoner (Raquel Welch) and July Johnson. As

Professionals in Western Film and Fiction

Mace Bishop says before returning the bag containing $10,000 from his own quiet robbery from the Val Verde Bank to July Johnson and then collapsing to the ground, dead from a gunshot wound, "It almost worked."

In fact, a number of Westerns featuring preacher or minister characters exhibit stress lines in their presentation. Rarely is a religious figure portrayed "straight" without the film's running the risk of veering into sentimentality and mawkishness. Sometimes the religious leader is shown as ineffectual and indecisive, as in *High Noon*; or simply as irrelevant to the main concerns of the men who fight over cattle, cards, or rails. Occasionally, as in *Canadian Pacific*, *The Bravados*, or *Nevada Smith*, a priest or minister is shown in a strong, positive light. But more often the character is, as mentioned, shown as irrelevant or ineffectual—or as a poseur masquerading as a religious—as in *Two Mules for Sister Sara* for example. An unusual but oddly effective case of such masquerade is the French-produced *Guns for San Sebastian* [*La bataille de San Sebastian*, Henri Verneuil, 1968].

In this south-of-the-border Western, Anthony Quinn plays, with his accustomed verve, Leon Alastray, a rebel against the Mexican government who undergoes a series of peripeteias until he ends up, for much of the narrative, in the desolate village of San Sebastian where he is mistakenly assumed to be the new priest. Despite his protests that he is not a priest, the villagers, who had been hiding in the hills from fear of the fierce Yaqui Indians, set him up as their parish leader and begin to rebuild their village, specifically its agricultural base. The clear reference to *The Magnificent Seven* with its "villagers versus bandits" plot is complicated here by the presence of yet another band, rebellious riders led by Teclo (Charles Bronson), who were originally villagers and who appear to be at least neutral in the fight but who in fact are in secret alliance with the Yaquis. A further layer of uncertainty is the role of the government forces. Although the government opposes the Yaqui incursions, their opposition has so far proven ineffectual, as was actually the case historically—the Yaquis were never really conquered by the Spanish or later by the Mexican authorities. Eventually, the problem is resolved by the villagers in a rather unorthodox fashion, through the good offices of "Father" Leon Alastray.

Alastray travels to the governor's palace to plead for military assistance against the Yaquis. He does not request troops but rather munitions, including cannon, averring that the villagers will fight for themselves (allusion of the Vietnam experience is perhaps intentional). By this time, the

3. Masquerades

villagers have suffered a defeat at the hands of the Yaquis (and, unbeknown to them, Teclo and his band), and they have lost faith in their "priest" and his assurances of eventual victory. When he returns with an escort of government troops and the munitions, their surprise does not allay all their concerns. Leon finally admits, although he had not hidden the truth previously (his protests that he was no priest were ignored), that he had assumed a false identity after the real priest (Sam Jaffe) was killed by bandits. He offers to lead the villagers against the Yaquis and Telco, using the munitions provided by the government. The priest question for the village is resolved as a new priest takes over in the parish, but he makes it quite clear to Leon that he is not a tool of the government or of the showy, pompous, and indifferent archbishop, played by the excellent Leon Askin. Austrian-born Askin (1907–2005) was a versatile actor of stage and screen who is now best known for his unforgettable General Burkhalter on the TV series *Hogan's Heroes*. He was well-regarded by such industry talents as Billy Wilder (https://pro-labs.imdb.com/name/nm0039169/bio?ref_= nm_subnv_persdet_bio).

Leon's masquerade as village priest is not, like the masquerade in *5 Card Stud*, a cynical ploy for revenge. A peculiar form of revenge does play a role in another professionals film with echoes of *Guns for San Sebastian*. In the first sequel to *The Magnificent Seven*, *Return of the Magnificent Seven*, Emilio Fernandez (Mapache of *The Wild Bunch* as well as an important Mexican director) plays a bandit chieftain/peasant leader who enslaves villager men to rebuild a village and a church once destroyed by bandits. In this he claims to honor his two dead sons, who in fact had hired Chris (Yul Brynner) to kill him because of his tyranny and abuse. His attempt to rebuild the church in their honor is an odd form of sublimated vengeance.

Leon is placed in the interesting position of not being taken at his word as he protests that he is no priest. Additionally, he gradually changes positively as a person due to his adoption of the priest role. He begins to value commitment to others and even to a cause. His masquerade career bears some similarity to an intriguing piece of fictional masquerade detailed in the great Mexican play *El gesticulador* by Rodolfo Usigli. In this mid–20th century work (1938), written during the period after the Mexican Revolution and serving as one of the important pieces of evaluative creative work addressing the effects of that Revolution, a man (the "gesticulator" of the title) appears to be an important officer from the Revolution who has settled into the life of a university professor. His masquerade is so convincing that the reader (or audience), to whom the masquerade is not revealed as such until near the end of the play, does not know whether to credit the man as an actual war veteran; furthermore, even when the pose is revealed, the man's reasons for having adopted it remain murky, and he seems to have taken on much of the real character of a revolutionary hero. The predicament for the reader is similar here to the position of the viewer, and the investigator, in the film *Anastasia* (Litvak), in which Ingrid Bergman played the actual impostor who pretended to be, or who actually believed herself to be, the surviving daughter of Tsar Nicholas and Tsarina Alexandra, who were executed by the Bolsheviks soon after the 1917 Russian Revolution.

A few Westerns follow the model of *Stars in My Crown* (Jacques Tourneur, 1950) by invoking the medieval image of the warrior-priest, the clergyman who fights evil with words and weapons (see Hall, K.E., *Stonewall Jackson and Religious Faith in Military Command* 110–11, 160–72). These include *The Persuader, Heaven with a Gun*, and the Clint Eastwood *Pale Rider*. Of the last three films mentioned, the Eastwood venture is the most compelling. The other two suffer from indifferent scripting and uneven directing. Nevertheless, they are of some interest because of their unusual protagonists.

Heaven with a Gun is a film from late in the career of the often underrated actor Glenn Ford, a performer with a gift for understatement and controlled emotion. His role as Jim Killian, a gunfighter turned preacher, does not hold up well when compared with his great appearances, as in Lang's *The Big Heat*, or Charles Vidor's *Gilda*. At times Ford seems bemused by his character and even unsure of whether to believe in the man's sincerity as he preaches homilies from the pulpit and coldly dispatches adversaries, as in a scene in the saloon when he outdraws (under the table) his former cellmate Mace (J.D. Cannon), hired by rancher Asa Beck (John Anderson) in an echo of *Shane*, to drive out the sheepherders attempting to live alongside his ranch.

Jim Killian is first shown trying to bury an elderly Indian sheepherder lynched by some of Beck's riders, led by his ungovernable son Coke (David Carradine). Besides his presentation as a highly capable gunman, this scene links Killian to justice and compassion, as well as to minority concerns. Killian also acquires a ward, the orphaned daughter of the Indian, Leloopa (Barbara Hershey), whose beauty and Candide-like vivaciousness

3. Masquerades

pose obvious problems for the would-be preacher. Nevertheless he perseveres in setting up a church in an old stable and inviting the townspeople to come to services. Among them is a Mormon and sheepman, Abraham Murdock (James Griffith), who will become critical to resolving the conflicts in the town, as he forms an alliance with cattleman Bart Paterson (Bill Bryant). As one would expect, Killian has friends among the less stellar citizens in the town, among them the owner of the saloon (appropriately named Road to Ruin), Madge (Carolyn Jones). His honesty and his unassuming manner (a Glenn Ford trademark) win him new friends, among them the well-respected shopkeeper Gus Sampson (Harry Townes).[2]

After Killian provides protection on the church premises for all parties in the conflict, Beck and his ranchers retaliate by burning the church. After deaths on both sides, including Mace and Coke, Killian decides to hang up his guns, to become a real preacher, and to find an unorthodox solution to the war. Beck and his men are planning to ambush the sheepmen and their newfound rancher ally Bart Paterson at the water source for both sides. Killian leads the townspeople to the river in alliance with Murdock and Paterson, confronting Beck with an impossible situation. He concedes defeat and the conflict is ended, with Killian staying on as town preacher.

A recent film starring Tom Berenger focuses on a similarly conflicted preacher, a man with a checkered past who prefers not to engage in gunplay but who is not necessarily averse to doing so when circumstances demand. *Lonesome Dove Church* (Terry Miles, 2014) is factually based, as it tells the story (fictionally embellished here) of the founding of the titular church in 1846 (Miles, T.).[3] John Shepherd (Berenger) would like to settle in one place and found his own church, but his rebellious son Isaac (Greyston Holt) is unstable and prone to violence, so that Shepherd must rescue him from a difficult entanglement with some gunmen. After the first rescue by Shepherd, the two become hunted men, and the road trip provides opportunities for Shepherd and Isaac to talk about their pasts, particularly about Shepherd's past, and for Shepherd to attempt to convey to the nearly belligerent Isaac the importance of his faith. Of course Shepherd's skill with a gun and his evident willingness to use it do not seem to mesh very cleanly with his avowals of religious faith. Despite the contradictions, though, Shepherd is quite piously dedicated to founding a church where he can settle, and he even extracts a promise from Isaac, who agrees to "one year of preaching with me" in exchange for his helping

Professionals in Western Film and Fiction

Isaac to escape from vengeful Butch Henley (Alex Zahara) and his thugs. Henley is a demonic double of John Shepherd, offering Biblical quotations in support of his ruthless greed.

After some further encounters with Henley's men, John and Isaac make their way to Grapevine, Texas, a typically rough-hewn frontier town which seems unpropitious for founding a church. Isaac goes to work as a bartender, while John finds work at a lumberyard run by Charles Stone (Serge Houde), who comes to admire his humble work ethic and his religious faith. Stone allies himself with John's project to build a church, showing him the burned-out remains of a hotel on a suitable lot. After Isaac reunites with his erstwhile lover Angie (Drea Whitburn) and drives his treacherous former partner Dutch (Geoff Gustafson) out of town, John and Isaac are reconciled. When Dutch is interrogated by Henley and killed after revealing the Shepherds' whereabouts, John's peaceful stint as pastor is violently interrupted. John and Isaac use guile and gunfighting skills to prevail over Henley and his gang and settle in the now-pacified community of Grapevine, still home today—factually—to the Lonesome Dove Church. This rather straightforward and reasonably effective little film presents in John Shepherd an odd amalgam of a man with a clearly violent past, given his skill with firearms, and a man who wishes to become a professional preacher. The narrative follows the familiar arc of the gunman (rather obscured in this case by the quiet exterior presented by the effective Tom Berenger) who must eliminate threats to his dream of a civilized, nonviolent life.

The preacher in *Stars in My Crown* (Jacques Tourneur, 1950) finds a nonviolent means of resolving the racial and economic crisis in the small Southern town of Walesburg. Although not a strictly generic Western, the film shades into Western movie territory because of its iconography—Colt revolvers, Western hats and clothes—and especially because of its conflict between a homesteader and a mining entrepreneur. Barry Atkinson, writing of McCrea's Westerns (along with Audie Murphy's and George Montgomery's), is rather dismissive: after summarizing the film, he comments: "Maybe McCrea was presenting a classic Western hero as a man of the cloth, but the end result was a pleasant-enough family-oriented picture that had little to do with the Old West" (Atkinson 147). We might note here, however, that, as James K. Folsom reminds us, "David B. Davis indicated the resemblances between the myth of the antebellum South and the myth of the West, which 'purified and regenerated' the original

3. *Masquerades*

myth 'by the casting off of apologies for slavery'" (Folsom, "Imaginative" 88) (Davis 114). Notwithstanding its generic uncertainty, the film directly contradicts the position ascribed by Jane Tompkins to *Riders of the Purple Sage* and by extension, to the Western, that "you can't live by Christian love because if you do you'll be destroyed" (Tompkins 33–34).

The settler-mining boss conflict, often seen in Westerns, is shifted here to a threat to a black farmer, living in the South in 1865, soon after the end of the Civil War, and a greedy storeowner who wants to buy his farm, or to take it by force if necessary, because it contains mica deposits. The farmer, Uncle Famous Prill, played by the pioneering and talented Afrohispanic Puerto Rican actor Juano Hernandez, does not wish to sell his farm because of its sentimental value to him and because of his pride in ownership. Soon he begins to endure threats from Klan members, clearly led by the storeowner, Lon Backett (Ed Begley).

Prill is a longtime friend of the preacher, Pastor Josiah Doziah Gray (Joel McCrea), and of his nephew John Kenyon (Dean Stockwell), and so Gray soon becomes involved in the dispute. Gray is shown early in the film walking into the Walesburg saloon (another bit of Western iconography)[4] and quieting the town rowdies by laying his twin Colts on the bar before beginning to preach from the Book of Genesis. This humorous scene would appear to foreshadow further use of violent threat by Gray, but in fact he only uses physical force on one important occasion, also early in the film, when he relieves bully Perry Lokey (Jack Lambert) of the whip with which he is tormenting Chloroform Wiggins (Arthur Hunnicutt), and uses the whip to tip Lokey face-down in the mud.

Bullies like Lokey are not the only townspeople with whom Gray has disagreements. In fact one of the most important divisions in the town's professional structure appears when the old and dying town physician, Dr. Daniel Kalbert Harris, Sr. (Lewis Stone), also a friend to Gray, cedes his position to his son, Dr. Daniel Kalbert Harris, Jr. (Charles Mitchell). The older doctor fits neatly into the frontier doctor stereotype from Western films, although he does not share the drunkenness of characters like Doc Boone from *Stagecoach*. Clearly the trusted town healer, Dr. Harris, Sr., evinces a philosophical weariness and humility not always seen in such stereotypical figures. Speaking of his son, he tells Gray: "Right now, he's a little long on education and a little short on sense. He's got a lot to learn. Even with that, he's a better doctor than I am" (Tourneur Ch. 8).

The younger doctor is highly educated and arrogantly cocky and is not at all happy about working in the small town, a position which he considers beneath his station. He is also very positivistic, disdaining any talk of religion or spirituality, and so he dismissively tries to banish Gray, who had come to see a dying woman at her request, from "his" sickroom. The rift between the two men gradually widens, becoming bitter when an outbreak of typhus threatens the town. The doctor blames Gray for not quarantining himself—his nephew John is the first to become ill. Soon, however, the doctor's beloved Faith Radmore Samuels (Amanda Blake, the future Kitty on *Gunsmoke*), the town schoolteacher, falls gravely ill, on the brink of death. Dr. Harris can do nothing more for her. Desperate, he appeals for Pastor Gray to visit her. After a time in her room, Gray sees her open her eyes and summons a grateful Dr. Harris, whose eyes are presumably opened to the power of prayer. The rift is healed, uniting three of the town professionals—doctor, pastor, and schoolteacher. All three are concerned with health and education, primary themes in the film: when the mysterious virus strikes the little town, it originates in the school's well, and its gradual disappearance coincides with the healing of the rifts in the town. Additionally, the most threatened character in the film, Uncle Famous, is a model of dignity, hard work, and good humor, serving as a mentor for John Kenyon, who will narrate the story in voice-over as an adult. The voice-over narration was provided by one of the more interesting actors of the era, Marshall Thompson.

Another of the town professionals, the jovial blacksmith Jed Isbell (Alan Hale, Jr.), has been a loyal friend to Gray for some time. When Ku Klux Klan thugs (one of whom is Lokey) burn Prill's farm, Jed and his sons arrive promptly, although too late to stop the fire, and promise to help restock the farm. Despite Jed's comical demurs to Gray's suggestions that he come to church, the blacksmith is clearly a spiritual and moral cousin to Gray and his family. When the conflict between Lon Backett and Uncle Famous turns potentially lethal, Jed and his sons ride up to Gray's house and offer their armed assistance to Gray and Prill.

Pastor Gray tells Jed that they are welcome to accompany him to the farm to assist Prill but that they must leave their weapons at home. Somewhat crestfallen, Jed and his sons depart for home. Gray proceeds alone to the farm, where Klansmen led by Backett are threatening to hang Prill. The pastor intercedes, not to stop the hanging, but instead to read a will purportedly dictated by Prill. This last testament, actually invented by Gray, generously leaves the farm and property of the old man to various

3. Masquerades

townspeople, all of whom happen to be present though masked in typical Klan garb. Rather implausibly, the masked thugs are shamed into leaving Prill's farm, and the heretofore vicious Lon apparently drops his insistence on buying the farm. A peaceful coexistence is reached between races in an idealistic ending (scarcely consonant with the history of the Reconstruction South), and the professional authority figures in the little post–Civil War town, the doctor, the preacher, and the schoolteacher will settle into a warm working arrangement.

A more traditional Western setting featuring religion and racial conflict appears in *Pillars of the Sky* (George Marshall, 1956), based on the novel *Frontier Fury* by Will Henry. Although the main character in this film is not the pastor figure but an army officer, the religious element runs throughout the narrative. Loosely based on the conflict in the Northwest, including southern Oregon, between the Army and tribes which included Yakimas and Wallawallas, in 1855–56 (see Utley and Washburn 179–85), the film presents a complex portrait of conflicting loyalties, with some Indians supporting the whites by working officially as Army scouts, and with still others caught between the vengeful Palouses led by Kamiakin (Michael Ansara, here playing a role similar to his work in *Only the Valiant*). Nearly all the Indians are presented as Christianized, although for some this conversion may be a veneer.

The film opens at a mission school for the Indians, run by Pastor Joseph Holden (Ward Bond, in one of his fatherly, less uproarious roles), who is also a physician, thus neatly encompassing two civil professional functions. The army officer, First Sgt. Emmett Bell (Jeff Chandler), appears at the outset to be just a very competent and straightforward leader of his men, in large part because of the type usually played by Chandler. Bell's strong and forthright exterior is soon revealed as less than solid: his attachment to alcohol and his rebelliousness have kept him from advancing in rank. Nevertheless, as one of his superiors, Major Donahue (Walter Coy) tells his commanding officer, Colonel Edson Stedlow, "[Bell is] a shame and a disgrace to his uniform, but if you had a hundred more like him, you could ride into hell and put out the fires." Stedlow, played in reliably stuffy, upright fashion by Willis Bouchey, does not respect Bell or his opinions, and shows signs of conducting himself foolishly like Col. Thursday (Henry Fonda) of *Fort Apache*. Additionally, as in *Little Big Horn* (Charles Marquis Warren, 1951), a romantic rivalry between Captain Tom Gaxton (Keith Andes) and Bell over the affections of Mrs. Calla Gaxton (Dorothy

Malone) threatens to result in tragedy. The story becomes a captivity narrative when Calla is taken hostage by the Palouses, and Emmett and Tom set out, under Stedlow's command, to attempt a rescue. Gradually Stedlow comes to respect Emmett's skill and judgment and thus avoids a full massacre along the lines depicted in *The Last Frontier*.

The narrative contains more than one surprising touch given its generic status. After being rescued, Calla decides that she really loves her husband and wishes to stay with him. The expected conclusion to the love triangle would have been for Tom to die in the attack—he is severely wounded but will recover—and for Calla to make a life with Emmett. Additionally, in a perhaps less surprising but still somewhat unusual resolution, Dr. Holden is killed by Kamiakin, who in turn is shot by Isaiah (Richard Hale), one of the moderate chiefs. Another narrative might have spared Holden, but in this case his death motivates (rather unconvincingly, though, given his recent rebelliousness) that Emmett assume the care of the mission, drawing on his long-rejected religious upbringing, and presumably reforming his rebellious lifestyle.

Kamiakin was not the unreasoning, murderous leader portrayed in the film. Historically his trajectory parallels that of Red Cloud, who also championed and waged war against the whites but who eventually retired to his reservation. Col. Stedlow appears to be loosely based on the historical Lt. Col. Edward J. Steptoe (for Steptoe, see Utley, et al. 183–85).

The preacher figures just discussed are only masqueraders in the sense of hiding or escaping from their prior violent life, but they are men with good intentions who sincerely wish to become stable civil professionals. Another benevolent masquerader of a different type is Major Ransome Callicut (Randolph Scott) in *Man Behind the Gun* (Felix Feist, 1953). Callicut first pretends to be an outlaw named Rick Bryce and then masquerades briefly as a schoolteacher, standing in for the real town schoolteacher Lora Roberts (Patrice Wymore). His masquerades are revealed to be covers—thus, a double masquerade—for his actual role as an undercover military agent working to stymie an attempt at a territorial coup in California. The film is filled with masquerades, as the putative villain, slavery advocate Senator Bram Creegan (Morris Ankrum) is set up as a straw man by the actual villain, Senator Mark Sheldon (Roy Roberts). For present purposes, the interesting masquerade in a rather routine film[5] is Scott's brief role-switch (and implied gender-shift, perhaps) as a schoolteacher, soon dropped due to events. The actual schoolteacher, Lora, at first

3. Masquerades

decides to retire in order to marry Captain Roy Giles (Philip Carey); but predictably she discovers that she really loves Callicut, deciding to marry him and remain a teacher in the army town.

In the hands of a better director, the implied shift in gender roles as Callicut adopts the schoolmarm role, however briefly, might have been linked to the actual gender masquerade at the end of the film, when Sgt. Walker (Dick Wesson) actually dons a dress and bonnet to pass as the wife of Cpl. Swenson (Alan Hale, Jr.) for a "Trojan Horse" attack on Sheldon's camp. If some sort of satirical or ironic commentary on professional gender roles was in fact intended, the point is not well made. (See also Atkinson's brief comments on the "irritation" of the Wesson scene [Atkinson 125–26].)

Arguably as well one could include in the masquerade category the *Kung Fu* television series with David Carradine, as the lead character is a monk trained in martial arts who flees to the post–Civil War American West after being sought for murder. This unusual cult series will be discussed at some length later in this study.

Clergymen are not the only Western figures to appear in masquerade.[6] A common stock character in Westerns, the piano player in saloons, is normally either a pallid fixture or a figure of fun, his piano a target for rambunctious cowhands, as attested in the admonition, "Don't shoot the piano player!" Oscar Wilde made this prescription famous but did not, according to his account, originate it:

> They [miners in Leadville, CO] ... took me to a dancing saloon, where I saw the only rational method of art criticism I have ever come across. Over the piano was printed a notice:
> PLEASE DO NOT SHOOT THE PIANIST.
> HE IS DOING HIS BEST [Wilde 180].

Wilde's hyperbolic witticism that "the mortality among pianists in that place is marvellous" (Wilde 180) could serve as an ironic subtext for the Mason Hawke novels by Robert Vaughan. Hawke is a classically trained pianist who moves from saloon to saloon playing piano in different towns. Far from being under threat of "mortality," it is Hawke who deals death as a highly skilled gunman who only fights reluctantly, as the narrator of *Hawke: The Law of a Fast Gun* observes, adding that "hot-headed hooligans would sometimes mistake the piano player for an easy mark" (Vaughan, R., *Law* 44–45). (The guitar-toting gunman Johnny Guitar [Sterling Hayden] might well agree. Like Hawke, Johnny adopted the musical role after bitter experience with violence [Ray].) A famed concert pianist who received raves in a European tour, Hawke left the tour to return to America to fight on the Confederate side. Disillusioned and fatigued after the war, he became an itinerant piano player in saloons (Vaughan, R., *Law* 16–17). He draws the attention of other civil professionals in the town of Braggadocio, Nebraska, as the local newspaper highlights one of his feats of saloon pacification and the editor discusses him with other town worthies. Thus Hawke is implicitly linked to the "civilized" part of the population (Vaughan, R., *Law* 64–65).

The five Hawke novels[7] rely at least in part on the ironic reversal of the saloon piano player's usual status as target of abuse of all sorts or merely of indifference. They also emphasize a subtler point about the cultural level or at least interest of many settlers in the West. Not all Westerners, even in the areas distant from large centers like San Francisco, were bumptious, ignorant rubes. In his article on Shakespeare on the frontier, Michael L. Greenwald observes that the desire for cultural elevation did not disappear just because settlers moved west: "[Shakespeare's] experience on the great frontier helps chronicle the zeal to establish a theatre by people who knew that a civilization must be built on something more substantial than gold dust, firearms, or territorial expansion" (Greenwald 45). Some of this interest in higher culture can be seen in Ford's *My Darling Clementine* (1946) and in *Tombstone* (George P. Cosmatos, 1993). In the Hawke novels some of the denizens of the places where Hawke works or plays piano (as, for example, at a funeral) demonstrate an unexpected level of cultural development. *Vendetta Trail* opens with a scene set in Nebraska City, Nebraska, in the establishment of Callie Mouchette, a transplant from New Orleans who appreciates "classical music" (Vaughan, R., *Vendetta* 2–3). Hawke normally insists that he be called a "pianist" and not an ordinary "piano player"; in this novel, he explains that "'Callie would know the difference'" (Vaughan, R., *Vendetta* 36). In this novel Hawke confronts members of an early version of the Mafia in New Orleans,[8] so that two groups of Eastern city people—Hawke, with his musical education, Southern-bred culture (*pace* the stereotype), and European experience; and the Northern, Italian immigrant criminals whose leader dresses elegantly despite his brutish nature, can oppose each other. This conflict is paralleled by the resolution of *The Law of a Fast Gun*, in which Hawke bests the former members of a Quantrill-like gang of raiders, led by one of his former comrades-in-arms from the Confederacy who has

3. Masquerades

been masquerading as a preacher (Gideon McCall). Hawke's victory in this novel serves to free him from his ties to the past, although it does not cure his restlessness.

The other professionals in *The Law of a Fast Gun* include the parson and the newspaper editor in Braggadocio. The parson is also in masquerade after a fashion, although unlike the Mitchum character in *5 Card Stud* he sincerely carries out his duties. He officiates at the funeral for prostitute Cindy Carey, killed in the saloon where Hawke plays, and defends her worth as a person (Vaughan, R., *Law* 69–70). Later, after a gunfight between some raiders and Hawke, McCall shows up at the saloon, surprising Hawke at "the juxtaposition of a parson and a bartender as a coda on what was already an unusual morning" (Vaughan, R., *Law* 112). The parson begins to reveal his true nature as he speaks of "the military preciseness" displayed by the raiders (Vaughan, R., *Law* 113). After a series of murders, including the marshal, Hawke and the bartender, Bob Gary, visit the parson because he will not officiate at any of the funerals. They find him embittered, with no religious faith and disheveled (Vaughan, R., *Law* 194–95). Hawke soon decides to move on to another town. As he is preparing to leave, the parson enters the bar, but not in the dress of a pastor. He is revealed as Jesse Cole, a raider with Quantrill and others (perhaps a veiled version of the Eastwood Josey Wales character). Cole was a priest before the Civil War and had been trying to bury his violent war deeds by returning to the cloth. In a nice touch of historical detail, he is carrying a Whitworth, the favored sniper rifle of the Confederates (Vaughan, R., *Law* 204–07). According to historian Wiley Sword, the Whitworth was chambered for a .45 and was "technologically advanced." It was imported from England and was instrumental in delaying the Union victory at Chattanooga. The snipers of CSA General John Bell Hood's division at Chattanooga were equipped with six Whitworths, at that time "the most accurate military firearm available in the world" (Sword 117–18). Here, Cole uses a Whitworth in an attempt to avenge the recent death of his wife and daughter and is killed in a gunfight. True to formula, Hawke cleans up the loose ends by dispatching the villains.

The newspaper editor also figures prominently in this novel. The publisher of the *Braggadocio Journal*, Vernon Clemmons, is a characteristic Western journalist in fiction—a voice for the community who tries to present the average town dweller's perspective on ranchers, outlaws, and economic progress. In historical fact, Larry Cebula notes, the familiar portrait of "the small-town editor" as "a fearless crusader for the truth" is largely the fabrication "of the journalists themselves" and of other authors like Horace Greeley. He contends that "the truth behind the image is that Western journalists were more often pawns than players in the politics of their communities," with little "editorial independence" (Cebula 28). The discrepancy noted by Cebula of course only makes the fictional versions of such journalists all the more attractive to readers and audiences.

In an incident probably modeled on the destruction of Dutton Peabody's *Shinbone Star* office in *The Man Who Shot Liberty Valance*, but with comic softening, a group of cowboys throw his type out in the street after he publishes an editorial criticizing their activities (Vaughan, R., *Law* 77–83). Clemmons reacts to this by posting a defiant sign on his window and by continuing to call for action against the raiders. He even tries to hire Hawke, now unemployed, as a newspaperman, making common cause with him on the basis of his education, intelligence, and "sophistication" (Vaughan, R., *Law* 124–25). Clemmons is also a typical small-town skeptic somewhat in the vein of pharmacist M. Homais in Flaubert's *Madame Bovary* or the narrator of Pérez Galdós's *Doña Perfecta*, opposed to religious hypocrisy, although admittedly he is not subject to the ironic treatment afforded such provincial "intellectuals" by 19th century novelists like Flaubert[9] or Galdós (Vaughan, R., *Law* 152–54). Other professionals in the book include the town doctor, who has a relatively minor presence.

A story by Vaughan that preceded the Hawke novels, "The Piano Man" (2002), names the piano player Jones and shows him using a Whitworth rifle[10]—signaling his Confederate origins—instead of Colt revolvers. The setting is "a Kansas town whose name he had not yet bothered to learn" (Vaughan, R., "The Piano Man" 230). This is a somewhat Cervantesque remark—like the narrator at the beginning of *Don Quijote*, who says that his unlikely hero is from a town "whose name I do not wish to recall ['*de cuyo nombre no quiero acordarme*']" (Cervantes 21), the narrator of Vaughan's tale is intentionally mysterious about the town's name—sets the stage for an apparent repetition of the kinds of mishaps that have caused Jones to drift for half a decade. As in the Hawke novels, the piano player is a European-trained concert pianist who has become an itinerant saloon player with hidden gunfighting talents. In this story, he soon runs afoul of the local bully, Callous Cal Cole, whose showy, alliterative name signals his mock-villain nature. The ordinarily named Jones bluffs him out of the saloon by threatening him with a shotgun, which he does not

3. Masquerades

in fact have a grip on behind the bar. Cole soon reacts viciously by kidnapping the town schoolteacher, holding a gun to her head, and calling Jones into the street. Instead of facing him in the street, Jones fires from an upstairs window, killing Cole with one shot to the head and freeing the schoolteacher. The story is particularly engaging because of its O. Henry–like ending, where it is revealed that the fiancé of the teacher, Miss Dover, is named David Eisenhower (Vaughan, R., "The Piano Man" 247) (hence the reason for the strategy of withholding the name of the town, Abilene, to increase the surprise effect).

In *Ride with the Devil* (2004), Mason Hawke confronts a former Civil War acquaintance, Titus Culpepper, who has turned vigilante, heading a group called the Salcedo Regulators Brigade who enforce a ruthless brand of justice in the town of Salcedo, Texas. Hawke and Culpepper had last fought together at Chickamauga in September 1863 (a Confederate victory and one of the bloodiest battles of the war), after which, Culpepper says, he "joined up with Quantrill and Bloody Bill Anderson," ruthless pro–Confederate irregular or guerrilla leaders whom Culpepper praises as "the real fighters" on the Confederate side (for Quantrill, see Leslie and Schultz). Hawke is indebted to Culpepper, who, he says, "saved my life" in the battle of Gettysburg (July 1–3, 1863) (Vaughan, R., *Ride* 20–21). As in *The Law of a Fast Gun*, a former Quantrill rider threatens the rule of law, unofficially represented, or supported, by Hawke, who becomes a force for coexistence between erstwhile enemies.

Early in the novel, the Brigade is supported by the town mayor and neophyte newspaper publisher Cyrus Green, who favors its tough enforcement of order in the town. His *Salcedo Advocate* also backs Culpepper's candidacy for Congress (Vaughan, R., *Ride* 26–27). Green had worked for a Southern paper (*Richmond Dispatch*) during the war and had tried to start his own paper in several places. As a former Confederate, he naturally supports ex-Confederate soldier and irregular Culpepper (Vaughan, R., *Ride* 28–29). He begins to turn against the Regulators over a tax being collected to finance them (Vaughan, R., *Ride* 104–05).

The town also features a cultured doctor and an undertaker among its professional class. The undertaker is given less attention in the narrative than is Doctor Urban, who is linked to the mayor-editor Green through their regular games of chess. The doctor is also a veteran of the war, working on a merchant ship "throughout the entire Civil War," and, like Hawke, Green, and Wright, expresses a conciliatory or neutral attitude towards the conflict. The doctor also endured a shipwreck ordeal, a detail included in the novel to highlight his positive qualities of endurance and courage. The unity among the former veterans and the newspaper editor Green is symbolized by the editor's recall of "'a song the soldiers used to sing,'" identified as "Lorena" and played by Hawke. The song was beloved by both North and South (Vaughan, R., *Ride* 89–94) (for "Lorena," see Hall, K.E., "*The Searchers*: Image and Sound" 54–56, 65).

Unusually, though, one of the most important civil professionals in Salcedo, the town blacksmith, is a former boxer and Buffalo Soldier named Ken Wright. An important sign of former Confederate Hawke's conciliatory attitude is his nearly instantaneous friendship with the former soldier, whose Northern affiliations and his race would likely antagonize many dedicated Southern partisans. Wright is shown to be an expert archer, demonstrating his skill for an old Buffalo Soldier friend, Moses Gillespie, who now cooks for cattle drovers (Vaughan, R., *Ride* 149).

Perhaps this detail in Wright's résumé pays homage to the character Jake (Woody Strode), the African-American scout and bow expert in *The Professionals* (Richard Brooks, 1966). A clear echo of that film can be found late in the novel, when Hawke enlists Wright and his bow and dynamite, of which he keeps a stock, in the final battle with the Regulators, paralleling Jake's use of bow and dynamite in Raza's camp in the film (Vaughan, R., *Ride* 251–56). In any event, the positive presentation of these two characters (one of whom, Moses, dies violently) strengthens the unifying, Reconstruction-friendly ethos shared by Hawke and other townspeople. Additionally, the warm friendship between the two Buffalo Soldier veterans contrasts sharply with the suspicion and the eventual hostility between the two Civil War veterans and former comrades, Hawke and Culpepper. The ill treatment afforded Ken and Moses by characters associated with Culpepper similarly highlights the unreconstructed attitudes of the Regulators, most particularly Culpepper. The death of the cook Moses in the course of a shootout between some drunken cowboys and members of the Brigade contributes to a "'call ... to arms'" in an editorial written by Cyrus Green (Vaughan, R., *Ride* 174). The eventual resolution of the conflict entails a showdown between Culpepper and Hawke, and of course Hawke prevails and then leaves town.

The Hawke novel *Showdown at Dead End Canyon* (Vaughan, R., *Showdown*) is more traditionally generic, with less emphasis on Hawke's veteran status and more recourse to borrowings from the Western genre.

3. Masquerades

Thus, the novel begins with a ruthless, unprincipled gunman in the mold of Wilson (Jack Palance) from *Shane*. The gunman, Dancer, provokes two cowboys in a bar into a hopeless contest, killing them both. Dancer is employed by Bailey McPherson, a rapacious woman who has designs on much more land to add to her holdings. Her diminutive stature might recall the feisty saloon owner in *Silverado* (Lawrence Kasdan, 1985), Stella (Linda Hunt), but the description of Bailey strays from this model, as Stella was scarcely the harpy described by the novel's narrator:

> Although very small, Bailey McPherson was well-proportioned for her height, and at first glance one might have compared her to a Dresden doll. But upon closer examination there was something awry about her, like an imperfection in fine crystal. One could see a disquieting edge, a hardness in the set of her mouth, and a malevolent glint in her eyes [Vaughan, R., *Showdown* 42].

Physical description aside, Bailey recalls much more the grasping Jessica Drummond (Barbara Stanwyck) in *Forty Guns* (Samuel Fuller, 1957), a hard woman who also hires a dangerous gunman, Griff Bonell (Barry Sullivan). Even so, Bailey is irredeemably evil, as is Dancer, while the pair from the Fuller film eventually find redemption through tragedy and through their love for each other. Bailey and Dancer want to use corruptly "legal" methods to push ranchers off their land and will employ violence if necessary, tactics recalling those employed by villains in Depression-era Westerns and echoed in latter-day nostalgic Westerns such as *Silverado*. A chief stratagem used by Bailey and Dancer is hemming off ranchers from their water sources.

Another clearly generic echo in the novel is the presence of a cultured Englishman having a turn as a rancher. Like John H. Tunstall in the Lincoln County War, Sir James Spencer Dorchester represents a contrast between the wildness of the frontier and the civilization of Europe, a motif played out time and time again in the Billy the Kid tales based on the Lincoln County War. In this case, unlike the ill-fated Tunstall, Dorchester has a daughter, not an adopted son figure (Billy); and Dorchester eventually will succeed in keeping his ranch on the Green River. His daughter Pamela is, like Dorchester, no shrinking violet to be intimidated by Bailey and Dancer, despite being kidnapped on Bailey's orders and then being rescued by Hawke, who kills her two kidnappers. Additionally Dorchester and Pamela provide adequate balancing for Hawke, who plays Dorchester's piano, gaining an appreciative audience and, for a time, a job as pianist on the Union Pacific Railroad thanks to Dorchester's connections. The job is short-lived due to Hawke's accustomed direct intervention in an unpleasant situation, as he roughly throws a belligerent man from the train (Vaughan, R., *Showdown* 118–20).

Not surprisingly, the narrative leads into a final confrontation between Dancer and Hawke. The preparations for this encounter include a scene of psychological one-upmanship between the two at a meeting of ranchers intruded upon by Bailey and Dancer. Dancer moves around the parlor where the meeting is held "without taking his eyes off Hawke," and Hawke reciprocates: "Hawke walked over to the service table, all the while returning Dancer's stare" (Vaughan, R., *Showdown* 214–15). This shadow-play reprises, in a different setting, the scene at Starrett's farm in *Shane* when Wilson accompanies Ryker, slowly getting off his horse while staring at Shane, who calmly watches him from a vantage point near the farmhouse. Soon afterward, Dancer dispatches Bailey and is in turn killed by Hawke, who moves on from his foreman job at the Dorchester outfit.

The final Hawke novel to be discussed here is *The King Hill War* (Vaughan, R., *King Hill*), in which Hawke again assists landowners (here, sheepherders) being fenced off from the open range, in this case by a man named Joshua Creed, who has suborned a lawyer named Felix Gilmore to "legalize" his depredations. The novel is heavily indebted to *Shane*, with several scenes clearly reprising the film. More backstory is provided for Hawke, including the revelations that his father, Colonel Jefferson Tinsdale Hawke, was killed at Fredericksburg (a Confederate victory; for the battle, see *The Fredericksburg Campaign: Decision on the Rappahannock*), and that Mason had been engaged to be married, but his fiancée did not survive the war. In the same context Hawke's rebirth as a ruthless killer is noted: "And somewhere, in the din and crash of battle, the new, soulless, and very deadly Mason Hawke was born" (Vaughan, R., *King Hill* 34).

The sheep men are led by Ian McGregor, who had been sergeant major of Hawke's regiment during the war, and whose wife, Cynthia, had been engaged to Hawke's brother Gordon, killed in the war. Cynthia appeals to Mason Hawke for help in their predicament (Vaughan, R., *King Hill* 26–28). As expected in a Hawke novel, the former Confederates Hawke and McGregor find common cause with Union veterans. Ian McGregor urges the former enemies to join together in the cause of keeping their rights as sheep men:

> "Boys, I know that some of us fought for the North and some for the South. But we are all united in our memories. I wonder if you would all join me in a toast to all

3. Masquerades

our friends, those that are separated from us now by distance, and those who gave their last full measure of devotion" [Vaughan, R., *King Hill* 101].

As in many other Westerns, former Civil War enemies learn to put aside their differences. Even in such cases, sensitivities still exist. A good example is Torrey (Elisha J. Cook, Jr.), in *Shane*, a vocal Rebel whose touchiness everyone in the community approaches with good humor, even teasing him at times. His touchiness is the weak point exploited by Wilson to kill him. As in *Shane*, the rapacious cattleman hires an outside gunman to settle things. Like Wilson, Clay Morgan is ruthless and highly skilled and cares little about disrupting business as usual in the town.

The novel borrows from *Shane* in its broad plot outlines as well as in some specific ways. As in the Stevens film, the chivalrous outsider and the wife of the threatened landowner are clearly attracted to each other, and they dance together at a function attended by the woman's husband. Incidentally, this courtly love atmosphere is augmented by the introduction of a Montague-Capulet style rivalry between one of the rancher boys, Jesse Carlisle, and Hannah McGregor. The two actually quote from *Romeo and Juliet* in one of their encounters (Vaughan, R., *King Hill* 151–52). As already noted, the hired gun is in the Wilson mold and has the interesting name Clay Morgan, perhaps inspired by the two gunmen hired by the town of Warlock in *Warlock* (Edward Dmytryk, 1959), Clay Blaisedell (Henry Fonda) and Tom Morgan (Anthony Quinn). Morgan is shown as more dismissive of his employer than is Wilson, but both men are hired to effect removal of a group of undesirables (from the ranchers' point of view). In this novel, the ally of the undesirables—the sheep men, who include, incidentally, a group of Basques—is the itinerant pianist Mason Hawke, who makes a distinction between being "a professional gunfighter" like Morgan and simply a man who has engaged in gunfights: "'I have never been paid for the use of my guns.... On the other hand, I have been paid to play the piano'" (Vaughan, R., *King Hill* 175).

In an odd echo of another culture, Hawke the itinerant piano player, paid for his musical skills but repeatedly called upon to exercise his gunplay skills, recalls a Japanese popular culture hero, Zatoichi, the blind swordsman who makes a living as an itinerant masseur and gambler, living among the world of the Tokugawa-era yakuza. Besides his appeal as an action hero, his popularity in Japan, like that of other such "vagabond" heroes, as Gregory Barrett terms them, stems from his itinerant lifestyle, affording to audiences a fantasy escape from "their circumscribed social

Professionals in Western Film and Fiction

circle": "Vagabonds ... give vicarious pleasure to modern [Japanese] office workers and others who only travel with fellow workers or go to places where they have some social connections" (Barrett 84). So Zatoichi and his fellows are, in this sense, Japanese equivalents to the lone Westerner traveling from town to town, from fight to fight.

Zatoichi's adventures have been chronicled in films, television, and fiction, with a long-running film series starring Katsu Shintaro (see Barrett 84–87 for a brief introduction), and more recently in a film by auteur director and star Kitano Takeshi, *The Blind Swordsman: Zatoichi* (2003) (see Hall, K., "*Blind Swordsman: Zatoichi* by Kitano Takeshi: Not a Mere 'Entertainment'"). Like Hawke, Zatoichi plies a trade unrelated to his true skills as a fighter (he is an invincible swordsman despite his blindness), and he is called upon to use his sword skills usually to defend or to rescue people mistreated by the yakuza. Also like Hawke the professional piano player, Zatoichi persistently surprises his adversaries, who underestimate his skills because of appearances. For example, in the first Zatoichi film with Katsu, he stays at the home of a yakuza *oyabun* (boss), and everyone knows he is blind. The boss has told his men about Zatoichi's prowess, but they don't take him seriously. Finally, when one of them speaks condescendingly of him, Zatoichi makes a little speech about his pride and about his capabilities, and then tosses a lit candle in the air which he splits in half with one sword stroke. Zatoichi normally tries to shrug off challenges to combat or to warn off adversaries but is quite ruthless when provoked; similarly, Hawke usually provides examples of his gun prowess only when pushed into action, and the results are predictably lethal.

The Sharpshooter novels by Tobias Cole (pseudonym of Cameron Judd) are somewhat similar to the Hawke series, as a former soldier becomes a civil professional in an attempt to eschew a life of violence. Unlike Hawke, the Sharpshooter character (a former Civil War sniper for the Union) has turned to writing, concentrating on memoirs of his experiences and on writing about life in the West. True to the formula of Western fiction, though, he is unable to stay out of trouble and must become involved in adventures, as in the *Repentance Creek* entry in the series. In an opening reminiscent of Ford's *Stagecoach*, the train in which Wells is riding is attacked by bandits led by a desperado named Barco, and Wells admits to having been a sniper in the late conflict but wrestles with the morality of killing Barco if not fired on first. This qualm ends up getting

3. Masquerades

the stage driver killed and Wells himself injured by a bullet. Wells allies himself with the local sheriff in pursuing Barco, but he still intends to write for publication and continues to hedge at taking up arms in an active fashion.

Wells has come to the area to meet with a rancher and possible publishing patron named Walter Gage (Cole, *Repentance* 66–67). He begins his stay by a visit to the library, where he meets a woman who turns out to be key to the mystery of Barco. Soon he reads an account of the train incident written by the local newspaperman, Pembrook Jones, who becomes an important secondary character in the novel (Cole, *Repentance* 80–82). Wells praises the veracity of the article but shrinks at its hero-worshipping tone. This is a clever criticism by Cole (Cameron Judd) of the accustomed bombastic style of frontier journalism and dime novels so brilliantly skewered in Ford's Dutton Peabody (Edmond O'Brien, *The Man Who Shot Liberty Valance*) and Eastwood's Beauchamp (Saul Rubinek, *Unforgiven*)[11] and parodied throughout in the voice-over narration of Jack Crabb (Dustin Hoffman, Penn's *Little Big Man*). As an aspiring writer, the reluctant man of action, Wells, is very aware of the disparity between fact and presentation, or image, and so he provides criticism of the practice of journalism by a professional already engaged in it, from a perspective rather unusual in such cases. Additionally, the chestnut about the crusading journalist in Western towns is sidelined to some extent by the focus on the informational nature of the newspaper: Wells is worried because his role in the recent shooting will be revealed, making him a target for revenge (Cole, *Repentance* 82). Of course all is put right by the end of the novel. In the final chapter we learn that Wells's latest novel is a somewhat fictionalized account of the recent adventure narrated by him in the novel we are reading and that he has agreed to work part-time as a deputy while continuing his career as a writer. Thus, unlike the dime-novel writer who invents stories or, at best, records and inflates events observed by him (like Beauchamp), Wells actually writes his own life and lives his own writings (Cole, *Repentance* 280–82).

In *The Sharpshooter: Brimstone* (2003), Wells confronts his difficult past as a prisoner at the notorious Andersonville prison in Georgia. When the book begins, Wells muses on his newfound fame as an author with a family who has taken him in after a train accident:

> I'd cleansed out the pollution of my Andersonville nightmare through the pages of that novel. I had not anticipated that thousands upon thousands of others across

the nation would make that story their own, turning me ... into a relatively noted literary figure [Cole, *Brimstone* 9].

Soon, Wells will have to confront that "nightmare" in the person of one of his fellow inmates, Amos Broughton. As in the Hawke novels, the damaged psyche of Civil War veterans becomes an important focus. Unlike Wells, Broughton, the sheriff of Starnes, Kansas, where Wells comes to visit him, has been unable to live with the trauma caused by Andersonville (for a recent study of the prison and its Commandant, see Ruhlman). He suffers from insomnia and anxiety and has turned to surreptitious drinking. He also displays a mysterious hatred of an itinerant preacher named Killian, who has an active camp meeting not far from Starnes. He even steals Wells's sniper rifle, which he keeps with him even though the Civil War has ended, for an apparent attempt on Killian's life. Killian is partially vindicated by the end of the novel, having been suspected of betraying his comrades at Andersonville when in fact he was trying to protect his brother who had unwittingly put his comrades in danger.

Brimstone also includes as a secondary character a local newspaperman named Mark Taylor Smith. He is a pretentious, overdressed, and irritating young man who clearly wants to impress his father, the editor of the newspaper, the *Bleeker County Herald*, for which he tries mightily to report (Cole, *Brimstone* 81–82). His paper has an adversarial relationship with Amos and his deputy Leroy, and Wells forms a very negative opinion of the aspiring journalist, "Smith, the runt of a newspaperman" (Cole, *Brimstone* 106). Despite his unattractive qualities, Smith turns out to have a newspaperman's nose for the truth behind appearances, as his suspicions about Killian prove. After Smith is injured in a stabbing incident, he redeems himself somewhat by his courtesy to Mrs. Broughton while he and Wells prepare an article for the newspaper which will publicize Amos's threats to Killian's life. As Wells muses wryly, "Maybe Mark Taylor Smith should get stabbed a little more often. It seemed to do his personality some good" (Cole, *Brimstone* 283). Throughout much of the novel, Smith has mistakenly assumed that he and Wells are professional kin, so to speak, because both are writers. Wells is not just a writer, of course; he has a difficult personal history as a war veteran and a former prisoner of war, and he easily perceives the flaws in Smith's personality. In *The Sharpshooter: Gold Fever* (2003), Wells works on a second novel and searches for an artist who was a fellow prisoner in Andersonville.

Rather like Wells, the hero of the TNT production *Crossfire Trail*,

3. *Masquerades*

Rafe Covington (Tom Selleck) is a former sharpshooter in the Civil War, returning home. Like many veterans of this and other wars as depicted in film and fiction, he returns to a society that has changed since he left it, and not always for the better. In this instance, he had made a promise to one of his friends, a man named Charles Rodney, who died on the ship where they both had been working after the war ended, to take care of his farm or ranch in his stead. Like Macreedy (Spencer Tracy) in *Bad Day at Black Rock*, Rafe tries to fulfill his promise to a comrade in arms even when faced with seemingly insurmountable obstacles. When Rafe travels to the ranch, he discovers that the unscrupulous saloon owner Bruce Barkow (Mark Harmon) is trying to gain ownership of the ranch by marrying Ann Rodney (Virginia Madsen), the widow of Charles, and has lied to her about what really happened to him. The conflict escalates, following the pattern of films like *Shane*, leading Barkow to hire Beau Dorn (Brad Johnson), a supposedly unstoppable assassin, to get rid of Rafe and his allies Joe (Wilford Brimley) and Rock (David O'Hara). The film reads essentially like a "returning veteran" film set after World War II, with the common plot of the veteran who returns to find that his wife has left him, or is about to leave him, and that the job he once had, or the home he once lived in, is no longer his. In this case one veteran attempts to fill the void left by another's death, becoming a changeling figure who finally succeeds in replacing, even surpassing, the position occupied by his former friend.

In this 2001 film, the Civil War veteran receives very positive treatment from the narrative, perhaps reflecting the attitudes of at least some sectors of American society at that time about the first Gulf War, the most recent major conflict which had taken American troops abroad. As in many films soon after World War II, the veteran is treated positively in the screenplay. As James I. Deutsch observes in his article on Civil War veterans in American movies,

> The Civil War veterans in the films ... of 1945 to 1955, like their counterparts from World War II, almost always received sympathetic treatment from Hollywood. They may have turned to crime, they may be emotionally unstable, but they are depicted as victims of forces beyond their control—scarred by a war that had to be fought for the causes of freedom and democracy [Deutsch 134].

As Deutsch also notes, this perspective began to shift later in the decade, as the 1956 film *The Searchers* demonstrates (Deutsch 134).

Professionals in Western Film and Fiction

While the Tom Selleck character returned home with a mission, Ray Milland plays a rather mysterious, or masquerading, Civil War veteran with marksman skills in *Copper Canyon* (John Farrow, 1950). He becomes embroiled in a conflict between the miners in Coppertown, primarily former Confederates, and a crooked cabal of Unionists. A former Confederate with the assumed name of Corporal Johnny Carter (Ray Milland), Col. Desmond maintains his masquerade as a traveling marksman who performs in a stage show because he does not want to become involved in violent conflicts, as well as from concern about false accusations against him for stealing money from a Union fort. Following common generic practice, the film features a "good" woman, Caroline Desmond (Mona Freeman), and a "bad" woman, saloon owner Lisa Roselle (Hedy Lamarr). Also like some other Westerns before the 1960s and the peak of the civil rights movement, this film treats the Confederates sympathetically and presents them as oppressed or cheated by rascally Yankees. (Instead of farmers and ranchers, the film sets up an opposition between miners and speculators.) In its treatment of the Reconstruction period the 1950 film seems a throwback to 1930s examples like *The Lawless Nineties* or the two Jesse James films featuring Henry Hull as Major Cobb. The Farrow film also lines up ideologically with a number of John Ford's films such as his Cavalry Trilogy, discussed by Westbrook and Brown. As noted in their article, in filming James Warner Bellah's stories, some of which were the basis of his Cavalry Trilogy,

> ... Ford introduced Southern characters and story lines that reinforce a particular stance towards efforts to effect a reconciliation between the North and the South in the decades following the Civil War. In the movement between prose and screen, the racial underpinnings of the Civil War were uniformly excluded, with the focus instead on the iconography and mythology of the "Lost Cause" [Westbrook and Brown 171].

At the end of Farrow's film, the rifts in the town are healed, and the good will even extends to romance. Caroline, widow of Tom Desmond, the colonel's brother, will wed Captain Ord (Harry Carey, Jr.), a stalwart Union soldier. Johnny and Lisa leave town on the stage (perhaps as a comic nod to the departure of Ringo and Dallas from "civilization" in *Stagecoach*), headed for San Francisco and a career in saloon management, to be financed by the $20,000 that Johnny (Col. Desmond) had been accused of stealing and which, he tells Lisa, is hidden in his gun case.

Also featuring a mining context are the Brady Kenton novels (written

3. Masquerades

by Cameron Judd), about a journalist in the West who embroils himself in rather Gothic entanglements. The Western setting of the Kenton novels is somewhat secondary to their qualities as melodramatic suspense tales of the Gothic type, revolving around hidden identities, mysterious deaths and disappearances, and progeny of unclear origin. Certainly a novel like *The Quest of Brady Kenton* is not as typically "Western" as the usual production of Matt Braun or Johnny D. Boggs, two authors who painstakingly fill their work with period authenticity. This is not to say that a novel like *The Quest* lacks Western authenticity; instead, the Western setting is more of a backdrop for a Conan Doyle–like narrative.

The Quest opens in a very Western setting: Leadville, Colorado, whose boom as a mining town led to its fame and to visits by European luminaries like Oscar Wilde.

> Along with the rough life of the town, an upper class developed alongside the silver boom. Horace Tabor, who owned a general mercantile store with his wife Augusta, invested in mining with incredible success. Making millions from silver mining, he built and opened the famous Opera House in 1879, as well as the Bank of Leadville and the Tabor Grand Hotel. Along the way, he infamously left his wife and married the young "Baby Doe." He rose from local to state to national political figure, built a mansion in Denver, Colorado, and lived a very wealthy lifestyle. His Tabor Opera House presented an astounding variety of talent. The world-famous magician Harry Houdini, John Philip Sousa, the British wit Oscar Wilde, the great actress Sarah Bernhardt and many wonderful operatic performers "trod the boards" of The Tabor during its heyday ... [*Leadville's Rich Colorado History*].

In the novel, a man named Alex Gunnison, whom we soon discover to be an associate of Brady Kenton, is about to deliver a speech in his stead; the site for the speech faces the Tabor Grand Hotel.[12] So the journalists, and the newspaper editor who introduces Gunnison, are placed at the center of one of the West's most solidly prosperous towns and are identified by extension as adjuncts to or at least as approved associates of one of its great fortunes, the Tabor mining empire. This mining empire was the basis of the Leadville boom, which led to the establishment of a theater there: "In 1878 the discovery of silver at Leadville began another boom. When H.A.W. Tabor, the new and fabulous millionaire, owner of the Matchless Mine and many others, built a lavish opera house, he hired the unbeatable Jack Langrishe to run it for him" (Cochran 335).

Brady Kenton appears to be missing and has a difficult history with his employer. The formal structure of the novel recalls Conan Doyle as well in that Gunnison is a Dr. Watson to the mercurial Kenton's Holmes.

Professionals in Western Film and Fiction

And Kenton has his Moriarty in Paul Kevington, half-brother of Rachel Frye (née Kevington), who has come West in search of Brady Kenton, paralleling Brady's search for his wife Victoria, thought to be dead but eventually found to be living in England. This convoluted storyline, filled with even more complications than detailed here, patently qualifies the novel as Gothic melodrama. The novel also contains the plot twist of the foreigner, Kevington, impersonating a dead Texas Ranger—in other words, a "civilized" Easterner—actually a Briton—successfully pretending to be a tough Western lawman. He is finally discovered because a Ranger acquaintance of the dead man avers to Rachel Frye that the description of the man purporting to be Jessup Best does not match the real man. The novel is rather unusual as well because, unlike the journalist characters in other Westerns, Brady Kenton is the focus of celebrity, with other journalists reporting on him as they would on dime-novel gunfighters. Disappearing and reappearing mysteriously, he engages in physical derring-do, including a fight aboard a train, filling the role of a dime-novel hero.

At nearly the other pole from Brady Kenton is Maurice Dumas, the newspaperman of Elmore Leonard's *Gunsights*, in which journalists follow and even try to foment a feud between two tough Westerners. The two men, Brendan Early and Dana Moon, are friends, and the journalists wonder whether or not they will end up on opposing sides in the Rincon Mountain War. The satire of contemporary media hype is clear enough: the journalists treat serious events like sports matches, complete with manufactured or at least putative rivalries, winners and losers in an exciting contest, and so forth. Unlike many other fictional treatments of journalists in the West, in which one journalist appears as a witness and perhaps a participant in events (as in *The Last Manhunt*), in this case Maurice Dumas is the most prominent of a large gang of journalists and other media figures. The narrative even features in an important secondary role the historical photographer from Tombstone, C.S. Fly, whose shop and boardinghouse abutted the site of the famous events near the O.K. Corral. Fly had a shop and a boardinghouse on Fremont Street in Tombstone at the time of the famous gunfight. Doc Holliday roomed at the boardinghouse (Guinn 104–05). Fly also participated in the aftermath of the gunfight, in fact removing the dying Billy Clanton's firearm from his possession (Guinn 231). (For Fly's photography career, see Vaughan). Leonard inserts him into the novel as a photojournalist, showing him, for

3. Masquerades

example, taking pictures of a lynched activist named Armando Duro and mentioning in passing his political aspirations and connections with John Slaughter, sheriff of Tombstone (Leonard 157). Historically, Fly was elected sheriff of Cochise County (the county housing Tombstone and Benson) in November 1894 and was backed by John Slaughter. He served until 1896 (Vaughan, T. 314–15).

The novel's Rincon Mountain War (set near Benson, Arizona, not far from Tombstone), like the many rancher-homesteader conflicts in Westerns (*Shane*, *Heaven's Gate*) pits larger profit interests against small business ones. In this case, the mining industry wishes to push out the small farmers and other homesteaders in the mountainous areas containing minerals. So the conflict is somewhat of a reversal of the type of struggle represented by the Johnson County War of 1892,[13] in which ranchers like the fictional Ryker in *Shane* see the homesteaders as interlopers on established boundaries. As Ryker (Emile Meyer) forcefully relates to Joe Starrett (Van Heflin), "We made this country! We found it and we made it.... We made a safe range out of this. Some of us died doin' it, but we made it.... And then people move in who've never had to rawhide it through the old days. Fence off my range, and fence me off from water" (Stevens 10 [1:08:30]). Unlike the fight in *Shane*, though, which remains isolated within the rough boundaries of the town and surrounding community, the Rincon Mountain War is treated like a gladiatorial contest between two men and their followers. The bread and circuses here will be provided, presumably, by all the newspapers (a long list) and the famous photographer, Fly, who have come to witness and in some cases perhaps to help incite the battle. As the narrator reports, the news organizations may need an "'angle'" but would rather have sensationalism: "But it would be far better if Personalities [*sic*] were involved" (Leonard 39). Questions about land rights and mining leases don't sell papers, but bigger-than-life characters do:

> This was, in part, the reason Dana Moon and Brendan Early were elected to be the principal antagonists, bound to come together sooner or later, which would be the climax, the Big Story: two living legends in a fight to the finish [Leonard 39–40].

The "living legends" may not be too interested in cooperating, either in interviews or by actually fighting each other (they are longtime friends), but this doesn't matter too much to the journalists, with the exception of the enterprising Maurice Dumas (Leonard 40–42). Dumas, from the *Chicago Times*, begins to gain the confidence of the main "actors" because he "asked straight questions and didn't know any better when he got direct answers" (Leonard 42).

A contrasting set of journalist characters peoples *Death Head Crossing* by James Reasoner. Ostensibly focusing on Hell Jackson, a feared gunfighter, the narrative develops into a mystery about the murder of an old man which is investigated by Jackson and a visiting newspaperman from New York, Everett Sidney Howard. Howard, who at the beginning of the novel is predictably fascinated by the exploits of the mysterious Jackson, becomes acquainted with the local newspaper publishers, the Grahams, Malcolm and Rosalie. A subplot concerns a ranch run by a transplanted Easterner, Benjamin Tillman from Philadelphia, and Howard's romantic interest in his cousin Deborah, which leads to a violently jealous reaction from Benjamin (Reasoner 160–65). After a series of murders blamed on a madman called the Hand of God, the ingenuous Howard, who had been working for the *Death Head Weekly Journal* (edited by the Grahams), learns in a revelation typical of melodrama that the true killers, and thieves of considerable property including the lucrative ranch, are the Grahams, who are not brother and sister but are instead lovers. Graham had served as the Hand of God killer behind a mask. Graham also reveals to Howard that he and his "sister" are not from Dallas, as they had claimed, but from New York, like Howard. Not true Westerners, then, they are dark doubles of the Easterner Howard, and additionally they are in league with Tillman's venal relatives from Philadelphia in stealing his ranch after killing him and Deborah. Like Plummer in *The Lawless Nineties*, the Grahams are criminals masquerading as reformers, in this case as the voice of the community.

A Western notable both for its artificiality and for an excellent cast working with unusual material is *The Fastest Gun Alive* (Russell Rouse, 1956), with Glenn Ford as storekeeper George Temple in the small town of Cross Creek. Married, with his wife Dora (Jeanne Crain) expecting, he is clearly uncomfortable with his position in the town. Ford plays the role with his usual subtle, nervous intelligence, conveying Temple's resentment at the treatment he receives from the other men in the town, who belittle him for his profession and his teetotaling. He displays considerable irritation (underplayed by the skillful Ford) at his role as a humble shopkeeper. We discover that he has a drinking problem and has been abstemious for the four years spent in Cross Creek. Of course the viewer suspects as well that he is the titular "fastest gun alive," but his reasons for secrecy are unclear and, as we learn near the end of the film, subject to misinterpretation. According

3. Masquerades

to the usual Western plot configuration, such a gunman should be trying to hang up his guns because he is tired of killing or has had too many confrontations with eager gun hands (like the Gregory Peck character in *The Gunfighter*). The notches on his gun would also lend credence to such an interpretation. These six notches are prominently displayed when he loses patience with his role as shopkeeper and stalks off to the saloon to drink. His drinking in turn leads him to show off his matchless speed and accuracy to the townspeople, sprinkled with comments about where to aim at an opponent which imply that he has faced and killed men in the past. One of the townsmen who examines his gun notes the six notches on its grip. We also know that he will likely have an opportunity soon, as Vinnie Harold (Broderick Crawford, working in his accustomed ferocious mode), rather of an evil double of Temple, is on his way to the town, running with his gang from a posse, and already shown to have killed a man named Fallon in a gunfight provoked by the obsessed Harold.

While the gang is headed for the town, the conflicted Temple goes to the local church during Sunday services—in a scene reminiscent of *High Noon*—and announces his decision to leave town and to leave his gun with the Methodist pastor. Dora had been trying to persuade him to give up his gun, and she decides to go with him. (The long-suffering Dora is, to a degree, the type identified by Ronna Privett as "the worn-down, bedraggled wife or widow of some less-than-heroic western settler" [Privett 83].) Then the congregation, led by Lou Glover (Leif Erickson), intervene to convince him to stay, swearing individual oaths never to reveal his prowess and so to prevent his fame from inviting challenges. Unlike Will Kane, Temple chooses at this point to hang up his guns and so is accepted by the congregation. Eventually he must fight, like Kane, but the townspeople in this film are presented with the destruction of their town as the alternative to fighting, a dilemma not faced by the people of Hadleyville.

As the members of the congregation are pronouncing the oaths, the gang arrives in town and meets a small boy in the saloon (not in church where his parents are). He tells them about the fastest gun alive, showing them two silver dollars George had shot on the fly from some distance, a nearly impossible feat. Harold threatens to burn the town if Temple does not come out of the church. Meantime Temple has revealed to the congregation that his real reason for moving from town to town is that he is afraid of challenges because he has never faced a man in a gunfight. He reveals that his father was a famous marshal (George Kebler) who had "cleaned up

Abilene" and had taught him to shoot until he became even faster than his father, who was killed in a gunfight. The notches on his father's gun record his kills, not Temple's (whose real name is George Kebler, Jr.). So the film subverts the viewer's expectations, and the projected contest becomes an unwrapping of psychological dilemmas or defects harbored by both George and Vinnie. The final gunfight is left unresolved on screen until the closing scene of the film, when a funeral is shown for both men. Only then do we learn that one of the graves, George's, is empty except for some clothes and his gun. He and Dora will remain in Cross Creek as shopkeepers. Presumably, and rather implausibly, George's conflicts are now resolved.

Like George Temple, Steve Dancy, the hero of James D. Best's Shopkeeper novels, is a handy man with a gun but is not a professional gunfighter. Neither is he a conflicted, alcoholic wanderer like Temple. Instead, in the first novel of the series (*The Shopkeeper*), he is an Easterner who has come out West (to Colorado) to get away from family conflict and to live on the very large fortune he has amassed through smart investment and speculation. Soon embroiled despite his initial intentions in a savage local political and economic war, he displays his gun skills in a street fight with two tough brothers, the Cutlers, both of whom he kills. The reader learns that Dancy is a wealthy gun dealer and gunsmith but, like Temple, has never (until now) participated in a gunfight.

Dancy is as deadly with a banknote as with a gun. He proves himself a devious manipulator who declares war on the local boss, Washburn, a man with political ambitions who controls many local figures and institutions. Dancy begins to undermine Washburn's position by buying up debt owed to Washburn and taking control of some of his enterprises—a bank, a store, and so forth. Dancy hires some of Pinkertons' best men for protection and undertakes to defend the interests of men like Jeff Sharp, a wealthy miner opposed to Washburn. In a lethal countermove, Washburn hires notorious sniper Sprague to kill a gubernatorial hopeful (Bolton) and to intimidate Dancy and his allies.

Dancy turns the Eastern tenderfoot motif on its head. His Pinkerton companions, all tough Westerners, soon discover that not only is he expert with, and about, firearms, but that he also has excellent woodsman skills. (Usually the lack of outdoors expertise signals tenderfoot status in Western tales.) When the best of the Pinkerton hunters kills some game birds, Dancy offers to clean one and is told his help is not needed. So he wagers the man that he can clean his bird in much shorter order than the hunter

3. Masquerades

can. Dancy demonstrates his prowess by cleaning the bird with a highly practiced and rapid technique that leads the hunter to ask him for pointers. Quite at home on the trail, Dancy blends an Eastern knowledge of finance, including a deviousness appropriate to the cutthroat Gilded Age world, with a Westerner's skill set. Thus he is arguably a "new man" for the frontier, with his avowed interest in bringing civilized mores to rough areas like the Colorado mining country.

Nevertheless Dancy is not a fully trained Westerner, as an incident not long after the bird episode demonstrates. When he confronts two of Washburn's bodyguards and disarms one of them of his revolver, while his companion, Pinkerton lead detective McAllen, bloodies the other and then disarms Dancy's opponent of his hidden weapons, Dancy learns an important lesson about facing down such ruthless men. McAllen observes that Dancy opened his attack verbally when he should have been physically forceful from the start. The incident is reminiscent of the scene in Kasdan's *Wyatt Earp* (1994) when Ed Masterson (Bill Pullman) confronts some drunken cowboys in Dodge City, trying to talk them into disarming. Wyatt Earp (Kevin Costner) intervenes, buffaloing one of them (hitting him over the head with his gun barrel). Earp shows Masterson the hidden gun in the cowboy's belt and advises the lawman to find another line of work, saying "You're too affable."[14] Dancy's first-person narrative makes a similar point as he observes that "I had been lulled by old habits, habits that were harmless in my previous life [back East] but now might prove fatal" (Best 124–25).

During the novel Dancy and the Pinkertons, seen here in a light more positive than their history might indicate and certainly more positively than in films about the James brothers,[15] pursue an assassin named Sprague, hired by Washburn. Dancy must also contend with a Ma Barker–like character, Mrs. Bolton, of whose daughter Jenny he becomes enamored. As the narrative sorts itself out, Sprague and Washburn are killed, and Mrs. Bolton is sent packing to San Francisco. Jenny turns out to be vengeful and murderous and has no interest in Dancy, who settles for the moment into the life of a successful businessman. The Dancy character reverses the stereotype of the capitalist or the speculator who operates from motives of greed. The conservative point of view of the novel displays Dancy and his wealth as a benefit to society because he defeats grasping capitalists and politicians like Washburn.

As in *The Lawless Nineties*, professionals may appear undercover or incognito in plots analogous to contemporary setting crime films. Many of

Professionals in Western Film and Fiction

these professionals are Pinkerton men or federal agents, as in *Station West*; or military investigators, as in *Westbound*. Some are more unofficial, like the James Stewart railroad investigator in *Night Passage*. A more unconventional type is the private citizen with a professional background seeking justice or revenge, as in *Warpath* (Byron Haskin, 1951). Edmond O'Brien, appearing here in one of three Haskin-O'Brien Westerns (the others were *Silver City* and *Denver & Rio Grande*), is John Vickers, an embittered former army captain and lawyer (thus combining military and civil professional roles) who searches for three men who robbed a bank and fired the shot that paralyzed his fiancée, leading eventually to her death. The Vickers character parallels, from a different time setting, other damaged war-veteran, *noir* avenger roles which appeared after World War II: *Cornered* (Dick Powell) *Dead Reckoning* (Humphrey Bogart), for example, both of which featured World War II veterans seeking some form of retribution within a quest structure.

Warpath fits easily into the damaged veteran subgenre, and it even bears some similarities in plot development to some characteristic examples of the subgenre dealing with World War II. Besides the films already mentioned above, *Backfire* (Vincent Sherman, 1950), also featuring O'Brien in an important role, deals with recuperating war veteran Bob Corey (Gordon MacRae) whose friend Steve Connelly, played by O'Brien, disappears and is accused of killing a prominent gambler. The typically convoluted plot is resolved when yet another veteran, Ben Arno (Dane Clark), a member of the same infantry company as Bob and Steve, is revealed as the killer. The themes of loyalty and betrayal conflated with criminality, as well as the presence of paralysis as a plot element (Steve is nearly paralyzed from a confrontation with Ben), are motifs running through films of the subgenre, whether concerning World War II or the Civil War. *Cornered* also features a traumatized veteran, in this case a Canadian, Laurence Gerard (Dick Powell), trained as an electrical engineer, who had been fighting Germans in Europe for the British. His French wife was executed as a Resistance member on the orders of a shadowy figure, Marcel Jarnac (a sinister portrayal by Luther Adler). The film details Gerard's efforts to find Jarnac and avenge his wife. Gerard suffers from flashbacks and near-seizures because of his trauma, losing touch at times with his surroundings. Like Vickers, he is haunted by his wife's death and displays instability. When confronted finally by Jarnac, whom he does not recognize, he comments on the effects of war on one's recall: "War does something to your memory. Gets sharper. You forget the way people look

3. Masquerades

and—remember the important things." Like Vickers, Gerard is a civil professional—from a different era—whose war service is a dangerous zone for his personality.

Unlike these two war vet films set in the 1940s, when the war had recently ended and the nation was living through an uncertain peace, *Warpath* features a recent war veteran, from the Civil War, who finds it rather convenient to enlist as a private with the 7th Cavalry, part of an army technically at war with the Sioux and their allies, not long before the 1876 battle at Little Big Horn. Instead of having to fit into a civilian society and search for his malefactors there, he is provided with the ability to function quite easily as an underachieving private—his comrades and superiors soon perceive that he is much more qualified than his rank attests—while serving under the man he suspects of being one of the robbers, Sergeant O'Hara (Forrest Tucker).

During his unorthodox investigation at Fort Abraham Lincoln (near Bismarck, ND), Vickers meets the camp sutler, a civilian professional whose daughter Molly (Polly Bergen) he had defended in a fight over her honor with O'Hara. (This was the fort from which Custer left on his ill-fated last command journey. It has been restored and preserved as a museum site.) The storeowner, Sam Quade (Dean Jagger), is outwardly courteous but is reluctant for Molly to come into contact with too many soldiers. This fatherly concern is soon suspect[16] as Vickers learns from Molly that one of her father's frequent visitors is O'Hara. After O'Hara and Vickers are detailed to a reconnaissance mission and must return by stealth to get help when their troop is stranded among numerous Sioux, Vickers suspects O'Hara of trying to kill him during their escape. Additionally, O'Hara openly resents Vickers for his newfound hero status and his promotion to top sergeant, thus outranking O'Hara.[17] Soon O'Hara deserts, while Quade sells his store, taking his daughter with him to join a wagon train being escorted by the troop commanded by Vickers. Captured by the Sioux, O'Hara redeems himself by sacrificing his life to enable Vickers and some of his men, as well as Molly, to escape, while Quade selflessly rides through hostile lines to try to warn Custer about the thousands of Indians surrounding his command. Vickers has lost his desire for vengeance and so is fit to marry Molly and to assume a lieutenant's bar in the Army. In this film, then, two of the major characters are professionals (lawyer and salesman), and the law and the usual Army justice structure have relatively little to do with the resolution of the conflicts.

Professionals in Western Film and Fiction

Sam Quade fits into a series of shady sutlers, merchants, Indian agents, and bar owners who represent the commonly noted American, and particularly frontier, suspicion of profiteers and capitalists. Unlike the sunnily positive storeowner played by Jack Kruschen in *McLintock!*, these professionals are portrayed as threats to the civil community. Two such characters of particularly sinister bent were played by the fine character actor John McIntire in two Anthony Mann Westerns with James Stewart, *Winchester '73* and *The Far Country*. In *Winchester '73*, McIntire plays Joe Lamont, a duplicitous gambler and a sort of traveling salesman who sells guns and liquor to the Indians and is killed after winning the titular rifle in a card game. Although Lamont is not officially an Indian agent, his character recalls crooked Indian agents in other films. As the article in *The BFI Companion to the Western*, "Indian Agent," observes, "That stock figure of the Western, the corrupt Indian agent, ... has a basis in history," but, the article cautions, "Not all were corrupt," and concludes, "If the stereotype persisted, this may owe less to historical truth, and more to Hollywood's preference for individual villainy over complex social conditions as the cause of such events as Indian wars" (Buscombe 155). In *The Far Country*, McIntire's character Gannon actually runs a criminal enterprise in the North Country, swindling miners and maintaining a monopoly on sales of goods, rather like the Humphrey Bogart saloon owner Whip McCord in *The Oklahoma Kid* (Lloyd Bacon, 1939) or the corrupt mining engineer Alex McNamara (Randolph Scott) in *The Spoilers*. All three characters die at the hand of the films' heroes.

John Ford Westerns also featured such nefarious portrayals, such as Silas Meacham (Grant Withers), the crooked Indian agent in *Fort Apache* who, like the McIntire gun salesman, dies at the hands of the Indians, but not before being upbraided and deprived of his illegal liquor at the command of Col. Thursday (Henry Fonda); and Jerem Futterman (Peter Mamakos), a trader who makes the fatal mistake of trying to backshoot Ethan Edwards (John Wayne) in *The Searchers* only to suffer the same fate himself. In this respect as in others, as has been noted quite often in the literature on the film, Ethan does not match the heroic stereotype, summarized by Joseph J. Waldmeir in his article on Westerns and knighthood: "Chosen by passing tests of physical strength, the gaining of a heraldic identification, the quest, courtesy to fallen or disarmed foe (one does not shoot one's enemy in the back), all are part and parcel of chivalric tradition" (Waldmeir 116). Arguably Ethan meets only one of these criteria, the

3. Masquerades

strength test, as even the quest motif is vitiated by his threats against Debbie, the object of the quest.

A John Wayne Western from Republic, *In Old California* (William McGann, 1942) presents an interesting case of conflict between a venal and dictatorial saloon owner, a man who also owns just about everything in the town of Sacramento (like, in later films, Murphy in *Chisum* or Gannon in *The Far Country*), Britt Dawson (Albert Dekker), and newcomer from Boston Tom Craig (John Wayne), a druggist who wants to set up shop in the early boomtown period. The film is set on the virtual eve of the famous California Gold Rush—a prospector actually runs into town with news of the first big strike—and so one of the central motifs of the film is the concern over property rights, ownership, and capital. Such focus is hardly unusual in a Western, but in this case the disputes and conflicts revolve almost obsessively around these themes, to the point that law and order, in the form of officials, seems more or less secondary, an afterthought. Even the newly appointed U.S. marshal does little about egregious breaches of law—he will not investigate a murder charge but will lock up Tom for disorderly conduct. No implication of corruption is made about the marshal; he merely seems uninterested. When Tom arrives in town, having had previous confrontations with Britt, he is frozen out of the rental market (he wants to open a store) until Lacey (Binnie Barnes), who owns an old store next to the town saloon, agrees to rent to him for half his profits.

Here the masculine-dominated saloon world comes into direct conflict with the more female-oriented ambience of stores and shops. This familiar opposition is sharply and dramatically focused in *Shane*, as Matthew J. Costello observes: "Grafton's Mercantile and Saloon becomes a locus for much of the imagery concerning masculinity. The store and saloon are separated by a swinging gate similar to a fence.... Ryker's men [ranchers] occupy the saloon while the settlers occupy the store" (Costello, "'I Didn't Expect'" 265–66). In the present instance, Lacey moves from her subaltern existence in Britt's saloon to a full partnership in Tom's store.

Again, the terms of the rental and its context say nothing explicitly about any emotional or romantic motive from either party. Britt certainly interprets the rental in a possessively jealous manner until Lacey reassures him that she is only interested in the profits from the drugstore, which should thrive in the newly booming town. She even suggests that she and

Professionals in Western Film and Fiction

Tom can charge a dollar per pill, a price that Tom had already told her was too high.

As in many such narratives, Tom also becomes involved in a romantic entanglement. At first Lacey and Britt are more or less engaged, and Tom becomes engaged to a very sprightly and pretty woman with very obvious blue-blood background or at least pretensions, Ellen (Helen Parrish). Tom and Ellen seem to match each other, given Tom's Boston origins and education as a pharmacist, and he plans to go to San Francisco to marry her. But the seasoned Western viewer might suspect that Tom is actually more suited to Lacey (as part of his shift to the Western environment), and if this be the case, two obstacles must be removed, in keeping with such narrative examples: Britt and Ellen. Many "town-building" Westerns fit roughly the pattern of Greek New Comedy, which, following Northrop Frye's concept, often featured a romantic entanglement which is resolved after the removal of obstacles (such as rival suitors) and which resulted in the formation of a new social order within the comedy (see Frye 163–65). This removal is accomplished in the case of Ellen by her issuing an ultimatum to Tom which he declines to satisfy, stating that his duty to the community (assisting with an epidemic at the mining camp) is more important; and in Britt's case, by his repentance of his actions on his deathbed after being shot in a robbery attempt on the wagon train with supplies for the mining camp, led by Tom.

A less morally attractive storeowner is found in *Firecreek* (Vincent McEveety, 1967). This cynical town Western features established stars like James Stewart and Henry Fonda in unheroic roles. Other dependable Western actors like Ed Begley and Dean Jagger fill supporting roles, all of them unappealing in one way or another. Begley plays the circuit-riding Preacher Broyles, a bombastic Calvinist who is mocked by members of the gang of range riders led by Bob Larkin (Henry Fonda, playing against type as in Leone's *Once Upon a Time in the West*). When he is unhorsed by the gang and assisted in mounting his horse by part-time sheriff Cobb (James Stewart), he reacts sharply, without humor, to an attempted bit of levity by the sheriff. Much later in the film, the quiet storeowner Mr. Wittier (Dean Jagger) (a former lawyer) tries to convince the desperate sheriff, who is steeling himself to act against Larkin and his men, that he should simply leave the town to its own devices and perhaps even move on to another place. Wittier, who has been shown studiously observing events in the town, explains to Cobb why he moved to the desolate town of

3. Masquerades

Firecreek: "I found myself unable to cope with making important decisions, so I came to Firecreek because I could live out each day here without my word having any importance" (McEveety Ch. 19). Presumably the work of lawyering was too filled with argument and tension for Wittier. Clearly he, like others in the town but in a more pronounced manner, suffers from the spiritual ailment of abulia, lack of will, discussed at length by Spanish writers of the so-called Generation of 1898, who were at least in part trying to account for the lack of initiative which they perceived in the Spain of their time.[18]

Although many examples of merchants can be found in Westerns, the viewpoint of the genre on storeowners is not always so jaundiced. In a forthrightly conservative film like *McLintock!*, the town businessman, well-established and with ties to families in the community, is a positive asset, thus storeowner Birnbaum (Jack Kruschen). A more complex treatment of the town provider of goods is to be found in *Shane*, a fictionalized presentation of the notorious Johnson County War in Wyoming. Here the storeowner (and saloon owner) Sam Grafton (Paul McVey) is a decent enough man who tries very hard to stay out of taking sides in the fight between ranchers and homesteaders. Hence he has the respect of all in the community, to the point that he can be quite clear about fights in his store-saloon: he will not tolerate them, as he tells Shane and Joe Starrett after they engage in an epic fight with Chris (Ben Johnson) and other henchmen of grasping rancher Ryker (Emile Meyer). Grafton is only mollified when Starrett and Shane offer to pay damages (and because he quietly sympathizes with them). Respect for property rights in this film is a double-edged sword: while such respect is the basis of the conflict in the town, it is also the protection for the ethical businessman. The businessman is the necessary linchpin for the preservation of the community, a theme appropriate for the period of the film's release. Grafton's store is the setting for the resolution of conflicts about property and political organization in the town.

The routine film *Trouble in Sundown* (David Howard, 1939) concerns a well-respected, elderly banker in the town of Sundown who is framed for robbing his own bank and killing the bank guard by locking him in the safe overnight, resulting in his suffocation. The banker, John Cameron (Howard Hickman), is protected by honest, courageous rancher Clint Bradford (George O'Brien) against attempts to kill him or to arrest him. The real criminal, Ross Daggett (Cy Kendall), and his two henchmen Dusty

Professionals in Western Film and Fiction

(Ward Bond) and Tex (Monte Montague), are finally exposed and arrested during Cameron's trial through a risky stratagem, essentially restaging the locked-safe maneuver, executed by Clint and his associates.

Another film notable for its inclusion of the storeowner and other town characters is *Open Range* (Kevin Costner, 2003). This adaptation of the Lauran Paine novel approaches the familiar cattleman-homesteader conflict from a different angle, focusing on the antagonism between "free-grazers," that is, roving cattlemen who graze off common land and then move on, and established ranchers who claim such land as their own. In this film the free-grazers are led by Boss Spearman (Robert Duvall) and Charlie Wade (Kevin Costner), and the disputatious and grasping rancher, an Irishman named Baxter, is played by Michael Gambon. A series of escalating confrontations leads first to the arrest and injury of the giant Mose (Abraham Benrubi) and then to the death of Mose and the grazers' beloved dog Tig, and the near-death of Button (Diego Luna), at the hands of hired gunmen for Baxter. Baxter, who controls the town and its lawman Marshal Poole (James Russo), tells Boss dismissively that "times have changed" regarding free land for grazers. Boss insists on his right to roam where he will and swears revenge for the outrages. As the film unfolds we learn that Charlie has a Jesse James–like past, having joined a killing squad during the war (side not specified) and then, unlike James, hiring on as gunmen for "men just like Baxter."

From the town dwellers' perspective, the balance begins to shift morally in favor of the grazers after Charlie and Boss rescue a drover's dog (actually his daughter's) from raging waters after an epic downpour. Harmonville (a set built on the Negoda Reservation in Alberta, Canada) is a typically unromanticized frontier town following recent Western movie protocol, but not sleazily presented as in some cases. The drover insists to the hostile bartender who does not want to serve Boss and Charlie that they are good men, telling him about the dog. When the bartender, whose bar is owned by Baxter, demurs, Boss and Charlie react with some violence but are supported by the drover and by several men in the bar who know the drover. In addition to these allies, Boss and Charlie have begun to cement a friendship with Sue Barlow (Annette Bening), sister to the town doctor, who is caring for the concussed Button. Also friendly to them is the peppery stableman Percy (Michael Jeter), who has already made it clear that he does not like Baxter. So the roving grazers gradually become enveloped in relationships with the townspeople, whose loyalties

3. Masquerades

are sometimes ambiguously presented but who, in the main, turn out to be opposed to Baxter and his minions. The more nuanced presentation of the townspeople in this film contrasts with the archly unidimensional caricature in *Lawman* (Michael Winner, 1971) of the craven town dwellers who try to resist a marshal (Burt Lancaster) from another town who tries to arrest members of the ranching concern run by Vincent Bronson (Lee J. Cobb). The marshal, Jared Maddox, tells storekeeper Luther Harris (Walter Brooke), one of the townspeople trying to run him out of town because of their fear of Bronson, "You want the law but you don't want it to put a hole in your pocket" (Winner).

Gradually Charlie becomes romantically involved with Sue, whose brother does not trust him, and he tells Sue enough about his past for her to come to an informed decision about him. She chooses to disregard his past because she sees moral goodness behind the tough exterior. Sue is a quasi-professional, serving as unofficial nurse in her brother's home office, and her role in the narrative is a variation on "the sweet civilizer, like Molly in *The Virginian*, who serves to work her domestic wiles on the western landscape and on the hero" (Privett 83).[19] She also accepts Charlie's statement on the morning of the upcoming showdown with Baxter that "men are going to die today, and I'm going to kill them" as inevitable under the dire circumstances. As Jim Kitses points out, "In contrast to the genre's countless heroines who beg the hero to avoid violent tests, Bening's lucid Sue can make the distinction, and is consequently instrumental in Charlie's rebirth and their successful union" (Kitses, *Horizons West* 8–9).

When the final, protracted shootout unfolds, Boss and Charlie are aided at first by the stableman, who signals to them from his elevated perch when threats appear and also fires at Baxter's men in support of the two. Eventually, when Sue and Button enter the arena, the café owner and even the milquetoast storeowner attack Baxter's men. Thus the entire town becomes involved in the fight, finding solidarity against the common enemy as in films like *Seven Samurai* and its Western epigones beginning with the Kennedy-era *The Magnificent Seven*. The stocky café man blasts a gunman with his double-barrel through the window, remarking, "We're closed."

Doc Barlow and his sister Sue are the most important professional team in the town. Sue is in fact the more instrumental in assisting Boss and his men, as Doc is more or less abducted by the Baxters after Boss and Charlie ambush several of them. As in other small frontier towns, the doctor serves also as the pharmacist: his door sign advertises "compounding of preparations" as well as medical services. Both Barlow and Sue (not a doctor but clearly with experience akin to a modern RN) display a high level of competence, successfully treating Button for a concussion and other injuries. Like other such professionals, they have come West from a more settled society: Sue tells Charlie and Boss that her mother's tea set is about the only thing that survived the journey. The tea set, partially broken by Charlie when he is startled from a nightmare, becomes a symbol of the growing closeness between him and Sue. As in *The Virginian*, Sue is the "good woman" who will tame the outcast Charlie. She fits neatly into one of the categories proposed by Peggy A. McCormack in her useful article on women in Westerns: "The prototypical good woman in society is either the unmarried school marm [like Molly Stark] or the respectable married woman, often a cavalry officer's wife" (McCormack, P.A. 15).[20]

Charlie asks the stableman to sell his property if he dies and to buy a new set from a catalogue in Peterson's store. The final shot of the film, over the credits, shows a new tea set in Sue's house, but now it stands for the future life of marriage between Charlie and Sue. Incidentally, the storeowner and his wife may sell fine goods, but in a realistic touch not often seen in Westerns, Peterson admits to Boss that he has never even tasted the Swiss chocolate he sells because he can't afford it. Boss buys bars of the chocolate and expensive Havana cigars before the gunfight because he wants to experience such luxuries: "Shame to go forever without takin' the taste of somethin'." Before giving the storeowner some of his own chocolate to sample, Boss chides him for not enjoying life enough, telling him that "[it] Sit[s] right here in front of you, and you never even tried it (Costner Ch. 12)."

If Charlie is "tamed" by the influence of Sue and the counsel of his elder father-figure Boss, Jimmy Ringo (Gregory Peck) in *The Gunfighter* (Henry King, 1950) dies, as Charlie might have, without the reintegration Charlie will presumably enjoy. Like Charlie, Ringo promises to return to his wife, the schoolteacher Peg, and his son Jimmy Jr., after a time apart from them—in Charlie's case, after finishing his stock drive; in Ringo's, after a year in which to prove himself rehabilitated. Kostas Myrsiades compares Peg's conditional acceptance of Ringo to the "test" assigned to Odysseus by Penelope upon his return to Ithaca (Myrsiades 287). Unlike Charlie, Ringo is killed before he can embark on his year of purification.

3. Masquerades

He had finally achieved a meeting of minds with Peg (Helen Westcott), who, like Mark Strett (Millard Mitchell), the tough marshal (and ex-gunfighter and outlaw) in Cayenne, the town to which Ringo has returned, had tried to leave her past behind by becoming a useful member of society. Both Peggy and Mark carry symbolic surnames. Peggy has changed her last name to Walsh in an attempt to "wash" away her past, while Mark Strett has gone "straight" in his attempt to escape from the vicious circle implied by his association with Ringo. Peg has become a respected civil professional, schoolteacher to the many children of Cayenne, and, like Mark, has hidden her past from the townspeople. She had refused to meet with Ringo until her friend Molly (Jean Parker), the widow of another outlaw, Bucky, convinces her that Ringo has changed.

Despite his best intentions, Ringo is still a disruptive force: his very presence in the town leads to the cancellation of school for the town's children, as the boys "play hooky" because of their fascination with the famous gunfighter in their midst. Peg is, or purports to be, given the later revelation that she had tried to refashion herself, a typical schoolmarm: proper, stern but even-humored, virtuous (despite her attractiveness, noted by saloon singer Molly). She might well fit the character sketched rather wryly by Josh Billings: "She wears her hair either cut short or hanging in ringlets, and is as prim and proper in everything as a pair of improved Fairbank Platform Scales.... She is the paragon of propriety and had rather be three years behind in styles than to spell one word wrong or to parse a sentence incorrectly.... She is stepmother to more bad boys' children than anybody else and has the patience of Job with naughty boys and stupid girls" (qtd. in Furness 349). Peg's attempt to rein in her boy Jimmy Jr., despite whatever "patience" she may display, is unavailing. Discovering Jimmy outside the Palace Bar where Ringo is watching the clock, she marches him home and locks him in his upstairs room. Soon enough he climbs out the window, down a tree, and heads back to form part of the cheering section outside the saloon. This seemingly trivial incident positions the boy for an encounter with his estranged (and unacknowledged) father, Jim Ringo. The encounter helps to bridge the gap between Ringo and Peg. And, as Myrsiades notes, Ringo tries to steer the boy away from his fascination with the deadly lifestyle which until now he has adopted (Myrsiades 285–86). After Ringo is killed, Peg and Jimmy are united with Mark at his funeral service: schoolteacher and marshal will overwrite their murky pasts by merging into the civil community.

4

Encroachments of Culture
The Frontier in History and Fiction

A persistent thread in Westerns is the existence of cultured individuals among the rough and ready members of mining, cattle, and gambling communities. The affinity of miners for Shakespeare and for theatrical performance more generally is well attested.[1] In some cases actors or impresarios may appear as examples of civil professionals in Western film and fiction. Apart from the commoner Shakespeare references, sometimes a gunfighting or other "action" character is shown to have familiarity with literature or with "classical" music.

The mining town of Tombstone (now a tourism-driven ghost town)[2] has served as the setting for numerous films and fictions about the famous "gunfight at the O.K. Corral" between the Earp brothers and John "Doc" Holliday, and the Clanton gang, on October 26, 1881.[3] Sometimes featured in these tales is the "opera house" built in Tombstone, as in other mining towns like Leadville. These establishments were more properly theaters:

> All over the West, towns built elaborate gilt-and-plush theaters grandiosely called opera houses. A few of these jewel-box theaters still survive in former boomtowns such as Nevada City, California; Tombstone, Arizona; and Aspen, Central City, and Leadville, Colorado [Carrell 100].

A staple of Tombstone films is the presence of traveling performers in the Bird Cage Theatre. In some instances these are Shakespearean actors; in others they are professionals of a lighter sort: comedians or musical revue performers. The performers intersect the violent ambience of Tombstone in differing ways. One of the less complex interactions occurs in two relatively recent films, *Wyatt Earp* (Lawrence Kasdan, 1994) and *Tombstone* (George P. Cosmatos, 1993).

In both films Wyatt Earp begins an affair with a traveling performer

4. Encroachments of Culture

named Josephine (Sadie or Josie) Marcus. The essential relationship here is accurate enough: Sadie Marcus was a song-and-dance girl with a troupe from San Francisco that played in Tombstone. Earp became romantically involved with her and left his mistress Mattie (perhaps a common-law wife) for Sadie. Later married, Earp and Sadie lived out the rest of their lives together, Sadie surviving Wyatt by a number of years and becoming the custodian of his legend (see Tefertiller 69–72, 100, 335–37). Neither film attempts to dress up Sadie by making her into any sort of accomplished actress. The Kasdan film, which does mention her Jewish ancestry (not noted in the Cosmatos film), is more restrained in its presentation of Sadie (or Josie, as she is called in the films), as she is played here by delicately beautiful Joanna Going. The prejudice perhaps felt but hidden away by the more "proper" townspeople of Tombstone is put into drug-addicted and vengeful Mattie's mouth as she hisses at Josie, calling her "Wyatt's hebe whore."

A useful article about Wyatt and Josie which highlights her background in the California Jewish community is "Wyatt and Josie Earp: Fact, Fiction, and Myth," by the Dillon brothers. According to the Dillons, Ms. Marcus was "called Josie by her childhood friends and family, but Sadie by Wyatt." She "was the adventurous daughter of a Jewish San Francisco family" who eventually arranged for herself and Wyatt (a Gentile) to be buried in the family's section of the Jewish cemetery in Colma, California (Dillon and Dillon 27, 30, 38).

The Kasdan Josie makes quite an issue of not wanting to see Wyatt involved in further violence and in seeming somewhat sympathetic to the tragic plight of Mattie (Mare Winningham), who is dying of opiate addiction. Wyatt first sees Josie performing in the Gilbert and Sullivan *H.M.S. Pinafore* in Dodge City, where he is unable to meet her because of an incident in the street. Later he meets her in Tombstone and begins an affair with her. In *Tombstone*, Josie is played by the more earthily erotic and openly emotive Dana Delany, and she is also displayed being photographed in scanty clothing by Tombstone photographer C.S. Fly,[4] a scene shown with some temporal sleight-of-hand as simultaneous with the famous gunfight. Lee Ann Westman summarizes the distinctiveness of this version of Josie in a paragraph which begins: "Josephine Marcus is a 'spirited actress' who lives on her own, travels, rides out on the Western landscape without the protection of a male, and is sexually aggressive" (Westman 77).

Tombstone films have also featured Shakespearean actors as traveling performers. The most famous example of this type is the Granville

Professionals in Western Film and Fiction

Thorndyke character (Alan Mowbray) in *My Darling Clementine* (John Ford, 1946). Eric C. Brown clarifies the origin of the character's name: "[It] combines two famous early twentieth-century Shakespearean actors—Harley Granville Barker and Sibyl Thorndike" (Brown 141). The drunken actor haltingly recites Hamlet's well-known soliloquy, which intersects with the plot of the narrative about Holliday, the Earps, and the Clantons (see Simmon). When Ike Clanton interrupts him rudely, Doc Holliday (the very underrated Victor Mature) intervenes and even finishes part of the speech for him. Mary P. Nichols emphasizes the doubling of Doc Holliday in the person of the actor: "Thorndyke serves as a comic version of Doc—an easterner who knows Shakespeare but goes West and mingles with 'tavern louts'" (Nichols 79–80). Mature's Doc Holliday interpretation emphasizes the Eastern, educated aspect of the dentist (in this version, a surgeon, and from Boston, not Georgia as was the real man); as Simmon comments, "a *noir* Hamlet ... a doctor turned consumptive (a 'city disease' in the West), a doctor who fails when his skills are tested" (Simmon 119). Tag Gallagher links the Hamlet soliloquy directly to Wyatt Earp and his pursuit of "vengeance duty," observing that "duty ... as a myopic, negative quality, is an obsessive theme throughout Ford's oeuvre, while the major theme of *My Darling Clementine* is wrapped around musing over whether one can ever have the right or duty to kill, whether one should 'be or not be' (i.e., the staging of Shakespeare's *Hamlet* soliloquy)" (Gallagher, "Shoot-Out" 305). This Doc Holliday, suffused with *accidie*[5] and rejecting any opportunity for happiness or even peace because of his self-hatred, is a highly Romantic interpretation, strongly rendered by Mature.

Other Doc Holliday incarnations vary in their emphasis, but in all cases this civil professional character features elements of the real Holliday: his tuberculosis, his Eastern origins, his deadly temper, and his skill with firearms.[6] Holliday interpretations after Mature's range from the stolidly vengeful yet loyal Kirk Douglas (*Gunfight at the O.K. Corral*) to the humorously cynical, ruthless Jason Robards (*Hour of the Gun*), through the bizarre but fascinating caricature by Val Kilmer (*Tombstone*) to one of the better, more realistic portrayals of Holliday by Dennis Quaid in *Wyatt Earp*. Quaid's Holliday has a reasonably authentic Georgia accent, and the actor is about the right size and weight to play the real Doc; additionally, Quaid provides his role with a raspy, twangy delivery and a sarcastically weary demeanor which befit a man suffering from tuberculosis and active alcoholism. The script also provides for Holliday to explain

4. Encroachments of Culture

when first meeting Earp, in Fort Griffin, Texas, that he "was proud to be a dentist" but that now he is "a sporting man." He even admonishes Earp to "take good care" of his teeth as "they cannot be replaced" (Kasdan, *Wyatt Earp* Ch. 26). Kirk Douglas's florid Holliday also refers specifically to his former profession. In fact, as the script has it, the Douglas Holliday first met Earp not in Fort Griffin but some years before, when he extracted a tooth for him. Here Holliday explains that he gave up dentistry because his patients did not like his coughing—actually a pretty accurate biographical statement.

Other theatrical interventions in the Tombstone story on film include an appearance by entertainer Eddie Foy[7] (played by Eddie Foy, Jr., in *Frontier Marshal* [Allan Dwan, 1939])[8] and a visit by an aspiring Shakespearean actor, Mr. Fabian (played by Billy Zane, in *Tombstone*) which ends in fatal disaster. As Richard Burt observes, Fabian recites part of the St. Crispin's Day speech from *Henry V* (Burt 34n26). Perhaps tellingly, in his brief appearance at the Bird Cage Theatre he does not include the "band of brothers" part of that speech. As with neobaroque suppression devices, which emphasize a term by its replacement (see Acosta Cruz 200), or with the device of *omissio* more generally, the lack of this reference may lead the viewer to consider that the brothers Earp will not be a unified band once the Tombstone tale is told. The seeds for discord are already planted in the extended Earp family as Wyatt and Mattie watch another skit by the troupe, "Faust: Or, the Devil's Bargain," in which the Devil is played by Josie. When she removes her mask and bows to the audience, clearly flirting with Wyatt from the stage, he is clearly transfixed, to Mattie's obvious chagrin. The Faust reference is comically underlined with reference to Wyatt as he exclaims, "I'll be damned," and the sardonic Holliday quips, "You may indeed. If you get lucky."

Eventually, as happened historically, Wyatt and Josie are married. The fate of the fictional actor Mr. Fabian is not so positive. One of the Cowboys (the gang which includes, at least in this film, members of the Clanton family, Johnny Ringo, and Curly Bill Brocious) kills him when he tries to keep them from stealing Josie's watch. Unlike the mournful Thorndyke, who is humiliated but not physically harmed and who leaves Tombstone on the stage, Fabian is ridiculed and ultimately murdered.

A comical take on the mythmaking motif (so familiar to Tombstone tales) is the story "Mark and Bill" by Loren D. Estleman. The story, set in Chicago at the time of the World's Fair, imagines a face-off between Mark

Twain and Buffalo Bill Cody, mediated (and spurred on) by fellow mythic figure and mythmaker Theodore Roosevelt. The "duel" is to be fought with the preferred weapon of each participant: a Winchester for Cody, humor for Twain. Roosevelt serves as a mediator, advisor, and facilitator, as befits his statesman's qualifications. As each shot for Cody becomes more difficult, so too Twain is faced with increasingly difficult marks for his humor. Finally Twain prevails by making Cody's jealous wife laugh and thereby helps to patch up the strained marriage. So the entire little story actually qualifies as a comedy along Northrop Frye's lines, in which "green world" comedies end in a wedding or in the reaffirmation of love between characters (Frye 163–64, 182–83).

An important contemporary to Mark Twain, Eastern-born Stephen Crane (1871–1900) wrote several stories about the West, but his treatment of the Western myth and its mythmakers differed from Twain's genial mockery. One influential critic of Crane's work counters the common notion "that Crane wrote about the West only to laugh at it" by arguing "that his essential attitude toward 'The Passing of the West' was not parodic, not satiric—but serious, sympathetic, and even tragic" (Deamer 111–12). While Jules Zanger, writing about "The Bride Comes to Yellow Sky," does not deny the "parodic" nature of Crane's treatment (Crane, "The Bride Comes to Yellow Sky"), he does contend that Crane was not merely satirizing the form of the dime-novel, with its well-known exaggerations and falsifications, but instead was criticizing the "countermyth" for the West proposed by Eastern intellectuals like Theodore Roosevelt and Owen Wister (Zanger 157–58). Zanger states, "I believe that 'Bride,' beyond its parodic deflating of a minor popular juvenile form [the dime-novel], was a response to what was in 1898 a much broader and more significant issue: the transformation of an American myth of the West, not by reality, but by an alternative myth empowering and justifying the extension of an eastern, bourgeois hegemony of values," identified with figures like Theodore Roosevelt (Zanger 157–58) (see also Will).

Jamie Robertson observes that in stories like "Blue Hotel" (Crane, "The Blue Hotel") Crane presents the stereotypical Western "ideal of rugged individualism" only to show that its time has passed. As Robertson notes too, "The most perceptive character is the Easterner, an outsider who ... has not bought the myth" (Robertson, J. 255). The immigrant Swede who tries despite his trepidation to live the myth, provoking a fight with Irish barkeep Scully's volatile son Johnnie, later dies at the hands of

4. Encroachments of Culture

a slick gambler who seems like a parody of Doc Holliday—cultured and ruthless but seemingly assimilated or accepted into his community. Robertson concludes that "the Swede is convinced that he is fulfilling the possibilities of manhood in the real West, and the stock scene in the saloon where he meets his death [at the gambler's hands] is a parody of a scene from a dime novel" (Robertson, J. 255–56). As Diana C. Reep observes, "The saloon as killing ground exemplifies the frontier clash between the Eastern values of restraint, consensus, and negotiation and the Western values of independence and spontaneous action" (Reep 210). Kolb observes that in Crane's story, [Our] best tale of this West, a West created by the perceiver," the Swede "finally creates a Nebraska in which his murder is not only possible but inevitable," and this despite the fact that civilization has already reached the little town of Fort Romper (Kolb 125).

A contrasting vision of the Easterner-tenderfoot trope is offered by *The Big Country* (William Wyler, 1958), a large-palette film which includes an important schoolteacher character (Julie Maragon [Jean Simmons]). The plot plays on the Wister palimpsest, with Molly the Eastern schoolmarm in *The Virginian* becoming Jim McKay (Gregory Peck), an Eastern sailor and scion of a shipbuilding family, and his eventual love-interest, Julie, an actual Eastern schoolmarm who has already acclimated to the West, becoming the heir to a ranch which is the center of conflict between two bitterly opposed families. Their eventual union will resolve the divide presented by David W. Noble with respect to the work of Owen Wister,

> ... for the American middle-class reader, the West, or America, was not to be pure nature, pure barbarism, pure savagery. It was to be a civilization married to nature; ... a civilization able to transcend its own rules when it was necessary to fight for survival. And so into the symbolic West comes Molly Stark Wood, eastern bred and refined ... [Noble 155].

The Virginian character from the Wister work becomes here Steve Leech (Charlton Heston), the foreman of the Terrill ranch and a man who eventually finds common ground with McKay. The complex narrative can be read as a Cold War allegory, with the Big Muddy (Julie's ranch) as the Berlin fought over by NATO and Soviets; but it also fits uncannily well into the Western genre argued by Thomas Deegan to descend from the novels of Sir Walter Scott.[9] The two warring families fit neatly into Scott's dichotomies between Highlanders and Lowlanders, between wilderness (or barbarism) and civilization, as presented by Deegan (572–73). The Hannasseys (Rufus [Burl Ives], patriarch) are uncouth, rough, and semiliterate, and they live high up in a canyon, an elevated wilderness setting, while the Terrills (Major Henry [Charles Bickford], patriarch) live down below, run the town, and have pretensions of high culture. The contrast is deceptive, though, as Rufus is anything but illiterate and uncultured and protests to respect "true gentlemen" like Julie's late father; he also lives by a strict moral code (perhaps an unusual one, but consistent nonetheless) and is not a "hypocrite," as he calls Major Terrill, to whom he also refers to as a "high-toned skunk." Despite Rufus's roughness and potential for violence, he is one of the more attractive characters in the film because of his forthrightness and quickness to right perceived excesses, as in his intervention against his son Buck (Chuck Connors) when he tries to rape Julie.[10]

In any case, the film uses as a plot element the contrast between the supposed competence of the Westerner as opposed to the presumed ineptness of the Easterner. Douglas Pye mentions this film as exhibiting "both possibilities" of the Easterner type—ineptness and toughness due to adaptation to the West in his discussion cited earlier (Pye, "Genre and History" 120). In fact Easterner McKay is highly competent, as he demonstrates by using a compass to "navigate" the nearly featureless wilderness, a metaphorical sea surrounding town and ranch. When a rancher asks him knowingly if he's ever seen such "big country," McKay responds, "Yes, I have," to the bemusement of his friendly interlocutor. McKay simply does not share certain preconceptions about proving manhood and courage which entrap men like Terrill, and so he soon proves himself to perceptive watchers like the ranch hand Ramón (played by the superb Alfonso Bedoya)[11] (significantly, a Mexican and thus not a member of the "white aristocracy"), who tells Julie and the spoiled Scarlett O'Hara–Jezebel type Patricia Terrill (Carroll Baker) that "such a man is rare." Sinyard's evaluation of McKay is useful here: "Jim McKay is a most unusual Western hero, a dude from back East who never looks like a cowboy at any stage and who, in his resolute refusal to conform to the expectations of his new community, dares to be exasperating rather than exciting" (Sinyard 168–69). Unusually this film displays two civil professionals—a shipbuilder (as we assume), McKay, and a teacher, Julie—who attract each other like magnets in a society filled with people very unlike them. Sinyard observes that "the victors at the end of the film are an intriguingly diverse trio to be carrying the message of a western: a pacifist Easterner (McKay), an educated schoolteacher (Julie), and a peaceful Mexican (Ramon)" (Sinyard 179).

5

Professionals as Civilization Meets Barbarism

A central motif of many Westerns is the contrast, sometimes overstated or oversimplified, between civilization and barbarism.[1] Often this is treated in terms of soldiers versus Indians, townspeople versus ranchers, and so forth. An unusual subset of the motif is the opposition between mainstream Christian establishments and Mormonism. Much of this opposition in the 19th century focused on polygamy: "The most persistent criticism made of Mormon polygamy was that its threat to monogamy placed civilization in peril" (Handley 11) (see also Heinze, R. 63–64); and this concern was expressed in terms of "'barbarism'" (Hardy 40) (qtd. Handley 11). As several studies including Handley's demonstrate, Zane Grey presented the Mormon-Protestant dichotomy in more than one novel, most notably in *Riders of the Purple Sage*, adapted to film most recently in 1995 (previously in 1941 and 1925). The 1995 adaptation stars Ed Harris as Lassiter and Amy Madigan as Jane Withersteen. The narrative contains an important professional character, the leader of the local Mormon community, Pastor Dyer (G.D. Spradlin). Dyer is an intolerant and obsessed cleric who clearly has secrets to protect. The hawkish Spradlin (1920–2011), well known to devotees of Francis Ford Coppola films (*Godfather Part II*, *Apocalypse Now*) as an edgy character actor, brings a combined menace and sniveling cowardice to the role.

The first Dyer scene in the film is set in the church during one of his sermons. In an apostrophe directed at Jane, Dyer upbraids her for not having married and essentially calls her an apostate. Dyer appears overly accusatory and histrionic in this scene, and the viewer may well suspect that he has some hidden motivation or conflict. Only gradually is this clarified, as his role in the mistreatment of Millie Erne is revealed. At first he is suspected of forced polygamy by taking her away from her husband, a telling suspicion regarding his religion. The narrative progresses from total irony (in the sense of no revelation to the viewer, as would be the case with dramatic irony[2]) through gradual, small revelations about the Millie story. Lassiter has come to Jane's ranch in search of answers about Millie, but he will not tell her why, and Jane will not tell him anything about Millie. Eventually the truth is revealed, by Jane principally, that Millie and her daughter were stolen by the pastor for Jane's father, now deceased: the Millie Erne story is shown to be a family secret, part of a dark past, obscured or repressed as in *noir* films like *Pursued* or *Marnie*. (In these two *noir* epitomes the repressed but domineering characters [like Dyer] are played by Dean Jagger [*Pursued*] and by Louise Latham [*Marnie*].) Dyer also tries to facilitate, through cajolery and threats, the marriage of Tull and Jane. Clearly his function in the community has devolved to that of procurer, or pimp, for predatory males. Perhaps of significance as well is the fact that this complex narrative contains no other professionals—no doctors, no lawyers, not even a bartender—so that the focus is kept squarely on the contrast between one kind of professional, the corrupt pastor, and another, the wandering gunman, both men likely self-taught. Dyer could be considered an example of a "Yankee Indian," a term coined by James Fenimore Cooper to describe whites who have become "fallen pilgrims without mission" (Williams, D. 101). Williams summarizes the type:

> At best, the Yankee Indian is loyal only to clan interests, and neutral to all else. At worst, the Yankee Indian actively preys on all those not of the clan. He represents a cultural primitiveness beneath both Indian and white societies [Williams, D. 101].

The depraved Dyer might well be thought of as a predatory figure, the worst-case sketched by Williams. Between these two poles are the semi-professionalized "riders" who tend the cattle and carry out less innocuous tasks, like hunting down deviants from community orthodoxy.

The sinister and cloistered atmosphere of this range fable is not dissimilar to a later tale, a memorable episode ("Return of the Archons") from the original *Star Trek* series in which a rigid groupthink orthodoxy is enforced by faceless, cloaked Lawgivers armed with sonic disruptors. All this is set in a Luddite community that follows the will of Landru, a sonorously voiced prophet or oracle whose lined features bespeak wisdom. Through the efforts of Kirk, Spock, and company, the figure is revealed

5. Professionals as Civilization Meets Barbarism

to be a computer projection of the founder of the colony, with his Solonic pronouncements now corrupted by relentless binary logic. In the case of *Riders of the Purple Sage* the violent avengers led by Tull echo the Danites, a band of vigilantes of enduring mythic but temporary historical valence (see Cornwall and Arrington 147–49). A contrasting reading is offered by Cathryn Halverson, who maintains that while the larger Mormon community of the novel indeed tries to enforce conformity, and Lassiter and his companions do resist this, the outcome is not a victory for "individuality over community" but rather a successful attempt "to form a tiny new community from five erstwhile isolates: Venters the 'black fox' outcast, Lassiter the lone gunman, Jane the rebel Mormon daughter, Bess the mysterious Masked Rider, and Fay the orphan Gentile" (Halverson 56).

Similar to Dyer as a failed or hypocritical pastor, but in quite a different context, is the Rev. Daniel McCain of the short story "Anonymous" by Randy Lee Eickhoff. This preacher figure, married to a rather prudish woman named Judith, encounters the witness-narrator,[3] Sam Wheeler, in a stagecoach that will stop in Dodge City, where Wheeler runs the newspaper. As in Ford's *Stagecoach* and in other Westerns using this device, the stagecoach (or train) journey allows a multifaceted group of characters representing roles typical to the genre to be introduced within a confined space in which their personalities can be brought into relief.[4] In this case the conflict arises (as it does in part in the Ford film) from the presence of a prostitute, Flo, in the coach, where her eroticism reveals a hidden feature of Daniel's nature. The coach becomes for him a frontier lion's den, which will lead to his demise. The Reverend is coded as a figure of hidden conflict even before Flo gets on the stage: "Quiet fires seemed to burn in the depths of his black eyes set in deep sockets" (Eickhoff 161). Soon his obsession with Flo becomes clear enough (Eickhoff 166). This will lead to his eventual downfall: he hangs himself after an apparently carnal encounter with Flo in the boarding house where the passengers stay on arrival. This "son of Cain" dies, like his "father," an outcast, eventually buried in a nameless grave ("anonymous") and disowned by his disgusted widow.

A conflicted pastor is played memorably by Donald Sutherland in the recent *Forsaken* (Jon Cassar, 2015), a rather self-consciously "traditional" Western albeit with some interesting twists on the formula. Kiefer Sutherland inhabits a very traditional role—the gunfighter who wants to hang up his guns. His backstory, however, is somewhat unusual, and he only volunteers it late in the film, after refusing to talk to his estranged pastor father about the circumstances of his violent career.[5] During much of the film, the aged but still energetically forceful preacher alternately berates his son John Henry Clayton (the repetition of the three parts of the name recalls gunfighter figure John Wesley Hardin, perhaps) for his long absence of several years after the Civil War had ended and tries to tease out of him the reasons for his spiral into gun violence. Sickened by his accidental killing of a young boy during a gunfight, John has returned to his father's farm in an attempt to escape the deadly round of killings.

For a time John Henry and his father reach an uneasy stalemate, with his father trying to convince him of spiritual imperatives and John denying any divinity at all. In scenes echoing *Shane*, John doggedly works at clearing a field, anchored by a large tree stump. The narrative revises its model, though, as the father refuses to work with the son at the field-clearing, which had been urged by the deceased mother. (In *Shane*, Joe Starrett and Shane work together to tear out a recalcitrant stump, with Marian and Joey watching admiringly.[6]) Here, one almost might think that little Joey has moved away, become a Shane-like figure, and returned to his old homestead to square off with his widower father. John Henry is clearly a traumatized war veteran, with his violent acts stemming primarily from his war experiences. A similar case could be made for Shane, at least allegorically, as he is displayed early in the film reacting violently to Joey's (unloaded) rifle being cocked and to a random noise in the farmhouse. His gunfighting career has left him traumatized, causing him to react to aural stimuli in a fashion similar to sufferers from "shell-shock." And, in fact, Dennis Cutchins makes this very point regarding the viewer response to the film on its release (and to the novel on which it was based): "Ex-soldiers trying to resume their old lives in the late 1940s and early 1950s had a unique perspective on Schaffer's [sic] 1949 novel and Stevens's film about a gunfighter who longs to live a normal life" (Cutchins 182).[7]

John Clayton tries mightily to adopt another path, even attempting to follow his father's way of Christian resignation in the face of evil. In this film the evil is represented by James McCurdy (Brian Cox), a typical out-of-control land-grabber familiar to viewers of Westerns. Again, though, the film deviates from the expected, as we learn that McCurdy and the Reverend Clayton are former friends, and the Reverend tries to intercede with him in favor of a farm family headed by Tom Watson (Greg Ellis), a love rival of John Henry's. After some of McCurdy's men attack

5. Professionals as Civilization Meets Barbarism

and nearly kill the Reverend Clayton (against McCurdy's wishes), John Henry Clayton once again takes up his guns and goes after them, despite the remonstrances of his father. The well-mounted and nicely played gunfight scene in the saloon leads to a street showdown scene between John and the hired gun for McCurdy, the Southerner Gentleman Dave Turner (Michael Wincott). Again, though, expectations are wittily diverted, as John first tries to convince Turner that they do not need to fight and can remain friends, of a sort. (Besides their profession, or way of life, they have a common link, as both fought at Shiloh, though on opposite sides of the battle line.) When Turner responds that he is not employed to "walk away," as John had suggested, John then asks permission to retrieve a Colt from the saloon because the LeMat gun in his holster is too unwieldy. Produced in limited quantities for the Confederacy, the LeMat revolver, named for its inventor, New Orleans doctor Jean Alexandre François LeMat, was an innovative pistol which was used by some Confederate officers, notably Generals Beauregard and Stuart (Sanders 69). Stuart W. Sanders observes: "Known widely as the 'grapeshot revolver,' the LeMat was an intricate percussion handgun featuring a pistol barrel astride a short shotgun barrel" (Sanders 66). In the film, Clayton obtains the gun from the local storeowner, who comments on its interesting qualities.

When John re-enters the saloon, he is fired upon by McCurdy, whom he kills with dispatch. John goes back out to the street and calmly reminds Turner that he is no longer employed. So the fight ends quietly. Both pastor and gunfighter are discussed in the voice-over epilogue, which owes something to Eastwood's *Unforgiven*.

A much more positive version of the preacher or pastor character in Westerns is to be found in *Heaven with a Gun* and *The Persuader*. In each film, Glenn Ford and William Talman, respectively, play pastors who have reformed from their gunslinging past and who endeavor to resolve intractable problems in a peaceful manner. A similar type of character or story outline, treated unusually, appears in the cult TV series *Kung Fu* (1972–75), in which the late David Carradine played a Shaolin monk who tries to hide out in the post–Civil War American West after being sought for murder in his native China.[8] As in many Westerns, the hero in this series, named Kwai-Chang Caine, tries to "hang up his guns"—in this case, his martial arts skills—and simply to fit into the new environment to which he has come. But events force him repeatedly to intervene in disputes or to escape from pursuit by the authorities, both American and Chinese.

Professionals in Western Film and Fiction

The Caine character, an odd type of civil professional (a Chinese priest trained in physical combat techniques), is an amalgam of the gunfighter-turned-farmer of *Shane*, the gunfighter challenged by pretenders to his title (*The Gunfighter*), and the more unusual gunfighter-turned-preacher of *Heaven with a Gun* and similar films. As a mixture of these types, and because of the countercultural thrust of the series—like the cult hit *Billy Jack* (Tom Laughlin, 1971), it was an example of the anti–Vietnam-War themed entertainment meant to appeal to young adult viewers—Caine represents an intriguing attempt to update the Western for a new audience. Paul Green comments:

> David Carradine's performance as Chinese-American Shaolin monk Kwai Chang Caine was in stark contrast to the prevalent Hollywood Western hero of the time. Carradine's unconventional lifestyle added to the mystique of the character who preached peace and love but wasn't averse to defending himself in spectacular fashion when required [Green 127].

The pilot for the series (dir. Jerry Thorpe) highlighted the Chinese past of Caine, a man of mixed ancestry (Chinese mother, American father)—a motif tying the character to Western outsiders of mixed ancestry like Nevada Smith—and focused as well on the plight of the Chinese workers on the railroads. Caine becomes their defender but is betrayed by one of their number (played by typecast James Hong), motivated by greed and perhaps by fear of reprisals against the community that tries to harbor him. The pilot film draws a clear line between the "civilized" railroad owner Dillon [Barry Sullivan] and his men and the "barbarian" Chinese—of course, these tags are deceptive, as the Chinese, especially Caine, conduct themselves in a much more civilized manner than most of the Westerners. (The sole Caucasian who tries to act ethically, the mining engineer McKay [Wayne Maunder], is killed on orders from Dillon.) Tracked down by a bounty hunter dispatched from China (played by David Chow, the martial arts choreographer for the episode), Caine must fight to the death. Of course he prevails, but true to Western, and serial, form, he wanders off to new adventures, believing that he cannot stay with the workers' community. A version of the Wandering Jew character type, Caine moves from place to place during the series, becoming involved despite his intentions in local disputes and forming relationships of varying importance and length.[9] In a rather unusual way, Caine reverses "The Man Who Knows Indians" motif, as he is literally a man of two worlds—half-Chinese, half-Anglo, and also peaceful but warlike, with his

5. Professionals as Civilization Meets Barbarism

Shaolin training—by defending Chinese against white "invasion" or violation.[10]

One of these relationships is formed with a complexly deceptive preacher, Serenity Jones (John Carradine, father of David), whose mute assistant Sunny Jim is played by Robert Carradine (brother of David).[11] In the episode "Dark Angel" (dir. Jerry Thorpe), Serenity comes into contact with Caine after the death of a drifter who had made a gold strike on Apache land. Serenity expresses to Caine his desire to build a church, although in fact he has mixed motives, wanting to see the "bright lights" of New York before—or instead of—building the church. Caine gives him the map to the gold strike, and Serenity is captured by the Apaches and blinded. His blindness leads to his spiritual regeneration with Caine's help, and finally he and his derelict charges build the church. So he becomes not a mountebank but a true civil professional, an enlightened pastor to the town. Or perhaps Serenity was not fully enlightened, at least for very long. His second and final appearance is near the end of the series' run, in "Ambush" (dir. Gordon Hessler), where he plays an ambiguous game, enlisting Caine to escort him to meet an old flame who, he discovers, has a silver-smuggling scheme (Hessler). Serenity is willing to help her, ostensibly to keep his church going. At the end of the episode, his status is somewhat uncertain.

Caine functions here as elsewhere as a kind of spiritual physician, healing dysfunction in towns and other communities. So in "The Stone" (dir. Robert Butler) he helps an estranged, or at least separated, couple to reunite. One of them is an Armenian immigrant, Zolly (Gregory Sierra), working as a pianist in the town saloon.

Caine often finds allies in professional characters who have been marginalized—so, in "The Ancient Warrior" (dir. Robert Butler), he is assisted by Judge Marcus (Will Geer), whose tolerant juridical views are not shared by the fascistic sheriff Aldon Poole and his willing allies. (Caine also serves as a bridge or buffer between whites and Indians, in this episode and others.) In "The Third Man" (dir. Charles S. Dubin), he is assisted by the town undertaker, who had until recently acted in an underhanded and corrupt manner, in recovering the gambling winnings of the dead husband of Mrs. Gallagher (Sheree North). In "Blood Brother" (dir. Jerry Thorpe), an episode reminiscent of *Bad Day at Black Rock* (John Sturges, 1954), in which John J. Macreedy (Spencer Tracy) searches for Japanese-American farmer Komoko, Caine tries to learn the fate of his Shaolin Temple friend, and warm rival, Lin Wu (Yuen Kam), who had settled in a small Western town. He soon suspects that Lin Wu may have been murdered by a group of bigoted young men led by a jealous Greg Dundee (Robert Urich), who has been courting a young woman, Livvie (Kathleen Lloyd). Livvie had been treated for headaches by Wu, using techniques learned at the Shaolin Temple. Despite an attempted coverup by Greg's father Benjamin (John Anderson), the men are indicted for murder, and Caine discovers from information offered at the inquest by the decent and diligent sheriff (Clu Gulager) that Wu had treated many people in the community and had become a respected member of the town, a professional physician with Chinese training.

"Blood of the Dragon," a two-part episode from the third and final year of the series (dir. Richard Lang), features a doctor character who plays a sometimes ambiguous role in the story of an old love affair and its consequences for the present of Caine and his extended family (his grandfather has died under suspicious circumstances). Dr. George Baxter (Eddie Albert) is a typical Western doctor figure—kindly, elderly, and methodical in his care of the community. In this instance, though, he shares a destructive secret with the town's most important inhabitant, Mrs. Sara Kingsley (Patricia Neal). As he sometimes did in his long career, Albert plays a character who seems cowardly or, at best, indecisive. This is highly ironic given Albert's own heroism during World War II. As the entry on Albert in the *Scribner Encyclopedia of American Lives* explains,

> In 1942 Albert joined the U.S. Navy and was assigned to the USS *Sheridan*. He drove a landing craft vehicle in the first invasion wave at the Battle of Tarawa in 1943 [a particularly savage battle, dubbed The Battle of Bloody Beach], rescuing seventy marines who were wounded or stranded on the beachhead, a feat for which he was awarded the Bronze Star [Byrne 6].

Perhaps Albert understood cowardice as only the brave can.

Baxter was once in love with Sara and knows the truth about the parents of her two wards, who in fact are her grandchildren from a brief liaison with Caine's grandfather. Baxter is reluctant to oppose Sara's ruthless plan to eliminate Caine to protect her secret (besides being merciless she is a racist and also incestuous). When he discovers the wanted poster for Caine, he does not actively turn him in, instead allowing Margit (Season Hubley) to see the poster and to betray him from fear for her brother Johnny (played by Edward Albert, son of Eddie Albert). The doctor's office is a convenient venue for other characters to meet and for secrets to be

5. Professionals as Civilization Meets Barbarism

revealed. Eventually, the doctor's basic decency wins out, as he warns Caine about staying in town and provides moral support for Margit after her brother is killed trying to defend Caine.

In "The Vanishing Image" (dir. Barry Crane), another episode from the third season, Caine allies himself with another marginalized professional, played by veteran character actor Lew Ayres. He is photographer J.D. Beaumont, who wanders the countryside trying to capture as many images as possible of the desert landscape and its inhabitants as he can before time runs out for him. Beaumont is partner in a photography shop with a man named Hobbs, who stays in town taking care of the business and taking pictures of townspeople, while Beaumont pursues his quixotic quest. Caine has sought out Beaumont after Hobbs gave him a picture of his brother Danny and some men, but Caine has never met Danny and would like Beaumont to identify him. The path of the two men intersects with an Indian named Matoska who tries to steal food and is stopped by Caine, becoming friends with Caine and Beaumont. Nevertheless the Indian is frightened of the camera, afraid it will steal his spirit. He discovers that Beaumont had taken a photograph of him without his knowledge, and so a conflict is established which will only be resolved later in the episode.

Caine discovers as well that Beaumont is dying from the mercury vapors used in processing his pictures; the scenes with Beaumont are intercut with flashbacks to an old man (Benson Fong) who used to collect pottery shards and bric-a-brac from the Shaolin Temple to build a shrine. Like Beaumont, he has dedicated his life to a project that others may not understand. Beaumont's project, like Edward Abbey's in the 20th century, is to record as much as possible of the Western landscape. His self-appointed mission takes him from his work as a town-based professional to an itinerant life in the wilderness. In this unusual instance, the town professional is bifurcated into two characters: one, Hobbs, the traditional town-dweller who serves and profits from townspeople, drifters (like Caine), and traveling salesmen and others; the other, Beaumont, a professional who himself becomes essentially a drifter, like Caine, experiencing as much as possible of the landscape and life outside the town. Significantly, both professionals are shown to be duplicitous or manipulative, if harmlessly so, as they take pictures either unbeknown to their subjects, like Beaumont, or leverage their subjects into sitting for photographs, like Hobbs.

Professionals in Western Film and Fiction

Photographers are rather infrequent characters in Westerns, although photographs sometimes play an important role, as in films about Jesse James, with photos of the dead raiders at Northfield. Before the photograph became the preferred technology, the painter, like George Catlin (see Masters), was the recorder of life in the West, and particularly of the culture of the earlier inhabitants, the Indians or Native Americans. Such artists rarely appear in Western fiction, being supplanted by the photographer, the journalist, or the new hybrid, the photojournalist.

Occasionally the photographer actually appears in a Western film, as in *Wyatt Earp* and *Tombstone*, where the C.S. Fly of Fly's Photography, part of the site of the famous gunfight, is shown taking photographs of Josie Marcus, Wyatt's lover and future wife, at the time of the gunfight an actress only a step up from a lowly showgirl. Similarly, a photographer appears briefly in *Geronimo* (Walter Hill, 1998) to record images of the Apaches.

In the recent *Hostiles* (Scott Cooper, 2017), Jeremiah Wilks (Bill Camp), a journalist from *Harpers' Weekly*, engages in a touchy discussion with Captain Joseph Blocker (Christian Bale) (Cooper, S. Ch. 2) about the justice of imprisoning Apaches and members of other tribes, even those who have been captured in hostilities. One of these is the Cheyenne chief Yellow Hawk (Wes Studi), for whom Blocker has a fierce hatred. Blocker angrily (but coldly) lectures Wilks about the fearsome atrocities committed by Yellow Hawk and his men before his long prison sentence (seven years to date). Blocker is ordered by Colonel Abraham Biggs (Stephen Lang), commander of the (fictional) Fort Berringer in New Mexico, to escort the dying Yellow Hawk and his family to their ancestral land in Montana. The film is set in 1892 during the presidency of Republican Benjamin Harrison, at the very end of the Indian Wars, and Blocker is due to retire soon after a long, hard, and violent career. The journey by Yellow Hawk and his little band replicates in microcosm the tragically epic journey (1878–79) of the Cheyennes to their eventual reservation in Wyoming (see Greene). Supporters of tribes like the Cheyennes have been working towards a more humane arrangement for them. As James R. Allison III shows, this backing from whites was not without a paternalistic or even patronizing dimension, or even a self-serving one: "To the Northern Cheyenne's white supporters, the 1884 reservation was a crucial step in the project to settle this 'most fierce and warlike tribe,' circumscribing the Cheyenne in a tightly controlled spatial logic that segregated the tribe

5. Professionals as Civilization Meets Barbarism

from the wild and chaotic frontier conditions so they could be managed to meet white expectations" (Allison 93).[12] At the presidential level, administrations of the period grappled with the interests of various groups in trying to find ethical solutions:

> In [Grover] Cleveland's two [Democratic] administrations [1885–89, 1893–97], and to a lesser extent in the intervening [Republican] one of Benjamin Harrison [1889–93], the executive office ... tried to act as the conscience of a nation, identifying the immorality of landed monopolies, inaugurating modern conservation policy, and seeking, in vain, a viable path for the integration of American tribes into American society [Heinze, A.R. 81].

Without explicitly stating the East-West divide in the sensibilities of the two antagonists, the film shows an arrogant, sarcastic, and intellectually condescending Wilks (in a gemlike performance by Bill Camp) being confronted by the experienced, battle-wearied Westerner who scolds him for making light of his assertions. The disagreement is provoked by Wilks's taunting query of Blocker, "Now that I'm in your esteemed company, Captain, I must ask, is it true you took more scalps than Sitting Bull himself?" (Cooper, S. Ch. 2). The firmly authoritative Colonel Biggs is not inclined to debate the matter, and he orders Blocker to arrange to escort the Cheyennes and then, when Blocker objects to the order, explains to him that he should think about his pension, which a court martial would surely threaten. So Blocker reluctantly accedes. Before departing, the troopers are photographed with their charges by Wilks (Cooper, S. Ch. 3).[13]

Nevertheless a photographer is rarely even a character in Westerns with more than a cameo appearance. *The Missing* (Ron Howard, 2003) is an exception. Based on the novel by Thomas Eidson, the narrative, in novel and film, provides "a mix of the captivity narrative, the gothic mode, and feminist writing" (Bischoff and Noçon 117). The film's plot follows the attempt of Maggie (Cate Blanchett) to recover her daughter Lily (Evan Rachel Wood) from the Apaches and white slavers who have kidnapped her. A recasting of the storyline of Cooper's *Last of the Mohicans*, which also features a kidnapping and an attempted rescue, the film presents, as Bischoff and Noçon observe, a Natty Bumppo–like hero, Samuel Jones (Tommy Lee Jones), who is needed to effect the rescue (Bischoff, et al. 119).

Lily is not the only captive of the renegades, however. Among the coterie of kidnapped whites is the ill-fated traveling photographer Russell J. Wittick (Ray McKinnon). He continues to ply his trade as a captive, apparently hoping to placate his captors by photographing them, perhaps also stalling for time. He is shown photographing a group of Apaches and their captives. Later he attempts to show the Brujo's photograph to him. The Brujo ["Sorcerer"] (Eric Schweig), who has been suspicious of the spirit-stealing photographs all along, reacts violently, poisoning him with a powder blown in his face and telling him, "Take your bad luck to your grave." The photographer is soon shown developing plates, and he begins bleeding from the eyes, dying soon afterward. The Brujo had attacked his sight, metonymically destroying the "vision" in his camera.

This episode in the narrative is perhaps loosely based on the real experiences of C.S. Fly, who photographed "enemy" Apaches in the field, much more successfully and safely than the unfortunate Wittick. These were the Chiricahuas, including Geronimo, during General Crook's campaign in 1886. One of Crook's officers commented skeptically on Fly's audacity:

> Captain John G. Bourke ... described how Fly, with such "'nerve' that would have reflected undying glory on a Chicago drummer [salesman], cooly asked 'Geronimo' and the warriors with him to change positions, and turn their heads or faces, to improve the negative." Bourke also said Fly "was a d————d fool for going into the camp and that he'd never come out" [Van Orden 323].

Not long after these events, Jones, Maggie, and Dot (her younger daughter), who are tracking the Apaches, discover the dead body and wrecked camera of the photographer. Jones retrieves the photo showing captors and captives, which becomes a recent proof of life of Lily, because she is shown in the photo.

The accomplished short-story writer Frank Bonham focuses in his tale "The Green Moustache" not on a photographer but on a man with related skills, a pictorial artist. This man, named Finn Stephens, is arrested for horse-stealing after the stolen animal plays out on him. The local sheriff, a man named Hannaford, is a bit of a dreamer who embellishes his prisoners' biographies in his own mind but who is also a competent lawman. He is also somewhat narcissistic, with a yellow moustache imitating Custer's and a tendency to "pose in front of a mirror with his hand tucked in his coat" in the familiar Napoleonic style of the era (Bonham 214–15).

While rummaging through the prisoner's bag, Hannaford finds a set of painting accessories. The next day, after some sulphur fumes from mining blow into town, the sheriff discovers his prisoner choking and

5. Professionals as Civilization Meets Barbarism

complaining of asthma, so he calls in the local doctor, Doc Jenkins, who prepares a "cure" using some crystals of saltpeter, some of which he leaves with the prisoner in case of another attack. In better spirits, the prisoner admires the angle of Hannaford's jaw and, despite being sentenced to hang, sketches a charcoal portrait of him. The sheriff is susceptible to such flattery, as the narrator has already intimated. When the prisoner asks for materials for pigments to make a full portrait, the sheriff obliges; tellingly, the image "was not the man Hangtown knew, but the one who now and then posed before a mirror" (Bonham 217). The impressionable sheriff is convinced that the prisoner is "a sincere and intelligent man" and regrets that he is to hang (Bonham 218). Early in the morning, Hannaford wakes to an explosion and discovers that the prisoner has blown a hole in his jail cell, escaping with the sheriff's horse. He had used the charcoal, sulphur (for yellow pigmentation for the moustache in the portrait), and saltpeter to make a black powder charge. In a picaresque touch, the artist had tinted the moustache in the sheriff's portrait green (Bonham 218).

Barbarism and civilization are also examined, though in a different fashion, in the short story "War Shirt" by Dorothy M. Johnson. A captivity narrative told from an outsider's perspective, the tale concerns the efforts of Francis Mason to bring back his lost brother from Indian captivity. He has heard of a medicine man called Medicine Mark, a man with an unusual facial marking like the one his brother had. He wants to find out whether or not his brother, if he is in fact this man, has "gone native" to the extent that he will not wish to return to white society with him. He enlists the aid of a hard-bitten scout, Bije Wilcox, and they locate the medicine man. But the outcome of the encounter is enigmatic, as Mason leaves without explicit identification of his brother and with ambiguous observations about his "civilized" status relative to Medicine Mark's "barbarism," a tag which does not fit his conduct in following the precepts of "the golden rule" (Johnson, D.M. 125–26).

A captivity narrative not revolving around Indians but featuring a prominent professional character, in this case an aspiring journalist, is *The Last Manhunt*, a novel appearing in the "Ralph Compton" series and authored by Joseph A. West. The journalist, a young Easterner named Lester A. Booker, comes out West on a mission familiar to readers and viewers of Westerns: he is in search of a story about a legendary lawman, in this case Ransom (Rance) March.[14] March's legend is dime-novel material,[15] with all the clichés about the noble fast draw who saves virginal damsels and soiled doves from death and from fates worse than death. In reality, as the crestfallen Booker (whom for some reason many characters in the novel, as if secretly conferring, persist in calling Archibald in a mocking tone) soon discovers, March is rather disreputable, with a reputation close to that of a backshooter, a hard drinker who is physically not very striking. As a type of *Bildungsroman*, the novel shows the dual process of the hardening of Booker into the ways of the real West, with its toughness and unforgiving landscape and people, and of Booker's growing realization that if March is not the idealized, silly dime-novel hero of Booker's favorite fictions, he is most certainly heroic in a rougher sense. Like J.B. Books of *The Shootist*, March has no illusions about gunfights—they are brutal affairs—and he will not be bullied or stand by to watch defenseless people harmed. Books (whose name is indicative of his fictive nature) is quite hard-nosed about the reasons for his actions; he says clearly that he only tried to defend his interests: "'I won't be wronged, I won't be insulted, and I won't be laid a hand on. I don't do these things to other people, and I require the same from them'" (see Hall, K., "*Gringo Viejo*" 139). His reputation for shooting first, and even backshooting, is accurate enough, but Booker gradually understands that March did such things out of necessity, not preference.

The captivity aspect of the novel, which highlights its focus on barbarism and civilization—not only the West versus the East, but more importantly the fissures within the West itself—results from the serial kidnappings and killings of people across the area where March lives. Mary P. Nichols cautions against drawing neat dichotomies between East and West, arguing rather that East and West are more properly located within characters: "It is not that East and West are two 'value systems' that a self-contained man can for a moment internalize, but that in East and West Ford [in *My Darling Clementine*] has externalized the tensions within human beings [like Wyatt Earp and Doc Holliday] that form more or less precarious balances at all moments of life" (Nichols 83).

The culprit in *The Last Manhunt* is a bizarre character nicknamed The Gravedigger, who buries his captives alive, claiming that he will resurrect them later. A former undertaker who was once hanged and buried but did not die, he believes himself to be immortal and shows "vampiric" tendencies. He is also preternaturally strong. March goes in pursuit of The Gravedigger and his gang, whom he has recruited with the promise

5. Professionals as Civilization Meets Barbarism

of gold of which he claims to know the location, because some friends of March's were killed in the criminal's characteristic manner. Booker insists on accompanying him. Their peripeteia includes captures by and escapes from The Gravedigger and his men. Booker finally becomes somewhat of an epigone of March, learning to be tough and ruthless. He eventually dispatches The Gravedigger by burying him alive as he had done to so many captives, and March kills most of the gang, dying in the process. As Booker's musings, reflected through the narrator at the end of the novel,[16] summarize: "City fathers didn't hire saints as town marshals. They wanted killers who knew how to get the drop on a man" (West, J.A. 269). More optimistic about the character of a man like March than is Eastwood's *Unforgiven*, which features a similar encounter between Eastern journalist and Western gunman, *The Last Manhunt* rather easily forgives March's tough-minded ruthlessness and even shades into glorifying him as a hero in a way less ambiguous than does *Unforgiven*. Although the journalist in *Unforgiven*, Beauchamp "is fascinated with murderous violence and its structuring codes in a manner disguised as scholarly," this fascination is implicitly investigated by the film's complex narrative voice, which seems to set up a parallel, as William Beard suggests, between Beauchamp and the viewer. Beard sees Beauchamp's preoccupation with violence as nearly obsessive rather than purely "scholarly," "suggesting rather a passionate inner compulsion," like the viewer watching Munny (Eastwood) on a "homicidal rampage" at the end of the film (Beard 59–60).

March may be an unlikely hero, perhaps even unattractive as an antihero, but he is still close enough to the Western hero type that he is quite far from the antiheroic protagonist of some contemporary films. As David L. McNaron observes,

> No Western antihero would ever do what Edward Fox's consummate professional assassin does in *Day of the Jackal* (1973), that is, kill the woman he slept with [a French countess, played by Delphine Seyrig] simply to eliminate someone who can identify him. Though not amoral, the western hero was never a do-gooder altruist. He doesn't draw first, but he finds his completion in the act of violence ... [McNaron 152].

The superlative thriller mentioned above was directed by Austrian emigré Fred Zinnemann of *High Noon* fame. Despite its typically generic qualities, though, *The Last Manhunt* does examine, as does *The Missing*, the "savagery" hidden within the Western experience. Both Westerns exemplify the scenario sketched by John G. Cawelti: "The Western story is set at a certain moment in the development of American civilization, namely at that point when savagery and lawlessness are in decline before the advancing wave of law and order, but are still strong enough to pose a local and momentarily significant challenge" (Cawelti, "Savagery, Civilization and the Western Hero" 57).

6

Professionals Across the Border
Mexican Revolution Fiction and "Professional Westerns"

Some varieties of Latin-American fiction bear similarities to Western novels and stories. In part this is because both American Westerns and Latin-American regionalist novels concern themselves with the questions of civilization, barbarism, and the frontier. In addition, the generic forms of many regionalist novels and other 19th century Latin-American prose texts are parallel, or roughly so, to the traditional types of narrative used in Westerns as popular fictions. Beginning with hybrid forms like *Facundo: civilización y barbarie* (Domingo Faustino Sarmiento, 1845),[1] and continuing through several early fictions of the Mexican Revolution, such narratives are populated, like Westerns, with recognizable character types: bandits, lawmen, civil professionals, ranchers, and of course rebels and revolutionaries.[2] Selected fiction and film about the Mexican Revolution will also be discussed. Important as well to fictions about Mexico and its revolutionary past are Westerns belonging to the "cycle" identified by Noël Carroll in "The Professional Western: South of the Border." These include, according to Carroll, *Vera Cruz, The Magnificent Seven, The Professionals*, and *The Wild Bunch*. The list might well be expanded to include films like *Red Sun* (Terence Young, 1971).

Richard C. Robertson observes that "the professional plot line emerged in the 1960s during the Vietnam era and parallels the military platoon specialties of the United States Army" (Robertson, R.C. 174) (for the "cycles" concept, see Grindon). Thomas Schatz sees the professional Western as a response to "the psychological Western," of which *High Noon*

Professionals in Western Film and Fiction

was an example. In the professional Western, the psychological approach is sidestepped, and "the Westerner either works for pay and sells his special talents to the community that must evaluate his work on its own terms or else he becomes an outlaw.... Consequently, many recent Westerns incorporate a group that is led by an aging but still charismatic hero figure and whose demand of payment, either as professional killers or as outlaws, undercuts the classic Westerner's moral code" (Schatz, "The Western" 442; see also Schatz 32).

A rather different formulation of the "south of the border" Western is offered by Gary Hoppenstand, who does not emphasize the professionals angle but instead situates some examples of Western or, in his terminology, "frontier" films and fictions geographically, with articulation points at the Canadian and the Mexican borders:

> Indeed, conducting a close review of the genre, it soon becomes obvious that the frontier adventure story is comprised of "Northerns" and "Southerns," in addition to Westerns. A useful example of a Southern movie is director Andrew V. McLaglen's *The Undefeated* (1969) [Hoppenstand 123].

Hoppenstand observes that:

> [I]n both real history and the fictionalized cinema founded in that history, Confederate soldiers journeyed South instead of West to seek spiritual regeneration, denying Frederick Jackson Turner's fundamental mythology of the West as an "escape valve" for those seeking a better life previously denied in the East [Hoppenstand 124].

The professionals referenced here are not the civil professionals which appear in many Westerns. Nor are these men the familiar professionals of law enforcement in Western towns. Instead they are Western counterparts of the mercenaries of today, often in Western contexts, former soldiers or lawmen. As professionals, these fighters usually work for money, although one of the contrastive elements sometimes introduced into the storylines is the ironic decision of some of these characters to work despite the lack of monetary reward, as in *The Magnificent Seven*, or their decision to work in such a fashion so as to deny themselves a reward, as in *The Professionals*.[3] In some cases an added dimension is the variance between members of the professional group (apart from the usual disagreements about tactics), as in *Vera Cruz*, with its ambiguous moral contrast between the two leading professionals Ben (Gary Cooper) and Joe (Burt Lancaster) (see Williams, T., "Some").

In the case of *Vera Cruz* both professionals are driven by ambition

6. Professionals Across the Border

and desire for monetary reward; as Williams observes, "Joe and Ben are ... mirror images of each other in terms of being motivated by economic gain throughout most of the film" (Williams, T., "Some" 35). Set in Mexico the year after the end of our Civil War but during the remaining years of the French Intervention in Mexico, when French Emperor Louis Napoleon installed Archduke Maximilian as emperor there, the film seems at first glance to concern subject matter later treated (and romanticized) in *The Undefeated* (Andrew McLaglen, 1969).[4] That film presented in a highly fictionalized fashion the expedition by some Confederate civilians and former soldiers (notably the Iron Brigade, led by Gen. Jo Shelby of Missouri, accompanied by Major John N. Edwards, mythologizer of Jesse James) to join up with Maximilian and eventually to set up a state or colony of their own instead of surrendering to the Union (see Rister and Casellas).[5] The expedition did not find success, particularly after the United States exerted influence pursuant to the Monroe Doctrine (Lavery 5–6). *Vera Cruz* treats this episode only tangentially and modifies its historical content, placing former Confederate Ben in an uneasy alliance with Joe and his men, who include among their number an African-American and a former Union soldier. Instead of a rehashing of historical fact and legend, the film may allegorize the exodus of Hollywood Blacklisters to Mexico during the 1950s (Williams, T., "Some" 35–36). In line also with the 1950s revision of the Western by directors like Anthony Mann and Budd Boetticher, this film features a "hero" (Ben) who is only marginally "better" than the "villain" (Joe).

Tony Williams (Williams, T., "Some" 35) discusses Cooper's concerns about playing a nearly villainous role and director Aldrich's relative success in shading the character. Richard Slotkin emphasizes the "professional" in Ben Trane and observes that in the final gunfight with Joe Erin "Trane does not win because he is a *morally* better man, but because he is a faster man with a gun" (Slotkin, *Gunfighter Nation* 438) (original emphasis). Both men, of course, are highly proficient in the use of weaponry and in other military areas, and the men in Joe's gang certainly qualify as a mercenary band of specialists, or, from their perspective, a group of professionals trained in techniques later to be termed "counterinsurgency" tactics. The term as applied to this film is Richard Slotkin's; he discusses the film in the context of the involvement of the United States—following France—in Indochina and types the film as an example of "the counterinsurgency scenario" (Slotkin, *Gunfighter Nation* 435–40) (cited in Carroll 62*n*1).

Professionals in Western Film and Fiction

The 1960 Western *The Magnificent Seven* (John Sturges), a reworking of Kurosawa's great masterpiece *Seven Samurai* (*Shichinin no samurai*, 1954), is less skeptical of the benefits for Mexico of American involvement, and its group of professionals foreshadows the increasing use of special forces by the Kennedy Administration in Vietnam.[6] Richard Slotkin cautions however that this presentation is not "prophetic" but rather that "movie and policy address similar ideological concerns and use the same mythological language..." (Slotkin, *Gunfighter Nation* 485–86). He also observes that "the premise for *The Magnificent Seven* begins with the classic trope of American myth/ideology: the translation of class differences into racial difference, and the projection of an internal social conflict into a war beyond the borders" (Slotkin, *Gunfighter Nation* 475). Comparisons with the source material, Kurosawa's legendary epic, are inevitable, and Slotkin offers interesting plot differences between the two (see esp. 481–82), but the most obvious difference between the two films, that in the original, no racial or ethnic distinctions exist between samurai and villagers, obscures the class distinction stressed repeatedly in the Japanese film.[7]

In Japan, samurai and commoners were sharply distinguished, as the samurai belonged to an aristocratic upper class. Like most, if not all, aristocracies, the samurai had humbler origins: "Despite their aristocratic pretensions, the samurai began essentially as a class of men at arms who sold their swords to various local landholders in exchange for a payment of rice" (Von Mueller 56). Tada hints at less mercenary motives for the samurais' defense of the peasantry, calling them "the pioneers of Japan" whose motive in opposing "the old central authority in Kyoto ... was clearly to protect the immigrant rice farmers in the Kanto area from the unfair policies of the central government" (Tada 49). Desser observes that "in the chaotic pre–Tokugawa era of civil war and banditry" (the period fictionalized in the Kurosawa film) not only do "unemployed Samurai (*ronin*) roam the land" but that

> related to the interiorized moral systems of a chaotic period is the idea of crossing class boundaries. Distinctions between Samurai and peasant, held up as fairly absolute in theory, become, in practice, no longer so clear [Desser, *Samurai Films* 140].

Until the end of the Tokugawa Bakufu or "shogunate" (1615–1868), samurai had certain legal rights not given to commoners, among them the right to wear two swords (see Galloway 14) and even to execute commoners who did not show them proper respect. The rights exercised by samurai

6. Professionals Across the Border

began to be abrogated beginning especially in 1871, after the Meiji Restoration of 1868: "Samurai lost the right of *kirisute-gomen* [切り捨て御免], that is, of using their swords on the lower orders with impunity.... After this, it was not unduly surprising that in March 1876 ... a law was issued banning the wearing of swords entirely" (Beasley 112). Paul Varley comments that, during the pre–Meiji period,

> [the samurai] alone ... enjoyed the privilege of wearing swords ... and had the theoretical (although presumably seldom exercised) right to cut down any member of another class who chanced to offend or displease them [Varley 121].

The Tokugawa law did state that "common people who behave unbecomingly to the samurai or who do not show respect to their superiors may be cut down on the spot" (Benedict 64). (See also Hurst 520, 522.) The 17th century *Code of the Samurai* [*Bushido Shoshinshu*], "written for novice knights" by Taira Shigesuke (1639–1730) (Cleary xvi), prescribes honest and humane treatment of those not in one's social class: "...even if you are of low rank [as a samurai], as a warrior you should not abuse or mistreat the other three classes" (Cleary 46).

The samurai of Kurosawa's film are more precisely ronin,[8] masterless men displaced usually by war and (often) the concomitant destruction of their clan, but they still perceive a distinction in class between themselves and the farmers. As Emmett Early observes in the chapter on Kurosawa in his book *The Alienated War Veteran in Film and Literature*,

> ... Akira Kurosawa captured in his films about the Japanese samurai a character who has worked as a professional warrior and who, when the battles are over, is "discharged" from military service and left to survive on his own. The war veteran in Japan in the period following the end of World War II, when Kurosawa made these films, was forced to adjust to the reality of defeat [Early 13].

Tada Michitaro makes the interesting observation that "like bureaucracies anywhere, the Japanese *han* ["clans"] had no qualms about firing unnecessary or unwanted employees, and in the Japanese case these men became the leaderless samurai, the *ronin*" (Tada 56). So the displacement of the ronin was not always attributable to war as films would often imply.

Much of the tension between villagers and ronin in *Seven Samurai* centers on this class distinction, with the additional element of the association in the villagers' consciousness between the ronin and the destruction of war. One example of the effect on the Sturges film of eliminating this class distinction concerns the question of weapons. The villagers begin their quest for assistance, as the village elder suggests, by asking Chris (Yul Brynner) about buying weapons. He suggests hiring men, and of course this results in the recruitment of the Seven. Later in the village, when the gunmen are training the farmers to shoot, one of the farmers says he wishes they "had more guns," to which Bernardo replies, "You'll get more guns," and Chris explains to the puzzled villager, "Same way you got these. Calvera's men" (Sturges, *The Magnificent Seven* Ch. 8). This contrasts sharply and tellingly with Kurosawa's film. When Kikuchiyo (Toshirô Mifune), the farmer's son who wants to be a samurai, appears during the training period clothed in armor and bearing weapons, Kambei (Shimura Takashi), Chris's counterpart in this film, asks him sternly where he got the armor. A villager had given it to him, and Kambei and the ronin are shown a cache of weapons. They react with disgust and sadness, remarking that the villagers took the weapons from dead samurai, thus implicitly dishonoring the dead and transgressing a social taboo as well as reminding the samurai of their own possible fate. Aeon G. Skoble notes the incident but emphasizes a different, legalistic feature when discussing the fact "that the villagers ... have a supply of weapons, which they had taken from murdered ronin...." He speculates that "they may ... have internalized the law stating that only a samurai could go armed." He also states that "they literally have no idea how to use these weapons," which may well be true but misses the point in the film about the existence of the cache as shocking to the moral and class sensibilities of the samurai (Skoble 147n9).

Like the Kurosawa film, *The Magnificent Seven* avoids direct historical reference and no involvement by the larger government is contemplated to resolve the problems of the villagers. In the Sturges film, the villagers sound rather like the Wyoming homesteaders in *Shane*, one of whom (the dispirited Ernie Wright [Leonard Strong]) complains, "That's the trouble with this country. There ain't a marshal within a hundred-mile ride." *The Magnificent Seven* does allude indirectly to a historical context, as Chris mentions that he just came from Dodge (City) and Vin (Steve McQueen) says he has just left Tombstone, and in neither place is there employment now for men such as they. (Of course these men are not displaced in quite the same sense as are the ronin of the Kurosawa film, former vassals or retainers in a feudal system.) These references seem almost more tied to movie history than to real history, or at least so they would be perceived by audiences accustomed to tales of the Earps and Bat Masterson.

6. Professionals Across the Border

Allusions by the gunmen to Western towns in fact foreshadow their departure from the small town where they have little opportunity of employment.

The town in which the opening scenes of the film are set affords Chris and Vin an encounter with two civil professionals, a drummer (traveling salesman) who wants to pay for the burial of a man who died suddenly in front of him on the street, and the frustrated town undertaker (the ubiquitous Whit Bissell) who explains patiently that the man was an Indian, and the locals don't want Indians in their cemetery. This presentation of civil professionals may be an example of "the growing secularization of society" which Gary Day, referring to British society in the late 19th century, discusses in his article "The State of *Dracula*" (Day 84). Although parallels between British and American Western society of the time should not be pushed too far, it is noteworthy that the men concerned with burying the dead Indian in Sturges's film are the town undertaker and a traveling salesman, two civil professionals of sorts, and not the local pastor or priest, who is not even mentioned.

The drummer, clearly a Northerner by his accent and somewhat bemused at the odd atmosphere of this outlying town, protests volubly. Chris and Vin volunteer to take the hearse up to the cemetery, and their prowess and unflappable demeanor in the adventure impress not only the townspeople but also the villagers who have come to town seeking relief from the bandits.[9] As earlier noted, ethnicity or race is a prominent concern in this film, unlike its model, and as Slotkin has pointed out, the cemetery incident may allude to the "battles" over "the integration of Southern military graveyards" (Slotkin, *Gunfighter Nation* 475). Such political or ideological content is obscured in the Kurosawa film, although one may read it subtextually as critical of the militaristic ideology which produced the Japan of World War II.

Both *Vera Cruz*, set in 1866, and *The Magnificent Seven*, set roughly in the 1880s, precede in their timelines by several decades the Mexican Revolution of 1910. *The Professionals* is set in the midst of the Revolution,[10] although its exact date is indeterminate (but probably around 1917) and some of the references are fictionalized. In this film, as Slotkin notes, these professionals fit more precisely with the Special Forces model of the Vietnam War era; each member of the group possesses a particular skill-set and the group even qualifies as a version of the "ethnic platoon" (for this concept, see Slotkin, "Unit Pride").

Professionals in Western Film and Fiction

The "ethnic platoon" is also notable in two *Magnificent Seven* films, *Guns of the Magnificent Seven* (Paul Wendkos, 1969), whose group of Seven includes a Mexican (Reni Santoni) and an African-American (Bernie Casey)—the latter contrasted with another of the Seven, Slater (Joe Don Baker), a Confederate veteran; and the recent reboot *The Magnificent Seven* (Antoine Fuqua, 2016), whose contingent includes a Comanche (Martin Sensmeier) and a Mexican (Manuel Garcia-Rulfo) and is led by an African-American (Denzel Washington). The recent film, about which more later, also features a cross-section of sorts of society, with a woman (Haley Bennett) participating actively in the fighting and a mountain man–trapper type (Vincent D'Onofrio) working as one of the Seven. In her article on Primo Levi, Mirna Cicioni states more generally that "in 'professional plot' Westerns, the narrative tensions and oppositions are due to the different skills, ethnic identities, life histories, and personal conflicts that each member of the group brings to the job." With respect to the 1960 *The Magnificent Seven*, she notes that "the seven gunfighters are variations on generic stock characters" (Cicioni 159).

In *The Professionals*, Rico Fardan (Lee Marvin) is a small-arms expert; Dolworth (Burt Lancaster) is intimate with explosives; Jake (Woody Strode) is a skilled tracker and bow-and-arrow man; and Ehrengard (Robert Ryan) is a gifted horse wrangler. Also notable is the association of corporate villainy with railroads, a feature missing or understated in stories about Mexico and Western characters like Loomis's "Tough Hombre." Slotkin observes perceptively that:

> Grant's appealing invocation of the conventions of the captivity myth has masked other signs which Rico and Dahlberg [actually named Dolworth] ... and the audience ... ought to have recognized. In outlaw/gunfighter movies, and in Mexican Revolution movies, it is almost always the case that "good guys" ride horses and "bad guys" ride trains.... Moreover, ever since *Jesse James* [1940] it has been a given of such films that railroad barons [like Grant] are by nature and inclination tyrants who prosper by stealing land from small farmers or peasants [Slotkin, *Gunfighter Nation* 571–72].

Thus, Mr. Joe W. Grant (Ralph Bellamy) is coded as villainous from the beginning of the film, when he presents himself duplicitously as an aggrieved, innocent husband whose wife has been kidnapped by a ruthless Mexican revolutionary with a heavily symbolic name (or perhaps a *nom de guerre* like Pancho Villa), Jesus Raza (Jack Palance).

Civil professionals have limited importance in Brooks's film, the

6. Professionals Across the Border

exception being Ortega (Joe De Santis), Raza's urbane, bilingual aide, a man who appears to have a level of education and a demeanor commensurate perhaps with a lawyer.[11] Raza is a composite figure, although probably intended to represent a Villista, with the customary attribution to Villa's band of casual ruthlessness (his order to execute their prisoners, a detachment of *Colorados* [a Federal band who, as Dolworth explains to a shocked Ehrengard, have committed terrible atrocities, including the horrific murder of Fardan's wife, a survivor of an attack on her village]) (Brooks, R. Ch. 12).

The professional gunmen in *The Wild Bunch*, the widely studied, and debated, film by Sam Peckinpah, are like mirror-images of a band of Villistas, as they raid the small border town of Starbuck for a railroad payroll robbery but are ambushed (rather like the James gang in Northfield, Minnesota) and are chased into Mexico by a band of bounty hunters, echoing the fruitless Pershing expedition in pursuit of Pancho Villa after his retaliatory incursion into Columbus, New Mexico, in 1916 (see Katz, *The Life and Times of Pancho Villa* 560–80). Although the attentive viewer might note their military dress and their advanced weaponry (the Colt 1911 .45 carried by Pike [William Holden], for instance), the provenance of the arms is later made explicit by a German "adviser" in the camp of Mapache (Emilio Fernández), who observes that the "pistol" Pike wears is only issued to U.S. military personnel.

Although the vicious Mapache ("raccoon," thus a scavenger),[12] like the allegorically named Jesus Raza, is a composite figure, he works for the dissolute historical personage Victoriano Huerta, who had seized power in 1913 and had treacherously murdered elected President Francisco Madero and his vice-president Pino Suárez (after promising them safe conduct out of Mexico City) soon afterward. Bishop (Ernest Borgnine) contemptuously dismisses Mapache as "a killer for Huerta who calls himself a general." As Bredahl notes, "In *The Wild Bunch*, Harrigan of the railroad and Mapache of the Federales are the representatives of law and order, but they are vicious and corrupt" (Bredahl 294–95). The specific presence of Germans in Mapache's camp is a direct reference to the historical fact of German attempts to interfere in the Mexican conflict as World War I progressed in Europe. The German High Command likely reasoned that:

> the eventual entry of the United States into World War I, even in the spring of 1915, was a strong possibility. A friendly government in Mexico could give Ger-

many a base of operations in the Western Hemisphere and at the same time would keep the government of Woodrow Wilson occupied with matters closer to home [Meyer, M.C. 82].[13]

Very few civil professionals appear in *The Wild Bunch*, and those who do appear fill minor roles—banking officials and so on. An exception is the railroad magnate Harrigan (if we are to consider him a type of professional), whose characterization, in the superbly melodramatic hands of Albert Dekker, goes J.W. Grant one better (Neilson). Unlike Grant, Harrigan displays no smoothness or duplicity, ruthlessly and loudly threatening Deke Thornton (Robert Ryan, in one of his finest performances), a former member of the Bunch and reluctant head of the disreputable bounty hunters crew, with return to the dreaded Yuma Territorial Prison if he does not get rid of the Bunch within thirty days. Harrigan even kills one of the wounded Bunch members (played by Bo Hopkins). He also shows little regard for the innocent townspeople caught up in the crossfire. A grotesque organization man, Harrigan is the face of the railroad, sometimes presented as a haven for professionalism (as in *Whispering Smith* or *Night Passage*), or an opportunity for quick money gains by thieves (*Jesse James*), or as a positive factor in the opening of the West (*Kansas Pacific, Union Pacific*); but in this instance, the railroad is, as Allison Graham observes, a cold, soulless leviathan: "The railroad itself comes to represent the bureaucratic control of what was once a human frontier" (Graham, A. 67).

The consolidation of the frontier into corporatist hands centers the 2016 *The Magnificent Seven* (Antoine Fuqua). While civil professionals are not given explicit prominence in the script, certainly the vicious Bartholomew Bogue (Peter Sarsgaard), who tries to monopolize the entire town and its mine, is a professional entrepreneur who implements forcible takeovers. Bogue acts here in opposition to all civil authority, co-opting the town sheriff and trampling on the sanctuary aura of the church. The minister of that church, simply called the Preacher (Mark Ashworth) is marginalized by Bogue's ruthless display of force. Later, though, he takes an active hand in defending the town, even taking on the role of a warrior priest as he fights off some of Bogue's invading force. His burned-out church (destroyed on Bogue's orders at the beginning of the film) is the locus of some important events during the long invasion sequence, most notably the death of Bogue at the hands of Emma (Haley Bennett) as he almost shoots Chisholm (Denzel Washington) with a hidden revolver.

6. Professionals Across the Border

When the three survivors of the Seven ride out of town, the grateful pastor promises to give the four casualties among them a proper burial. Another civil professional in the town, the craven storekeeper, caves in to Bogue's demands and gives his henchmen free rein in his store and saloon—a significant contrast with the upstanding neutrality practiced by Grafton in *Shane*.

Although the latest iteration of *The Magnificent Seven* does not take place across the border with Mexico, numerous Westerns do involve southern border crossing. Often they connect with the Mexican Revolution of 1910, as do *The Professionals* and *The Wild Bunch*. The tumultuous Revolution, whose active military phase wound down by 1917, produced subgenres in the Mexican novel, short story, and drama. In some instances these works featured civil professionals, especially educated professionals like doctors and lawyers; and because of the nature of the violent conflict, often fought out in desert locations, for example in the northern states of Chihuahua and Sonora, these fictions share some features with the American Western, including iconography such as costumes, horses, trains, and of course guns.[14]

One of the most prominent writers of twentieth century Mexico was Mariano Azuela (1873–1952). Trained as a physician, he spent some time traveling with Revolutionary troops in the cadre of northern leader Pancho Villa in 1914.[15] Max Parra notes that "in October 1914, physician and novelist Mariano Azuela joined the troops of Villista general Julián Medina in Guadalajara with the rank of colonel." The "campaign notes" which became *Los de abajo* were serialized in an El Paso, Texas, newspaper beginning in October 1915 (Parra 23); see also Azuela, "*Cómo escribí* Los de abajo" 3, where Azuela states explicitly that he composed the novel "*en plena lucha*" [in the midst of battle]—often, though perhaps not in this case, an authorial pose to lend simultaneity to the events narrated or fictionalized (Azuela, "*Cómo escribí* Los de abajo" 3: 1268). Although Azuela had written novels and stories prior to this time, it was the Revolution of 1910–17 which fueled his greatest creativity, producing his one acknowledged masterpiece, *Los de abajo* (usually translated into English as "The Underdogs"),[16] a rigorously structured novel (Menton; Murad, "Foreshadowing") which follows the tragic course of a number of participants in the Revolution.

Jennifer Lei Jenkins advances a compelling argument for regarding this novel as a Western. In the process she contradicts the prevailing perspective of "scholars and critics on both sides of the Rio Bravo/Rio Grande [who] stubbornly deny the existence of a Mexican Western." Basing her argument in part on the work of Richard Slotkin, she asserts that "Azuela structured his 1915 novel ... as exactly the kind of cultural myth that Slotkin describes: one concerned with a people's sense of their history, their relationship to the land, and their nascent detachment from European influences—in short, a Western" (Jenkins 94). She points out that in the Azuela work "the morality" of "wilderness" versus "civilization" "is reversed" from the U.S. model or analogue, with wilderness made positive and civilization into a negative (Jenkins 96–97). Essentially, however, the building blocks of the two national myths are the same.

Although many of the characters in the novel are *campesinos* (peasants or country people) with little education, a few of the important participants in the narrative are highly educated, among them Luis Cervantes, a young man with medical training. To some extent this character, referred to disparagingly by some of the other characters as a *curro* (roughly, a "fop" or, in this context, a city-slicker),[17] may appear to be a surrogate for the author, who was an active physician.

Max Parra presents a compelling thesis that in fact Cervantes, whose "motive in urging Macías to join the Constitutionalist Army is simply greed," is not an authorial surrogate. Instead Azuela presents his ideas about revolution through the presence of two "incidental and passing figure[s]," Alberto Solís and Loco Valderrama (Parra 30–31). Arlyn Sánchez Silva states that "*Solís, a quien podemos identificar como el portavoz de Azuela, expresa tristemente su desilusión frente al proceso revolucionario*" ["Solís, whom we can identify as Azuela's mouthpiece, sadly expresses his disillusionment with the revolutionary process"] (Sánchez Silva 428). In this connection, note as well Azuela's own protestation about any identification with the Cervantes character:

> me ha sorprendido la similitud que se ha encontrado entre el tipo de Luis Cervantes y yo mismo.... En el [tipo] de Cervantes [he pretendido presentar] a uno de los especímenes más repugnantes de la fauna revolucionaria: el logrero de la revolución que sólo busca su medro personal y está listo a abandonar cualquier causa en cuanto la ve perdida.
>
> I have been surprised at the similarity that has been found between the Luis Cervantes type and me.... In the Cervantes [type] [I have attempted to present] one of the most repugnant specimens of revolutionary fauna: the opportunist of the revolution who only seeks his own prosperity and is ready to abandon any cause as soon as he sees it to be lost [Robe 216] [qtd. in Sández 81: 128].

6. Professionals Across the Border

Roberto Cantú comments regarding Luis Cervantes that "this fictitious character is not Azuela's double; on the contrary, he is a recurring type in Azuela's novels ... who appears under different names but with shared social-Darwinist [that is, essentially *positivista* in the Mexican context] ideologies and similar 'opportunist' proclivities (the object of contempt in Azuela's narrative)..." (Cantú xxiv). Porfirio Sánchez is especially dismissive of the Cervantes character, highlighting his opportunism (so unlike Azuela's perspective): "*Luis Cervantes es la figura más despreciable y baja de la novela, a pesar de ser uno de los que tiene más educación. Es, además, un cambia-chaquetas, lo suficientemente hipócrita para actuar como si de veras sintiera compasión por las miserias que sufre el pueblo*" [Luis Cervantes is the lowest and most despicable figure in the novel, despite being one of those who has the most education. He is, moreover, a turncoat, sufficiently hypocritical to act as if he truly felt compassion for the miseries that the people suffer] (Sánchez 186).

Luis Leal makes a convincing case for the influence of Azuela's profession on his novelistic practice (Leal, "Mariano"). Leal states that "... *podríamos decir que Azuela ve la realidad, en todos sus aspectos, con ojos de médico*" [we might say that Azuela sees reality, in all its aspects, with a doctor's eyes] (Leal, "Mariano" 303). Also according to Leal, the area in which Azuela's profession most influenced his fiction was "*la creación de los personajes*" [the creation of characters] (Leal, "Mariano" 301). In fact, Luis Cervantes contributes especially to the narrative, as Juan Pablo Dabove notes, as "a journalist" who tries to put Demetrio Macías (the hero of the novel) into an ill-fitting pigeonhole: "The ambition and manipulative style of Luis Cervantes (a journalist who joined Demetrio's gang as 'secretary') made Demetrio a *villista* [a follower of Pancho Villa], which he was not and never completely became" (Dabove 243–44).[18] James Seay Dean observes that "Luis Cervantes, the educated opportunist and sycophant attempts to impress Demetrio with puffed up reasons for joining the Revolution" (Dean 93). In the Western framework proposed for the novel by Jenkins, Luis Cervantes, "a foil to Demetrio,"[19] may undergo the "tests" befitting "the dude," but in the end he does not fit into the violence and the risk-taking of the Revolution and leaves for Texas (Jenkins 103).

According to Richard A. Hill, the term "dude" was originally related to clothing ("*duddes*, an eighth Century term for clothing") and was still associated with style when it became a popular term in North America:

"Virtually all scholarly sources agree that *dude* as in 'a well-dressed man,' made its debut in the last quarter of the 19th century, probably on the western frontier." Eventually, in its frontier sense of "greenhorn" the term "dude" was widely applied in Westerns (Hill, R.A. 321–23). James K. Folsom provides a good example of this aspect of the dude in a story by Owen Wister, "The Gift Horse," introducing his discussion with the statement: "The notion that the most contemptible, though admittedly not the most evil, member of Western society is the dupe rather than the villain is one ramification of the theme of the dude, who is by definition unknowing and easily preyed upon by the unscrupulous" (Folsom, *The American Western Novel* 120).

Luis Cervantes (whose surname recalls, certainly with more than a dose of irony, the great intellectual tradition of Spain, here perhaps set into counterpoint with the "underclass" in Mexico, and implicitly having degenerated to a state of irrelevance[20]) first appears in *Los de abajo* after a battle in which the *campesino* (peasant) protagonist, Demetrio Macías, has been wounded. His medical expertise prevails in treating the wound, revealing a fissure between his "high" culture and the "low" culture of Demetrio and his companions. David Laraway cautions however that the narrative does not necessarily elevate one above the other: "This is not to claim that Camila [one of Demetrio's companions] does not see the bacteria and the others do not see what Luis sees in Demetrio's wound simply because their powers of observation are not up to the task; rather, they have not been initiated into a world in which those entities are both meaningful and discernible in the requisite way" (Laraway 56–57). Azuela uses the Luis Cervantes character in this case to highlight the challenges of bridging the gap between cultures and eras within a single country during the course of revolutionary upheaval.

The contrast drawn by J. Patrick Duffey between the culture of "orality" as represented by characters like Demetrio and the culture of "literacy" as represented particularly by Luis Cervantes helps to illuminate the social and cultural gap within Mexican society at the time of the Revolution (Duffey). A letter from Luis, now relocated to El Paso, to Venancio the barber (a relatively literate member of Demetrio's band) opens the third and final part of the novel. Luis proposes that he and Venancio open a Mexican restaurant in El Paso. Despite Luis's medical education, his money-making schemes have been reduced to the unlikely possibility of becoming rich from such a risky enterprise. Whether consciously or not,

6. Professionals Across the Border

Azuela echoes Miguel de Cervantes, both in his inclusion of a barber friend for the literate Luis—paralleling the barber from Don Quijote's village—and in the strategy of including an ironic letter (an irony which escapes the letter's author) proposing schemes for getting rich or advancing in status, like the ghost-written exchanges between Sancho Panza and his wife, Teresa, in the Second Part of *Don Quijote*.

Duffey highlights the letter from Luis for its documentation of "the literate aspects of his character," essentially "objectivity" and "distance." In this connection, Duffey also mentions two other highly literate characters in the novel, the mad Valderrama, "a babbling poet who has lost his mind but not his taste for extravagant literary flourishes," and Alberto Solís, a revolutionary ideologue who dies at the end of the first part of the novel (Duffey 177).

Luis Leal connects the fictional Valderrama to Azuela's circle of friends: "*Tanto Valderrama como López Romero, y más tarde José María, en otro cuento de Azuela que lleva precisamente ese título, reflejan aspectos de la personalidad del licenciado José Becerra, íntimo amigo de Azuela*" [Both Valderrama and López Romero, and later José María, in another story by Azuela which bears that title precisely, reflect aspects of the personality of the lawyer José Becerra, an intimate friend of Azuela] (Leal, "*La Revolución Mexicana y el cuento*" 94). Leal cites an essay by Azuela, "*Los de abajo*," in which Azuela states that his friend "*el poeta laguense José Becerra* [the poet from Lagos, José Becerra]," was important to several of his fictions:

> *Por la amistad íntima que cultivé con él, por su vida aventurera y por sus maneras extravagantes, fue el hombre que más material humano me dio, no sólo para mis novelas de la revolución, sino para muchas anteriores y posteriores a ella.*
>
> Because of the intimate friendship that I cultivated with him, because of his adventuresome life and because of his extravagant manner, he was the man who gave me the greatest human material, not only for my novels of the Revolution, but also for many novels before and after it [Azuela, "*Los de abajo*" 3: 1084].

Azuela links Becerra to characters from his works *Los fracasados*, *Los caciques*, the story "José María," and specifically to Valderrama in *Los de abajo* (Azuela, "*Los de abajo*" 3: 1084). Jenkins observes that "Solís is as disillusioned by the rebels as Cervantes was by the Conservatives" and draws an interesting parallel to the standard narrative of Westerns, where "this [disillusioned] role typically falls to the Easterner, the gambler, or the disaffected gunfighter [as with Doc Holliday]," further noting that

"Azuela uses college men to articulate this disillusionment" (Jenkins 104). And Jenkins parallels Valderrama to the frontier madman (Jenkins 110).

An extreme amalgam of such intellectual revolutionaries who descend from idealism into selfishness or negativity can be found in the character Fernando in the film *Viva Zapata!* (Elia Kazan, 1952). Played with coldly sinister precision by the fine character actor Joseph Wiseman,[21] Fernando approaches Zapata's stronghold early in the film, at the beginning of Zapata's career, becoming a sort of Iago urging him forward in his fight against the dissolute and unprincipled Victoriano Huerta (Frank Silvera).[22] As the film progresses, Fernando attaches himself to the current winner in the Revolution, finally becoming an adviser to the eventual victor, Venustiano Carranza. Despite the portrayal of this unwholesome "intellectual" in the film, the cautionary words of Daniel Cosío Villegas about the role of intellectuals in the Mexican Revolution should be noted here: "...it is well to state that intellectuals allied to revolutionary leaders were not very numerous and that their influence was exceedingly limited" (Cosío Villegas 31). In his brief discussion of "the enigmatic Fernando [who] moves opportunistically from one side to another," Leo Braudy cites Kazan's 1952 letter to the *Saturday Review*, in which the director discusses the character (Braudy 39). In a more complete form than cited by Braudy, Kazan states that

> ... there is such a thing as a Communist mentality. We created a figure of this complexion in Fernando, whom the audience identify as "the man with the typewriter." He typifies the men who use the just grievances of the people for their own ends, who shift and twist their course, betray any friend or principle and promise to get power and keep it [Kazan 22].

For Kazan, as Jeremy G. Butler observes, Fernando mirrors Joseph Stalin, the extremely cynical and murderous tyrant who usurped the Russian Revolution from leaders like "the more progressive Trotsky." As "the only true villain" here, Butler suggests, "in Fernando we find cruelty, deceit and treachery in service to nothing more than hunger for power" (Butler, J.G. 244–45). Paul Vanderwood presents the evolution of Fernando in successive script treatments from "an insignificant character" to "a villain." The change occurred because "The studio felt that the public had to be assured beyond question that Zapata (liberal democrat) was right and that Fernando (opportunistic totalitarian) was wrong" (Vanderwood 194). Fernando begins idealistically, appearing to Zapata (Marlon Brando) and Eufemio (Anthony Quinn) with his typewriter, which he protests to the illiterate Eufemio, who is about to destroy it, fearing that Fernando might be armed, is a "sword of the mind," explaining that it is a "writing machine." He reads a high-sounding declaration to Zapata about Francisco Madero (the equally idealistic first revolutionary president, soon murdered on the orders of Victoriano Huerta) (Kazan, *Viva Zapata!* Ch. 5). By the end of the film, however, when Zapata renounces his political leadership position, he angrily tells Fernando: "You only destroy. That is your love." Zapata also remarks that "you will go to Obregón or Carranza"[23]; in other words, Fernando is a cynical opportunist. And in fact, when Zapata is ambushed on orders from Carranza, it is Fernando who spits out orders that his body be exhibited publicly to deflate his myth (Kazan, *Viva Zapata!* Ch. 26, 30).[24]

The cultural split between literacy and orality is illustrated in a different way in a rather recent novel by the late Mexican writer Carlos Fuentes (1928–2012), *Gringo viejo* (1985).[25] Based on the legendary (and debated) disappearance of journalist and fiction author Ambrose Bierce (1842–1914?) in Mexico in 1914,[26] the complex novel establishes not only a frontier between culture and history north of the Rio Grande (or Rio Bravo, for Mexicans) but also a division between literary and oral cultures, as personified by the literate Gringo (Bierce) and Harriet Winslow, a well-educated woman from the United States contracted by a rich Mexican *hacendado* family, the Mirandas, as governess for their children.

A central conflict in the narrative (in both novel and film) revolves around the written land grants issued during the colonial period, a theme also presented in Kazan's film.[27] General Tomás Arroyo, a Villa subcommander, finds the box of documents about which he had been told as a youth in the Miranda home (as an illegitimate son of the landowner), and he insists to the Gringo that despite his illiteracy he knows what they say about the indigenous title to the land (Fuentes 36–37). The documents become the *casus belli* between Arroyo and the Gringo, who perceives that they may be the catalyst he needs to force Arroyo to kill him, fulfilling his wish to die in Mexico.[28] The Gringo's own writings are interposed in the text, and Harriet (more clearly in the film based on the novel) learns the Gringo's identity, recognizing him as a famous author.[29] Harriet is a meta-character, based according to Fuentes himself, as Steven Boldy notes (Boldy 493), on an eponymous character from the Edith Wharton novel *False Dawn* (1924).

If the two characters, the Gringo and Harriet, may be considered civil professionals (author and governess), in a Mexican revolutionary setting, they are set off, or excluded, from the oral culture around them, rather as young lawyer Ransom Stoddard is fenced off from the semiliterate culture of Shinbone. This contrast is made even more explicit in the film, perhaps inevitably so, as the shadowy, slippery, undetermined figure of the Gringo is replaced by the very photogenic, cinematically appealing presence of Gregory Peck. Harriet, played by Jane Fonda, expresses in a scene of anagnorisis late in the film her surprise, or perhaps her relief, at the confirmation of her suspicions, at her discovery that the Gringo is indeed Ambrose Bierce. Copies of his books (brought with him to Mexico) in his room at the hacienda are her visual evidence and also are metonymic representations of the emphatic literacy of the Gringo and of Harriet, as opposed to the nearly unlettered society immediately surrounding them in Mexico. The film also adds an early scene in which the Gringo is shown at a book signing, an event that he subverts by denouncing his own career and by rudely dismissing the audience after throwing his books up in the air. Thus his presence as a writer is openly confirmed from the outset of the narrative, leaving the viewer in no doubt about the contrast between his lettered background and the unlettered milieu in which he lives, and dies, during the rest of the film.

Such cultural breaches as the orality/literacy divide often accompany or signal shifts in a country's perspective and may be reflected in popular media, as in the oddly similar point of contact between modern and traditional in *Once Upon a Time in China II* (1992, Tsui Hark), a martial arts film following the fictionalized exploits of the legendary Huang Fei-hong (Jet Li)[30] in the period of the Boxer Rebellion at the turn of the 20th century (for this rebellion, see Preston). In one episode of the film, Western-trained physician Sun Yat-sen (Zhang Tielin), leader of a failed revolt (and later of a successful one) asks for traditional healer Huang to aid him in helping patients: "Sun Yat-sen requests Huang's help when he runs out of anesthetic. Succeeding scenes show Sun's scalpels and Huang's needles jointly undergoing sterilization" (Williams, T., "Under" 14). Zixu Liu observes that, unlike the "Western doctor" who displays intolerance of Chinese medicine, "the two Chinese, Huang and Sun, are portrayed as being open minded, flexible, and willing to give credit to both Chinese and Western cultures" (Liu 542). The two cultures find, or attempt to find, an equilibrium against the backdrop of the Boxer Rebellion, the end of the imperial dynasty, and the coming of Sun's revolution. In the Mexican

6. Professionals Across the Border

instance, such balance seems lacking, at least in Azuela's novel, as Luis eventually yields to his "greed and opportunism" (Laraway 59). Unlike the idealized characterization of Sun Yat-sen presented in Tsui's film, the portrayal of the fictional Luis Cervantes shows the corrupting influence of ambition in times of turmoil.

A morally attractive professional character is the witness-protagonist of the political thriller *La sombra del caudillo* (1929) by Mexican journalist, political figure, and novelist Martín Luis Guzmán (1887–1976). As a participant in the Revolution and as a witness to some of the events narrated in the novel, Guzmán can be recognized in surrogate form as the politician Axkaná González (Castro Leal vii-xi) (Houck 147). Kessel Schwartz comments that "it may be argued that [Axkaná] González (his Mayan first name and Spanish second mark him as the heir of the best in two civilizations) presents the novelist's idea of his own role" (Schwartz 288).

The novel fictionalizes—in a thinly veiled fashion—the 1923 revolt led by Adolfo de la Huerta and the alleged coup attempt in 1927, supposedly led by presidential candidate General Francisco R. Serrano. The 1927 incident is summarized by Luis Leal, who notes that the scene depicted in the novel "*es una exacta pintura del hecho histórico ocurrido el tres de octubre de* 1927 ... *del fusilamiento de catorce prisioneros políticos ... en un lugar llamado Huitzilac. Entre los fusilados se encontraba ... el general Francisco R. Serrano, candidato a la presidencia de la República*" [is an exact portrait of the historical event which occurred on 3 October 1927 ... of the shooting of fourteen political prisoners ... in a place called Huitzilac. Among the executed was found ... General Francisco R. Serrano, candidate for the presidency of the Republic] (Leal, "*La Sombra*" 16).[31] Aguilar Camín and Meyer observe that "the spectacle was cathartic; Calles and Obregón [the president and the candidate to replace him], in executing Serrano and Gómez [an opposition candidate], eliminated not only two countrymen, comrades-in-arms since the beginning, but also their most faithful lieutenants, united by years of common risks, shared war, fidelity at all costs, and even family ties" (Aguilar Camín and Meyer 92). Although, as Leal notes, many of the characters can be identified or at least shown to parallel historical figures of the 1920s (see Leal, "*La Sombra*"), significantly the major character most parallel to the author is the only totally fictional one (Houck 147).

According to Lanin A. Gyurko, Guzmán produces a more universally applicable work by using the *roman à clef* device: "By writing a *roman à clef* instead of a historical novel, Guzmán produces a work which can apply not only to Mexico of other eras but also to the political situation, the struggle between tyranny and freedom, in other Latin American countries" (Gyurko, "Fuentes" 548). Luis Leal, in his article on the novel as a *roman à clef*, focuses on the difficulty in finding exact equivalents to the characters in the book (Leal, "*La Sombra*"). Serna Rodríguez observes however that Guzmán does tie the shadowy strongman of the book directly to then-president Álvaro Obregón, a former military leader turned politician:

> *El presidente Obregón no era precisamente un demócrata. Bien conocido es su fallido intento de reelección que, en vez de llevarlo a la silla presidencial, le deparó la muerte. Martín Luis Guzmán lo inmortalizaría como uno de los personajes de su célebre novela* La sombra del caudillo, *que echaron mano de prácticas autoritarias y violentas para hacerse del poder....*
>
> President Obregón was not precisely a democrat. Well known is his failed attempt at re-election that, instead of carrying him to the presidential chair, brought him death [by assassination]. Martín Luis Guzmán would immortalize him as one of the characters of his celebrated novel *La sombra del caudillo*, among those who seized on authoritarian and violent practices to acquire power... [Serna Rodríguez 137].

Axkaná, a "*diputado* [delegate or representative]," is presented as the "amigo inseparable" [inseparable friend] of Minister of War General Ignacio Aguirre. The narrator clearly separates the roles of the two men by highlighting their opposing communication styles: if Aguirre is ironic, perhaps even laconic, Axkaná is more effusive and discursive. So, *"Aguirre era el político militar; Axkaná, el político civil"*; or, loosely, the man of action versus the public intellectual (Guzmán 3). Gastón García Cantú characterizes Axkaná as the man who survives the horrific massacre of Aguirre and his supporters because Axkaná is the "*conciencia individual del drama que sustituye al coro trágico; símbolo que no puede morir por lo que representa para el entendimiento o la lamentación del país*" [individual conscience of the drama who stands in for the tragic chorus; a symbol who cannot die because of what he represents for the understanding or the lamentation of the country] (García Cantú 30). Mark I. Millington sees the contrast between Axkaná as intellectual and Aguirre as "man of action" as significant for the novel's message: "...keeping the strands—intellectual and revolutionary leadership—separate means that, while the denouement can echo historical events by depicting the assassination of the rebel leader, the intellect can be saved from the same fate ... the intellect is an absolute in *La sombra*" (Millington 42).

Axkaná is established in a dual mode as "*actor y espectador*" [actor

6. Professionals Across the Border

and spectator] of events; he apparently *"trataba de penetrar la esencia de ... emociones* [tried to penetrate the essence of emotions]" (Guzmán 33). As both witness and actor in events, his function is akin to the "observer-hero" (Buell) or "narrator as hero" (Thale) types, except that he does not narrate in first person but is himself observed by an omniscient narrator. As an intellectual and a civil professional within a narrative populated by military professionals and by political professionals who are anything but intellectuals, Axkaná attempts to search beneath the surface of events for a hidden meaning applicable to the period, *"la verdad nacional que pudiera esconderse debajo de todo aquello* [the national truth that might be hidden beneath all that]" (Guzmán 33).

During the decade or two following important events such as the Mexican Revolution, World War I, and the Russian Revolution, many nations (old and new) engaged in self-examination. In Latin America, this exercise produced works such as Samuel Ramos, *El perfil del hombre y la cultura en México* (1934; 1938) [*Profile of Man and Culture in Mexico*]; Jorge Mañach, *Indagación del choteo* (1928) [Cuba] [Investigation of *choteo* {wordplay}]; Ezequiel Martínez Estrada, *Radiografía de la pampa* (1933) [Argentina] [*X-Ray of the Pampa*]. This was the period in Mexico when the great murals were painted—famous muralists include Diego Rivera, José Clemente Orozco, and David Siqueiros—celebrating Mexican history and culture.[32] So Axkaná serves as a surrogate for the author not only as an observer of events, and as a public intellectual, but as a sort of embedded investigator, a mole within the secret network of Mexican political relations. Nevertheless, as Lanin A. Gyurko perceives, Axkaná fails in this enterprise, which Gyurko notes is probably impossible in the Mexico of that era. Gyurko sees Axkaná as the reflection of Aguirre or his *"alter ego"* and observes that "Axkaná, sensitive, altruistic, unwilling to participate in the corruption and graft and decadence that constantly swirl around him, is an indication that if circumstances were different, Aguirre would have the potential to become the politically enlightened and responsible leader that is the ideal of Guzmán." Unfortunately, Axkaná too finds himself "swept up in the atmosphere of moral turpitude" (Gyurko, "Fuentes" 559). Axkaná fails to change the prevailing gloomy ambience: "Instead, in Guzmán as in Azuela and later in Fuentes, it is the mere mask of idealism that is over and over again raised up" (Gyurko, "Twentieth-Century Fiction" 258).

In addition to Axkaná, a minor character in the novel represents civil professionalism, in the person of a young, enthusiastic journalist who accompanies Aguirre and his men as they escape to the putative safety of Toluca. Described as "casi un adolescente; por la ingenuidad del rostro, un niño" [almost an adolescent; from the ingenuousness of his countenance, a boy], the reporter for *El Gran Diario* requests of Aguirre that he be allowed to join the traveling group (Guzmán 210). After the supposed refuge in Toluca turns out to be a trap, the reporter dies along with Aguirre and his men. Like the reporter Mark Kellogg who accompanied Custer and his 7th Cavalry on their expedition to the Little Big Horn, the young reporter perishes because of his professional involvement.[33] Kellogg accompanied Custer "apparently because Custer's friend, Clement Lounsberry of the *Bismarck Tribune*, had illness in his family"; thus, "Mark Kellogg, surrogate for Custer's preferred journalist, became a shadowy part of that [Custer's] legend" (Saum 12).

The outcome of the massacre leaves Axkaná as the sole survivor, as a "symbol" for the country but, in simpler terms, as the only witness to the terrible event. Thus Guzmán uses the "lone survivor" trope familiar from Puritan captivity tales in North America and perpetuated in horror films like *The Texas Chainsaw Massacre* (Tobe Hooper, 1974) (see Williams, T., *Hearths* 186–87) and *Halloween* (John Carpenter, 1978). In such films, according to Carol J. Clover, the survivor is generally female: "The image of the distressed female most likely to linger in memory is the image of the one who did not die: the survivor, or Final Girl" (Clover 201–04) (see also Petridis 77). If we were to transpose the Puritan captivity tale, which concerned captivity usually of white women by Indians (see, for example, Fitzpatrick), into the Mexican post-revolutionary context of *La sombra del caudillo*, we might say that the highly civilized Axkaná is the Final Man who survives the captivity of his (relatively) civilized colleagues by the savage cohort led by Caudillo henchman Major Segura.[34]

A civilized professional, rather like Axkaná, who ventures into uncivilized or barbaric territory is lawyer Santos Luzardo, the protagonist of the famed regionalist novel *Doña Bárbara* (1929) by Venezuelan author and political figure Rómulo Gallegos (1884–1969). The heavily symbolic names given the two major characters point up the *"civilización y barbarie"* theme centering the novel.[35] Based thematically on the dictatorship of Juan Vicente Gómez (1857–1935) (Polanco Alcántara; Rourke), which lasted from 1908 until 1935 ("it is well known that Gallegos intended his Doña Bárbara character to represent the Venezuelan dictator Gómez"

6. Professionals Across the Border

[González 41]), the novel exhibits such features of allegory, besides its thematic links to a historical subtext, as the frequent renaming of figures from the author's acquaintance to constitute, as does *La sombra del caudillo*, a partial *roman à clef* (see, for example Englekirk 263–70; and for a fuller discussion of the allegorical nature of the novel Alonso Ch. 4). Its title character, a domineering and "primitive" ranch owner, bears comparison to figures from Westerns such as the similarly eroticized Jessica Drummond (Barbara Stanwyck) in Fuller's *Forty Guns* (1957), Altar Keane (Marlene Dietrich) from *Rancho Notorious* (Fritz Lang, 1952), or Vienna (Joan Crawford) from *Johnny Guitar* (Nicholas Ray, 1954) (for a recent and comprehensive discussion of the Doña Bárbara image, see Swier).

Although Gallegos was inspired in his creation of the Doña Bárbara character by the life of an extraordinary woman named Francisca Vázquez, known locally as Doña Pancha, as John E. Englekirk observed in 1948, "Gallegos himself will admit that he is no longer certain just how much of the story of Doña Bárbara is the story of Doña Pancha as he gathered it from the '*imaginación de la ciudad*' [imagination of the city]" (Englekirk 268–70). The tumultuous relationship between Santos and Doña Bárbara focuses the civilization versus barbarism theme, a motif also seen in novels of the Mexican Revolution, although perhaps not in such stark terms as in the Gallegos work.

"Civilized" values (or poses) are of little use in the often barbarous ambience of the early period of the Mexican Revolution, and for that matter of its immediate aftermath. Like the cultured, civilized Axkaná of *La sombra del caudillo*, Juan Ampudia in the unheralded but sophisticated novel of the Revolution *En el sendero de las mandrágoras* [On the mandrakes' path] (1920) by journalist Antonio Ancona Albertos (1883–1954) (Jarmy Sumano 57) is an intellectual caught up in the political maelstrom of the Revolution.[36]

Unlike the idealistic hero of the Guzmán novel, Ampudia is portrayed in the early years of the turmoil, with much of the novel set between 1911 and 1915, during the Madero and Huerta periods. Ampudia is a dreamy aesthete imbued with notions from the *fin-de-siècle*: Nietzsche, spiritism, abulia, and crank health notions like water cures. Like Huysmans's Des Esseintes in *A rebours* [*Against the Grain*, 1884] (see Knapp), he is a parody of the decadent type among early 20th century intellectuals, complete with alcoholism and poetic aspirations. He is described as "*neurasténico*" [neurasthenic] and refers to his own "*manía*" (Ancona Albertos 164, 151), and he bears comparison to the obsessed protagonist typical of Guy de Maupassant's stories about the fantastic double the "Horla" (see Brossillon). He is also an opportunistic journalist figure who wants to get ahead in the revolutionary rat race of the Madero and especially of the Huerta periods. He roams Mexico City and other spots of revolutionary activity, often with his two friends Pérez, a reporter, and Romualdo García, who becomes a general in the Venustiano Carranza "Constitutionalist" forces by employing his skills as a trickster and a thief, in a process rather reminiscent of the peasant Tobei in *Ugetsu monogatari* (Mizoguchi Kenji, 1953), who becomes a samurai commander through sheer bluster and opportunism. Pérez is a more or less clear-minded reporter who is very concerned about the state of Ampudia's health, while the unrealistic Ampudia alternately wishes to found a newspaper and to join the revolutionary forces, or perhaps just to retire to Veracruz or another suitable spot with his beloved Malvina, whom he pursues obsessively throughout the novel. These Three Musketeers provide an ironic perspective on the tragic events in Mexico, which include the *Decena Trágica*, the Tragic Ten Days when Mexico City became a war zone in 1913 (of which more later).

The epigraph to this somewhat odd but intriguing and unjustly neglected novel encapsulates the deadly challenge faced by the accidie-plagued protagonist Ampudia, who was, according to John Rutherford, based on the novel's author: "Ancona affirmed that his novel was largely autobiographical, which—in view of the portrayal of the protagonist—was honest and courageous of him" (Rutherford, *An Annotated Bibliography* 29).[37] Translated from the French of Anatole France's *La rôtisserie de la reine Pédauque* [*The Sign of the Queen Pedauque*], the epigraph reads:

> "Walk with care," said M. d'Asterac. "This pathway is somewhat dangerous, as it is lined by mandrakes which at night-time sing at the foot of the trees. They hide in the earth. Take care not to put your feet on them; you will get love sickness or thirst after wealth, and would be lost, because the passions inspired by mandrakes are unhappy" [France 34].[38]

The mandrake plant carried a symbolic weight:

> **Mandragora** (or **Mandrake**) A plant which was supposed to have various magic properties, a belief arising out of the likeness of its roots to the human form. Mandragora was also the name of the ghost of a devil, who appeared as a tiny black man, beardless and with unkempt hair.... For the primitive mind, the mandrake represented the soul in its negative and its minimal aspects [Cirlot 204].

6. Professionals Across the Border

Ampudia is identified with the mandrake both comically and tragically. On a visit to Monterrey, among a cadre of Carrancistas, Ampudia, in his favorite element, cultured, or pseudo-intellectually ironic dissipation, "*tuvo días de grato olvido al lado de Vicente Escobedo, el célebre 'Ego,' de los artículos humorísticos de 'México Nuevo,'*" [had days of pleasing oblivion at the side of Vicente Escobedo, the celebrated "Ego," of the humoristic articles of "New Mexico,"] who writes about Ampudia "*como un idealista. Había pisado una mandrágora, ¿eh? Y su pasión revolucionaria era melancólica*" [as an idealist. He had stepped on a mandrake, eh? And his revolutionary passion was melancholic] (Ancona Albertos 175). So this intellectual, or would-be intellectual, who is at the center of formative events in the Revolution—Carranza was to win out in the fight against Huerta and then against Villa and Zapata—is presented (here, comically) as the man who stepped on the mandrake, with "melancholic" results for his "revolutionary passion." Note the admonition in the France epigraph not to "put your feet on them [mandrakes]; you will get love sickness or thirst after wealth, and would be lost, because the passions inspired by mandrakes are unhappy."

One of Ampudia's periodic attempts to reform himself takes place while Mexico was spiraling away from a chance at reform, spinning down towards escalating revolutionary violence. Thus, while Ampudia writes of his efforts to restore his health by not drinking, waking early, and so forth, in the streets outside his hotel, fighting fills the streets in a rebellion against the duly elected Madero (Ancona Albertos 72–73). These events in Mexico, named for posterity *La Decena Trágica*, culminated in the betrayal of Madero by his military chief Victoriano Huerta, who allegedly had Madero and his vice-president Pino Suárez murdered after promising them safe-conduct (for *La Decena Trágica*, February 1913, see Knight, A., *Mexican* 43–44, and Silva Herzog, "*El gobierno de Madero y la Decena Trágica*"). The treacherous Huerta was the subject of a 1916 play by author Salvador Quevedo y Zubieta. In this little-known play, Huerta is effectively portrayed, according to Pedro Bravo-Elizondo: "*La caracterización de Huerta ... y sus secuaces está a la altura del mejor teatro latinoamericano de la época* [The characterization of Huerta ... and his followers is at the level of the best Latin-American theater of the period]" (Bravo-Elizondo 198) (see also Aub 172).

Later in the novel, Ampudia compares himself to Huerta after his own homicide of Malvina's lover Gregorio Ruiz, noting that his crime has not received the attention given Huerta's: "*porque a mi crimen han superado en interés, en crueldad y en cobardía, los que ha cometido Victoriano Huerta,—otro personaje de novela*" [because my crime has been surpassed in interest, in cruelty, and in cowardice, by those committed by Victoriano Huerta,—another character from a novel] (Ancona Albertos 100).[39] Despite the sordidness of his crime, however, Ampudia cannot resist converting the episode into a literary analogy: "*Y, por una asociación de ideas, frecuente en él que vivía en perpetuo análisis subconsciente—se acordó de 'El Inocente' de D'Annunzzio [sic], en la cruda realidad*" [And, by an association of ideas, frequent in one who lived in perpetual subconscious analysis—he recalled "The Innocent" by D'Annunzio, in crude reality] (Ancona Albertos 92). He also muses that he and Malvina had once read the book together (Ancona Albertos 93). *L'Innocente* by Gabriele D'Annunzio was published in 1891–92 and "is a first-person confession about an infanticide" and "deals mainly with issues of love and betrayal" (di Paolo 381). (Ampudia fantasizes killing Malvina's infant son after recalling the novel [Ancona Albertos 92–93]).

Not only does Ampudia have "melancholic passions" about the Revolution, he pines self-destructively after Malvina, who has gone with another man, whom, as we have noted, Ampudia eventually kills, seemingly with no legal consequences. As the novel progresses, Ampudia's identification with the mandrake's power becomes sinister and tragic. Near the end of the novel, Ampudia is dying, advised by Malvina to disengage himself from his ambitions within the Revolution, "*porque era un apasionado de la Revolución y 'las pasiones que inspira la mandrágora, son melancólicas'*" [because he was impassioned about the Revolution and "the passions inspired by mandrakes are melancholic"] (Ancona Albertos 216). Ampudia also recalls a dream he had while in La Habana (Havana, Cuba) with a "*cabalista*" [Kabbalist] and direct influence from the mandrakes (Ancona Albertos 217–20).

If Ampudia displays neurotically decadent tendencies regarding mandrakes and disease and death,[40] he also taps into the idealistic, chivalric tradition exemplified (or parodied) by the figure of Don Quijote. Ampudia's portrayal of himself (and the narrator's perspective on him) as connected to Don Quijote goes beyond a few offhand references. Ancona's novel contains repeated allusions to the Cervantes work which create parallels between the dreaminess of Ampudia and the fantasizing of Alonso Quijano (the apparent "real" name of Don Quijote).

6. Professionals Across the Border

The narrator refers explicitly to Don Quijote when relating one of the many fantastic aspirations of Ampudia, in this case a fantasy about moving to Italy with his current paramour María Luisa and living out an idealized, aristocratic life typical of the late 19th century fad for Italian cities and culture. In this fantasized idyll, Ampudia would flourish:

> Creíase eterno y dejaba rienda suelta al Amor y al optimismo. Pero, como Don Quijote, tenía rota la celada—con remiendos de jerez—y era su lanza de utópico el carcomido trancón de un roble.
>
> He believed himself eternal and gave free rein to Love and to optimism. But, like Don Quijote, he had a broken helmet—with mendings of sherry—and his utopian lance was the worm-eaten branch of an oak [Ancona Albertos 82].

On occasion during the novel the hopelessly unrealistic Ampudia is presented through the perspective (with indirect narrative) of his companions Pérez and García. When the three friends reunite in Mexico City in November 1914 (Ancona Albertos 181), Ampudia is described to Pérez by Romualdo García, the arriviste military man, as a man drowning in his own intellectualizing, in need of rescue from himself:

> Era el hombre que vivía, perpetuamente, en el sendero de las mandrágoras.... Y del mismo modo, lo hallara en las diversas etapas de la revolución: deprimido y filosofante. Por Dios, esto era imprescindible: remediarlo. ¿Para qué pensar minuto a minuto en la obra obsesionante y consumirse en el ideal, caballero en clavileño galopante, como si estuviérase enradado [sic] por días y por meses entre los muslos de una mujer?
>
> He was the man who lived, perpetually, on the path of the mandrakes.... And in the same way, he might be found in the diverse stages of the revolution: depressed and philosophizing. Good God, this was indispensable: rehabilitate him. Why think minute to minute about the obsessing work and consume oneself in the ideal, a knight on a galloping Clavileño, as if he were ensnared for days and months between the thighs of a woman? [Ancona Albertos 190].

Clavileño is the wooden horse ridden by the blindfolded Don Quijote and Sancho as one of the elaborate pranks played upon them by the Duke and Duchess in the Second Part of *Don Quijote* (1615). The name of the horse is a portmanteau word composed of *clavo* "nail" and *leño* "lumber." In this comical if rather cruel episode, the knight and his squire ride the "magical" horse through the empyrean spheres, an illusion achieved through the use of fireworks and other special effects. Of course the episode parodies Don Quijote's riding through the countryside of Spain on the decrepit Rocinante, accompanied by Sancho Panza riding his *asno* [ass or donkey]. Like Don Quijote traveling through Spain, Ampudia travels through the sites of revolutionary Mexico: "*Yerró de ciudad en ciudad*" [He wandered from city to city] (Ancona Albertos 181). Whether intentionally or not, Ancona's presentation of Ampudia as a feckless knight-errant taps ironically into a particular chivalric image, the wandering knight seeking combat and inspiration. Thus, as Helen Cooper observes of the knight's quest as seen in romances (like those of Chrétien de Troyes), "They [knights] may not know quite what to expect, but they seize the initiative, choose to act rather than let themselves be acted upon: they will 'take the adventure that shall fall to them,' or 'the adventure that God will send them'" (Cooper, H. 52–53).[41] This image is not restricted to European narratives. Akira Kurosawa employs it in his *Yojimbo* (1961), in which the *ronin* (masterless samurai), played by Toshiro Mifune, throws a stick in the air and proceeds in the direction to which it points after it falls. This motif can be traced to the Zen-inspired concept *musha-shugyyo* [武者修行], explained by authority Daisetz T. Suzuki[42]:

> There is another thing the swordsmen learned from Zen. In olden days they used to travel all over Japan in order to perfect themselves in their art by experiencing every form of hardship which might befall them and by undergoing training in the various schools of swordsmanship. The example was furnished by the Zen monks, who did the same thing before they attained final enlightenment. This practice is known among the monks as *angya* [行脚], "traveling on foot," whereas the swordsmen call it *musha-shugyō*, "training in warriorship" [Suzuki 128].

One of Ampudia's goals is to found a newspaper in his native Mérida, which would be a reformist's ideal. This is expressed in terms which essentially quote the archaic language parodied in the *Don Quijote* narrative. The paper would be "*Un órgano de regeneración universal que saliera de las prensas armado, como Don Quijote, para desfacer agravios, enderezar entuertos, enmendar sinrazones, mejorar abusos y satisfacer deudas*" [An organ of universal regeneration which would sally forth from the presses armed, like Don Quijote, to undo offenses, to make wrongs right, to rectify injustices, to ameliorate abuses and to satisfy debts] (Ancona Albertos 108). The laughably idealistic project and its contact with the ruder reality of the Mexico of the novel is not far distant from *Citizen Kane's* "Declaration of Principles" written by Charles Foster Kane (Orson Welles) for the *New York Inquirer*, the original of which is kept by his more cynical friend Jed Leland (Joseph Cotten), who requests the document as a record, suspecting that Kane may not live up to its high-sounding ideals: "I'd like to keep that particular piece of paper myself. I have a hunch it might turn

6. Professionals Across the Border

out to be something pretty important. A document.... Like the Declaration of Independence and the Constitution—and my first report card at school" (Welles Ch. 11).

Ampudia may criticize Madero for his naïveté regarding the treacherous Huerta (Ancona Albertos 74–75), but Ampudia is tragically similar to Madero; in fact, Ampudia possesses in heightened form Madero's perceived defects—indecision, flightiness, "crank" preoccupations. Historian Alan Knight provides the following description of the failed president:

> Francisco Madero, a short, balding landlord and businessman, scion of one of the richest families of northern Mexico, foreign educated, a devotee of spiritism and homeopathic medicine, but a genuine idealist who sought—by peaceful persuasion—to make a reality of Mexico's liberal-democratic tradition [Knight, A., *Mexican* 25].

One of Juan Ampudia's flings with homeopathy or naturopathy is the "water cure" based on recommendations by Leipzig physician Louis Kuhne:

> Juan ... era un revolucionario de tomo y lomo: en el campo de la lucha y en su propio cuerpo; y si Madero había revolucionado en México, Luis Kuhne revolucionó en las costumbres de Ampudia. Era su nueva obsesión.... Tomaba agua, por todas partes....
>
> Juan ... was a revolutionary to be reckoned with: in the field of the struggle and in his own body; and if Madero had done revolution in Mexico, Louis Kuhne revolutionized in Ampudia's habits. It was his new obsession.... He took water everywhere... [Ancona Albertos 188].

Kuhne (1835–1901) emphasized "physiognomy" in healing: "At the start of the twentieth century Louis Kuhne, a natural therapist from Leipzig, first proposed the idea that the natural and harmonious state of healthy organisms could be read from their physical appearances" (Peeters 450); but he was chiefly associated with "hydropathy" or a water cure ("Louis Kuhne"). Ampudia's recourse to such "cures" points to his essential rootlessness; he suffers from a malady similar to that of Des Esseintes and later of Roquentin (from *La nausée* [1938; Nausea] by Jean-Paul Sartre), compared by Lane Gormley: "In both cases [Des Esseintes and Roquentin, but applicable also to Ampudia], the 'solution' to the problem represented by the emotional and intellectual distance which separates the hero from those who surround him and his panic at finding himself alive, alone and without purpose in society is, at some level, the attempt to escape" (Gormley 183). Gormley's characterization of Des Esseintes fits Ampudia quite closely: "He is the bourgeois esthete, the middle class dandy who pines for an absolute and for an ideal in which he does not quite believe and which he does not quite know how to realize" (Gormley 186). Despite Ampudia's repeated attempts to believe in the Revolution and to act on his emotional attachment to it, he fails to join it fully, lacking the thoroughgoing cynicism and opportunism of a Luis Cervantes, or, perhaps, of a Romualdo García. Like Don Quijote, the knight-errant who must choose his path in life (a common feature of chivalry tales, which Quijote resolves early in the novel by following the path his horse Rocinante takes [see Baena for discussion and context with other works]), Ampudia reaches a crossroads:

> *Tenía frente a sí los caminos del Quijote y, a la espalda, otro, uno nuevo en el que don Alonso de Quijano no pensó sino hasta que, recobrado el juicio, quemó sus libros de caballería y se dispuso a bien morir. Ese nuevo camino, definido en la expresión vulgarísima de "desandar lo andado," parecióle a Ampudia algo inexistente o absurdo.*
>
> He had in front of him the paths of the Quijote and, at his back, another, a new one about which don Alonso de Quijano did not think until, his good judgment recovered, he burned his chivalry books and prepared to die well. That new path, defined in the highly vulgarian expression "backtracking your tracks," seemed to Ampudia something nonexistent or absurd[43] [Ancona Albertos 66].

A different portrait of the intellectual involved in, or observing, the Mexican Revolution appears in one of Mariano Azuela's less-studied novels—most attention falls on *Los de abajo*—*Andrés Pérez, maderista* (1911). The major character in the novel, narrated in first person, is journalist Andrés Pérez, who displays a pattern of fleeing from difficult situations in his career and personal life, beginning with a hurried visit to the country home of his friend Toño (Antonio) Reyes and his wife, María. Perhaps a less unattractive character than the later Luis Cervantes, Andrés is nonetheless a rather cynical and self-centered man who finds himself trapped in a public image as a revolutionary—a *maderista* or supporter of Francisco Madero (for Madero and his revolution, see Raun). As A.W. Woolsey observes, "*Andrés Pérez maderista es una novela corta de la cual el protagonista no era revolucionario al principio* [*Andrés Pérez maderista* is a short novel whose protagonist was not a revolutionary at the outset]" (Woolsey 344). The novel is set (and was published) in the very early days of the Revolution, when longtime dictator Porfirio Díaz was ousted, going into exile in Paris, as northern landowner and idealist Francisco Madero

6. Professionals Across the Border

and his vice-president Pino Suárez took power. Azuela commented that, in this work, he wanted to criticize the failures of the Madero revolution:

> La audacia y el cinismo con que los enemigos de la revolución chaquetearon en los propios momentos en que se consumó la derrota del régimen, me dieron el tema básico de la novela. En Andrés Pérez, maderista vertí todo mi desencanto.
>
> The audacity and the cynicism with which the enemies of the revolution changed sides in the very moments when the defeat of the {Porfirio Díaz} regime was consummated, gave me the basic theme of the novel. Into *Andrés Pérez, maderista* I poured all my disenchantment [Azuela, *Páginas autobiográficas* 115].

Andrés is cagey regarding his professional standards, as he is about his personal relationships. In an early exchange with his friend Toño, who suffers from consumption, he categorizes journalists as either mercenary hacks or idealistic cowards and fools:

> —Hay un malecillo entre los periodistas, Antonio amigo, que se llama, en términos decentes, miedo; pero como un malecillo vergonzante, suele ocultársele bajo una máscara, y esta máscara es la de la imbecilidad, las más de las veces.
>
> There is a little malady among journalists, friend Antonio, which is called, in decent terms, fear; but like a shameful little illness, it tends to be hidden beneath a mask, and this mask is that of imbecility, most of the time.

He further separates these workaday journalists from writers who seem to work *pro bono* or at least are not preoccupied with piecework wages. According to Andrés, such journalists belong to a type analogous to idealistic revolutionaries who suffer prison or death for no good reason:

> [Antonio says:]—*Calumnias á muchos de tus compañeras* [sic], *Andrés; hay escritores honorables que no escriben para eso.*
> —*Sí, pero estos regularmente no son periodistas de profesión.... Son iguales á ese pobre diablo de Serdán ... género especial de cándidos, que escriben para podrirse en una prisión.*
> —You're slandering many of your companions, Andrés; there are honorable writers who don't write for that (for money).
> —Yes, but these are regularly not journalists by profession. They are the same as that poor devil Serdán ... a special type of naïfs, who write so they can rot in a prison.

Andrés demurs when asked if he might fit into that latter group (Azuela, *Andrés Pérez* 28–29).

The reference to "Serdán" concerns an early, nonprofessional revolutionary (he was a shoemaker) from Puebla, Aquiles Serdán, who was killed in an abortive uprising in support of Madero. His uprising was reduced to a hopeless defense of his house against local police and *rurales*. He had overestimated his local support and had underestimated the strength of the authorities, and he was killed after hiding in the basement of his house. These events occurred on November 18, 1910. As Stanley R. Ross, whose account is followed here, summarizes:

> *Los hermanos Serdán y sus seguidores fueron así los primeros mártires de la revolución maderista. Don Francisco Madero ... escuchó ... con lágrimas en los ojos, el relato de la tragedia de Puebla. Embargado por la emoción, dijo estas palabras: "No importa; nos han enseñado a morir."*
>
> The Serdán brothers and their followers were thus the first martyrs of the Maderista revolution. Don Francisco Madero ... listened ... with tears in his eyes, to the tale of the Puebla tragedy. Overcome by emotion, he said these words: "It does not matter; they have taught us how to die" [Ross, S.R. 86–88] [see also LaFrance].

Besides being ironically prophetic regarding Madero's own fate, murdered on orders from Victoriano Huerta, Serdán's death is echoed in the Azuela novel by the fate of the consumptive Toño Reyes, who also dies in a revolutionary uprising.

Mislabeled as a revolutionary (specifically, a *"maderista"*), deliberately so in some cases and unwittingly in others, Andrés eventually tries to leave Mexico for a time to escape the hounding by the press and also by locals and is captured on his way out of the country. Freed by a local man with influence, he is drawn into a revolt in which Vicente, the manager of the late Antonio's home, is executed by a grasping arriviste "colonel."[44] Andrés has become, more or less against his will (unlike the willing impostor of the later play by Rodolfo Usigli, *El gesticulador* [1938], in which a professor assumes a false identity as a revolutionary hero), *"un supuesto líder revolucionario"* [a presumed revolutionary leader], as opposed to the hapless Vicente, *"el verdadero revolucionario"* [the true revolutionary] (Andino 147). The intellectualizing Andrés, who models his conduct to at least some extent on a character from a then-recent short story by Catalán author Víctor Català [Caterina Albert], *"El calvario de 'Mitus'"* (from the collection *Caires vius*), and who muses about Nietzsche and other recent luminaries, is, like Juan Ampudia, an early 20th century type: *"Representa ya al hombre moderno del siglo XX, urbano, egoísta, con una buena dosis de hedonismo y una moral voluble"* [He already represents the modern man of the 20th century, egotistical, with a good dose of hedonism and a fickle morality] (Coronado 94).

6. Professionals Across the Border

Like the unfortunate protagonist of the Usigli play, but in a different context, Andrés is quite aware of his imitation of a model; again, in his case the model is fictional and European. He uses the imitation as a stratagem to escape unwanted contacts among the inhabitants of the region where Antonio lives, many of whom have begun to mistake him for a revolutionary. So, in order to escape immersion in a false identity of others' choosing, he takes masochistic refuge in one of his own choosing:

> *imito al infeliz Mitus de Víctor Català, quien con una navajita enterrada en las carnes, volvía y revolvía, destrozaba, dislaceraba [sic] las fibrillas más sensibles, hasta acabar por encontrar la voluptosidad [sic] suprema en un espasmo de su propio dolor.*
>
> I imitate the unfortunate Mitus of Víctor Català, who with a scalpel buried in his flesh, turned and turned again, tore, shredded the most sensitive little fibers, until at the end finding supreme voluptuousness in a spasm of his own pain [Azuela, *Andrés Pérez* 49].

As with an Edgar Allan Poe character (see, for example, Saliba), the morbid Andrés is haunted by his (false) association with Madero, to the point of undergoing obsessive nightmares:

> *Y Madero siempre, siempre la odiosa palabra en mis oídos. Madero, la pesadilla que me asalta en sueños y á todas horas del día.... ¡Maldito sea Madero! ...*
>
> And Madero always, always the odious word in my ears. Madero, the nightmare that assaults me in dreams and at all hours of the day.... Madero be damned! ... [Azuela, *Andrés Pérez* 79].

Like a Gothic demon, the image of Madero threatens to smother the protagonist. Philip W. Martin states that "the origin of the word [nightmare] is in folklore, which variously supposes the bad dream to be accompanied by a stifling feeling in the sleeper's chest, or uses the word simply to refer to this discomfort" (Martin 206). Seemingly a "curse of Madero" is visited upon him, as his best attempts to escape being thought a revolutionary and eventually to escape the country come to naught.

After his arrest when trying to flee the country, he is freed by the good offices of a landowner named Don Octavio, who appears to be the representative of 19th century liberal values in the novel. Don Octavio and Andrés engage in a lengthy debate about the judicial system and other matters (Azuela, *Andrés Pérez* 93–100). Andrés becomes defensively oppositional and retreats into a rather flippant nihilism when asked about his "ideal," citing an anecdote about French Parnassian poet Théophile Gautier (1811–72):

Professionals in Western Film and Fiction

> —*Don Octavio, dicen que Teófilo Gautier ofrecía sus derechos de ciudadano, por ver á Julia Grisi en el baño.... Teofilo* [sic] *Gautier me es simpatico...*
>
> —Don Octavio, they say that Théophile Gautier offered his citizenship rights, to be able to see Julia Grisi in the bath.... Théophile Gautier is in sync with me...
> [Azuela, *Andrés Pérez* 100].

The reference is to Gautier's fascination with Julia (Giulia) Grisi, a "well-known opera singer" (Grant 102), expressed in his preface to his *Mademoiselle de Maupin* (1835):

> For myself, I am one of those to whom the superfluous is necessary.... I should most joyfully renounce my rights as a Frenchman and a citizen to see an authentic picture by Raphael, or a beautiful woman naked—the Princess Borghese, for example, when she has posed for Canova, or Julia Grisi when she enters the bath...
> [qtd.in Richardson 27].

Julia Grisi was also a topic in one of Gautier's poems, "*La Diva*" (1832), in which the poet sees Julia at the opera "and ends his poem regretting having given up painting in favour of poetry: only painting, he says, can hope to capture the essence of physical beauty" (Nurnberg 229).

The superficial and narcissistic Andrés fits neatly into a set of characters which includes Juan Ampudia as well as a certain "type" in Azuela's fiction:

> *Es este carácter* [Andrés] *una sátira contra los oportunistas, los revolucionarios de ocasión, los que no tienen ideas definitivas, sino que son los que siguen el camino que les promete, o parece prometerles, el mayor bien. Es un tipo que se desarrolla con frecuencia en otras novelas de Azuela; Andrés Pérez es un precursor de Pascual [in* Las tribulaciones de una familia decente*] y de cierta manera de Luis Cervantes.*
>
> This character is a satire against the opportunists, the sometime revolutionaries, those who don't have definitive ideas, but who are the ones who follow the path that promises them, or seems to promise them, the greatest good. It is a type that crops up frequently in other Azuela novels; Andrés Pérez is a precursor of Pascual and in a certain way of Luis Cervantes [Woolsey 344].

The wispy character Andrés Pérez, "*el primer antihéroe revolucionario de Azuela* [the first revolutionary antihero of Azuela]" (Santana 304), is linked to later Azuela characterization by Gerhard Herbst, who sees him as an indicator of Azuela's own worries about the Revolution. Herbst comments

> There is some correlation between Solís [the intellectual from *Los de abajo*] and ... the main character of *Andrés Pérez, maderista* (1911). Although inferior to *Los de abajo* ... it does have deep thoughts on the revolution and presents the first seeds of disenchantment.... Apparently Azuela had to face his personal dilemma early in

6. Professionals Across the Border

the revolution and this feeling increased to great bitterness when he left Mexico for a short time. Although sympathetic to the cause of the revolution, he had seen too much behind the scenery as a medical doctor to believe sincerely in the success of the movement. He thought it hopeless and a thorough prodigality [Herbst 160–61].

John Rutherford sees Andrés Pérez as a model for later characters:

... one of the recurring characteristics of the intellectual in the novels of the Mexican Revolution is already shown in his first appearance: the conflict in him between the calls of revolutionary duty and of romantic love affairs, between his feeling that the world needs to be changed and the temptation to take the easy way out, of escape into the oblivion that eroticism provides [Rutherford, *Mexican Society* 95].

As noted earlier, a different kind of intellectual figure is central to the very well-known play by Rodolfo Usigli, *El gesticulador* (1938). A chamber drama set during the administration of one of Mexico's most revered presidents, Lázaro Cárdenas, the play calls into question the success of the revolution and engages in generational discussions about its effects on a family whose paterfamilias is a professor recently employed in Mexico City but now retired to the country. César Rubio, whose field is Mexican Revolution history, plans to use his knowledge of the peccadilloes of local politicians and influential figures in his home town, to which he and his rather unwilling family have relocated, to obtain a teaching post or even a more lucrative sinecure. Of course with this tactic he reveals himself as no different from any of the corrupt functionaries of the post-revolutionary state (or of the prerevolutionary one, for that matter). Besides the members of his family, Rubio is counterpointed with a houseguest, another professor of Mexican history, from the United States, Oliver Bolton. This encounter allows Usigli to present perspectives from north and south of the border on the great revolutionary upheaval, which began in 1910.

Rubio will take on the identity of an eponymous general who mysteriously disappeared in 1914, at about the same time of the alleged disappearance of Ambrose Bierce in Mexico, supposedly executed on orders from Pancho Villa. This adoption of the identity of a disappeared (fictional) general parallels the murky disappearance of an actual historical figure, Bierce, who may himself have fictionalized his own disappearance in an elaborate scheme to "disappear" from public and private view (see Nickell, "Biography: The Disappearance of Ambrose Bierce" and Nickell, "Ambrose Bierce and Those 'Mysterious Disappearances' Legends"). The coincidence of the supposed date of the death of the two figures, General Rubio and

Bierce, only adds to the confusion or obfuscation; or, perhaps, to the seamlessness of the history/fiction nexus: "The pairing of Ambrose Bierce and César Rubio [the general] as Bolton's two research interests seems to legitimize the fiction historically" (Kronik 8). In any case, the history professor, Rubio, writes, or acts, himself into revolutionary "history" by assuming another identity, becoming yet another intellectual figure associated in some fashion with the Revolution who wears a mask, like Luis Cervantes, Solís, Ampudia, or Andrés Pérez. Professor Rubio may have mercenary motives for his fakery, but his fascination with the period is genuine. His Yankee counterpart, Oliver Bolton, may be loosely modeled on the actual historian from the University of California, Herbert E. Bolton (1870–1953), author of works such as *The Spanish Borderlands: A Chronicle of Old Florida and the Southwest* (1921), as Daniel Meyran suggests (Usigli 116*n*2).

Reluctant at the outset to discuss the disappeared General Rubio, or at least to reveal the outcome of his disappearance, Professor Rubio is gradually drawn into (or perhaps, draws Bolton into) a further discussion of the General's fate. Rubio soon acknowledges, or does not deny, that he is the General and that he has adopted the guise of a professor of Mexican history in order to hide in plain sight. Regarding Rubio's role in adopting the identity of the General, Catherine Larson comments that "the distinction between telling a blatant lie and neglecting to reveal the truth is illustrated early on in the play by César himself, as he counters his wife's accusation that he is a liar" (Larson, C. 23). Eventually the misguided professor will become inextricably merged with his mask: "*César pierde su identidad original, la de profesor de historia, y se convierte en César Rubio el general de la Revolución* [César loses his original identity, that of a history professor, and is converted into César Rubio the general of the Revolution]" (Amaya 13). Tragically, as Guillermo Schmidhuber comments, "*Este atrevimiento llega a costarle la vida, al pasar la gesticulación falsificada a constituir la nueva identidad del protagonista, convirtiéndose la máscara en carne* [This audacity {the identity pose} ends up costing him his life, once the falsified gesticulation passes over to constitute the new identity of the protagonist, converting the mask into flesh]" (Schmidhuber de la Mora 194). To a greater degree than Andrés Pérez, Rubio the intellectual or the professional man of letters loses his definition when confronted with the forces of revolution. And unlike Axkaná González, he does not stand apart from the "man of action," to repeat Millington's phrase

6. Professionals Across the Border

regarding Aguirre. Unfortunately for Professor Rubio, the attempt to merge in his invented persona the two wings of revolutionary activity—the intelligentsia and the frontline troops—leads to his inevitable downfall.

The Mexican history specialization adopted by the "General" (that is, himself), according to the fiction developed by the professor, is a natural fit for a new identity for the General, who would draw naturally on his own firsthand experience when presenting the Revolution to his students. In this way Usigli blends the experience of an observer of the Revolution, like the professor, with the active experience of a participant, like the fictional General. As Mark Frisch observes, Usigli's "plays, *El gesticulador* and *Corona de sombra* [a play about Maximilian and Carlotta], challenge the official view of history, underscores [sic] the subjective nature of history, and suggest that history, fiction, legend, and myth, often prove indistinguishable" (Frisch 133). Many of the same questions have been raised in connection to Westerns, which generally present legendary or mythic personalities sometimes based directly on historical personages. After a fashion, the professor functions like a mythmaking dime novelist, conflating "history, fiction, legend, and myth," although admittedly to a more radical degree than in most fictions of the Old West.

Rubio's adoption, or misappropriation, of the identity of an erstwhile leader of the revolution places him into conflict with his wife, Elena, and then, when the "truth" is revealed in the local newspaper, most dangerously with national and local party officials, who come to his house to discuss the revelation. These minor functionaries, including the designated representative of the party in the matter, are the corrupt faces of the central administration. Rubio has hinted darkly that he knows secrets about party officials and especially about a man named Navarro, who will play a sinister role in the drama. The officials of the ruling party have in many cases benefited from the gradual and inexorable betrayal of the expressed goals of the Revolution; as Mehl Penrose comments in his article on Usigli:

> En cuanto a la noción popular de la Revolución Mexicana, los ideales se perdieron a la ambición de algunos caudillos fuertes y corruptos y poco a poco ellos ganaron el respeto y la gloria de las masas mexicanas. En El gesticulador *Usigli nos intenta expresar su crítica de la corrupción e hipocresía políticas por una técnica metateatral en la cual encontramos muchas referencias históricas.*

> Concerning the popular notion of the Mexican Revolution, the ideals were lost to the ambition of some strong and corrupt leaders and little by little they earned respect and glory from the Mexican masses. In *El gesticulador* Usigli tries to

Professionals in Western Film and Fiction

express to us his criticism of the political corruption and hypocrisy through a metatheatrical technique in which we find many historical references [Penrose 131].

Ironically, the play is set in 1937–38, as Daniel Meyran notes, during the presidency of Lázaro Cárdenas (1934–40), a period of modernization and ideology, when land reform, one of the goals expressed in the 1917 Constitution (adopted during the Revolution), was pressed forward, and society and politics crystallized: *"Es entonces cuando se instalan todas las estructuras del México actual tanto en el nivel económico y social como en el nivel político, sindical y cultural* [It is then when all the structures of modern Mexico are installed, both on the economic level and on the political, unionist, and cultural level]" (Meyran 76). Thus the critique advanced by the play is even more corrosive given the reformist and progressive nature of the famous and revered Cárdenas administration, a presidential term which bears comparison in more than one respect to the contemporaneous presidency of Franklin D. Roosevelt (1933–45) in the United States. (Both presidents advanced progressive reformism and were charismatic, personalist leaders.) The inference to be drawn from the Usigli play would be that even in the most progressive and populist administration since the Revolution, corruption and hypocrisy still direct the course of the nation.

The conflicted professional in Usigli's play, as well as in Mexican Revolution fiction more generally, often works in opposition to the construction of a revolutionary state which is at odds with the professed ideals of the Revolution. In the American Western, the civil professional usually works toward an idealized civilization on the frontier, and as their fictional environment normally prescribes, these professionals usually assist in the creation of such perfectible societies.

Chapter Notes

Introduction

1. This designation, familiar to audiences or readers of Westerns, reflects popular culture more than strict historical fact:

> Terms [like gunfighter] were invented by late nineteenth century fiction writers whose words have since been projected back into the frontier period. "Gun-fighter" dates only to 1894, "gunfight" to 1898, "gun man" (in the western context) to 1903. "Gunslinger" [as Ryker calls Shane in the 1952 film] is strictly a philological latecomer dating from 1953 [Dykstra 511–12*n*32].

For some examples and discussion of "anachronistic speech" in Western films, see Ross, T.J. 160.

2. As one of the more prominent examples of the retrospective examination of Western legend, Ford's film follows a path explored previously by films such as *The Return of Frank James* (Fritz Lang, 1940), which contains, according to Ed Gallafent, "a shift from tradition (oral anecdote) to modernity (writing up Western legends for publication, to be 'telegraphed all over the country')" (Gallafent 24).

Chapter 1

1. For the growth of the professional class in the later 19th century, see Bédarida 50–51. Although the summary provided by Bédarida pertains specifically to England, the changes in class structure were mirrored in other countries of Western Europe and the Americas, in some cases more slowly than in England.

2. For Americans' attitudes toward urbanity and rurality, see Danbom. During the period associated with Westerns, the agrarian fascination grew as the nation developed: "The antiurban dimension of agrarianism in the 19th century became more prominent as the United States became more urban and industrial" (Danbom 22).

3. For a two-part study of the role of this tribe in the Indian wars, see Murphy, "The Place of the Northern Arapahoes in the Relations between the United States and the Indians of the Plains, 1851–1879" and Murphy, "The Place of the Northern Arapahoes in the Relations between the United States and the Indians of the Plains, 1851–1879."

4. Reid was quite good at portraying men with serious health challenges, conveying a stifled energy underneath a gruff exterior, as in his memorable turn as an accused embezzler in "The Case of the Ugly Duckling" from the first season of the *Perry Mason* TV series.

5. For accounts of heroism by military doctors on the frontier, see Wier.

6. For Red Cloud, see Larson, R.W., "Red Cloud. Part 1: The Warrior Years" and Larson, R.W., "Red Cloud. Part 2: The Reservation Years."

7. Whitney (1916–72) was capable of conveying bluster, as here, or slithering menace, as in his superb appearance in *The Big Heat* (Lang, *The Big Heat*) as a du-

plicitous bartender, or comic avarice and timidity, as *in Buchanan Rides Alone*. In the latter film he played the buffoonish Amos Agry, brother to the town boss.

8. These theories and practices included the use of carbolic acid as an antiseptic, a regimen which Dr. Garth promotes in the film. As Edgar observes in his article on Lister, "He applied the antiseptic principle in the use of various strengths of carbolic acid to the treatment of acute abscesses, carbuncles, boils, whitlows, and ordinary wounds" (Edgar 151).

9. For Joseph Lister (1827–1912), see Edgar and Bashford.

10. For Wallace (1827–1905), Union general, governor of New Mexico Territory, and author of *Ben-Hur: A Tale of the Christ* (1880), see Forbes; Jones; Theisen; and for a literary-biographical sketch, Eddings.

11. For Lister and Pasteur, see Edgar 149–52. A Warners biopic, *The Story of Louis Pasteur* (William Dieterle, 1936), stars Paul Muni as Pasteur, with an appearance by Halliwell Hobbes as Dr. Lister.

12. For more on Santiago (de Compostela), see Hall, K.E., *Stonewall Jackson and Religious Faith in Military Command* 125–30.

13. After firearms and horses appeared in the Americas, according to author William Brandon, the Cree brought along to the Great Plains "friends from southern Ontario, the Assiniboin, a sizable tribe that had separated not long before from the great Siouan-speaking nation known as the Dakota" (Brandon 325). For a factual account of mixed frontier marriage, focusing on the Sioux wife, see Gray.

14. Bell seemed to specialize in this kind of portrayal. A good example is his turn in the first season of the *Perry Mason* TV series (1957), in which he plays a genial, folksy man who lives in the country and has served as a tracker for law enforcement. His geniality hides his murderous resentment of the decedent in the case, whom he killed over a land dispute, obscuring his crime with tracking techniques ("The Case of the Lazy Lover").

15. Payton (1927–67) died at a very early age, plagued with addiction. See http://www.foxnews.com/entertainment/2018/08/16/former-50s-star-barbara-payton-endured-tragic-downfall-involving-drug-abuse-alcoholism.html and https://pro.imdb.com/name/nm0668510/?ref_=instant_nm_1.

16. The accomplished and innovative Stephen Hunter, author of numerous sniper thrillers featuring the Swagger men from Arkansas, provided a recent take on the Tom Doniphon character in his novel *G-Man* (2017), in which the titular character, Charles Swagger, is inserted into the famous stories about the FBI takedown of John Dillinger, Baby Face Nelson, and Pretty Boy Floyd. Swagger decides to fade from history in order to memorialize the heroic sacrifice of two FBI men; as his grandson Bob Lee Swagger explains of Charles, "'He had to erase himself from history and from the FBI'" (Hunter, S. 500). Another character in the novel pointedly quotes the "print the legend" line from the Ford film, of which Nick Memphis, longtime friend and colleague of Bob Lee, comments, "'Starring John Wayne, the Charles Swagger of the movies'" (Hunter, S. 457).

Chapter 2

1. Clum (1851–1932) was an important early figure in Arizona history. As Douglas Firth Anderson summarizes his frontier civilian career, Clum was an Indian agent at San Carlos Apache Agency (1874–1877), and editor of the *Arizona Citizen* (1877–1880). During his years in Tombstone, he was not only a newspaper editor (1880–1882), but also the postmaster (1880–1882, 1885–1886) and the mayor (1881) (Anderson 315). A fictionalized account of his San Carlos period, *Walk the Proud Land* (Jesse Hibbs, 1956), starred Audie Murphy and Anne Bancroft. See also Tate and Ryan.

2. J.A. Place contrasts the physicality of the two characters, to the detriment of Maxwell Scott (Place 221, 223).

3. For the topic of miscegenation in

Notes—Chapter 2

Westerns, see Pye, "Double Vision: Miscegenation and Point of View in *The Searchers*"; Eckstein; and Wood.

4. For a historical account of the construction of the railroad, see Boyd.

5. Beddoe (1903–91) had a long career in film and television, appearing in releases of many genres, including *The Narrow Margin* (Richard Fleischer, 1952) and in memorable episodes of the long-running *Perry Mason* television series.

6. For a discussion of the complex social nature of the period, see Susman and Griffin.

7. One of "The Big Four of the Central Pacific [Railroad]," "Crocker [1822–1888] was in charge of construction," much like the character in *Carson City* (Ambrose Illus.).

8. For a brief sketch of phrenology, including its arrival in the United States, see Pickard and Buley 222–26.

9. Michael Walker provides a sketch of the film's "Freudian design" (Walker, M. 154–55).

10. Also noticing the irony of the name, David Meuel comments as well on the *noir* elements in the characterization:

> One of the key narrative characteristics of film noir is its emphasis on the ambivalence and alienation of principal characters in an uncertain, sometimes threatening world. And, perhaps more fully than any character in a Daves western, Dr. Joe Frail—the man "with frail hope"—fits this description. On one hand, Frail is competent and kind.... On the other hand, he has a dark side [Meuel 164].

11. In his book *The Pulp Jungle*, Gruber identified "seven basic western stories." His names for these are: The Union Pacific Story, The Ranch Story, The Empire Story, The Revenge Story, Custer's Last Stand, The Outlaw Story, and The Marshal Story (Gruber 184–86). Jon Tuska offered a revision of this list in his *The American West in Film* (23–38). See also Boatright, cited as a source by Tuska (Tuska 23).

12. The same stagecoach appears in Ford's late film *The Man Who Shot Liberty Valance*, providing a deftly inserted bookend to his career and tying together the frontier experiences of the two films.

13. William Indick trenchantly comments:

> In the Western, our sympathies are generally drawn to the white outcasts of white society (as opposed to the red or brown outcasts). The hero is an outlaw, his woman a whore, and his friend a drunk [Indick 145].

14. In his study of names in Ford's *Stagecoach*, David Clandfield highlights the appropriateness of its doctor's name: "Josiah Boone ... has the ideal name for an obstetrician: *Josiah* means 'may God heal' ... [and] *Boone* recalls *boon*, 'blessings'" (Clandfield 35).

15. For a summary of the concept of *Bildungsroman*, including its fairly recent generalization from German literature, see Freese 31–37.

16. Marin (1899–1951) directed seven Westerns featuring Scott. Marin died shortly after finishing *Fort Worth* (Atkinson 116).

17. According to Peter Krapp, Greeley popularized this slogan although he did not actually originate it: "...it was John Babsone Soule who first coined the phrase, in an article for the *Terre Haute Express* in 1851." The exhortation "became the motto of Manifest Destiny when Horace Greeley reprinted the piece in the *New Yorker*" and has since been associated with Greeley (Krapp 605n6).

18. In his essay on samurai film, Tada Michitaro draws an interesting distinction between the geographical imperative of American Westerns and Japanese samurai films. In his formulation, the civilizing impetus of Japan flows in the reverse direction from that of America, because, due to their western Japanese origins, "The samurai were the true pioneers of Japan." If "the West is ... America's pioneer territory, ... in Japan it is the East." This geographical distinction should be borne in mind for our future discussion of *The Magnificent Seven* films and their origins in Kurosawa's great *Seven Samurai*. Extending the distinction to films, Tada states:

171

Notes—Chapter 2

I believe that the American westerns anticipate and reflect the progression of civilization from east to west in America; while the Japanese *chanbara* [swordplay] movies anticipate and reflect the flow of civilization in the opposite direction—they are, therefore, "easterns" [Tada 49–50].

For Wister and the tenderfoot, see Marovitz.

19. For an enjoyable upending of the Easterner as tenderfoot trope, see the novel *The Derby Man* by Gary McCarthy, discussed in my article "Newspapermen in the Western" (McCarthy) (Hall, K.E., "Newspapermen" 40–41).

20. Fritz Lang (1890–1976) was an internationally celebrated director before leaving Germany, having helmed great films such as the two-part *Die Nibelungen* (1924), *Metropolis* (1927), and *M* (1931). His work in Hollywood included film noir (*The Big Heat* [1951]) and Westerns such as *Western Union* (https://pro-labs.imdb.com/name/nm0000485/).

21. Anton Kaes discusses the experience of exile for Lang as informing his staging and treatment of characters; see Kaes in Works Cited.

22. Ray White summarizes the chief features of low-budget B Westerns:

> The B Western formula plots romanticized and glorified the American West, depicting the struggle between a hero and his sidekick and villains who stole cattle, land, and gold mines or who tried to take over valleys, towns, banks, and watering holes. The heroes always triumphed over the villains and departed the screen ready for action the following week [White 135].

For a neatly posed summary of the "two sides of the heroic character" in more complex Westerns, see Pippin 163*n*3.

23. The Harris character may recall, although a bit distantly, the historical figure of Moses Y. Beach, editor of the *New York Sun*, who was sent to Mexico on a clandestine mission by President Polk (see Nelson and Kross).

24. The film's use of Parkman's work is historically anachronistic, as the work was not published until 1849, after the termination of the Mexican-American War of 1846–48. Parkman's work does attempt to assess the war, however; see Lawrence. For more on Parkman, see Nye.

25. For the Johnson County War of 1892, see O'Neal and Smith.

26. Patrick McGee links the drunken Peabody with the inebriate Washington Dimsdale, marshal in *Destry Rides Again* (George Marshall, 1939), through similarities in their subjection to violence and their relationship in the *mise-en-scène*: "The critical scene before Ranse [James Stewart] goes out to face Liberty Valance in a gunfight, the one in which he looks over the body of the beaten and nearly dead newspaper editor [Peabody], echoes the scene in *Destry* when Tom [James Stewart] holds the dying Dimsdale in his arms" (McGee 133). For an account of some journalists in the midst of frontier wildness, see Myers, J.M. A study of the news business on the frontier is Barbara Cloud, *The Business of Newspapers on the Western Frontier* (Reno: University of Nevada Press, 1992).

27. See Saults for a summation of Edwards's life and influence. He provides an interesting précis of the paradoxical elements of his character (150).

28. For more on the Cobb character and on Edwards, see Hall, K.E., "Newspapermen" 37–38. See also Ray Lavery, "The Man Who Made a Folk-God out of Jo Shelby and Created a Legend for Jesse James," *Trail Guide* 6.4 (Dec. 1961): 1–15. Ed Gallafent comments of the Cobb character in both James films that he represents "a stock character of the Western—a newspaper proprietor, albeit in this case one of limited effectiveness [truer in the King film than in the Lang sequel]" (Gallafent 22).

29. A subtle hint as to the nature of the town is provided in the one building with a real name, the Herren Hotel, with the association of Herren ('Masters') with German National Socialism and the "master race" (Guthrie 285). Thanks to Dr. Steve Fritz, History Department, East Tennessee State University, for consulting

Notes—Chapter 3

with me on this point and for steering me in the direction of the autobiographical nature of the story. Several of Guthrie's tales were set in this town, based on the real Choteau, Montana (Ford, T.W. 129).

30. The story was filmed twice as a short feature, in 1912 and 1917 (Kirkland and O. Henry; Mills and O. Henry).

31. For a useful summary of the device from antiquity, see Hinckley. For its application to selected authors, see Fishburn (on Borges) Kuchta (Conrad and Coppola); and Hall, K., "'Chac Mool,' a Vampire Text: Stoker, Maupassant, and Other Antecedents" 32 (Fuentes, Stoker, and others).

32. For a brief summary of these incidents, see Underwood 39–41. For outlaw figures in American folklore, see Meyer, R.E.

33. Helen M. Lewis observes that "the Wayne character does not divorce": the usual resolution of his domestic difficulties is an eventual patching up of differences (Lewis 9).

34. See the comments by Kelly Jensen on the East vs. West divide in this film (Jensen 5–6), where she includes Birnbaum in the list of "real men" like McLintock.

35. See Gallafent 24 for these points.

36. For a study of banks and their role in the cattle industry, and thus in frontier progress, see Gressley.

Chapter 3

1. Brode (281) also notes the parallel with *The Night of the Hunter*.

2. Townes (1913–2001) was a versatile, expressive, and subtle actor who inhabited many roles. As Patrick King notes (Biography, Pro-Imdb database), he was a native of Huntsville, Alabama, returning there after his retirement as an actor and becoming an Episcopal priest. As King also observes, he was especially visible on television. His many roles included memorable appearances on *The Outer Limits* (the original series), *Perry Mason*, and *Star Trek*.

3. For an overview of religion on the frontier, see Hine 222–37.

4. For Westerns and iconography, see Buscombe, "The Idea of Genre in American Cinema" 14–25 (cited Neale 16).

5. For a summary of the film and a negative appraisal of its effectiveness, see Atkinson 125–27.

6. Brode uses the term "Western charade subgenre" (279). I prefer the term "masquerade" as it does not carry the implication of phoniness or the mountebank in the designation "charade." Some of the film and literary characters in Westerns who adopt masks are indeed phony, deceitful, or sinister—but others have solid and even moral personal reasons for their masquerades.

7. *Hawke: Ride with the Devil* (2004); *Hawke: Showdown at Dead End Canyon* (2005); *Hawke: Vendetta Trail* (2005); *Hawke: The Law of a Fast Gun* (2006); *Hawke: The King Hill War* (2007).

8. For the early history of the Mafia in New Orleans, see Asbury 406–23. Asbury summarizes the influence of the Matranga and Provenzano factions.

9. See, for example, the breathlessly pompous outburst by Homais on religion (Flaubert 112). See also Robert J. Niess, "On Listening to Homais," *French Review* 51.1 (1977): 22–28, and Hela Michot-Dietrich, "Homais, Homeopathy, and *Madame Bovary*," *Stanford French Review* 11.3 (1987): 313–21.

10. Jones's possession of this rifle would seem to point to service with the Confederacy, because the Confederate sharpshooters used this English rifle to great effect during the war. But the narrative specifies that Jones was one of Berdan's Sharpshooters in the conflict (Vaughan, R., "The Piano Man" 245). This unit was commanded by Bvt. Maj. Gen. Hiram Berdan. See Boatner 61, 917. For the Whitworth, see also John Anderson Morrow, *The Confederate Whitworth Sharpshooters*. A fine specimen of the innovative Whitworth can be viewed in the museum at the Visitor Center for the Chickamauga National Battlefield Park near Chattanooga, TN.

11. For a discussion of the role of language in *Unforgiven*, see Orr.

12. For a description of the Tabor Opera House in Leadville, see Cochran 335–36.

13. See the brief summary in McFerrin and Wills 69–70. A full account is Bill O'Neal, *The Johnson County War* (2004).

14. Ed Masterson was later killed in a tragic shooting seemingly predicted by the Earp of Kasdan's film. Marshal Masterson was shot and killed on April 9, 1878, in Dodge City, when attempting to disarm a man named Cowboy John (Jack) Wagner. For these details and further discussion of the incident and its aftermath, see Penn, C. 49ff. See also Myers, R.

15. For the Pinkertons and the James family, see Soltysiak; for a more expansive study including the Pinkerton agency and its role in labor disputes, see Weiss.

16. The fine character actor Dean Jagger made playing such men—outwardly strong and competent but hiding dangerous secrets or moral flaws—something of a specialty. Examples of such roles are his psychotic father in *Pursued* (Raoul Walsh, 1947) and his rather more sympathetic appearance as the physically powerful but morally spineless sheriff in *Bad Day at Black Rock* (John Sturges, 1954).

17. The script has an unfortunate anachronism at this point, as a soldier refers to Vickers as the new "topkick," an expression that was not used in the Army until 1918 (Merriam-Webster online).

18. The concept was first presented in Spain by Ángel Ganivet (1865–98), for whom "*Abulia* is simply a natural debilitation of the will in the absence of the vital convictions which provide its energy" (Shaw 224). According to Gayana Jurkevich, the term as used in Spain originated in French psychological theory (see Jurkevich 182–85). For Ganivet and his seminal work *Idearium español* (1897), see Krauel.

19. As *The BFI Companion to the Western* notes, "Along with the church, the school is a sure sign of a leap from wilderness to civilization" (Buscombe 215).

20. The trope of the "respectable" wife of a cavalry officer is cleverly tweaked in *Little Big Horn* (Charles Marquis Warren, 1951), where Marie Windsor plays a cavalry wife who is less than loyal. See Hall, K.E., "Custer and the 7th Cavalry" 15–16.

Chapter 4

1. A selection of articles in this area includes Greenwald, Brown, Davidson, Van Orman, Simmon, and Carrell (see Works Cited).

2. For a historical study of the fate of two Arizona mining towns, Tombstone and Jerome, see Clements.

3. For a recent, well-researched account of the gunfight, see Guinn.

4. For C.S. Fly, whose photography shop was near the gunfight location, see Vaughan, T.

5. Andrew Crislip writes of accidie or acedia,

> In the medieval Latin tradition of the seven deadly sins, acedia has generally been understood as the sin of sloth.... Moral theologians, intellectual historians, and cultural critics have variously understood acedia—or "accidie," among other English spellings—as the ancient depiction of a variety of psychological states, behaviors, or existential conditions: primarily laziness, ennui, or boredom [Crislip 144].

An explicit reference to the condition appears in the Ian Fleming novel *Live and Let Die*, in which the memorable villain Mr. Big tells his captive James Bond, "'Mister Bond, I suffer from "accidie," the deadly lethargy that envelops those who are sated, those who have no more desires'" (Fleming 51). Mature's sleepy-eyed performance accentuates his character's own "deadly lethargy," if for reasons different from those expressed by Mr. Big.

6. For Holliday, see Roberts and Tanner and DeArment.

7. Foy (1856–1928) was an accomplished entertainer who was to become world-renowned. (See the biography by Fields). His funeral in New Rochelle, New York, was attended by "more than 600 actors and neighbors" (Fields 236).

Notes—Chapter 5

8. Foy also can be heard singing inside Tombstone's Schieffelin Hall, whose marquee bills his show, in *Gunfight at the O.K. Corral*, but he does not appear onscreen. For Schieffelin Hall and other structures in Tombstone, some of which have undergone restoration, see McCormack, K.L. Foy was in Dodge City in 1878, during Wyatt's time there (Tefertiller 20, 23–24).

The Foy visit to Tombstone appears not to be a historical fact. Apparently it was an invention of Foy himself, whose "alleged trip to Tombstone (for the celebrated shoot-out at the OK Corral" was an example of "his 'tall tales' [which] tended to relate to actual historical events in which he claimed to have played a minor role" (Fields 103). Foy did appear at Dodge City in 1878, when Earp and Holliday were also there (Fields 25–30).

9. Mark Twain famously accused Scott of inspiring the rebellion in the South. The relationship of Scott's novels (particularly *Waverley*) to the chivalric spirit in the South is a contentious topic. See Orians, "Walter Scott, Mark Twain, and the Civil War" for a well-argued refutation of Twain's position. For more on chivalric survivals in the States, see Orians, "The Origin of the Ring Tournament in the United States."

10. Neil Sinyard's evaluation of Rufus parallels mine; he also remarks on Rufus's view of Buck: "A man of some principle and intelligence, Rufus seems to have harbored a lifelong disappointment with his son which in turn has fueled Buck's truculence" (Sinyard 176).

11. Mexican actor Alfonso Bedoya (1904–57) is most well-known for his template performance as the bandit who tells Fred C. Dobbs (Humphrey Bogart) in John Huston's *The Treasure of the Sierra Madre* (1948): *"Badges*? We don't need no stinkin' badges!"

Chapter 5

1. For a brief history of these terms, as well as useful sources, see Haberly 790–91.
2. For dramatic irony, see *The New Princeton Encyclopedia of Poetry and Poetics* 635, where it is noted that one facet of such irony is that "the spectators know more than the protagonist." See also Flickinger 202.
3. See Stanzel 10 for an example of such a "teller-character" from James's "The Aspern Papers."
4. The device is similar in structure and function to the ancient framing tale or "framework-story" form, familiar to readers of Chaucer and Boccaccio (see, for example Clawson and Hinckley). See also the entry "Framework-Story" (Harmon and Holman 224).
5. The film, competently directed by action specialist Cassar, is a reunion of sorts for veterans of *24*. These include Cassar, who directed many episodes, and of course Kiefer Sutherland, as well as actors Greg Ellis (who appeared in Season 3) and Michael Wincott (who appeared in the Season 9 reboot). The most important reunion, between Donald and Kiefer Sutherland, is actually their first on-screen collaboration. The father-son storyline in the film naturally acquires added resonance from their real-life relationship.
6. As David Desser observes, this important scene

> is downplayed in the film [*Shane*]. Its symbolic weight comes through more clearly in the novel by Jack Schaefer [Desser, "Kurosawa's" 64n11].

It is nevertheless significant in the narrative as a bridge scene showing the increasing acceptance of Shane by Starrett and his family. Regarding the scene in the novel, Ann-Janine Morey-Gaines observes:

> The invincible old tree stump is, like Shane, a resilient [*sic*] reminder of a wilder way of life and the order of things that preceded the domestication of the wilderness.... Only with Shane's cooperation is the triumph of the cultivated West over the wild secured [Morey-Gaines 139].

7. In the Kasdan *Wyatt Earp*, on the other hand, it is Lou Earp (Alison Elliott), widow of Morgan, who is traumatized, as she breaks out into hysterical sobbing at the sound of gunshots outside the train

carrying Morgan's body to California. Ironically, Lou is distraught by the shots fired by Wyatt as part of his vengeance for Morgan's murder.

8. For the Shaolin martial arts tradition, see Shahar.

9. For the Wandering Jew, see Russell and Briggs; and for a summation of the evolution of the character, see Mohr. A striking example of such a character appears in Ford's *The Searchers*: the merchant Futterman, "represented as an archetypal shuttler between worlds, that is, as a Jew" (Freedman 591). Curiously, Caine tells his new friend Han Fei (Benson Fong) that "I am called many names. I have chosen Caine"—a probable reference to his use of aliases, but intriguing in the light of the immortal Ahesverus figure, whose wanderings under different names and biographies have inspired works from Borges's "El inmortal" to the *Star Trek* episode "Requiem for Methuselah."

10. The phrase is Richard Slotkin's. He notes that in the later development of the motif in the 19th century, "The most mythologized military episodes of frontier expansion ... all have the same mythic structure: a small outnumbered group of white soldiers, led by a 'Man Who Knows Indians,' defends America against a dark-skinned enemy" (Slotkin, "Unit Pride" 473–74). See also FitzGerald and Kelly. *Saskatchewan* (Raoul Walsh, 1954) features a rather unusual example of the type, with Alan Ladd as Thomas O'Rourke, a Mountie who grew up among an Indian tribe and who is immediately shown traveling with his Indian "brother" Cajou (Jay Silverheels). Max Westbrook links the between-the-worlds experience of the Western hero to his condition as "both abstracted and alert" and observes that particularly "Among American Indian heroes, the combination of being both abstracted and alert is so recurrent that it could almost be called a characteristic of the race" (Westbrook 13).

11. Keith Carradine also appeared in the series as the younger Caine.

12. For a generally critical view of the treatment of Indians from a former Indian fighter, see Miles, N.A.

13. For the career of a historical photographer and journalist on the frontier, see Woolworth.

14. A similar outline for the journalist character appears in *The Magnificent Seven Ride!* and *Unforgiven*.

15. Booker reads to March and his friend Lafe from a novel called *Ransom March, Six-Gun Marshal* (West, J.A. 22).

16. For the concept of the "reflector-narrator," see Stanzel.

Chapter 6

1. Jaime Alazraki observes that:

> *Como el Martín Fierro, su contra-partida, el* Facundo *es un híbrido, un texto sui generis que comparte aristas con varios géneros. Ese polimorfismo, sin embargo, no invalida su carácter novel-ístico. La reserva de Unamuno y de muchos otros respecto a su valor histórico es justificada.*

> Like the Martín Fierro, its counterpart, the *Facundo* is a hybrid, a text *sui generis* which intersects with several genres. That polymorphism, nevertheless, does not invalidate its novelistic nature. The reserve of Unamuno and of many others with respect to its historical value is justified [Alazraki 16].

2. Fredrick B. Pike links the "schoolmarm" type directly to Sarmiento because of Sarmiento's courting of Horace Mann to assist him with the educational system in Argentina by providing him with "New England schoolmarms." Pike observes:

> Women schooteachers on the [U.S.] frontier came generally from the genteel elements of white American society, and their success in introducing refinements where barbarism had previously reigned impressed many upholders of civilized standards, among them the Argentine Domingo Faustino Sarmiento who served as his country's minister to Washington (1865–1868) and then as its president (1868–1874) (Pike 13).

3. For the connection to Mexico and its foreign relations with the United States

Notes—Chapter 6

during the time when these Westerns were released, see Fojas 30–31, 74.

4. For the French Intervention (1861–67), see McAllen and Haslip.

5. For a brief sketch of Shelby's career in Missouri, which led to his Mexican migration at the end of the war, see Phillips 13. Jasper Ridley provides a short summary of the stint of Shelby and his men in Mexico (Ridley 215). For a biography of Shelby, including extensive material on the Mexico expedition, see O'Flaherty. A useful summary of Edwards' varied career is found in Ray Lavery, "The Man Who Made a Folk-God out of Jo Shelby and Created a Legend for Jesse James."

6. David Desser classifies *Seven Samurai* as a professional Western (141).

7. David Desser discusses "class boundaries" in the Sturges film in terms of "*technological*" distinctions between the weaponry of the Americans and the Mexicans and ties the distinction to the crossing of the border between the U.S. and Mexico (Desser, *Samurai Films* 140–41) (emphasis in original). He also notes the "racial divide" in the Sturges film (19, 24) but qualifies this observation, averring that "the real divide is First World/Third World, North/South" and focusing on the "matter of access to power and the kind of technological resources possessed by America and lacking in Mexico/the Third World (Desser, "Remaking" 24). See also Corkin 181–82 and Slotkin, *Gunfighter Nation* 475.

8. [浪人] 'floating person' (Arnold, J.T., "E-Mail Communication"). In current, everyday usage in Japan, the term is now used to refer to students who do not pass entrance exams for higher education (Arnold, J.T., "E-Mail Communication") (Early 14).

9. This scene replaces the opening episode in the Kurosawa film, in which the lone samurai Kambei (Shimura Takashi) rescues a baby from a thief holding him hostage.

10. In the discussion below I follow several of Slotkin's points, including his use of the terms "Special Forces" and "platoon" as well as the points about specialization and the associations with the railroad (Slotkin, *Gunfighter Nation* 567–74).

11. Such professional advisors or aides to leaders like Zapata or Villa were common features of the Mexican Revolution.

12. Zuzana M. Pick also provides the translation of Mapache's name and provides an ideologically tinted summary of the image represented by Emilio Fernández but does not specifically tie the figure to a scavenger trope (Pick 8, 10).

13. For German intervention in Mexico see also Tuchman and Katz, "Alemania y Francisco Villa" as well as Herwig and Archer.

14. For a brief presentation of icons in the Western, see Marsden.

15. For Villa, see Katz, *The Life and Times of Pancho Villa*. A recent article on Villa as "icon" is Gollnick. For an interesting comparison between the careers of two medical participants in the Revolution, see von Feilitzsch.

16. William H. Beezley (cited Jenkins 100*n*4) employs the term "los de abajo" in connection with the bullfight tradition in Mexico: "Los de arriba (the topcats) had no trouble separating themselves from los de abajo (the underdogs); the gente decente have a sense of identity as strong as those who belong to the pueblo" (Beezley 5). For the translation challenges with the title and the work, see Murad, "*Los de Abajo* vs. *The Underdogs*: The Translation of Mariano Azuela's Masterpiece."

17. Jenkins observes that when Cervantes first appears, he is shot in the foot by Pancracio, who fails to understand his password ("Carranza"), so that he is "literally a 'tenderfoot'" (Jenkins 103). For a discussion of Cervantes in the context of Mexican concepts of masculinity, see Harris 656–58. The most recent translator of the novel into English, Sergio Waisman, opts for leaving "the term *curro* untranslated, noting the lack of a "direct English equivalent" while explaining that it is "a derogatory label applied to someone from the upper classes precisely because this individual thinks too highly of himself and looks down with contempt at poor, rural,

Notes—Chapter 6

mestizo, and/or indigenous Mexicans" (Waisman xvi).

18. Hazera says that "Demetrio Macías, the protagonist of *The Underdogs*, is a composite of the revolutionary leaders Azuela knew intimately" (Hazera 347).

19. Timothy Murad directly contrasts Demetrio's heroics and Cervantes's unsuitability to warring in terms of their skill with horses. He points to the battle at Zacatecas (Chapter XXI of *Los de abajo*), in which "Cervantes' ineffectiveness in the battle is ... mirrored in his twice being unhorsed," and observes that "Demetrio's bravery and superb horsemanship stand in striking contrast to Cervantes' incompetence" (Murad, "Animal Imagery and Structural Unity in Mariano Azuela's *Los de Abajo*" 209–10).

20. The irony of the name has not escaped critical notice:

> At his core, Luis is not an idealist. He is just a wordsmith. After all, his name is Cervantes. And we are in the presence of satire [Canfield 151].

21. Canadian actor Wiseman (1918–2009) may be most familiar to American audiences as the urbanely evil Dr. No in the first James Bond film, *Dr. No* (1962).

22. Frank Silvera (1914–70) was an accomplished and versatile actor and a pioneer in augmenting the African-American presence in Hollywood (https://pro-labs.imdb.com/name/nm0798426/bio?ref_=nm_subnv_persdet_bio). The editor of *Negro Digest*, to which Silvera contributed a 1969 review of a James Baldwin work, lauded Silvera as "one of the most distinguished actors in the American theater" (Silvera 35). He appeared in numerous films and TV episodes. One of his more memorable roles was the tragic Jonathan Hyett in "The Case of the Fancy Figures," a *Perry Mason* episode from December 13, 1958 (https://pro-labs.imdb.com/name/nm0798426/?ref_=nm_subnv_overview).

23. Venustiano Carranza was the leader of the Constitutionalist forces. Alvaro Obregón was his leading general who later became President of Mexico.

24. For criticism of the film in terms of its "Americanized" Zapata character, presumably lending it a quality of inauthenticity, see Alonzo 94–98.

25. The critical bibliography on Fuentes is extensive. For this novel, one might begin with Gyurko, "Self and Double in Fuentes' *Gringo viejo*"; and Boldy. See also my article, Hall, K., "*Gringo Viejo*" and comments on journalists in the Fuentes novel in Hall, K.E., "Newspapermen."

26. For a good discussion of the debated factuality of the disappearance, see Nickell, "Biography: The Disappearance of Ambrose Bierce." For Bierce, see O'Connor and Fatout.

27. As Steven Boldy observes (Boldy 489–90), historian Enrique Krauze criticized Fuentes for misrepresenting Mexican reality in *Gringo viejo*, particularly his shifting of southern Mexican (Zapatista) grievances about land ownership to northern Mexico, where the Villa forces had little concern with the problem (Krauze 26). See also Gunn 62–63.

28. The theme of patricide is central to the novel. See Chrzanowski and Boling.

29. For discussion of the film and some of its differences from the novel, see Pick 16–21.

30. Huang Fei-hong [Wong Fei Hung in Cantonese] has become legendary through accretions of popular storytelling: "Huang Feihong (1847–1924) is a real historical figure. One of the 'Ten Tigers of Guangdong,' he was a respectable kung-fu master of the school of Southern Shaolin Temple" (Lo 81*n*4). Many films have been made about the master, who has become symbolic of traditional Chinese martial arts discipline and of virtues like rectitude, generosity, courage, and tolerance. The Cantonese title of this Tsui Hark film is *Wong Fei Hung II: Nam yee tung chi keung*. [Wong Fei Hung II: A man should be strong in himself]. Thanks to my friend Win-chiat Lee, of Wake Forest University, for assistance with the translation.

31. For a detailed recounting of the incident, including clarification of its background, see Silva Herzog, "Durante la presidencia del general Plutarco Elías Calles. Sucesos que es menester recordar,"

Notes—Chapter 6

in Works Cited. See also Johnson, W.W. 396–98.

32. Georgina García Gutiérrez Vélez establishes a parallel between Diego Rivera and writer Carlos Fuentes as leaders of two twentieth century "Renacimientos" [Renaissances] in Mexico.

33. For Kellogg, see Barnard.

34. After the Aguirristas have been kidnapped and are about to be shot, Emilio Olivier, leader of the left wing of the faction, reminds Aguirre ruefully that he might well have listened to him when he counseled an uprising (*"madrugar,"* literally "waking up early") before the Caudillo and his henchmen could react (Guzmán 233). In a meeting held among the Aguirristas before they were betrayed, Olivier had warned, *"'Pues bien, la política de México, política de pistola, sólo conjuga un verbo: madrugar'"* ["'Well now, the politics of Mexico, politics of the pistol, only conjugates one verb: *madrugar*'"] (Guzmán 199).

35. For a discussion of the name symbolism, see González.

36. According to John Rutherford, "The most complete and penetrating study of the revolutionary intellectual in all the novels, including those of Azuela, is that made by Ancona Albertos in the two volumes of his undeservedly ignored work" (Rutherford, *Mexican Society* 103). The discussion which follows concerns the second volume of the novel, which focuses on the early Revolution. For the earlier first volume, see Rutherford, "The Novel of the Mexican Revolution" 103–08.

37. See Rutherford, *Mexican Society* 103–11 for a discussion of the novel and its protagonist which coincides in several respects with my own analysis.

38. Rutherford observes that "Ancona Albertos displays great admiration for Anatole France without showing any discernible literary dependence on him" (Rutherford, *Mexican Society* 76).

39. Jorge Aguilar Mora discusses the presentation of *La Decena Trágica* in the Ancona novel as well as in other novels of the Mexican Revolution (Aguilar Mora 82–84).

40. Ampudia can be compared to, and possibly was influenced by (as perhaps was his creator as well) Des Esseintes, protagonist of *A rebours* by Huysmans, whose melancholy and listlessness is characterized as *"acédie"* (accidie or abulia) by Anne Larue in her article *"A Rebours, roman de la chute acédiaste."*

41. I am indebted to Dr. Joshua Reid of the Department of Literature and Language, East Tennessee State University, for this source, as well as for pointing me to the specifically named 'adventure' motif, discussed in depth, as he notes, in Auerbach 133–36. See also Cavallaro 40ff.

42. I am indebted for this reference to Eddy von Mueller, "Naked Swords: The Zen Warrior Tradition and the Intertextual Odyssey of the Nameless Ronin in *Seven Samurai, Yojimbo,* and *Sanjuro,*" *Post Script* 20.1 (2000): 53–67. He uses Suzuki's terminology about *Yojimbo* and observes: "The film almost immediately invokes zen: the ronin, with no path, lets the random throw of a stick show him the way" (Von Mueller 58).

43. Ampudia's memory is hazy here. Don Quijote did recover his sanity at the end of Part 2 (1615), but his books, many of them at least, had already been burned early in Part 1 (1605), at the orders of the village priest.

44. For a brief summary and evaluation of the novel, see Schwartz 274.

Works Cited

Acosta Cruz, María. *The Discourse of Excess: The Latin American Neobaroque and James Joyce.* Diss. State University of New York at Binghamton, 1984. Ann Arbor: University of Michigan, 1985.
Aguilar Camín, Héctor, and Lorenzo Meyer. *In the Shadow of the Mexican Revolution: Contemporary Mexican History, 1910–1989.* Trans. Luis Alberto Fierro. Austin: University of Texas Press, 1993. Trans. of *A la sombra de la Revolución Mexicana.*
Aguilar Mora, Jorge. *Una muerte sencilla, justa, eterna: cultura y guerra durante la Revolución Mexicana.* México: Ediciones Era, 1990.
Alazraki, Jaime. "Facundo, de Sarmiento, y la novela hispanoamericana del dictador." *Casa de las Américas* 30.180 (May–June 1990): 14–28.
Aldrich, Robert, dir. *Vera Cruz.* 1954. Digital videodisc. With Gary Cooper, Burt Lancaster, Cesar Romero, and Morris Ankrum. Hecht-Lancaster-MGM, 2001.
Allison, James R. III. "Beyond the Violence: Indian Agriculture, White Removal, and the Unlikely Construction of the Northern Cheyenne Reservation, 1876–1900." *Great Plains Quarterly* 32.2 (Spring 2012): 91–111.
Alonso, Carlos J. *The Spanish American Regional Novel: Modernity and Autochthony.* 1990. Cambridge: Cambridge University Press, 2000.
Alonzo, Juan J. *Badmen, Bandits, and Folk Heroes: The Ambivalence of Mexican American Identity in Literature and Film.* Tucson: University of Arizona Press, 2009.
Amaya, Carlos. "Desdoblamiento y pérdida de identidad en *El gesticulador* y *A pesar del oscuro silencio*." *Revista de Humanidades* 2 (Spring 1997): 11–18.
Ambrose, Stephen E. *Nothing Like It in the World: The Men Who Built the Transcontinental Railroad, 1863–1869.* New York: Simon, 2000.
Ancona Albertos, Antonio. *En el sendero de las mandrágoras.* N.p., n.d. [1920].
Anderson, Douglas Firth. "Protestantism, Progress, and Prosperity: John P. Clum and 'Civilizing' the U.S. Southwest, 1871–1886." *Western Historical Quarterly* 33.3 (Autumn 2002): 315–35. http://www.jstor.org/stable/4144840.
Andino, Alberto. "Los juegos políticos, clasistas y étnicos en las novelas de Mariano Azuela sobre la Revolución mexicana." *Cuadernos Hispanoamericanos* 370 (April 1981): 144–50.
Archainbaud, George, dir. *The Woman of the Town.* 1943. VHS tape. With Albert Dekker, Claire Trevor, and Barry Sullivan. United Artists–United American Video, 1990.
Arnold, Jack, dir. *No Name on the Bullet.* 1959. Digital videodisc. With Audie Murphy, Joan Evans, Charles Drake, and Edgar Stehli. Universal, 2004.
Arnold, Junko Tezuka. E-Mail Communication, 2016.
_____. E-Mail Communication, August 24, 2018.
_____. E-Mail Communication, August 31, 2018.

Works Cited

Asbury, Herbert. *The French Quarter: An Informal History of the New Orleans Underworld.* 1936. Garden City, NJ: Garden City Publishing Co., 1938.
Atkinson, Barry. *Six-Gun Law: The Westerns of Randolph Scott, Audie Murphy, Joel McCrea and George Montgomery.* Baltimore: Midnight Marquee Press, 2015.
Aub, Max. "Los orígenes de la novela de la Revolución Mexicana." *Panorama de la actual literatura latinoamericana: ciclo organizado por el Centro de Investigaciones Literarias, Casa de las Américas.* La Habana: Casa de las Américas, 1969. 168–73.
Auerbach, Erich. *Mimesis: The Representation of Reality in Western Literature.* Trans. Willard R. Trask. 1968. Princeton: Princeton, NJ: University Press, 1974.
Azuela, Mariano. *Andrés Pérez, maderista: novela precursora.* Rpt. University of Michigan Library. 2017. México: Imprenta de Blanco y Botas, 1911.
―――. "Cómo escribí *Los de abajo*." *Obras completas.* Vol. 3. México: Fondo de Cultura Económica, 1958. 1267–68.
―――. "Los de abajo." *Obras completas.* Vol. 3. México: Fondo de Cultura Económica, 1958. 1077–99.
―――. *Páginas autobiográficas.* Pref. Francisco Monterde. 1974. México: Fondo de Cultura Económica, 1998.
―――. *Las tribulaciones de una familia decente.* 3rd ed. México: Ediciones Botas, 1947.
Bacon, Lloyd, dir. *The Great Sioux Uprising.* With Jeff Chandler, Faith Domergue, Lyle Bettger, and Peter Whitney. Universal, 1953.
―――, dir. *The Oklahoma Kid.* With James Cagney, Humphrey Bogart, Rosemary Lane, and Donald Crisp. Warner Bros., 1939.
Baena, Julio. "Trabajo y aventura: el criterio del caballo." *Cervantes* 10.1 (1990): 51–57.
Baker, Brian. *Masculinity in Fiction and Film: Representing Men in Popular Genres, 1945–2000.* London: Continuum, 2006.
Bandy, Mary Lea, and Kevin Stoehr. *Ride, Boldly Ride: The Evolution of the American Western.* Foreword by Clint Eastwood. Berkeley: University of California Press, 2012.
Barnard, Sandy. *I Go with Custer: The Life and Death of Reporter Mark Kellogg.* Bismarck: Bismarck Tribune, 1996.
Barrett, Gregory. *Archetypes in Japanese Film: The Sociopolitical and Religious Significance of the Principal Heroes and Heroines.* Selinsgrove: Susquehanna University Press–Associated University Press, 1989.
Bartlett, John. *Familiar Quotations: A Collection of Passages, Phrases and Proverbs Traced to Their Sources in Ancient and Modern Literature.* 16th ed. Gen. ed. Justin Kaplan. Boston: Little, Brown, 1992.
Bashford, Henry. "The Coming of Antisepsis." *History Today* 1.4 (April 1951): 37–41.
Beard, William. *Persistence of Double Vision: Essays on Clint Eastwood.* Edmonton: University of Alberta Press, 2000.
Beasley, W.G. *The Modern History of Japan.* 2nd ed. New York: Praeger, 1974.
Bédarida, François. *A Social History of England, 1851–1900.* 2nd ed. Trans. A.S. Forster and Jeffrey Hodgkinson. London: Routledge, 1991.
Beezley, William H. "Judas at the Jockey Club and Other Episodes of Porfirian Mexico." Lincoln: University of Nebraska Press, 1987.
Benedict, Ruth. *The Chrysanthemum and the Sword: Patterns of Japanese Culture.* 1967. Boston: Houghton Mifflin, 1989.
Benson, Jackson J. *Under the Big Sky: A Biography of A.B. Guthrie, Jr.* Lincoln: University of Nebraska Press, 2009.
Berg, Charles Ramírez. "The Margin as Center: The Multicultural Dynamics of John Ford's Westerns." *John Ford Made Westerns: Filming the Legend in the Sound Era.* Ed. Gaylyn Studlar and Matthew Bernstein. Bloomington: Indiana University Press, 2001. 75–101.

Works Cited

Bergstrom, Janet. "Alternation, Segmentation, Hypnosis." Interview with Raymond Bellour. Trans. Susan Suleiman. *Camera Obscura* 3/4 (1979): 70–103.
Bernstein, Matthew. *Walter Wanger, Hollywood Independent*. Berkeley: University of California Press, 1994.
Best, James D. *The Shopkeeper: A Steve Dancy Tale*. Tucson: Wheatmark, 2008.
Bischoff, Peter, and Peter Noçon. "*The Missing*: Gender-and Ethnicity-Correct Constructs." *Studies in the Western* 12 (2004): 117–22.
Biskind, Peter. *Seeing is Believing: How Hollywood Taught Us to Stop Worrying and Love the Fifties*. New York: Pantheon, 1983.
Boatner, Mark Mayo III. *The Civil War Dictionary*. New York: David McKay, 1959.
Boatright, Mody C. "The Formula in Cowboy Fiction and Drama." *Western Folklore* 28 (April 1969): 136–45.
Boetticher, Budd, dir. *Buchanan Rides Alone*. 1958. Digital videodisc. With Randolph Scott, Craig Stevens, and Peter Whitney. Columbia-Sony, 2008.
———, dir. *Decision at Sundown*. 1957. Digital videodisc. With Randolph Scott, Noah Beery, Jr., Ray Teal, Karen Steele, and John Archer. Columbia-Sony, 2008.
———, dir. *Ride Lonesome*. 1959. Digital videodisc. With Randolph Scott, Karen Steele, James Best, and Pernell Roberts. Columbia-Sony, 2008.
———, dir. *Westbound*. With Randolph Scott, Virginia Mayo, Karen Steele, and Andrew Duggan. Warner Bros., 1959.
Boldy, Steven. "Intertextuality in Carlos Fuentes's *Gringo viejo*." *Romance Quarterly* 39.4 (November 1992): 489–500.
Boling, Becky. "Parricide and Revolution: Fuentes's 'El Día de las Madres' and *Gringo Viejo*." *Hispanófila* 32.2 [95] (1989): 73–81.
Bonham, Frank. "The Green Moustache." *Liberty* magazine, 1946. *The Best Western Stories of Frank Bonham*. Ed. Bill Pronzini and Martin H. Greenberg. Athens: Swallow Press/Ohio University Press, 1989. 214–18.
Borges, Jorge Luis. "El inmortal." *El Aleph*. Buenos Aires: Emecé, 1996. 7–37.
Boyd, Consuelo. "Twenty Years to Nogales: The Building of the Guaymas-Nogales Railroad." *Journal of Arizona History* 22.3 (Autumn 1981): 295–324. http://www.jstor.org/stable/41695612. Accessed 10/21/2016.
Brandon, William. *Indians*. Boston: Houghton Mifflin, 1987. Rpt. of *The American Heritage Book of Indians* (American Heritage: 1961).
Braudy, Leo. "'The Director, That Miserable Son of a Bitch': Kazan, *Viva Zapata!* and the Problem of Authority." *Kazan Revisited*. Ed. Lisa Dombrowski. Middletown: Wesleyan University Press, 2011. 36–42.
Bravo-Elizondo, Pedro. "*El concepto de la revolución y de lo mexicano en* El gesticulador." *Texto Crítico* 10.29 (Spring 1984): 197–205.
Bredahl, A. Carl, Jr. "After Words: The Western Movies of John Ford and Sam Peckinpah." *Seeing Beyond: Movies, Visions, and Values*. Ed. Richard P. Sugg. New York: Golden String, 2001. 281–302.
Brode, Douglas. *Dream West: Politics and Religion in Cowboy Movies*. Austin: University of Texas Press, 2013.
Brooks, Bill. *Dakota Lawman: Killing Mr. Sunday*. New York: HarperTorch–HarperCollins, 2005.
———. *Dakota Lawman: Last Stand at Sweet Sorrow*. New York: HarperTorch–HarperCollins, 2005.
Brooks, Richard, dir. *The Professionals*. 1966. Digital videodisc. With Lee Marvin, Burt Lancaster, Robert Ryan, Woody Strode, Jack Palance, Claudia Cardinale, Joe De Santis, and Ralph Bellamy. Columbia-Sony, 2005.
Brossillon, Celine. "The Figure of the 'Horla' in Guy de Maupassant's Short Stories: From Isolation and Alienation to Annihilation." *Dix-Neuf* 21.1 (2017): 16–30.

Works Cited

Brown, Eric C. "The Bard Comes to Yellow Sky: Shakespeare's Tempestuous Western." *Shakespeare in Performance.* Ed. Eric C. Brown and Estelle Rivier. Newcastle upon Tyne: Cambridge Scholars, 2013. 138–54.

Buell, Lawrence. "Observer-Hero Narrative." *Texas Studies in Literature and Language* 21 (Spring 1979): 93–111.

Burt, Richard. "Shakespeare, 'Glo-Cali-Zation,' Race, and the Small Screens of Post-Popular Culture." *Shakespeare, the Movie II: Popularizing the Plays on Film, TV, Video, and DVD.* Ed. Richard Burt and Lynda E. Boose. London: Routledge, 2003. 14–36.

Buscombe, Edward. "The Idea of Genre in American Cinema." *Screen* 11.2 (1970), 33–45. *Film Genre Reader IV.* Ed. Barry Keith Grant. Austin: University of Texas Press, 2012.

———. *Stagecoach.* London: British Film Institute, 1992.

———, ed. *The BFI Companion to the Western.* New York: Athenaeum-MacMillan, 1988.

Butler, David, dir. *The Command.* With Guy Madison, Joan Weldon, Carl Benton Reid, and James Whitmore. Warner Bros., 1954.

Butler, Jeremy G. "*Viva Zapata!*: HUAC and the Mexican Revolution." *The Steinbeck Question: New Essays in Criticism.* Ed. Donald R. Noble. Troy: Whitston, 1993. 239–49.

Butler, Robert, dir. "The Ancient Warrior." *Kung Fu.* Television series. Digital videodisc. With David Carradine, Keye Luke, Philip Ahn, Chief Dan George, Victor French, Denver Pyle, G.D. Spradlin, Will Geer, Gary Busey, and Radames Pera. ABC-Warner Bros., 2004. 3 May 1973.

———, dir. "The Stone." *Kung Fu.* Television series. Digital videodisc. With David Carradine, Keye Luke, Philip Ahn, Moses Gunn, Gregory Sierra, Keith Carradine, and Radames Pera. ABC–Warner Bros., 2004. 12 April 1973.

Byrne, John J. "Albert, Eddie." *Scribner Encyclopedia of American Lives.* New York: Scribner's, 2003–2005. 5–7.

Cameron, Ken, dir. *Oldest Living Confederate Widow Tells All.* 1993. Digital videodisc. With Diane Lane, Donald Sutherland, and Cicely Tyson. Konigsberg/Sanitsky–CBS–Mill Creek, 2017.

Canfield, J. Douglas. "Mavericks on the Border: The Early Southwest in Historical Fiction and Film." Lexington: University Press of Kentucky, 2001.

Cantú, Roberto. "Introduction." *Equestrian Rebels: Critical Perspectives on Mariano Azuela and the Novel of the Mexican Revolution.* Ed. Roberto Cantú. Newcastle upon Tyne: Cambridge Scholars, 2016. x–xxxiv.

Carpenter, John, dir. *Halloween.* 1978. Digital Blu-ray videodisc. With Jamie Lee Curtis and Donald Pleasance. Compass International Pictures–Starz–Anchor Bay, 2007.

Carrell, Jennifer Lee. "How the Bard Won the West." *Smithsonian* 29.5 (August 1998): 98–107.

Carroll, Noël. "The Professional Western: South of the Border." *Back in the Saddle Again: New Essays on the Western.* Ed. Edward Buscombe and Roberta A. Pearson. London: BFI Publishing, 1998. 46–62.

Casellas, Roberto. "Confederate Colonists in Mexico." *Americas* 27.9 (September 1975): 8–15.

Cass, David S., Sr., dir. *Lone Rider.* Film for television. With Lou Diamond Phillips, Stacy Keach, and Vincent Spano. Larry Levinson Productions, 2008.

Cassar, Jon, dir. *Forsaken.* Digital Blu-ray videodisc. With Kiefer Sutherland, Donald Sutherland, Michael Wincott, Brian Cox, Aaron Poole, and Demi Moore. Momentum, 2015.

Castel, Albert. "The Fort Pillow Massacre: A Fresh Examination of the Evidence." *Civil War History* 4.1 (March 1958): 37–50.

Works Cited

Castro Leal, Antonio. "Prólogo." *La sombra del caudillo*. 1929. By Martín Luis Guzmán. México: Editorial Porrúa, 1977. vii–xvi.
Català, Víctor [Caterina Albert i Paradís]. "El Calvari d'en 'Mitus'." *Obres completes*. Ed. Tomàs Tebé. 2nd ed. Barcelona: Editorial Selecta, 1972. 607–31.
Catton, Bruce. *Never Call Retreat*. 1965. New York: Washington Square–Simon, 1967.
Cavallaro, Dani. *The Chivalric Romance and the Essence of Fiction*. Jefferson: McFarland, 2016.
Cawelti, John G. "Savagery, Civilization and the Western Hero." John G. Cawelti, *The Six-Gun Mystique* (1971): 38–47. *Focus on the Western*. Ed. Jack Nachbar. Englewood Cliffs: Prentice, 1974. 57–63.
———. *The Six-Gun Mystique*. 2nd ed. Bowling Green: Bowling Green University Popular Press, 1984.
Cebula, Larry. "'For Want of the Actual Necessaries of Life.'" *Journal of the West* 36.4 (October 1997): 28–35.
Cervantes Saavedra, Miguel de. *El ingenioso hidalgo don Quijote de la Mancha*. Ed. Tom Lathrop. Newark: Juan de la Cuesta Hispanic Monographs, 2012.
Chamberlain, Kathleen P. "In the Shadow of Billy the Kid: Susan McSween and the Lincoln County War." *Montana* 55.4 (Winter 2005): 36–53.
Chrzanowski, Joseph. "Patricide and the Double in Carlos Fuentes's *Gringo Viejo*." *International Fiction Review* 16.1 (Winter 1989): 11–16.
Cicioni, Mirna. "Levi's Western: 'Professional Plot' and History in *If Not Now, When?*" *New Reflections on Primo Levi: Before and After Auschwitz*. Ed. Risa Sodi and Millicent Marcus. New York: Palgrave Macmillan, 2011. 157–70.
Cirlot, J.E. *A Dictionary of Symbols*. Trans. Jack Sage. Trans. from *Diccionario de símbolos tradicionales*. 2nd. ed. New York: Routledge & Kegan Paul Ltd., 1971. New York: Barnes and Noble, 1995.
Clandfield, David. "*Stagecoach* (1939)." Rpt. from "The Onomastic Code of *Stagecoach*," *Literature/Film Quarterly* 5 (Spring 1977). *Western Movies*. Ed. William T. Pilkington and Don Graham. Albuquerque: University of New Mexico Press, 1979. 31–39.
Clawson, W.H. "The Framework of *The Canterbury Tales*." *University of Toronto Quarterly* 20.2 (January 1950): 137–54.
Cleary, Thomas. *Code of the Samurai: A Modern Translation of the* Bushido Shoshinsu. Boston: Tuttle, 1999.
Clements, Eric L. "Bust and Bust in the Mining West." *Journal of the West* 35.4 (October 1996): 40–53.
Cloud, Barbara. *The Business of Newspapers on the Western Frontier*. Reno: University of Nevada Press, 1992.
Clover, Carol J. "Her Body, Himself: Gender in the Slasher Film." *Representations* 20 (Autumn 1987): 187–228. http://www.jstor.org/stable/2928507. Accessed 8/24/2017.
Cochran, Alice. "Jack Langrishe and the Theater of the Mining Frontier." *Colorado Magazine* 46.4 (1969): 324–37.
Cole, Tobias [Cameron Judd]. *The Sharpshooter: Brimstone*. New York: HarperTorch–HarperCollins, 2003.
———. *The Sharpshooter: Gold Fever*. New York: HarperTorch–HarperCollins, 2003.
———. *The Sharpshooter: Repentance Creek*. New York: HarperTorch–HarperCollins, 2003.
Cook, Pam, ed. *The Cinema Book*. London: BFI, 1985.
———. "Women." *The BFI Companion to the Western*. Ed. Edward Buscombe. New York: Athenaeum-MacMillan, 1988. 240–43.
Cooper, Helen. *The English Romance in Time: Transforming Motifs from Geoffrey of Monmouth to the Death of Shakespeare*. Oxford: Oxford University Press, 2004.
Cooper, Scott, dir. *Hostiles*. Digital Blu-ray videodisc. With Christian Bale, Wes Studi, Rosamund Pike, Stephen Lang, and Bill Camp. Lionsgate, 2017.

Works Cited

Coppola, Francis Ford, dir. *The Godfather Part III.* 1990. Digital videodisc. With Al Pacino, Eli Wallach, and Andy Garcia. Zoetrope-Paramount, 2005.
Corkin, Stanley. *Cowboys as Cold Warriors: The Western and U. S. History.* Philadelphia: Temple University Press, 2004.
Cornwall, Rebecca Foster, and Leonard J. Arrington. "Perpetuation of a Myth: Mormon Danites in Five Western Novels, 1840–90." *Brigham Young University Studies* 23.2 (Spring 1983): 147–65.
Coronado, Juan. "*Independencia y revolución (la historia de la novela)*." *Literatura Mexicana* 21.1 (2010): 83–99.
Cosío Villegas, Daniel. "Politics and Mexican Intellectuals." *The Intellectual in Politics.* Ed. H. Malcolm Macdonald. Austin: University of Texas Press, 1966. 24–34.
Cosmatos, George P., dir. *Tombstone.* Digital videodisc. With Kurt Russell, Val Kilmer, and Stephen Lang. Hollywood Pictures, 1993.
Costello, Matthew J. "'I Didn't Expect to Find Any Fences Around Here': Cultural Ambiguity and Containment in *Shane.*" *Journal of American Culture* 27.3 (2004): 261–70.
———. "Rewriting *High Noon*: Transformations in American Popular Political Culture During the Cold War, 1952–68." *Hollywood's West: The American Frontier in Film, Television, and History.* Ed. Peter C. Rollins and John E. O'Connor. Lexington: University Press of Kentucky, 2005. 175–97.
Costner, Kevin, dir. *Open Range.* Digital videodisc. With Kevin Costner, Robert Duvall, Annette Bening, Michael Gambon, and Abraham Benrubi. Touchstone, 2004.
Coursen, David F. "John Ford's Wilderness: *The Man Who Shot Liberty Valance.*" *Sight and Sound* 47.4 (Autumn 1978): 237–41.
Crane, Barry, dir. "The Vanishing Image." *Kung Fu.* Television series. Digital videodisc. With David Carradine, Keye Luke, Philip Ahn, Lew Ayres, Tom Nardini, Benson Fong, and Radames Pera. ABC–Warner Bros., 2004. 20 December 1974.
Crane, Stephen. "The Blue Hotel." *The Portable Stephen Crane.* Ed. Joseph Katz. 1969. New York: Penguin, 1977. 418–48.
———. "The Bride Comes to Yellow Sky." *The Portable Stephen Crane.* Ed. Joseph Katz. 1969. New York: Penguin, 1977. 391–402.
Crislip, Andrew. "The Sin of Sloth or the Illness of the Demons? The Demon of Acedia in Early Christian Monasticism." *Harvard Theological Review* 98.2 (April 2005): 143–69.
Cromwell, John, dir. *Dead Reckoning.* With Humphrey Bogart, Lizabeth Scott, and Morris Carnovsky. Columbia, 1947.
Cubillos, Bernardita M., and Carmen Sofía Brenes. "Pious Heroes of the Fordian Western: Action Patterns That Define Heroism in *My Darling Clementine* (1946) and *The Man Who Shot Liberty Valance* (1962)." *Journal of the West* 54.2 (Spring 2015): 9–24.
Curtiz, Michael, dir. *Dodge City.* 1939. Digital videodisc. With Errol Flynn, Olivia de Havilland, Alan Hale, and Henry Travers. Warner Bros., 2005.
Cutchins, Dennis. "*Shane* and *Man on Fire*: George Stevens' Enduring Legacy of Spirituality and Violence." *Adaptation Studies: New Approaches.* Ed. Christa Albrecht-Crane and Dennis Cutchins. Madison: Fairleigh Dickinson University Press, 2010. 180–94.
Dabove, Juan Pablo. *Nightmares of the Lettered City: Banditry and Literature in Latin America, 1816–1929.* Pittsburgh: University of Pittsburgh Press, 2007.
Danbom, David B. "Why Americans Value Rural Life." *Rural Development Perspectives* 12.1 (1995): 19–23.
Daves, Delmer. *Broken Arrow.* 1950. Digital videodisc. With James Stewart, Jeff Chandler, and Debra Paget. Twentieth Century Fox, 2007.

Works Cited

———. *The Hanging Tree*. With Gary Cooper, Maria Schell, Karl Malden, George C. Scott, Ben Piazza, and Karl Swenson. Warner Bros., 1959.
Davidson, Levette J. "Shakespeare in the Rockies." *Shakespeare Quarterly* 4.1 (January 1953): 39–49. http://www.jstor.org/stable/2866555. Accessed 12/15/2016.
Davis, David D. "Ten-Gallon Hero." *American Quarterly* 6.2 (Summer 1954): 111–25.
Day, Gary. "The State of *Dracula*: Bureaucracy and the Vampire." *Rereading Victorian Fiction*. Ed. Alice Jenkins and Juliet John. Basingstoke: Palgrave, 2000. 81–95.
De Toth, André, dir. *Carson City*. 1952. Digital videodisc. With Randolph Scott, Raymond Massey, Larry Keating, and Don Beddoe. Warner Bros., 2010.
———, dir. *Riding Shotgun*. 1954. Digital videodisc. With Randolph Scott, Wayne Morris, Joan Weldon, and James Bell. Warner Bros., 2006.
Deamer, Robert G. "Stephen Crane and the Western Myth." *Western American Literature* 7 (1972): 111–23.
Dean, James Seay. "Extreme Unction for Past Power and Glory: Four Fictions on the Mexican Revolution." *Revista de Estudios Hispánicos* 17.1 (January 1983): 89–106.
Deegan, Thomas. "Walter Scott and the American Western Film." *Scott in Carnival*. Ed. J. H. Alexander and David Hewitt. Aberdeen: Assn. for Scottish Lit. Studies, 1993. 569–80.
DeMille, Cecil B., dir. *Union Pacific*. 1939. Digital videodisc. With Barbara Stanwyck, Joel McCrea, Brian Donlevy, Akim Tamiroff, and Robert Preston. Universal, 2006.
Desser, David. "Kurosawa's 'Eastern Western': *Sanjuro* and the Influence of *Shane*." *Film Criticism* 8.1 (Fall 1983): 54–65.
———. "Remaking *Seven Samurai* in World Cinema." *East Asian Cinemas: Exploring Transnational Connections on Film*. Ed. Leon Hunt and Wing-Fai Leung. London: I. B. Tauris, 2006. 15–27.
———. *The Samurai Films of Akira Kurosawa*. Ann Arbor: University of Michigan Research Press, 1983.
Deutsch, James I. "After Johnny Came Marching Home: The Representation of Civil War Veterans in American Film." *Irish Journal of American Studies* 2 (December 1993): 129–39. http://www.jstor.org/stable/30003030. Accessed 02/14/2012.
di Paolo, Maria Grazia. "D'Annunzio's *Giuliana*. Mistress and Muse." *Italica* 88.3 (2011): 381–96.
Dieterle, William, dir. *The Story of Louis Pasteur*. With Paul Muni, Josephine Hutchinson, Fritz Lieber, Porter Hall, and Halliwell Hobbes. Warner Bros., 1936.
Dillon, Brian Dervin, and David Erin Dillon. "Wyatt and Josie Earp: Fact, Fiction, and Myth." *Western States Jewish History* 48.1 (Fall 2015): 27–44.
Dmytryk, Edward, dir. *Cornered*. 1945. Digital videodisc. With Dick Powell, Walter Slezak, Morris Carnovsky, and Luther Adler. RKO–Warner Bros., 2010.
———, dir. *Crossfire*. 1947. Digital videodisc. With Robert Mitchum, Robert Young, Robert Ryan, Sam Levene, and Gloria Grahame. Warner Bros.–Turner Entertainment, 2005.
———, dir. *Warlock*. 1959. Digital videodisc. With Richard Widmark, Henry Fonda, and Anthony Quinn. Twentieth Century Fox, 2005.
Douglas, Gordon, dir. *Only the Valiant*. 1950. Digital videodisc. With Gregory Peck, Barbara Payton, Ward Bond, Gig Young, Lon Chaney, Jr., Herbert Heyes, and Michael Ansara. Republic, 2008.
Dubin, Charles S., dir. "The Third Man." *Kung Fu*. Television series. Digital videodisc. With David Carradine, Keye Luke, Philip Ahn, Ed Nelson, Sheree North, and Radames Pera. ABC–Warner Bros., 2004. 26 April 1973.
Duffey, J. Patrick. "A War of Words: Orality and Literacy in Mariano Azuela's *Los de Abajo*." *Romance Notes* 38.2 (1998): 173–78.
Dwan, Allan, dir. *Frontier Marshal*. 1939. Digital videodisc. With Randolph Scott, Cesar

Works Cited

Romero, Nancy Kelly, John Carradine, and Binnie Barnes. Twentieth Century Fox, 2012.
Dykstra, Robert R. "Overdosing on Dodge City." *Western Historical Quarterly* 27.4 (Winter 1996): 505–14. http://www.jstor.org/stable/970535. Accessed 01/17/2014.
Early, Emmett. *The Alienated War Veteran in Film and Literature*. Jefferson: McFarland, 2014.
Eastwood, Clint, dir. *Pale Rider*. 1985. Digital videodisc. With Clint Eastwood, Michael Moriarty, Richard Dysart, and Carrie Snodgress. Warner Bros., 2000.
Eckstein, Arthur M. "Incest and Miscegenation in *The Searchers* (1956) and *The Unforgiven* (1959)." *The Searchers: Essays and Reflections on John Ford's Classic Western*. Ed. and Introduction Arthur M. Eckstein, ed. Peter Lehman. Detroit: Wayne State University Press, 2004. 197–221.
Eddings, Dennis W. "Lew Wallace." *Nineteenth Century American Fiction Writers*. Ed. Kent P. Ljungquist. Detroit: Gale, 1999. 278–83.
Edgar, Irving I. "Modern Surgery and Lord Lister." *Journal of the History of Medicine and Allied Sciences* 16.2 (April 1961): 145–60. http://www.jstor.org/stable/24620815. Accessed 6/12/2017.
Eickhoff, Randy Lee. "Anonymous." *Boot Hill: An Anthology of the West*. Ed. Robert J. Randisi. New York: Tom Doherty Associates, 2002. 161–80.
Eidson, Thomas. *The Missing*. New York: Random House, 2003. Rpt. of *The Last Ride*. 1995.
Engel, Leonard. "Mythic Space and Monument Valley: Another Look at John Ford's *Stagecoach*." *Literature/Film Quarterly* 3.22 (1994): 174–80.
Engelhardt, Tom. *The End of Victory Culture: Cold War America and the Disillusioning of a Generation*. 2nd paperback ed. Amherst: University of Massachusetts Press, 1998.
Englekirk, John E. "Doña Bárbara, Legend of the Llano." *Hispania* 31.3 (August 1948): 259–70. http://www.jstor.org/stable/333036. Accessed 11/17/2017.
Enright, Ray, dir. *The Spoilers*. 1942. Digital videodisc. With Marlene Dietrich, Randolph Scott, and John Wayne. Universal, 2004.
_____. *Trail Street*. With Randolph Scott, Robert Ryan, George "Gabby" Hayes, and Anne Jeffreys. RKO, 1947.
Erisman, Fred. "*Stagecoach* in Space: The Legacy of *Firefly*." *Extrapolation* 47.2 (Summer 2006): 249–58.
Etulain, Richard W. *Telling Western Stories: From Buffalo Bill to Larry McMurtry*. Albuquerque: University of New Mexico Press, 1965.
Fairlamb, Brian. "'ONE IN A THOUSAND': Western Stars, Heroes and Their Guns." *CineAction!* 46 (1998): 18–25.
Farrow, John, dir. *Copper Canyon*. With Ray Milland, Hedy Lamarr, Macdonald Carey, Frank Faylen, and Mona Freeman. Paramount, 1950.
Fatout, Paul. "Ambrose Bierce (1842–1914)." *American Literary Realism* 1 (1967): 13–19.
Feist, Felix, dir. *The Man Behind the Gun*. 1953. Digital videodisc. With Randolph Scott, Roy Roberts, Patrice Wymore, and Philip Carey. Warner Bros., 2006.
Fenton, Leslie, dir. *Whispering Smith*. 1948. Digital videodisc. With Alan Ladd, Robert Preston, Brenda Marshall, Donald Crisp, and William Demarest. Paramount-Universal, 2014.
Fields, Armond. *Eddie Foy: A Biography of the Early Popular Stage Comedian*. Jefferson: McFarland, 1999.
Fishburn, Evelyn. "Traces of the *Thousand and One Nights* in Borges." *Variaciones Borges* 17 (2004): 143–58.
FitzGerald, Michael Ray. "The Indianized White Man and the Anglicized Indian: Imperial and Anti-Imperial Discourse in NBC's *Daniel Boone*, 1964–1970." *Journal of American Culture* 37.3 (September 2014): 281–89.

Works Cited

Fitzpatrick, Tara. "The Figure of Captivity: The Cultural Work of the Puritan Captivity Narrative." *American Literary History* 3.1 (Spring 1991): 1–26. http://www.jstor.org/stable/489730. Accessed 8/23/2017.

Flaubert, Gustave. *Madame Bovary.* 1856. Paris: Garnier-Flammarion, 1966.

Fleischer, Richard, dir. *The Narrow Margin.* 1952. Digital videodisc. With Charles McGraw, Marie Windsor, Jacqueline White, and Don Beddoe. RKO-Warner, 2005.

Fleming, Ian. *Live and Let Die.* New York: Signet, 1954.

Flickinger, Roy C. "Dramatic Irony in Terence." *Classical Weekly* 3.24 (23 April 1910): 202–05. http://www.jstor.org/stable/4386219. Accessed 5/28/2016.

Fojas, Camilla. *Border Bandits: Hollywood on the Southern Frontier.* Austin: University of Texas Press, 2008.

Folsom, James K. *The American Western Novel.* New Haven: College and University Press, 1966.

——. "Imaginative Safety Valves: Frontier Themes in the Literature of the Gilded Age." *The Frontier Experience and the American Dream: Essays on American Literature.* Ed. David Mogen, Mark Busby, and Paul Bryant. College Station: Texas A&M University Press, 1989. 87–94.

Forbes, John D. "Lew Wallace, Romantic." *Indiana Magazine of History* 44.4 (December 1948): 385–92. http://www.jstor.org/stable/27787717. Accessed 6/1/2017.

Ford, John, dir. *Fort Apache.* 1948. Digital Blu-ray videodisc. With John Wayne, Henry Fonda, Ward Bond, John Agar, Shirley Temple, and Pedro Armendariz. Argosy–Warner Bros., 2012.

——, dir. *The Horse Soldiers.* 1959. Digital videodisc. With John Wayne, William Holden, Constance Towers, Carleton Young, Basil Ruysdael, and Althea Gibson. Mirisch-MGM, 2001.

——, dir. *The Man Who Shot Liberty Valance.* 1962. Digital videodisc. With James Stewart, John Wayne, Lee Marvin, Vera Miles, Andy Devine, Carleton Young, John Carradine, and Edmond O'Brien. Paramount, 2001.

——, dir. *My Darling Clementine.* 1946. Digital videodisc. With Henry Fonda, Victor Mature, Linda Darnell, and Walter Brennan. Twentieth Century Fox, 2003.

——, dir. *Rio Grande.* 1950. Digital videodisc. With John Wayne, Maureen O'Hara, Ben Johnson, and Victor McLaglen. Argosy-Republic, 2002.

——, dir. *The Searchers.* 1956. Digital Blu-ray videodisc. With John Wayne, Jeffrey Hunter, Natalie Wood, Ward Bond, Henry Brandon, Karl Swenson, and Olive Carey. Warner Bros., 2006.

Ford, Thomas W. *A.B. Guthrie, Jr.* Boston: Twayne–G.K. Hall, 1981.

Foster, Gaines M. "The Fort Pillow Massacre: An Essay Review." *Louisiana History* 48.2 (April 2007): 227–30.

Fowler, Gene, Jr., dir. *The Oregon Trail.* With Fred MacMurray, John Carradine, William Bishop, Henry Hull, Gloria Talbott, and Nina Shipman. Twentieth Century Fox, 1959.

France, Anatole. *The Queen Pedauque.* Trans. Jos. A.V. Stritzko. Introduction James Branch Cabell. Project Gutenberg, 2004. Project Gutenberg. Web.

The Fredericksburg Campaign: Decision on the Rappahannock. Ed. Gary W. Gallagher. Chapel Hill: University of North Carolina Press, 1995.

Freedman, Jonathan. "The Affect of the Market: Economic and Racial Exchange in *The Searchers.*" *American Literary History* 12.3 (2000): 585–99.

Freese, Peter. "The 'Journey of Life' in American Fiction." *The Journey of Life in American Life and Literature.* Heidelberg: Universitätsverlag Winter, 2015. 17–63.

French, Philip. *Westerns: Aspects of a Movie Genre.* Rev. ed. New York: Oxford University Press, 1977.

Frisch, Mark. "Re-Reading the Past: Fiction and Historical Discourse in Borges and

Works Cited

Rodolfo Usigli's *El Gesticulador* and *Corona de Sombra.*" *Variaciones Borges* 32 (2011): 133–48.
Frye, Northrop. *Anatomy of Criticism: Four Essays.* 1957. Princeton: Princeton University Press, 1973.
Fuentes, Carlos. *Gringo viejo.* 1985. México: Fondo de Cultura Económica, 1986.
Fuller, Samuel, dir. *Forty Guns.* 1957. Digital videodisc. With Barbara Stanwyck, Barry Sullivan, Dean Jagger, Gene Barry, Eve Brent, Gerald Miton, and John Ericson. Twentieth Century Fox, 2005.
Fuqua, Antoine, dir. *The Magnificent Seven.* Digital Blu-ray videodisc. With Denzel Washington, Chris Pratt, Haley Bennett, Peter Sarsgaard, Ethan Hawke, Lee Byung-Hun, Vincent D'Onofrio, Manuel Garcia-Rulfo, Mark Ashworth, and Martin Sensmeier. MGM-Columbia, 2016.
Furness, Edna L. "Image of the Schoolteacher in Western Literature." *Arizona Quarterly* 18 (1962): 346–57.
Gale, Robert L. "Ernest Haycox." *Fifty Western Writers: A Bio-Bibliographical Sourcebook.* Ed. Fred Erisman and Richard W. Etulain. Westport: Greenwood, 1982. 183–93.
Gallafent, Edward. "Going Straight: The Past and the Future in *The Return of Frank James* (1940)." *Movie* 3 (December 2011): 22–28.
Gallagher, Tag. *John Ford: The Man and His Films.* Berkeley: University of California Press, 1986.
―――. "Shoot-Out at the Genre Corral: Problems in the 'Evolution' of the Western." *Film Genre Reader IV.* Ed. Barry Keith Grant. Austin: University of Texas Press, 2012. 298–312.
Gallegos, Rómulo. *Doña Bárbara.* Ed. Domingo Miliani. 1997. Madrid: Cátedra, 2007.
Galloway, Patrick. *Stray Dogs & Lone Wolves: The Samurai Film Handbook.* 2005. Berkeley: Stone Bridge Press, 2010.
Gannon, Barbara A. "*Fort Pillow: A Civil War Massacre and Public Memory.*" *Civil War History* 53.3 (September 2007): 304–06.
García Cantú, Gastón. "La sombra de Obregón." *Vuelta* 69 (1982): 30–35.
Gollnick, Brian. "Pancho Villa: Icon of Insurgency." *Latin American Icons: Fame Across Borders.* Ed. Patrick O'Connor and Dianna C. Niebylski. Nashville: Vanderbilt University Press, 2014. 21–33.
González, Alfonso. "Onomastics and Creativity in *Doña Bárbara* and *Pedro Páramo.*" *Names* 21 (1974): 40–45.
Gormley, Lane. "From Des Esseintes to Roquentin: Toward a New Decadence?" *Kentucky Romance Quarterly* 27 (1980): 179–87.
Graebner, Norman A. "The Mexican War: A Study in Causation." *Pacific Historical Review* 49.3 (August 1980): 405–26. http://www.jstor.org/stable/3638563. Accessed 4/21/2018.
Graham, Allison. "The Final Go-Around: Peckinpah's Wild Bunch at the End of the Frontier." *Mosaic* 16.1–2 (Winter-Spring 1983): 55–70.
Graham, Kathleen A. "The Role of the Town Bank in the Agrarian United States." *Financial History* (Fall 2004): 14–17.
Grant, Richard B. *Théophile Gautier.* Twayne's World Authors Series. New York: G.K. Hall–Twayne, 1975.
Gray, John S. "The Story of Mrs. Picotte-Galpin, a Sioux Heroine Eagle Woman Learns About White Ways and Racial Conflict, 1820–1868." *Montana* 36.2 (Spring 1986): 2–21.
Green, Paul. *Encyclopedia of Weird Westerns: Supernatural and Science Fiction Elements in Novels, Pulps, Comics, Films, Television, and Games.* Jefferson: McFarland, 2009.
Greene, Jerome A. "The Coming Home Trail." *Kansas History* 38.4 (Winter 2015/2016): 223–28.

Works Cited

Greenwald, Michael L. "Rough-Hewn Stages: Shakespeare on the American Frontier." *Shakespeare and Renaissance Association of West Virginia* 8 (1983): 38–48.
Gressley, Gene M. *Bankers and Cattlemen.* New York: Knopf, 1966.
Grindon, Leger. "Cycles and Clusters: The Shape of Film Genre History." *Film Genre Reader IV.* Ed. Barry Keith Grant and Roberta A. Pearson. Austin: University of Texas Press, 2012. 42–59.
Gruber, Frank. *The Pulp Jungle.* Los Angeles: Sherbourne Press, 1967.
Guinn, Jeff. *The Last Gunfight: The Real Story of the Shootout at the O.K. Corral—and How It Changed the American West.* New York: Simon, 2011.
Gunn, Drewey Wayne. "A Labyrinth of Mirrors: Literary Sources of *The Old Gringo/Gringo Viejo.*" *Revista de Estudios Hispánicos* 27.1 (January 1992): 61–79.
Guthrie, A.B., Jr. "First Principal." *Gunsmoke,* 1953. *The Arbor House Treasury of Great Western Stories.* Ed. Bill Pronzini and Martin H. Greenberg. 1982. New York: Arbor House, 1989. 285–93.
Gutiérrez Vélez, Georgina García. "Carlos Fuentes y Diego Rivera: protagonistas creadores de los 'Renacimientos' en México." *The Reptant Eagle: Essays on Carlos Fuentes and the Art of the Novel.* Ed. Roberto Cantú. Newcastle upon Tyne: Cambridge Scholars, 2015. 144–69.
Guzmán, Martín Luis. *La sombra del caudillo.* 1929. Prólogo de Antonio Castro Leal. México: Porrúa, 1977.
Gyurko, Lanin A. "Fuentes, Guzmán, and the Mexican Political Novel." *Ibero-Amerikanisches Archiv* 16.4 (1990): 545–610.
_____. "Self and Double in Fuentes' *Gringo viejo.*" *Ibero-Amerikanisches Archiv* 17.2–3 (1991): 175–244.
_____. "Twentieth-Century Fiction." *Mexican Literature: A History.* Ed. David William Foster. Austin: University of Texas Press, 1994. 243–303.
Haberly, David T. "Scotland on the Pampas: A Conjectural History of *Facundo.*" *Bulletin of Spanish Studies* 83.6 (September 2006): 789–813.
Haid, Charles, dir. *Riders of the Purple Sage.* 1995. Digital videodisc. With Ed Harris, Amy Madigan, and G.D. Spradlin. TNT–Warner Bros., 2012.
Hall, Ken. "*Blind Swordsman: Zatoichi* by Kitano Takeshi: Not a Mere 'Entertainment.'" *Asian Cinema* 16.2 (Fall/Winter 2005): 45–62.
_____. "'Chac Mool,' a Vampire Text: Stoker, Maupassant, and Other Antecedents." *Studies in Honor of Lanin A. Gyurko.* Ed. Ken Hall and Ruth Muñoz-Hjelm. Newark: Juan de la Cuesta, 2009. 319–33. Juan de la Cuesta Hispanic Monographs 32.
_____. "*Gringo Viejo* and the Elegiac Western." *University of Dayton Review* 23.2 (Spring 1995): 137–47.
Hall, Kenneth E. "Custer and the 7th Cavalry." *Studies in the Western* 23 (2015): 7–20.
_____. "From *The Iron Horse* to *Hell on Wheels*: The Transcontinental Railroad in the Western." *Studies in the Western* 22 (2014): 11–22.
_____. "Newspapermen in the Western." *Studies in the Western* 13 (2005): 31–50.
_____. "*The Searchers*: Image and Sound." *Studies in the Western* 18 (2010): 51–65.
_____. *Stonewall Jackson and Religious Faith in Military Command.* Jefferson: McFarland, 2005.
Halverson, Cathryn. "Violent Housekeepers: Rewriting Domesticity in *Riders of the Purple Sage.*" *Rocky Mountain Review of Language and Literature* 56.1 (2002): 37–53. http://www.jstor.org/stable/1348012. Accessed 9/13/2013.
Handley, William R. "Distinctions Without Differences: Zane Grey and the Mormon Question." *Arizona Quarterly* 57.1 (Spring 2001): 1–33.
Hardy, B. Carmon. *Solemn Covenant: The Mormon Polygamous Passage.* Urbana: University of Illinois Press, 1992.

Works Cited

Harmon, William and C. Hugh Holman. *A Handbook to Literature*. 8th ed. Upper Saddle River: Prentice, 2000.
Harris, Chris. "Mariano Azuela's *Los de Abajo*: Patriarchal Masculinity and Mexican Gender Regimes Under Fire." *Bulletin of Hispanic Studies* 87.6 (2010): 645–66.
Haskin, Byron, dir. *Denver & Rio Grande*. 1952. Digital Blu-ray videodisc. With Edmond O'Brien, Sterling Hayden, Dean Jagger, Laura Elliot, and Lyle Bettger. Paramount-Olive, 2012.
———, dir. *Silver City*. 1951. Digital Blu-ray videodisc. With Edmond O'Brien, Yvonne De Carlo, Barry Fitzgerald, Richard Arlen, and Laura Elliott. Paramount-Olive, 2012.
———, dir. *Warpath*. With Edmond O'Brien, Dean Jagger, Forrest Tucker, and Polly Bergen. Paramount, 1951.
Haslip, Joan. *The Crown of Mexico: Maximilian and His Empress Carlota*. New York: Holt, 1971.
Hathaway, Henry, dir. *5 Card Stud*. 1968. Digital videodisc. With Dean Martin, Robert Mitchum, Yaphet Kotto, Inger Stevens, and Roddy McDowall. Paramount, 2002.
———, dir. *Nevada Smith*. 1966. Digital videodisc. With Steve McQueen, Brian Keith, Karl Malden, Suzanne Pleshette, Arthur Kennedy, Martin Landau, Raf Vallone, and Howard Da Silva. Paramount, 2007.
———, dir. *The Sons of Katie Elder*. 1965. Digital videodisc. With John Wayne, Dean Martin, Earl Holliman, Dennis Hopper, John Doucette, James Gregory, Rhys Williams, Michael Anderson, Jr., Martha Hyer, and Jeremy Slate. Paramount, 2001.
Hawks, Howard, dir. *El Dorado*. 1966. Digital Blu-ray videodisc. With John Wayne, Robert Mitchum, James Caan, Arthur Hunnicutt, Ed Asner, Paul Fix, Christopher George, Michele Carey, Charlene Holt, R.G. Armstrong, and Anthony Rogers. Paramount–Warner Bros., 2014.
Haycox, Ernest. "High Wind." 1934. *The Arbor House Treasury of Great Western Stories*. Ed. Bill Pronzini and Martin H. Greenberg. 1982. New York: Arbor House, 1989. 257–70.
Hazera, Lydia D. "The Making of Two Guerrilla Generals in Azuela's *The Underdogs* and Traven's Jungle Novels." *B. Traven: Life and Work*. Ed. Ernst Schürer and Philip Jenkins. University Park: Penn State University Press, 1987. 345–56.
Heffernan, Jeanne. "'Poised Between Savagery and Civilization': Forging Political Communities in Ford's Westerns." *Perspectives on Political Science* 28.3 (Summer 1999): 147–51.
Heinze, Andrew R. "The Morality of Reservation: Western Lands in the Cleveland Period, 1885–1897." *Journal of the West* 31.3 (July 1992): 81–89.
Heinze, Rüdiger. "American Outsiders at the Center: Mormons and the West." *Crisscrossing Borders in Literature of the American West*. Ed. Reginald Dyck and Cheli Reutter. New York: Palgrave Macmillan–St. Martin's, 2009.
Henry, Will. *Frontier Fury*. New York: Leisure-Dorchester, 2008.
Herbst, Gerhard Raymond. *Mexican Society as Seen through the Literary Works of Mariano Azuela*. Diss. Ann Arbor: University of Michigan, 1973.
Herwig, Holger H., and Christon I. Archer. "Global Gambit: A German General Staff Assessment of Mexican Affairs, November 1913." *Mexican Studies/Estudios Mexicanos* 1.2 (Summer 1985): 303–27. http://www.jstor.org/stable/1052040. Accessed 12/15/2016.
Hessler, Gordon, dir. "Ambush." *Kung Fu*. Television series. Digital videodisc. With David Carradine, Keye Luke, John Carradine, Rhonda Fleming, Timothy Carey, Pat Morita, and Radames Pera. ABC–Warner Bros., 2004. 4 April 1975.
Hibbs, Jesse, dir. *Walk the Proud Land*. With Audie Murphy, Anne Bancroft, and Charles Drake. Universal, 1956.
Hill, Richard A. "You've Come a Long Way, Dude—a History." *American Speech* 69.3 (Autumn 1994): 321–27. http://www.jstor.org/stable/455525. Accessed 11/22/2017.

Works Cited

Hill, Walter. *Geronimo: An American Legend.* 1993. Digital videodisc. With Jason Patric, Wes Studi, Gene Hackman, and Matt Damon. Walter Hill–Neil Canton–Columbia, 1998.

Hinckley, Henry Barrett. "The Framing-Tale." *Modern Language Notes* 49.2 (February 1934): 69–80. http://www.jstor.org/stable/2912740. Accessed 7/07/2017.

Hine, Robert V. *The American West: An Interpretive History.* Boston: Little, 1973.

Hitchcock, Alfred, dir. *Marnie.* 1964. Digital videodisc. With Tippi Hedren, Sean Connery, Diane Baker, Martin Gabel, and Louise Latham. Universal, 2006.

Homans, Peter. "Puritanism Revisited: An Analysis of the Contemporary Screen-Image Western." *Studies in Public Communication* 3 (1961): 73–84.

Hooper, Tobe, dir. *The Texas Chainsaw Massacre.* 1974. Digital Blu-ray videodisc. With Marilyn Burns and Gunnar Hansen. Vortex-Dark Sky Films, 2014.

Hoppenstand, Gary. "Hollywood Cowboys and Confederates in Mexico: Andrew V. McLaglen's *The Undefeated* (1969)." *Popular Culture Review* 14.1 (2003): 121–28.

Houck, Helen Phipps. "Las obras novelescas de Martín Luis Guzmán." *Revista Iberoamericana* 3 (1941): 139–58.

Howard, David, dir. *Legion of the Lawless.* 1940. Digital videodisc. With George O'Brien, Virginia Vale, Herbert Heywood, Norman Willis, Hugh Sothern, Eddy Waller, and Bud Osborne. RKO–Grapevine Video, 2014.

———, dir. *Trouble in Sundown.* With George O'Brien, Howard Hickman, Rosalind Keith, Ward Bond, Chill Wills, Cy Kendall, and Monte Montague. RKO, 1939.

Howard, Ron, dir. *The Missing.* Digital videodisc. With Cate Blanchett, Tommy Lee Jones, Aaron Eckhart, Evan Rachel Wood, Eric Schweig, and Ray McKinnon. Columbia, 2004.

Humberstone, H. Bruce, dir. *Ten Wanted Men.* With Randolph Scott, Jocelyn Brando, Richard Boone, and Alfonso Bedoya. Ranown-Columbia, 1955.

Hunter, Evan. "The Killing at Triple Tree." 1953. *A Century of Great Western Stories.* Ed. John Jakes. New York: Forge–Tom Doherty, 2000. 258–69.

Hunter, Stephen. *G-Man: A Bob Lee Swagger Novel.* New York: Putnam's, 2017.

Hurst, G. Cameron III. "Death, Honor, and Loyality [sic]: The Bushidō Ideal." *Philosophy East and West* 40.4 (October 1990): 511–27. http://www.jstor.org/stable/1399355. Accessed 11/21/2016.

Huston, John. *The Treasure of the Sierra Madre.* 1947. Digital Blu-ray videodisc. With Humphrey Bogart, Walter Huston, Tim Holt, Bruce Bennett, and Alfonso Bedoya. Warner Bros., 2010.

———. *The Unforgiven.* 1960. Digital videodisc. With Burt Lancaster, Audrey Hepburn, Lillian Gish, Audie Murphy, Joseph Wiseman, Charles Bickford, and Albert Salmi. Hecht-Hill-Lancaster-MGM, 2003.

Indick, William. *The Psychology of the Western: How the American Psyche Plays Out on Screen.* Jefferson: McFarland, 2008.

Ingrassia, Catherine. "'I'm not Kicking, I'm Talking': Discursive Economies in the Western." *Film Criticism* 20 (Spring 1996): 4–14.

Jarmy Sumano, Myriam. "Ancona Albertos, Antonio." *Diccionario de escritores mexicanos siglo XX. Desde las generaciones del Ateneo y novelistas de la Revolución hasta nuestros días.* Ed. Aurora M. Ocampo. Tomo 1 (A-Ch). México: Universidad Nacional Autónoma de México, 1988. 57.

Jenkins, Jennifer Lei. "The Mexican Revolution as Western Vengeance Quest: Azuela's *Los de Abajo.*" *Paradoxa: Studies in World Literary Genres* 19 (2004): 94–115.

Jensen, Kelly. "Acceptable Violence: How the Cowboys 'Civilized' the U.S." *The Image of Violence in Literature, Media, and Society II.* Ed. Will Wright and Steven Kaplan. Pueblo: Society for the Interdisciplinary Study of Social Imagery, Colorado State University-Pueblo, 2007. 3–7.

Works Cited

Johnson, Dorothy M. "War Shirt." *Indian Country*. Foreword Jack Schaefer. Lincoln: University of Nebraska Press, 1996. 108–26.
Johnson, William Weber. *Heroic Mexico: The Violent Emergence of a Modern Nation*. Garden City: Doubleday, 1968.
Jones, Oakah L. "Lew Wallace: Hoosier Governor of Territorial New Mexico, 1878–81." *New Mexico Historical Review* 60.2 (1985): 129–58.
Judd, Cameron. *The Quest of Brady Kenton/Kenton's Challenge*. New York: St. Martin's, 2001.
Jurkevich, Gayana. "*Abulia*, Nineteenth Century Psychology and the Generation of 1898." *Hispanic Review* 60.2 (Spring 1992): 181–94. http://www.jstor.org/stable/474109. Accessed 2/26/2018.
Kaes, Anton. "A Stranger in the House: Fritz Lang's *Fury* and the Cinema of Exile." *New German Critique* 89 (Spring–Summer 2003): 33–58.
Kaminsky, Stuart M. *American Film Genres: Approaches to a Critical Theory of Popular Film*. N.p.: Pflaum Publishing, 1974.
Kane, Joseph, dir. *King of the Pecos*. 1936. Digital Blu-ray videodisc. With John Wayne, Muriel Evans, Cy Kendall, Jack Clifford, Arthur Aylesworth, and Herbert Heywood. Republic/Paramount-Olive, 2013.
———, dir. *The Lawless Nineties*. With John Wayne, Ann Rutherford, and George Hayes. Republic, 1936.
Karlson, Phil, dir. *The Phenix City Story*. 1955. Digital videodisc. With Richard Kiley, John McIntire, Edward Andrews, and Kathryn Grant. Allied Artists–Warner Bros.–TCM, 2010.
Kasdan, Lawrence, dir. *Silverado*. 1985. Digital videodisc. With Kevin Costner, Kevin Kline, Scott Glenn, John Cleese, Danny Glover, Rosanna Arquette, Linda Hunt, Brian Dennehy, and Jeff Goldblum. Columbia, 1999.
———, dir. *Wyatt Earp*. 1994. Digital Blu-ray videodisc. With Kevin Costner, Dennis Quaid, Joanna Going, Michael Madsen, Gene Hackman, and Mare Winningham. Warner Bros., 2011.
Katz, Friedrich. "Alemania y Francisco Villa." *Historia Mexicana* 12.45 (July 1962): 88–102.
———. *The Life and Times of Pancho Villa*. Stanford: Stanford University Press, 1998.
Katzin, Lee H., dir. *Heaven with a Gun*. With Glenn Ford, Carolyn Jones, Barbara Hershey, John Anderson, David Carradine, James Griffith, Harry Townes, and Bill Bryant. King Bros.–MGM, 1969.
Katzman, David M. "The Children of Abraham and Hannah: Grocer, Doctor, Entrepreneur: The Summerfields of Lawrence, Kansas." *Kansas History* 37.1 (Spring 2014): 2–19.
Kazan, Elia. "Elia Kazan on 'Zapata.'" Letter to the editor. *Saturday Review* 5 April 1952: 22–23.
———, dir. *Panic in the Streets*. 1950. Digital videodisc. With Richard Widmark, Paul Douglas, Jack Palance, Zero Mostel, and Barbara Bel Geddes. 20th Century Fox, 2004.
———, dir. *Viva Zapata!* 1952. Digital Blu-ray videodisc. With Marlon Brando, Anthony Quinn, Joseph Wiseman, Jean Peters, and Frank Silvera. 20th Century Fox, 2013.
Kelly, Thomas O., II. "Whites and Indians and White Indians: *The Last of the Mohicans* from James Fenimore Cooper to Daniel Day Lewis." *James Fenimore Cooper* 11 (1997): 64–68.
Kennedy, Burt, dir. *Return of The Magnificent Seven*. 1966. Digital Blu-ray videodisc. With Yul Brynner, Warren Oates, Claude Akins, Robert Fuller, Emilio Fernandez, and Fernando Rey. MGM–20th Century Fox, 2010.
King, Henry, dir. *The Bravados*. 1958. Digital videodisc. With Gregory Peck, Joan Collins, Stephen Boyd, Albert Salmi, and Henry Silva. Twentieth Century Fox, 2005.

Works Cited

———, dir. *The Gunfighter.* 1950. Digital videodisc. With Gregory Peck, Helen Westcott, Millard Mitchell, Jean Parker, Karl Malden, and Skip Homeier. Twentieth Century Fox, 2008.

———, dir. *Jesse James.* 1939. Digital videodisc. With Tyrone Power, Henry Fonda, Randolph Scott, and Henry Hull. Twentieth Century Fox, 2006.

Kirkland, Hardee, dir. "Friends in San Rosario." Selig–General Film Company, 1912. https://pro-labs.imdb.com/title/tt1152327/.

Kitano, Takeshi, dir. *The Blind Swordsman: Zatoichi.* 2003. Digital videodisc. With Kitano Takeshi and Tadanobu Asano. Bandai Visual/Tokyo Film/Dentsu/TV Asahi/Saito Entertainment/Office Kitano-Miramax, 2004.

Kitses, Jim. *Horizons West: Anthony Mann, Budd Boetticher, Sam Peckinpah: Studies of Authorship Within the Western.* Bloomington: Indiana University Press, 1969.

———. *Horizons West: Directing the Western from John Ford to Clint Eastwood.* Rev. ed. London: British Film Institute, 2004.

Klapp, Orrin E. "The Creation of Popular Heroes." *American Journal of Sociology* 54.2 (September 1948): 135–41. http://www.jstor.org/stable/2771362. Accessed 07/13/2015.

Knapp, Bettina L. "Huysmans's 'Against the Grain': The Willed Exile of the Introverted Decadent." *Nineteenth Century French Studies* 20.1–2 (Fall–Winter 1991–1992): 203–21.

Knight, Alan. *The Mexican Revolution: A Very Short Introduction.* Oxford: Oxford University Press, 2016.

———. *The Mexican Revolution: Porfirians, Liberals and Peasants.* 1986. Lincoln: University of Nebraska Press, 1990.

Knight, Oliver. "The Frontier Newspaper as a Catalyst of Social Change." *Pacific Northwest Quarterly* 58 (April 1967): 74–81.

Kolb, Harold J., Jr. "Mark Twain and the Myth of the West." *The Mythologizing of Mark Twain.* Ed. Sara deSaussure Davis and Philip D. Beidler. Tuscaloosa: University of Alabama Press, 1984. 119–35.

Krapp, Peter. "*Unforgiven*: Fausse Reconnaissance." *South Atlantic Quarterly* 101.3 (Summer 2002): 589–607.

Krauel, Javier. "Ángel Ganivet's *Idearium Español* as *Fin-de-Siècle* Imperial Melancholia." *Revista Hispánica Moderna* 65.2 (2012): 181–97.

Krauze, Enrique. "La comedia mexicana de Carlos Fuentes." *Vuelta* 139 (June 1988): 15–27.

Kronik, John W. "Usigli's *El gesticulador* and the Fiction of Truth." *Latin American Theatre Review* 11.1 (1977): 5–16.

Kross, Peter. "New York Newspaperman Moses Beach Undertook a Secret Mission for President James K. Polk at the Height of the War with Mexico. Mission to Mexico—Moses Y. Beach, Secret Agent." *Military Heritage* 13.5 (February 2012): 16+.

Kuchta, Todd M. "Framing the 'Horror': Voice and Voice-Over in *Heart of Darkness* and *Apocalypse Now.*" *Studies in the Humanities* 21.1 (June 1994): 45–59.

Kurosawa, Akira, dir. *Seven Samurai.* 1954. Digital videodisc. With Mifune Toshiro and Shimura Takashi. Janus-Toho-Criterion, 1998.

LaFrance, David G. "*Madero, Serdán y los albores del movimiento revolucionario en Puebla.*" *Historia Mexicana* 29.3 (July 1979): 472–512.

Lanfield, Sidney, dir. *Station West.* With Dick Powell, Jane Greer, Agnes Moorhead, Burl Ives, Tom Powers, and Raymond Burr. RKO, 1948.

Lang, Fritz, dir. *The Big Heat.* 1953. Digital videodisc. With Glenn Ford, Gloria Grahame, Lee Marvin, Alexander Scourby, Jocelyn Brando, Peter Whitney, and Jeanette Nolan. Columbia Pictures, 2001.

———, dir. *Rancho Notorious.* With Marlene Dietrich, Arthur Kennedy, and Mel Ferrer. RKO, 1952.

Works Cited

———, dir. *The Return of Frank James*. 1940. Digital videodisc. With Henry Fonda, Gene Tierney, Henry Hull, and John Carradine. Twentieth Century Fox, 2006.

———, dir. *Western Union*. With Robert Young, John Carradine, Randolph Scott, Slim Summerville, Virginia Gilmore, Barton MacLane, and Dean Jagger. Twentieth Century Fox, 1941.

Lang, Richard, dir. "Blood of the Dragon: Part 1." *Kung Fu*. Television series. Digital videodisc. With David Carradine, Keye Luke, Philip Ahn, Patricia Neal, Eddie Albert, Season Hubley, Edward Albert, Clyde Kusatsu, Dean Jagger, and Radames Pera. ABC–Warner Bros., 2004. 14 September 1974.

———, dir. "Blood of the Dragon: Part 2." *Kung Fu*. Television series. Digital videodisc. With David Carradine, Keye Luke, Philip Ahn, Patricia Neal, Eddie Albert, Season Hubley, Edward Albert, Clyde Kusatsu, and Radames Pera. ABC–Warner Bros., 2004. 14 September 1974.

Laraway, David. "Doctoring the Revolution: Medical Discourse and Interpretation in *Los de Abajo* and *El Aguila y la Serpiente*." *Hispanófila* 127 (September 1999): 53–65.

Larson, Catherine. "'No Conoces el Precio de las Palabras': Language and Meaning in Usigli's *El Gesticulador*." *Latin American Theatre Review* 20.1 (Fall 1986): 21–28.

Larson, Robert W. "Red Cloud. Part 1: The Warrior Years." *Montana* 47.1 (March 1997): 22–31.

———. "Red Cloud. Part 2: The Reservation Years." *Montana* 47.2 (June 1997): 14–25.

Larue, Anne. "*A rebours*, roman de la chute acédiaste." *Joris-Karl Huysmans*. Ed. Marc Smeets. Amsterdam: Rodopi, 2003. 41–53.

Lassiter, Karl [Robert Vardeman]. "After Blackjack Dropped." *Lost Trails*. Ed. Martin H. Greenberg and Russell Davis. New York: Kensington-Pinnacle, 2007. 36–51.

Laughlin, Tom, dir. *Billy Jack*. With Tom Laughlin, Delores Taylor, and Clark Howat. Eaves Movie Ranch–Warner Bros., 1971.

Laughton, Charles, dir. *The Night of the Hunter*. 1955. Digital videodisc. With Robert Mitchum, Shelley Winters, and Lillian Gish. Paul Gregory Productions–United Artists-MGM, 2000.

Lavery, Ray. "The Man Who Made a Folk-God Out of Jo Shelby and Created a Legend for Jesse James." *Trail Guide* 6.4 (December 1961): 1–15.

Lawrence, Nicholas. "Francis Parkman's *The Oregon Trail* and the U.S.–Mexican War: Appropriations of Counter-Imperial Dissent." *Western American Literature* 43.4 (Winter 2009): 373–91.

Leadville's Rich Colorado History. Website, 2016. http://www.leadvilletwinlakes.com/history. Accessed 7/9/2016.

Leal, Luis. "Mariano Azuela, novelista médico." *Revista Hispánica Moderna* 28.2/4 (April-October 1962): 295–303. http://www.jstor.org/stable/30202692. Accessed 10/12/2015.

———. "La Revolución Mexicana y el cuento." *La Revolución y las letras: Dos estudios sobre la novela y el cuento de la Revolución Mexicana*. By Luis Leal and Edmundo Valadés. Lecturas Mexicanas. Tercera Serie: 14. México, D. F.: Dirección General de Publicaciones del Consejo Nacional para la Cultura y las Artes, 1990. 89–117.

———. "'La Sombra del Caudillo,' Roman à Clef." *Modern Language Journal* 36.1 (January 1952): 16–21. http://www.jstor.org/stable/318307. Accessed 07/14/2016.

Lee, Win-chiat. "E-Mail Communication." 9 November 2016.

Lehman, Peter. "How the West Wasn't Won: The Repression of Capitalism in John Ford's Westerns." *John Ford Made Westerns: Filming the Legend in the Sound Era*. Ed. Gaylyn Studlar and Matthew Bernstein. Bloomington: Indiana University Press, 2001. 132–52.

Lenihan, John H. "Classics and Social Commentary: Postwar Westerns, 1946–1960." *Journal of the West* 22 (1983): 34–42.

———. *Showdown: Confronting Modern America in the Western Film*. Urbana: University of Illinois Press, 1980.

Works Cited

———. "Western Film and the American Dream: The Cinematic Frontier of Sam Peckinpah." *The Frontier Experience and the American Dream: Essays on American Literature*. Ed. David Mogen, Mark Busby, and Paul Bryant. College Station: Texas A&M University Press, 1989. 226–35.

———. "The Western Heroism of Randolph Scott." *Shooting Stars: Heroes and Heroines of Western Film*. Ed. Archie P. McDonald. Bloomington: Indiana University Press, 1987. 42–59.

Leonard, Elmore. *Gunsights*. 1979. New York: HarperTorch–HarperCollins, 2002.

Leone, Sergio, dir. *Once Upon a Time in the West*. 1969. Digital videodisc. With Henry Fonda, Charles Bronson, Claudia Cardinale, and Jason Robards. Paramount, 2003.

LeRoy, Mervyn, dir. *Strange Lady in Town*. With Greer Garson, Dana Andrews, Cameron Mitchell, Nick Adams, Lois Smith, Walter Hampden, Pedro Gonzalez Gonzalez, and Ralph Moody. Warner Bros., 1955.

Leslie, Edward E. *The Devil Knows How to Ride: The True Story of William Clarke Quantrill and His Confederate Raiders*. 1996. New York: Da Capo, 1998.

Levin, Henry, dir. *The Man from Colorado*. 1948. Digital videodisc. With Glenn Ford, William Holden, Ellen Drew, and Edgar Buchanan. Columbia, 2004.

Lewis, Helen M. "Virgins, Widows, and Whores: The Bride Pool of the John Wayne Westerns." *Love in Western Film and Television: Lonely Hearts and Happy Trails*. Ed. Sue Matheson. New York: Palgrave Macmillan, 2013. 7–17.

Litvak, Anatole, dir. *Anastasia*. With Ingrid Bergman, Yul Brynner, Helen Hayes, and Akim Tamiroff. Twentieth Century Fox, 1956.

Liu, Zixu. "*Once Upon a Time in China*: Nationalism, Modernity, and Cinematic Representation." *Frontiers of Literary Studies in China* 8.4 (2014): 532–54.

Lively, Robert L. "Remapping the Feminine in Joss Whedon's *Firefly*." *Channeling the Future: Essays on Science Fiction and Fantasy Television*. Ed. Lincoln Geraghty. Lanham: Scarecrow, 2009. 183–97.

Livingstone, David W. "Spiritedness, Reason, and the Founding of Law and Order: John Ford's *The Man Who Shot Liberty Valance*." *Perspectives on Political Science* 38.4 (2009): 217–27.

Lo, Kwai-cheung. "*Once Upon a Time*: Technology Comes to Presence in China." *Modern Chinese Literature* 7.2 (Fall 1993): 79–96.

Long, E. Hudson. "O. Henry as a Regional Artist." *Essays on American Literature in Honor of Jay B. Hubbell*. Ed. Clarence Gohdes. Durham: Duke University Press, 1967. 229–40.

Loomis, Noel M. "Tough Hombre." *Heading West: Western Stories*. 1999. Foreword Bill Pronzini. New York: Dorchester, 2007. 55–69.

"Louis Kuhne," 2017. https://en.wikipedia.org/wiki/Louis_Kuhne. Accessed 7/3/2018.

Lowry, Dick, dir. *Last Stand at Saber River*. 1997. Digital videodisc. With Tom Selleck, Suzy Amis, David Dukes, Keith Carradine, and David Carradine. Turner–Warner Bros., 2009.

Loy, R. Philip. "The Frontier and the West." *The Columbia Companion to American History on Film: How the Movies Have Portrayed the American Past*. Ed. Peter C. Rollins. New York: Columbia University Press, 2003. 578–82.

———. *Westerns and American Culture, 1930–1955*. Jefferson: McFarland, 2001.

Lyon, Francis D., dir. *The Oklahoman*. With Joel McCrea, Barbara Hale, Michael Pate, Douglas Dick, Brad Dexter, Gloria Talbott, and Anthony Caruso. Allied Artists, 1957.

Lyon, William H. "The Significance of Newspapers on the Western Frontier." *Journal of the West* 19.2 (April 1980): 3–13.

Maio, Barbara. "Between Past and Future: Hybrid Design in *Firefly* and *Serenity*." *Investigating* Firefly *and* Serenity: *Science Fiction on the Frontier*. Ed. Rhonda V. Wilcox and Tanya R. Cochran. London: I. B. Tauris, 2008. 201–11.

Works Cited

Mañach, Jorge. *Indagación del choteo.* 1928. Miami: Mnemosyne Publishing, 1969.
Mangold, James, dir. *Cop Land.* 1997. Digital videodisc. With Sylvester Stallone, Ray Liotta, Harvey Keitel, Robert De Niro, Peter Berg, Annabella Sciorra, Robert Patrick, Janeane Garofalo, and Michael Rapaport. Miramax, 2004.
____, dir. "*Cop Land*: The Making of an Urban Western," 1997. *Cop Land.* Digital videodisc. Miramax, 2004.
Mankiewicz, Ben. "Now Showing." TV short, recorded 4/25/2015. *Canadian Pacific,* 1949, Twentieth Century Fox. Dir. Edwin L. Marin. TMC, 2015.
Mann, Anthony, dir. *The Far Country.* 1954. Digital videodisc. With James Stewart, Ruth Roman, Corinne Calvert, Walter Brennan, John McIntire, and Jay C. Flippen. Universal, 2003.
____, dir. *The Tin Star.* 1957. Digital videodisc. With Henry Fonda, Anthony Perkins, Neville Brand, John McIntire, Betsy Palmer, and Lee Van Cleef. Paramount, 2004.
____, dir. *Winchester '73.* Digital videodisc. 1950. With James Stewart, Shelley Winters, Stephen McNally, Millard Mitchell, Dan Duryea, Will Geer, and John McIntire. Universal, 2003.
Marek, Michael W. "*Firefly*: So 'Pretty' It Did not Die." *Sith, Slayers, Stargates, and Cyborgs: Modern Mythology in the New Millennium.* Ed. John Perlich and David Whitt. New York: Peter Lang, 2008. 99–120.
Marin, Edwin L., dir. *Canadian Pacific.* With Randolph Scott, Jane Wyatt, Victor Jory, Nancy Olson, and John Hamilton. Twentieth Century Fox, 1949.
____, dir. *The Cariboo Trail.* With Randolph Scott, Victor Jory, Bill Williams, Gabby Hayes, Karin Booth, Douglas Kennedy, Foo Lee Tung, and Tony Hughes. Twentieth Century Fox, 1950.
____, dir. *Fort Worth.* 1951. Digital videodisc. With Randolph Scott, David Brian, Phyllis Thaxter, Ray Teal, and Dick Jones. Warner Bros., 2006.
Marini, John. "Western Justice: John Ford and Sam Peckinpah on the Defense of the Heroic." *The California Republic: Institutions, Statesmanship, and Policies.* Ed. Brian P. Janiskee and Ken Masugi. Lanham: Rowman and Littlefield, 2004. 265–78.
Markusen, Ann. "Cold War Workers, Cold War Communities." *Rethinking Cold War Culture.* Ed. Peter J. Kuznick and James Gilbert. Washington: Smithsonian Books, 2010. 35–60.
Marovitz, Sanford E. "Testament of a Patriot: The Virginian, the Tenderfoot, and Owen Wister." *Texas Studies in Literature and Language* 15.3 (1973): 551–75. Rpt. in *Studies in the Western* 19 (2011): 117–30.
Marsden, Michael T. "Iconology of the Western Romance." *Icons of America.* Ed. Ray B. Browne and Marshall Fishwick. Bowling Green: Popular Press, 1978. 284–91.
Marshall, George, dir. *Destry Rides Again.* 1939. Digital videodisc. With James Stewart, Marlene Dietrich, Brian Donlevy, and Charles Winninger. Universal, 2012.
____, dir. *Pillars of the Sky.* With Jeff Chandler, Ward Bond, Dorothy Malone, Keith Andes, Michael Ansara, and Walter Coy. Universal-International, 1956.
Marshall, Ian. "The Easterner in Western Literature—and in the Western Literature Association." *Western American Literature* 26.3 (1991): 229–35.
Martin, Phillip W. "Nightmare." *The Handbook of the Gothic.* Ed. Marie Mulvey-Roberts. 2nd ed. Washington Square: New York University Press, 2009. 206–07.
Martínez Estrada, Ezequiel. *Radiografía de la pampa.* 1933. Buenos Aires: Losada, 1968.
Masters, Joshua J. "Reading the Book of Nature, Inscribing the Savage Mind: George Catlin and the Textualization of the American West." *American Studies* 46.2 (Summer 2005): 63–89.
Maté, Rudolph, dir. *The Violent Men.* 1954. Digital videodisc. With Glenn Ford, Edward G. Robinson, Barbara Stanwyck, Brian Keith, Dianne Foster, May Wynn, Basil Ruysdael, Richard Jaeckel, and Raymond Greenleaf. Columbia, 2005.

Works Cited

McAllen, M.M. *Maximilian and Carlota: Europe's Last Empire in Mexico*. New York: Trinity University Press, 2014.

McBride, Joseph. *Searching for John Ford: A Life*. New York: St. Martin's, 2001.

McCarey, Leo, dir. *The Bells of St. Mary's*. With Bing Crosby, Ingrid Bergman, Henry Travers, and Rhys Williams. RKO, 1945.

McCarthy, Gary. *The Derby Man*. Garden City: Doubleday, 1976.

McClintock, Thomas C. "British Newspapers and the Oregon Treaty of 1846." *Oregon Historical Quarterly* 104.1 (Spring 2003): 96–109.

McCormack, Kara L. "Safeguarding Its Past, Securing Its Future: Preservation and Performance in Tombstone, Arizona." *Journal of Arizona History* 54.2 (Summer 2013): 175–200.

McCormack, Peggy A. "Women in Westerns: Four Archetypal Characterizations." *RE: Artes Liberales* 8.2 (Spring 1982): 15–23.

McCowan, George, dir. *The Magnificent Seven Ride!* 1972. Digital videodisc. With Lee Van Cleef, Stefanie Powers, Michael Callan, and Pedro Armendariz, Jr. Mirisch-MGM, 2007.

McDermott, John D. "Guardians of the Pacific Telegraphs." *Annals of Wyoming* 83.1 (Winter 2011): 21–31.

McEveety, Vincent, dir. *Firecreek*. 1967. Digital videodisc. With James Stewart, Henry Fonda, Gary Lockwood, Dean Jagger, Ed Begley, Inger Stevens, Barbara Luna, Jack Elam, John Qualen, and Jay C. Flippen. National General–Warner Bros., 2006.

McFerrin, Randy, and Douglas Wills. "High Noon on the Western Range: A Property Rights Analysis of the Johnson County War." *Journal of Economic History* 67.1 (March 2007): 69–92. http://www.jstor.org/stable/4501134. Accessed 10/23/2015.

McGann, William, dir. *In Old California*. 1942. Digital Blu-ray videodisc. With John Wayne, Binnie Barnes, Albert Dekker, Helen Parrish, and Patsy Kelly. Republic, 2013.

McGee, Patrick. *From Shane to Kill Bill: Rethinking The Western*. Malden: Blackwell, 2007.

McLaglen, Andrew V., dir. *Bandolero!*. With James Stewart, Dean Martin, George Kennedy, Raquel Welch, Will Geer, and Andrew Prine. Twentieth Century Fox, 1968.

_____, dir. *Chisum*. 1970. Digital videodisc. With John Wayne, Ben Johnson, Forrest Tucker, Christopher George, Geoffrey Deuel, and Andrew Prine. Warner Bros., 2007.

_____, dir. *McLintock!* 1963. Digital videodisc. With John Wayne, Maureen O'Hara, Stefanie Powers, Patrick Wayne, Jack Kruschen, Jerry van Dyke, and Yvonne De Carlo. Paramount, 2005.

_____, dir. *The Undefeated*. 1969. Digital videodisc. With John Wayne, Rock Hudson, and Ben Johnson. Twentieth Century Fox, 2003.

McNaron, David L. "From Dollars to Iron: The Currency of Clint Eastwood's Westerns." *The Philosophy of the Western*. Ed. Jennifer McMahon and B. Steve Csaki. Lexington: University Press of Kentucky, 2010. 149–69.

Menton, Seymour. "*La estructura épica de* Los de abajo *y un prólogo especulativo*." *Hispania* 50.4 (December 1967): 1001–011. http://www.jstor.org/stable/338857. Accessed 5/26/2016.

Merk, Frederick. "The Oregon Question in the Webster-Ashburton Negotiations." *The Mississippi Valley Historical Review* 43.3 (December 1956): 379–404. http://www.jstor.org/stable/1893529. Accessed 4/21/2018.

Metz, Walter. "Have You Written a Ford, Lately? Gender, Genre and the Film Adaptations of Dorothy Johnson's Western Literature." *Literature/Film Quarterly* 31.3 (2003): 209–20.

Meuel, David. *The Noir Western: Darkness on the Range, 1943–1962*. Jefferson: McFarland, 2015.

Works Cited

Meyer, Michael C. "The Mexican-German Conspiracy of 1915." *Americas* 23.1 (July 1966): 76–89. http://www.jstor.org/stable/980141. Accessed 10/17/2016.
Meyer, Richard E. "The Outlaw: A Distinctive American Folktype." *Journal of the Folklore Institute* 17 (1980): 94–124.
Meyran, Daniel. "Introducción." *El gesticulador.* Ed. Daniel Meyran. By Rodolfo Usigli. Madrid: Cátedra, 2014. 9–112.
Michot-Dietrich, Hela. "Homais, Homeopathy, and *Madame Bovary.*" *Stanford French Review* 11.3 (1987): 313–21.
Miles, Nelson Appleton. "The Future of the Indian Question." *North American Review,* January 1891. *North American Review* 258.4 (July 1973): 75–78.
Miles, Terry, dir. *Lonesome Dove Church.* With Tom Berenger, Greyston Holt, Alex Zahara, Serge Houde, Drea Whitburn, and Geoff Gustafson. Nasser Group, North-Lionsgate, 2014.
Millington, Mark L. "Mexican Revolutionary Politics and the Role of the Intellectual in Martín Luis Guzmán's *La Sombra del Caudillo* and José Revueltas's *Los Días Terrenales.*" *Journal of Romance Studies* 7.2 (Summer 2007): 35–52.
Mills, Thomas R., dir. "Friends in San Rosario." Vitagraph–General Film Company, 1917. https://pro-labs.imdb.com/title/tt0181546/.
Misumi, Kenji, dir. *The Tale of Zatoichi* [*Zatoichi monogatari*]. 1962. Digital videodisc. With Katsu Shintaro. Daiei-Home Vision Entertainment, 2002.
Mitchell, Lee Clark. *Westerns: Making the Man in Fiction and Film.* Chicago: University of Chicago Press, 1996.
Mizoguchi, Kenji, dir. *Ugetsu Monogatari.* With Kyo Machiko, Mori Masayuki, Mito Mitsuko, Tanaka Kinuyo, and Ozawa Eitaro. Daiei, 1953.
Mohr, Hans-Ulrich. "Wandering Jew." *The Handbook of the Gothic.* Ed. Marie Mulvey-Roberts. 2nd ed. Washington Square: New York University Press, 2009. 257–59.
Morey-Gaines, Ann-Janine. "Of Menace and Men: The Sexual Tensions of the American Frontier Metaphor." *Soundings* 67.2 (1981): 132–49.
Morrow, John Anderson. *The Confederate Whitworth Sharpshooters.* 2nd ed. N.p.: N.p., 2002.
Muelsch, Elisabeth-Christine. "A Prostitute Is a Prostitute Is a Prostitute? From the Third Republic to the Great Depression—Outsiders in 'Boule de Suif' and *Stagecoach.*" *Excavatio* 22.1–2 (Summer 2007): 61–72.
Murad, Timothy. "Animal Imagery and Structural Unity in Mariano Azuela's *Los de Abajo.*" *Journal of Spanish Studies: Twentieth Century* 7 (1979): 207–22.
———. "Foreshadowing, Duplication, and Structural Unity in Mariano Azuela's *Los de Abajo.*" *Hispania* 64.4 (December 1981): 550–56. http://www.jstor.org/stable/341334. Accessed 6/16/2016.
———. "*Los de Abajo* vs. *The Underdogs*: The Translation of Mariano Azuela's Masterpiece." *Hispania* 65.4 (December 1982): 554–61. http://www.jstor.org/stable/342375. Accessed 11/25/2017.
Murphy, James C. "The Place of the Northern Arapahoes in the Relations Between the United States and the Indians of the Plains, 1851–1879." *Annals of Wyoming* 41.1 (January 1969): 33–61.
———. "The Place of the Northern Arapahoes in the Relations Between the United States and the Indians of the Plains, 1851–1879." *Annals of Wyoming* 41.2 (April 1969): 203–59.
Myers, John Myers. *Print in a Wild Land.* Garden City: Doubleday, 1967.
Myers, Roger. "A Closer Look at the Murder of Ed Masterson." *Quarterly of the National Association for Outlaw and Lawman History* (April–June 2005): 36–47.
Myrsiades, Kostas. "Reading *The Gunfighter* as Homeric Epic." *College Literature* 34.2 (Spring 2007): 279–300.

Works Cited

Nash, Gerald D. *Creating the West: Historical Interpretations 1890–1990.* Albuquerque: University of New Mexico Press, 1991.

Nazarro, Ray, dir. *Kansas Pacific.* 1953. Digital videodisc. With Sterling Hayden, Clayton Moore, Eve Miller, and Barton MacLane. Allied Artists–Alpha Video, 2005.

Neale, Steve. *Genre and Hollywood.* 2000. London: Routledge, 2005.

Neilson, James, dir. *Night Passage.* 1957. Digital videodisc. With James Stewart, Audie Murphy, Dan Duryea, Dianne Foster, Elaine Stewart, and Brandon De Wilde. Universal, 2003.

Nelson, Anna Kasten. "Mission to Mexico—Moses Y. Beach, Secret Agent." *New York Historical Society Quarterly* 59.3 (1975): 226–45.

Nevins, Francis M. "Through the Great Depression on Horseback: Legal Themes in Western Films of the 1930s." *Legal Reelism: Movies as Legal Texts.* Ed. John Denvir. Urbana: University of Illinois Press, 1996. 44–69.

The New Princeton Encyclopedia of Poetry and Poetics. Enlarged ed. Ed. Alex Preminger and T. V. F. Brogan. New York: MJF Books, 1993.

Nichols, Mary P. "Heroes and Political Communities in John Ford's Westerns: The Role of Wyatt Earp in *My Darling Clementine.*" *Perspectives on Political Science* 31.2 (Spring 2002): 78–84.

Nickell, Joe. "Ambrose Bierce and Those 'Mysterious Disappearances' Legends." *Indiana Folklore* 13.1–2 (1980): 112–22.

———. "Biography: The Disappearance of Ambrose Bierce." *Literary Investigation: Texts, Sources, and "Factual" Substructs of Literature and Interpretation.* Diss. University of Kentucky. 1987. Ann Arbor: UMI, 1987. 19–53.

Niess, Robert J. "On Listening to Homais." *French Review* 51.1 (October 1977): 22–8. http://www.jstor.org/stable/389603. Accessed 7/9/2016.

Noble, David W. *The Progressive Mind, 1890–1917.* 1970. Chicago: Rand, 1973.

Nurnberg, Monica J. "Inspiration and Aspiration: Gautier's '*La Diva*' and Musset's '*Une Soirée perdue.*'" *Australian Journal of French Studies* 15.5 (December 1978): 229–42.

Nyby, Christian, dir. *The Thing from Another World.* 1951. Digital videodisc. With Kenneth Tobey, Margaret Sheridan, Robert Cornthwaite, James Arness, and Douglas Spencer. RKO-Turner, 2003.

Nye, Russel B. "Parkman, Red Fate, and White Civilization." *Essays on American Literature in Honor of Jay B. Hubbell.* Ed. Clarence Gohdes. Durham: Duke University Press, 1967. 152–63.

O. Henry [William Sydney Porter]. "Friends in San Rosario." *41 Stories by O. Henry.* Ed. Burton Raffel. New York: Signet Classic–NAL–Penguin, 1984. 200–13.

———. "A Municipal Report." *The Complete Works of O. Henry.* Ed. William Lyon Phelps. Garden City: Garden City Books, 1937. 1509–21.

O'Connor, Richard. *Ambrose Bierce: A Biography.* Boston: Little, Brown, 1967.

O'Flaherty, Daniel. *General Jo Shelby: Undefeated Rebel.* Chapel Hill: University of North Carolina Press, 1954.

O'Leary, Mrs. James L. "Henry Chatillon." *Bulletin of the Missouri Historical Society* 22.2 (1966): 123–42.

O'Neal, Bill. *The Johnson County War.* Austin: Eakin Press, 2004.

O'Quinn, Trueman. "O. Henry in Austin." *Southwestern Historical Quarterly* 43.2 (October 1939): 143–57.

Orians, G. Harrison. "The Origin of the Ring Tournament in the United States." *Maryland Historical Magazine* 36 (1941): 263–77.

———. "Walter Scott, Mark Twain, and the Civil War." *South Atlantic Quarterly* 40 (1941): 342–59.

Orr, Stanley. "'A Man of Notoriously Vicious and Intemperate Disposition': Western Noir

Works Cited

and the Tenderfoot's Revenge in *Unforgiven.*" *New Essays on Clint Eastwood.* Ed. Leonard Engel. Foreword Drucilla Cornell. Salt Lake City: University of Utah Press, 2012. 148–67.

Parra, Max. *Writing Pancho Villa's Revolution: Rebels in the Literary Imagination of Mexico.* Austin: University of Texas Press, 2005.

Pearson, Sidney A., Jr. "It is Tough to Be the Second Toughest Guy in a Tough Town: Ask the Man Who Shot Liberty Valance." *Perspectives on Political Science* 36.1 (Winter 2007): 23–28.

Peckinpah, Sam, dir. *Bring Me the Head of Alfredo Garcia.* 1974. Digital videodisc. With Warren Oates, Isela Vega, and Emilio Fernández. MGM–Martin Baum–Sam Peckinpah, 2005.

———, dir. *The Wild Bunch.* 1969. Digital Blu-ray videodisc. With William Holden, Ernest Borgnine, Warren Oates, Ben Johnson, Edmond O'Brien, Robert Ryan, Emilio Fernandez, Albert Dekker, Jaime Sanchez, Strother Martin, Bo Hopkins, and L. Q. Jones. Warner Bros., 2007.

Peek, Wendy Chapman. "The Romance of Competence: Rethinking Masculinity in the Western." *Journal of Popular Film and Television* 30.4 (Winter 2003): 206–19.

Peeters, Evert. "Authenticity and Asceticism: Discourse and Performance in Nude Culture and Health Reform in Belgium, 1920–1940." *Journal of the History of Sexuality* 15.3 (September 2006): 432–61. http://www.jstor.org/stable/4629671. Accessed 7/3/2018.

Penn, Arthur, dir. *Little Big Man.* 1970. Digital videodisc. With Dustin Hoffman, Faye Dunaway, Martin Balsam, Jeff Corey, and Chief Dan George. Cinema Center Films–Paramount, 2003.

Penn, Chris. "Gunfire in Dodge City: The Night Ed Masterson Was Killed." *Wild West* 17.4 (December 2004): 48–53.

Penrose, Mehls. "*La historia en dos obras de Rodolfo Usigli, o el juego entre la fantasía y la realidad.*" *Mester* 27 (1998): 129–40.

Petridis, Sotiris. "A Historical Approach to the Slasher Film: The Classical Period, the Post-Slasher Films, and the Neoslashers." *Film International* 12.1 (2014): 76–84.

Phillips, Christopher. "The Hard-Line War: The Ideological Basis of Irregular Warfare in the Western Border States." *The Civil War Guerrilla: Unfolding the Black Flag in History, Memory, and Myth.* Ed. Joseph M. Beilein, Jr., and Matthew C. Hulbert. Lexington: University Press of Kentucky, 2015. 13–41.

Pichel, Irving, dir. *Santa Fe.* 1951. Digital videodisc. With Randolph Scott, Janis Carter, Jerome Courtland, Warner Baxter, Peter Thompson, and John Archer. Columbia, 2005.

Pick, Zuzana M. "A Romance with Mexico: The Epic Spectacle of the Revolution." *Canadian Journal of Film Studies/Revue Canadienne D'Etudes Cinématographiques* 9.22 (Fall 2000): 3–22.

Pickard, Madge E., and R. Carlyle Buley. *The Midwest Pioneer, His Ills, Cures, and Doctors.* 1945. New York: H. Schuman, 1946. http://hdl.handle.net/2027/uiuo.ark:/13960/t5h99817g.

Pierson, David. "Turner Network Television's Made-for-TV Western Films: Engaging Audiences through Genre and Themes." *Hollywood's West: The American Frontier in Film, Television, and History.* Ed. Peter C. Rollins and John E. O'Connor. Lexington: University Press of Kentucky, 2005. 281–99.

Pike, Fredrick B. *The United States and Latin America: Myths and Stereotypes of Civilization and Nature.* Austin: University of Texas Press, 1992.

Pippin, Robert B. *Hollywood Westerns and American Myth: The Importance of Howard Hawks and John Ford for Political Philosophy.* New Haven: Yale University Press, 2010.

Pizzello, Chris. "High Noon Hits the Jersey Turnpike." *American Cinematographer* September 1997: 54–64.

Works Cited

Place, J.A. *The Western Films of John Ford*. Secaucus: Citadel, 1974.
Polanco Alcántara, Tomás. *Juan Vicente Gómez: aproximación a una biografía*. Caracas: Grijalbo, 1990.
Preston, Diana. *The Boxer Rebellion: The Dramatic Story of China's War on Foreigners That Shook the World in the Summer of 1900*. New York: Walker, 2000.
Privett, Ronna. "The Western Woman and the Cowboy Hero: Power and Stoicism in the Western Landscape." *Conference of College Teachers of English Studies* 70 (September 2005): 81–89.
Puenzo, Luis, dir. *Old Gringo*. 1989. Digital Blu-ray videodisc. With Gregory Peck, Jane Fonda, and Jimmy Smits. Columbia, 2015.
Pye, Douglas. "Double Vision: Miscegenation and Point of View in *The Searchers*." *The Book of Westerns*. Ed. Ian Cameron and Douglas Pye. New York: Continuum, 1996. 229–40.
———. "Genre and History: *Fort Apache* and *The Man Who Shot Liberty Valance*." *The Book of Westerns*. Ed. Ian Cameron and Douglas Pye. New York: Continuum, 1996. 111–22.
Quevedo y Zubieta, Salvador. *Huerta: drama histórico en cinco actos*. México: Andrés Botas, 1916.
Ramos, Samuel. *El perfil del hombre y la cultura en México*. Rev. ed. México: P. Robredo, 1938.
Rasch, Philip J. "Prelude to the Lincoln County War: The Murder of John Henry Tunstall." *Brand Book* 7 (1957): 78–96.
Raun, Gerald G. "The Madero Revolution." *Journal of Big Bend Studies* 18 (2006): 85–120.
Ray, Nicholas, dir. *Johnny Guitar*. With Joan Crawford, Sterling Hayden, Mercedes McCambridge, and Scott Brady. Republic, 1954.
Reasoner, James. *Death Head Crossing*. New York: Kensington-Pinnacle, 2007.
Reep, Diana C. "See What the Boys in the Back Room Will Have: The Saloon in Western Films." *Locales in American Popular Film*. Ed. Paul Loukides and Linda K. Fuller. Bowling Green: Popular, 1993. 204–20. Beyond the Stars: Studies in American Popular Film 4.
Richardson, Joanna. *Théophile Gautier: His Life and Times*. New York: Coward-McCann, 1959.
Ridley, Jasper. *Maximilian and Juárez*. New York: Ticknor, 1992.
Rister, Carl Coke. "Carlota, a Confederate Colony in Mexico." *Journal of Southern History* 11.1 (February 1945): 33–50. http://www.jstor.org/stable/2197956. Accessed 11/11/2016.
Robe, Stanley. *Los de abajo*. Ed. Jorge Ruffinelli. México: Fondo de Cultura Económica, 1992.
Roberts, Gary L. *Doc Holliday: The Life and Legend*. Hoboken: Wiley, 2007.
Robertson, Jamie. "Stephen Crane, Eastern Outsider in the West and Mexico." *Western \ American Literature* 13 (1978): 243–57.
Robertson, Richard C. "Just Dreamin' Out Loud: The Westerns of Burt Lancaster." *Shooting Stars: Heroes and Heroines of Western Film*. Ed. Archie P. McDonald. Bloomington: Indiana University Press, 1987. 165–81.
Ross, Dick, dir. *The Persuader*. VHS tape. With William Talman, James Craig, Darryl Hickman, and Georgia Lee. Allied Artists–World Wide Pictures, 1957.
Ross, Stanley R. "Un manifiesto de Aquiles Serdán." *Historia Mexicana* 5.3 (1955): 86–91.
Ross, T. J. "Fantasy and Form in the Western: From Hart to Peckinpah." *December* 12.1–2 (1970): 158–69.
Rourke, Thomas. *Gómez: Tyrant of the Andes*. New York: William Morrow, 1936.
Rouse, Russell, dir. *The Fastest Gun Alive*. With Glenn Ford, Broderick Crawford, Jeanne Crain, and Leif Erickson. MGM, 1956.

Works Cited

Ruhlman, R. Fred. *Captain Henry Wirz and Andersonville Prison: A Reappraisal.* Knoxville: University of Tennessee Press, 2006.
Russell, W.M.S., and Katharine M. Briggs. "The Legends of Lilith and of the Wandering Jew in Nineteenth Century Literature." *Folklore* 92.2 (1981): 131–40. http://www.jstor.org/stable/1259465. Accessed 7/10/16.
Rutherford, John. *An Annotated Bibliography of the Novels of the Mexican Revolution of 1910–1917. In English and Spanish.* Troy: Whitson, 1972.
———. *Mexican Society during the Revolution: A Literary Approach.* Oxford: Clarendon, 1971.
———. "The Novel of the Mexican Revolution." *The Cambridge History of Latin American Literature, II: The Twentieth Century.* Ed. Roberto González Echevarría and Enrique Pupo-Walker. Cambridge: Cambridge University Press, 1996. 213–25.
Ryan, Pat M. "Trail-Blazer of Civilization: John P. Clum's Tucson and Tombstone Years." *Journal of Arizona History* 6.2 (1965): 53–70.
Saliba, David R. "The Nightmare in Miniature: 'Ligeia.'" *American Transcendental Quarterly* 40 (1978): 367–78.
Sánchez, Porfirio. *"La Deshumanización del hombre en* Los de abajo.*" Cuadernos Americanos* 192 (January 1974): 179–91.
Sánchez Silva, Arlyn. *"Narradores y muralistas de la Revolución Mexicana: Mariano Azuela y Diego Rivera."* Studies in Honor of Enrique Amberson Imbert. Ed. Nancy Abraham Hall and Lanin A. Gyurko. Newark: Juan de la Cuesta, 2003. 419–36.
Sanders, Stuart W. "LeMat." *Civil War Times Illustrated* 37.6 (December 1998): 66–70.
Sández, Laura V. *"How to Do Things with* Activo Desencanto: *El discurso del desencanto en* Los de abajo *de Mariano Azuela."* Revista Iberoamericana 81.250 (January–March 2015): 125–39.
Santana, Jorge A. *"El oportunista en la narrativa de Mariano Azuela."* Cuadernos Hispanoamericanos 275 (1973): 297–330.
Sarmiento, Domingo Faustino. *Facundo: Or, Civilization and Barbarism.* Trans. Mary Mann. New York: Penguin, 1998.
———. *Facundo.* Ed. Roberto Yahni. Madrid: Cátedra, 2006.
Saults, Dan. "Let Us Discuss a Man: A Study of John Newman Edwards." *Missouri Historical Society. Bulletin* 19.2 (January 1963): 150–60.
Saum, Lewis O. "Colonel Custer's Copperhead: The 'Mysterious' Mark Kellogg." *Montana* 28.4 (Autumn 1978): 12–25. http://www.jstor.org/stable/4518327. Accessed 8/22/2017.
Schatz, Thomas. "The Western." *Handbook of American Film Genres.* Ed. Wes D. Gehring. New York: Greenwood, 1988. 25–46.
———. "The Western." *Popular Culture: An Introductory Text.* Ed. Jack Nachbar and Kevin Lause. Bowling Green: Popular, 1992. 430–44.
Schmidhuber de la Mora, Guillermo. *El advenimiento del teatro mexicano.* San Luis Potosí, México: Ponciano Arriaga, 1999.
Schramm, Wilbur L. "A New Englander on the Road to Oregon." *New England Quarterly* 13.1 (March 1940): 49–64. http://www.jstor.org/stable/360681. Accessed 4/20/2018.
Schultz, Duane. *Quantrill's War: The Life and Times of William Clarke Quantrill, 1837–1865.* New York: St. Martin's Griffin, 1996.
Schwartz, Kessel. *From Colonial Times to the Mexican Revolution and Beyond.* Coral Gables, Florida: University of Miami Press, 1972. Vol. 1 of *A New History of Spanish American Fiction.*
Serna Rodríguez, Ana María. *"Prensa y sociedad en las décadas revolucionarias (1910–1940)."* Secuencia 88.1 (January–April 2014): 111–49.
Shahar, Meir. *The Shaolin Monastery: History, Religion, and the Chinese Martial Arts.* Honolulu: University of Hawaii Press, 2008.
Shaw, D.L. "Ganivet's *España filosófica contemporánea* and the Interpretation of the Gen-

Works Cited

eration of 1898." *Hispanic Review* 28.3 (July 1960): 220–32. http://www.jstor.org/stable/470749. Accessed 2/26/2018.

Sherman, George, dir. *Big Jake*. 1971. Digital videodisc. With John Wayne, Maureen O'Hara, Richard Boone, Patrick Wayne, and Chris Mitchum. Batjac-Paramount, 2005.

Sherman, Vincent, dir. *Backfire*. 1950. Digital videodisc. With Gordon MacRae, Virginia Mayo, Viveca Lindfors, and Dane Clark. Warner Bros., 2010.

Shooting Stars: Heroes and Heroines of Western Film. Ed. Archie P. McDonald. Bloomington: Indiana University Press, 1987.

Sickels, Robert C. "Beyond the Blessings of Civilization: John Ford's *Stagecoach* and the Myth of the Western Frontier." *John Ford in Focus: Essays on the Filmmaker's Life and Work*. Ed. Kevin L. Stoehr and Michael C. Connolly. Jefferson: McFarland, 2008. 142–52.

Siegel, Don, dir. *The Shootist*. 1976. Digital videodisc. With John Wayne, Ron Howard, Lauren Bacall, Richard Boone, Hugh O'Brian, James Stewart, and Henry Morgan. Paramount, 2001.

———, dir. *Two Mules for Sister Sara*. 1969. Digital videodisc. With Clint Eastwood and Shirley MacLaine, Albert Maltz, screenwriter. Malpaso–Warner Bros., 2003.

Silva Herzog, Jesús. "*Durante la presidencia del general Plutarco Elías Calles. Sucesos que es menester recordar*." *Memoria del Colegio Nacional* 8.4 (1978): 45–72.

———. "*El gobierno de Madero y la Decena Trágica*." *Cuadernos Americanos* 16.6 (1957): 153–80.

Silvera, Frank. "Towards a Theater of Understanding." *Negro Digest* 18.6 (April 1969): 33–35.

Simmon, Scott. "Concerning the Weary Legs of Wyatt Earp: The Classic Western according to Shakespeare." *Literature/Film Quarterly* 24.2 (1996): 114–27.

Sinyard, Neil. *A Wonderful Heart: The Films of William Wyler*. Jefferson: McFarland, 2013.

Siodmak, Robert, dir. *Criss Cross*. 1948. Digital videodisc. With Burt Lancaster, Yvonne De Carlo, Dan Duryea, and Stephen McNally. Universal, 2004.

Siska, William C. "Realism and Romanticism in the Films of John Ford." *Wide Angle* 2.4 (Summer 1978): 8–13.

Skoble, Aeon G. "Order Without Law: *The Magnificent Seven*, East and West." *The Philosophy of the Western*. Ed. Jennifer McMahon and B. Steve Csaki. Lexington: University Press of Kentucky, 2010. 139–47.

Slotkin, Richard. "The Continuity of Forms: Myth and Genre in Warner Bros.' *The Charge of the Light Brigade*." *Representations* 29 (Winter 1990): 1–23.

———. *Gunfighter Nation: The Myth of the Frontier in Twentieth-Century America*. 1992. New York: Harper Perennial–HarperCollins, 1993.

———. "Unit Pride: Ethnic Platoons and the Myths of American Nationality." *American Literary History* 13.3 (2001): 469–98.

Smith, Helena Huntington. *The War on Powder River*. New York: McGraw, 1966.

Smyth, J. E. "The Organization Woman behind *The Man in the Gray Flannel Suit*." *Camera Obscura* 27.2 (2012): 61–91.

———. *Reconstructing American Historical Cinema: From* Cimarron *to* Citizen Kane. Lexington: University Press of Kentucky, 2006.

Soltysiak, Harry A. "The Pinkerton Bomb." *American History Illustrated* 27.2 (1992): 52–55, 73–74.

Stanfield, Peter. *Hollywood, Westerns and the 1930s: The Lost Trail*. Exeter: University of Exeter Press, 2001.

Stanzel, Franz K. "Teller-Characters and Reflector-Characters in Narrative Theory." *Poetics Today* 2.2 (Winter 1981): 5–15. Narratology III: Narration and Perspective in Fiction.

Works Cited

Steckmesser, Kent L. "Robin Hood and the American Outlaw: A Note on History and Folklore." *Journal of American Folklore* 79 (1966): 348–55. https://www.jstor.org/stable/538043. Accessed 08/1/2018.
Stevens, George, dir. *Shane.* 1952. Digital videodisc. With Alan Ladd, Jean Arthur, Van Heflin, Brandon De Wilde, Jack Palance, Emile Meyer, Elisha J. Cook, Jr., and John Anderson. Paramount, 2000.
Stokesbury, James L. "Francis Parkman on the Oregon Trail." *American History Illustrated* 8.8 (December 1973): 4+.
Studlar, Gaylyn. "'Be a Proud, Glorified Dreg': Class, Gender, and Frontier Democracy in *Stagecoach.*" *John Ford's* Stagecoach. Ed. Barry Keith Grant. Cambridge: Cambridge University Press, 2003. 132–57.
Sturges, John, dir. *Bad Day at Black Rock.* 1954. Digital videodisc. With Spencer Tracy, Robert Ryan, Lee Marvin, Walter Brennan, Dean Jagger, Ernest Borgnine, and Anne Francis. Warner Bros., 2005.
———, dir. *Gunfight at the O.K. Corral.* 1956. Digital videodisc. With Burt Lancaster, Kirk Douglas, Rhonda Fleming, and Jo Van Fleet. Paramount, 2003.
———, dir. *Hour of the Gun.* 1967. Digital videodisc. With James Garner, Jason Robards, and Robert Ryan. Mirisch Corporation–MGM, 2005.
———, dir. *Last Train from Gun Hill.* 1959. Digital videodisc. With Kirk Douglas, Anthony Quinn, Carolyn Jones, and Earl Holliman. Paramount, 2004.
———, dir. *The Magnificent Seven.* 1960. Digital Blu-ray videodisc. With Yul Brynner, Steve McQueen, Charles Bronson, and Eli Wallach. Mirisch–MGM–20th Century Fox, 2010.
Susman, Warren, and Edward Griffin. "Did Success Spoil the United States? Dual Representations in Postwar America." *Recasting America: Culture and Politics in the Age of Cold War.* Ed. Lary May. Chicago: University of Chicago Press, 1989. 19–37.
Suzuki, Daisetz T. *Zen and Japanese Culture.* 1959. New York: Pantheon, 1960.
Swarthout, Glendon. *The Shootist.* 1975. Introduction Miles Swarthout. Lincoln: Bison–University of Nebraska Press, 2011.
Swier, Patricia L. "Intoxicating Outlaws: Dominance and Sexuality in Rómulo Gallegos' *Doña Bárbara.*" *The Woman in Latin American and Spanish Literature: Essays on Iconic Characters.* Ed. Eva Paulino Bueno and María Claudia André. Jefferson: McFarland, 2012. 30–45.
Sword, Wiley. *Mountains Touched with Fire: Chattanooga Besieged, 1863.* New York: St. Martin's, 1995.
Tada, Michitaro. "The Destiny of Samurai Films." *East-West Film Journal* 1.1 (December 1986): 48–58.
Tanner, Karen Holliday, and Robert K. DeArment. *Doc Holliday: A Family Portrait.* Norman: University of Oklahoma Press, 1998.
Tanner, Stephen L. "Richard Wheeler: Sierra and a Plea for Realism." *Studies in the Western* 11 (2003): 59–68.
Tate, Michael L. "John P. Clum and the Origins of an Apache Constabulary, 1874–1877." *American Indian Quarterly* 3.2 (Summer 1977): 99–120. http://www.jstor.org/stable/1184176.
Tefertiller, Casey. *Wyatt Earp: The Life Behind the Legend.* Foreword Angus Cameron. New York: Wiley, 1997.
Telotte, J.P. "*Serenity,* Genre, and Cinematization." *Science Fiction Film, Television, and Adaptation: Across the Screens.* Ed. J.P. Telotte and Gerald Duchovnay. New York: Routledge, 2012. 127–40.
Terrie, Philip G. "The Other Within: Indianization on *the Oregon Trail.*" *New England Quarterly* 64.3 (September 1991): 376–92. http://www.jstor.org/stable/366348. Accessed 4/20/2018.

Works Cited

Thale, Jerome. "The Narrator as Hero." *Twentieth-Century Literature* 3 (1957): 69–73.
Theisen, Lee Scott. "'My God, Did I Set All of This in Motion?' General Lew Wallace and *Ben-Hur*." *Journal of Popular Culture* 18.2 (Fall 1984): 33–41.
Thorpe, Jerry, dir. "Blood Brother." *Kung Fu*. Television series. Digital videodisc. With David Carradine, Keye Luke, Philip Ahn, Clu Gulager, John Anderson, Scott Hylands, Kathleen Lloyd, Robert Urich, Benson Fong, Yuen Kam, Richard Loo, and Radames Pera. ABC–Warner Bros., 2004. 18 January 1973.
____, dir. "Dark Angel." *Kung Fu*. Television series. Digital videodisc. With David Carradine, Keye Luke, Philip Ahn, John Carradine, Robert Carradine, Dean Jagger, and Radames Pera. ABC–Warner Bros., 2004. 11 November 1972.
____, dir. "Pilot." *Kung Fu*. 1972. Television series. Digital videodisc. With David Carradine, Keye Luke, Philip Ahn, Albert Salmi, Barry Sullivan, Benson Fong, David Chow, Radames Pera, James Hong, Richard Loo, and Wayne Maunder. ABC–Warner Bros., 2004. 22 February 1972.
Tompkins, Jane. *West of Everything: The Inner Life of Westerns*. New York: Oxford University Press, 1992.
Tourneur, Jacques, dir. *Stars in My Crown*. 1950. Digital videodisc. With Joel McCrea, Ellen Drew, Dean Stockwell, Ed Begley, Alan Hale, Lewis Stone, James Mitchell, Amanda Blake, Juano Hernandez, Jack Lambert, and Marshall Thompson. MGM–Warner Bros., 2011.
Tsui, Hark, dir. *Once Upon a Time in China II*. 1992. Digital videodisc. With Jet Li, Rosamund Kwan, and Donnie Yen. Columbia Tristar, 2001.
Tuchman, Barbara. *The Zimmermann Telegram*. 2nd ed. New York: Ballantine, 1995.
Tuska, Jon. *The American West in Film: Critical Approaches to the Western*. Westport: Greenwood, 1985.
Underwood, Deen. "Susan McSween Barber: Cattle Queen of New Mexico." *Password* 41.1 (March 1996): 39–43.
Usigli, Rodolfo. *El gesticulador*. Play first published 1938. Ed. Daniel Meyran. Madrid: Cátedra, 2014.
Utley, Robert M. "Billy the Kid and the Lincoln County War." *New Mexico Historical Review* 61.2 (April 1986): 93–120.
Utley, Robert M., and Wilcomb E. Washburn. *Indian Wars*. New York: Houghton Mifflin, 2002.
Vanderwood, Paul. "An American Cold Warrior: *Viva Zapata!*" *American History / American Film: Interpreting the Hollywood Image*. Ed. John E. O'Connor and Martin Jackson. New York: Frederick Ungar, 1979. 183–202.
Van Orden, Jay. "C.S. Fly at Cañon de los Embudos: American Indians as Enemy in the Field: A Photographic First." *Journal of Arizona History* 30.3 (1989): 319–46.
Van Orman, Richard A. "The Bard in the West." *Western Historical Quarterly* 5.1 (January 1974): 29–38.
Varley, H. Paul. *Samurai*. In collaboration with Ivan Morris and Nobuko Morris. New York: Laurel-Dell, 1970.
Varner, Paul. *Historical Dictionary of Westerns in Cinema*. Lanham: Scarecrow, 2008.
Vaughan, Robert. *Hawke: Ride with the Devil*. New York: HarperTorch–HarperCollins, 2004.
____. *Hawke: Showdown at Dead End Canyon*. New York: HarperTorch–HarperCollins, 2005.
____. *Hawke: The King Hill War*. New York: Harper–HarperCollins, 2007.
____. *Hawke: The Law of a Fast Gun*. New York: HarperTorch–HarperCollins, 2006.
____. *Hawke: Vendetta Trail*. New York: HarperTorch–HarperCollins, 2005.
____. "The Piano Man." *Boot Hill: An Anthology of the West*. Ed. Robert J. Randisi. New York: Tom Doherty Associates, 2002. 229–47.

Works Cited

Vaughan, Thomas. "C.S. Fly: Pioneer Photojournalist." *Journal of Arizona History* 30.3 (Autumn 1989): 303–18. http://www.jstor.org/stable/41695766. Accessed 10/23/2015.
Verneuil, Henri, dir. *Guns for San Sebastian*. With Anthony Quinn, Anjanette Comer, Charles Bronson, Sam Jaffe, Silvia Pinal, Leon Askin, and Jaime Fernandez. CIPRA–MGM, 1968.
Vidor, Charles. *Gilda*. 1946. Digital videodisc. With Rita Hayworth, Glenn Ford, and George Macready. Columbia, 2000.
Vidor, King, dir. *Duel in the Sun*. 1946. Digital videodisc. With Gregory Peck, Jennifer Jones, Joseph Cotten, Lionel Barrymore, Herbert Marshall, Lillian Gish, Walter Huston, and Charles Bickford. MGM, 2004.
von Feilitzsch, Heribert. "Medical Doctor, Occultist, Revolutionary, Spy: Arnold Krumm-Heller and the Mexican Revolution." *Equestrian Rebels: Critical Perspectives on Mariano Azuela and the Novel of the Mexican Revolution*. Ed. Roberto Cantú. Newcastle upon Tyne: Cambridge Scholars, 2016. 287–305.
Von Mueller, Eddy. "Naked Swords: The Zen Warrior Tradition and the Intertextual Odyssey of the Nameless Ronin in *Seven Samurai, Yojimbo*, and *Sanjuro*." *Post Script* 20.1 (2000): 53–67.
Waisman, Sergio. "Introduction." *The Underdogs: A Novel of the Mexican Revolution*. New York: Penguin Classics, 2008. xi-xvii. Trans. of *Los de abajo* (1915). Trans. Sergio Waisman.
Waldmeir, Joseph J. "The Cowboy, Knight, and Popular Taste." *Southern Folklore Quarterly* 22.3 (September 1958): 113–20.
Walker, Michael. "The Westerns of Delmer Daves." *The Book of Westerns*. Ed. Ian Cameron and Douglas Pye. New York: Continuum, 1996. 123–60.
Walker, Warren S. "The Frontiersman as Recluse and Redeemer." *New York Folklore Quarterly* 16 (1960): 110–22.
Walsh, Raoul, dir. *Pursued*. 1947. Digital videodisc. With Robert Mitchum, Teresa Wright, Dean Jagger, Judith Anderson, Alan Hale, and John Rodney. Republic, 2003.
———, dir. *Saskatchewan* [*O'Rourke of the Royal Mounted*]. With Alan Ladd, Jay Silverheels, Shelley Winters, J. Carroll Naish, and Hugh O'Brian. Universal-International, 1954.
Warren, Charles Marquis, dir. *Little Big Horn*. 1951. Digital videodisc. With Lloyd Bridges, Marie Windsor, and John Ireland. Lippert Pictures–VCI, 2005.
Weiss, Robert P. "Private Detective Agencies and Labour Discipline in the United States, 1855–1946." *Historical Journal* 29.1 (March 1986): 87–107. http://www.jstor.org/stable/2639257. Accessed 11/20/2016.
Welles, Orson, dir. *Citizen Kane*. 1941. Digital videodisc. With Orson Welles, Joseph Cotten, Dorothy Comingore, George Coulouris, Everett Sloane, Agnes Moorhead, Ray Collins, and Paul Stewart. RKO–Turner Entertainment–Warner Home Video, 2001.
Wellman, William A., dir. *The Conquerors*. With Richard Dix, Ann Harding, Guy Kibbee, and Edna May Oliver. RKO, 1932.
———, dir. *The Ox-Bow Incident*. 1942. Digital videodisc. With Henry Fonda, Dana Andrews, and Anthony Quinn. Twentieth Century Fox, 2003.
Wendkos, Paul, dir. *Guns of the Magnificent Seven*. 1969. Digital Blu-ray videodisc. With George Kennedy, James Whitmore, Michael Ansara, Joe Don Baker, Bernie Casey, and Reni Santoni. MGM–Twentieth Century Fox, 2010.
West, John O. "Billy the Kid, Hired Gun or Hero." *The Sunny Slopes of Long Ago*. Ed. William M. Hudson and Allen Maxwell. Nacogdoches: Southern Methodist University Press, 1966. 70–80. Publications of the Texas Folklore Society 33.
West, Joseph A. *The Last Manhunt*. A Ralph Compton Novel. New York: Signet, 2011.

Works Cited

Westbrook, Brett, and Kathleen A. Brown. "The Politics of Reconciliation in John Ford's Cavalry Trilogy: Adapting James Warner Bellah's Short Stories." *Westerns: Paperback Novels and Movies from Hollywood*. Ed. Paul Varner. Newcastle Cambridge Scholars, 2007. 170–90.

Westbrook, Max. "Mountain Home: The Hero in the American West." *The Westering Experience in American Literature: Bicentennial Essays*. Ed. Merrill Lewis and L. L. Lee. Bellingham: Bureau for Faculty Research, Western Washington University, 1977. 9–18.

Westman, Lee Ann. "Domesticity on the Range: Women and Men in *Tombstone*." *Interdisciplinary Humanities* 20.2 (Fall 2003): 73–79.

Whedon, Josh, dir. *Firefly*. Television series. With Nathan Fillion, Morena Baccarin, Alan Tudyk, Adam Baldwin, Jewel Staite, Gina Torres, Summer Glau, Sean Maher, and Ron Glass. Twentieth Century Fox, 2002–2003.

———, dir. *Serenity*. Digital videodisc. With Nathan Fillion, Morena Baccarin, Alan Tudyk, Adam Baldwin, Jewel Staite, Gina Torres, Summer Glau, Sean Maher, Ron Glass, and Chiwetel Ejiofor. Universal, 2005.

Wheeler, Richard S. *Deuces and Ladies Wild: A Santiago Toole Western*. 1991. Santa Fe: Sunstone Press, 2008.

———. *The Fate*. New York: Fawcett Gold Medal-Ballantine Books, 1992.

———. *The Final Tally*. 1991. New York: Ballantine Books, 2000.

———. *Incident at Fort Keogh: A Santiago Toole Western*. Santa Fe: Sunstone Press, 2008.

White, Ray. "The Good Guys Wore White Hats: The B Western in American Culture." *Wanted Dead or Alive: The American West in Popular Culture*. Ed. Richard Aquila. Urbana: University of Illinois Press, 1996. 135–59.

Wier, James A. "19th Century Army Doctors on the Frontier and in Nebraska." *Nebraska History* 61.2 (1980): 192–214.

Wilde, Oscar. "Lecture." *Impressions of America* (Sunderland: Keystone, 1906). *Oscar Wilde in America: The Interviews*. Ed. Matthew Hofer and Gary Scharnhorst. Urbana: University of Illinois Press, 2013. 177–81.

Will, Barbara. "The Nervous Origins of the American Western." *American Literature* 70.2 (June 1998): 293–316. http://www.jstor.org/stable/2902839. Accessed 4/29/2010.

Williams, Doug. "Pilgrims and the Promised Land: A Genealogy of the Western." 1998. *The Western Reader*. Ed. Jim Kitses and Gregg Rickman. New York: Proscenium, 1999. 93–114.

Williams, Mark. "Get/Away: Structure and Desire in *Rancho Notorious*." *Dietrich Icon*. Ed. Gerd Gemünden and Mary R Desjardins. Durham: Duke University Press, 2007. 259–86.

Williams, Tony. *Hearths of Darkness: The Family in the American Horror Film*. Cranbury, NJ: Associated University Presses, 1996.

———. "Some Further Thoughts on *Vera Cruz*." *Film International* 13.72 (2015): 30–40.

———. "Under 'Western Eyes': The Personal Journey of Huang Fei-Hong in *Once Upon a Time in China*." *Cinema Journal* 40.1 (Fall 2000): 3–24.

Wincer, Simon, dir. *Crossfire Trail*. 2001. Digital videodisc. With Tom Selleck, Virginia Madsen, Wilford Brimley, Mark Harmon, and Brad Johnson. TNT–Warner Bros., 2009.

Winner, Michael, dir. *Lawman*. With Burt Lancaster, Lee J. Cobb, Robert Ryan, and Walter Brooke. United Artists, 1971.

Winston, Colin M. "Between Rosas and Sarmiento: Notes on Nationalism in Peronist Thought." *Americas* 39.3 (January 1983): 305–32. http://www.jstor.org/stable/981228. Accessed 6/7/2015.

Wise, Robert, dir. *Blood on the Moon*. With Robert Mitchum, Robert Preston, Walter Brennan, Barbara Bel Geddes, and Phyllis Thaxter. RKO, 1948.

Works Cited

Wister, Owen. *The Virginian: Horseman of the Plains*. Ed. Robert Shulman. New York: Oxford University Press, 1998.

Wood, Robin. "*Duel in the Sun*: The Destruction of an Ideological System." *The Book of Westerns*. Ed. Ian Cameron and Douglas Pye. New York: Continuum, 1996. 189–95.

Woolsey, A. W. "*Los protagonistas de algunas novelas de Manuel* [sic] *Azuela*." *Hispania* 23.4 (December 1940): 341–48. https://www.jstor.org/stable/331941. Accessed 7/25/2018.

Woolworth, Alan R. "Adrian J. Ebell, Photographer and Journalist of the Dakota War of 1862." *Minnesota History* 54.2 (Summer 1994): 87–92.

Wyler, William, dir. *The Big Country*. 1958. Digital videodisc. With Gregory Peck, Burl Ives, Charles Bickford, Jean Simmons, Chuck Connors, Carroll Baker, Alfonso Bedoya, and Charlton Heston. United Artists–MGM, 2001.

Young, Terence, dir. *Dr. No*. 1962. Digital Blu-ray videodisc. With Sean Connery, Ursula Andress, Bernard Lee, and Joseph Wiseman. Albert R. Broccoli–Harry Saltzman–MGM, 2012.

____, dir. *Red Sun*. With Charles Bronson, Toshiro Mifune, Alain Delon, and Ursula Andress. Les Films Corona-National General, 1971.

Zanger, Jules. "Stephen Crane's 'Bride' as Countermyth of the West." *Great Plains Quarterly* 11.3 (Summer 1991): 157–65. http://www.jstor.org/stable/23531631.

Zinnemann, Fred, dir. *The Day of the Jackal*. 1973. Digital videodisc. With Edward Fox, Michel Lonsdale, Cyril Cusack, and Delphine Seyrig. Warwick Film Productions–Universal Productions France S.A./Universal, 1998.

____, dir. *High Noon*. 1952. Digital videodisc. With Gary Cooper, Grace Kelly, Katy Jurado, and Lloyd Bridges. Republic-Artisan, 2002.

Index

À rebours 179n40; see also Huysmans, Joris-Karl
Abbey, Edward 123
Abilene, Kansas 48, 56–57, 81, 96
Abilene Town (Marin) 48
abulia 103, 153, 174n18, 179n40; see also accidie
accidie (acedia, acédie) 110, 154, 174n5, 179n40; see also abulia
Adler, Luther 98
"After Blackjack Dropped" (Lassiter) 37
Against the Grain 153
Aguirre, Ignacio (*La sombra del caudillo*) 150–52, 167, 179n34
Ahesverus 176n9; see also Wandering Jew
Alastray, Leon (Guns for San Sebastian) 68–69
Alazraki, Jaime 176n1
Albert, Eddie 122
Aldrich, Robert 133
Alliance (*Firefly, Serenity*) 41–44
Ampudia, Juan 153–60, 162, 164, 166, 179n40, 179n43
anagnorisis 40, 148
Anastasia (Litvak) 70
Ancona Albertos, Antonio 153–60, 179n36, 179n38, 179n39
Anderson, Bloody Bill 81
Anderson, John 70, 122
Anderson, Michael, Jr. 47
Andersonville 10, 87–88
Andes, Keith 75
Andrés Pérez, maderista (Azuela) 80, 154, 157, 160–61, 163–66
Andrews, Dana 18, 32
angya (Zen) 158
Ankrum, Morris 76

"Anonymous" (Eickhoff) 117
Ansara, Michael 75
Apaches 26, 75, 100, 121, 124–26 170n1
Apocalypse Now (Coppola) 115
Arapahoes 10, 53, 169n3
Archainbaud, George 48, 65
Archer, John 15
Argentina 31, 61–62, 151, 176n2
Arlen, Richard 39
Arnold, Edward 47
assayers 34, 39
Ayres, Lew 123

Bacon, Lloyd 11, 100
Bad Day at Black Rock (Sturges) 31, 121, 174n16
Baker, Carroll 114
Baker, Joe Don 138
Baldwin, Peter 13
Bale, Christian 124
Bancroft, Anne 170n1
Bandolero! (McLaglen) 66–68
Barlow, Sue (*Open Range*) 104–6
Barnes, Binnie 101
Barry, Gene 46
Basques 85
Beauchamp (*Unforgiven*) 87, 129
Beddoe, Don 34–35, 171n5
Bedoya, Alfonso 114, 175n11
Beery, Noah, Jr. 15
Begley, Ed 73, 102
Bell, First Sgt. Emmett (*Pillars of the Sky*) 75–76
Bell, James 26, 170n14
Bellah, James Warner 10, 90
Bellamy, Ralph 138
Bellour, Raymond 19
Ben-Hur 170n10

Index

Bening, Annette 104–5
Bennett, Haley 138, 140
Benrubi, Abraham 104
Berdan, Bvt. Maj. Gen. Hiram 173n10
Berenger, Tom 71–72
Bergen, Polly 99
Bergman, Ingrid 70
Best, James D. 96
Bettger, Lyle 11–12
Bickford, Charles 114
Bierce, Ambrose 147–48, 165–66, 178n26
The Big Country (Wyler) 113–14
The Big Heat (Lang) 70, 169n7, 172n20
Bildungsroman 44, 128, 171n15
Billy Jack (Laughlin) 120
Bird Cage Theatre 108, 111
Birnbaum, Jake (*McClintock!*) 63–64, 103, 173n34
Bischoff, Peter 125
Bishop, William 53
Biskind, Peter 9, 21
Bissell, Whit 137
blacksmith 12, 29, 40, 47, 74, 82
Blaisedell, Clay (*Warlock*) 85
Blake, Amanda 74
Blanchett, Cate 125
Blocker, Capt. Joseph (*Hostiles*) 124–25
Blood on the Moon (Wise) 38
"The Blue Hotel" (Crane) 112–13
Boetticher, Budd 14, 16, 27, 43, 133
Bogart, Humphrey 98, 100, 175n11
Boggs, Johnny D. 90–91
Bogue, Bartholomew (*The Magnificent Seven* 2016) 140–41
Bolton, Oliver (*El gesticulador*) 165–66
Bond, Ward 75, 104
Bonell, Griff (*Forty Guns*) 46, 83
Bonham, Frank 126–27
Books, J.B. (*The Shootist*) 25, 28, 128
Boone, Doc (*Stagecoach*) 31, 39–43, 73, 171n14
Boone, Richard 28, 36
Borges, Jorge Luis 173n31, 176n9
Borgnine, Ernest 139
Bouchey, Willis 75
"Boule de Suif" (Maupassant) 42
Boxer Rebellion 148
Brando, Marlon 146
Braun, Matt 90–91
The Bravados (King) 68
Brennan, Walter 17

Brent, Eve 46
Brian, David 49
"The Bride Comes to Yellow Sky" (Crane) 112
Brighton, Dr. John (*The Oklahoman*) 28–29
Brimley, Wilford 89
Bring Me the Head of Alfredo Garcia (Peckinpah) 37
Brocious, Curly Bill 111
Brockie (*Forty Guns*) 46
Brodie, Steve 48
Broken Arrow (Daves) 12
Bronson, Charles 68
Brooke, Walter 105
Brooks, Bill 24–25; *Dakota Lawman: Killing Mr. Sunday* 25; *Dakota Lawman: Last Stand at Sweet Sorrow* 24–25
Brooks, Richard 6, 82, 138–39
Bryant, Bill 71
Brynner, Yul 69, 136
Buchanan, Edgar 17, 39
Buchanan Rides Alone 43, 169n7
Buenos Aires 61
Bumppo, Natty 33, 125
Buscombe, Edward 41, 100, 173n4, 174n19
Butler, David 10

Caine, Kwai-Chang 119–23, 176n9, 176n11
Calles, Plutarco Elías 149, 178n31
Callicut (*The Man Behind the Gun*) 76–77
Calvera (*The Magnificent Seven*) 136
Calvet, Corinne 17
Camp, Bill 124–25
Canadian Pacific (Marin) 32–33, 68
Cannon, J.D. 70
Capra, Frank 47
captivity narrative 76, 125–29, 138, 152
Capulet and Montagu 85
Cárdenas, Pres. Lázaro 165, 168
Carey, Harry, Jr. 90
Carey, Michele 9
Carey, Philip 77
The Cariboo Trail (Marin) 17
Carpenter, John 152
Carradine, David 45, 70, 77, 119–21
Carradine, John 51–53, 121
Carradine, Keith 45, 176n11

212

Index

Carradine, Robert 121
Carranza, Venustiano 146–47, 154–55, 177*n*17, 178*n*23
Carroll, Noël 131, 133
Carson City (De Toth) 34–36, 171*n*7
Caruso, Anthony 29
Casey, Bernie 138
Cassar, Jon 117, 175*n*5
Català, Víctor 162–63
Catholics 18, 44, 62
Catlin, George 124
Catton, Bruce 45
Cawelti, Jim 7, 129–30
Cervantes, Luis (*Los de abajo*) 142–46, 149, 160, 164, 166, 177*n*17, 178*n*19, 178*n*20
Cervantes, Miguel de 40, 80, 156, 160, 178*n*20
"Chac Mool" (Fuentes) 173*n*31
Chamberlain, Joshua Lawrence 11
Chandler, Jeff 11–12, 75
Chatillon, Henry 53
Chaucer, Geoffrey 40, 175*n*4
Cherokees 11, 28–29
Cheyennes 124–25
Chickamauga, battle of 81, 173*n*10
Chiricahuas 126
Chisum (McLaglen) 60–62, 64, 101
Chow, David 120
Churchill, Winston 49
Citizen Kane (Welles) 47, 158
civilización y barbarie 131, 152
Clantons (Tombstone, AZ) 30, 46, 92, 108, 110–11
Clark, Dane 98
Clavileño (*Don Quijote*) 157
Clayton, John Henry (*Forsaken*) 118–19
Cleef, Lee van 13
Cleveland, George 36
Cleveland, Pres. Grover 125
Clum, John 30, 170*n*1
Cobb, Lee J. 105
Cobb, Maj. Rufus (*Jesse James*) 55–56, 90, 172*n*28
Cochise 12
Code of the Samurai 135
Cody, Buffalo Bill 112
Cold War 39, 113
Cole, Tobias [Cameron Judd] 86–88; *see also* Judd, Cameron
Comanche 62, 64, 138
The Command (Butler) 10–11

Compton, Ralph 127
Confederates 10–11, 16, 45, 49, 56, 65, 67, 78–82, 84, 90, 119, 132–33, 138, 173*n*10
Connors, Chuck 114
The Conquerors (Wellman) 65
Conrad, Joseph 173*n*31
Constitutionalists (Mexico) 142, 154, 178*n*23
Cook, Elisha J., Jr. 85
Cooper, Gary 37–38, 41, 132–33
Cooper, Helen 158
Cooper, James Fenimore 33, 116, 125
Cooper, Scott 53, 124–25
Cop Land (Mangold) 14
Copper Canyon (Farrow) 90
Coppola, Francis Ford 115, 173*n*31
Cornered (Dmytryk) 98
Cornthwaite, Robert 33
Cosmatos, George 78, 108–9
Costner, Kevin 97, 104, 106
Cotten, Joseph 158
counterinsurgency 133
Covington, Rafe (sharpshooter) (*Crossfire Trail*) 89
Cox, Brian 118
Coy, Walter 75
Crain, Jeanne 94
Crane, Barry 123
Crane, Stephen 112–13; "The Blue Hotel" 112–13; "The Bride Comes to Yellow Sky" 112
Crawford, Broderick 95
Crawford, Joan 153
Criss Cross (Siodmak) 39
Crocker, Charles 34, 36, 171*n*7
Crossfire (Dmytryk) 17
Crossfire Trail (Wincer) 88–89
curro 142, 177*n*17
Curtiz, Michael 25–26
Custer, Gen. George Armstrong 55, 99, 126, 152, 171*n*11, 174*n*20

Dakota Lawman: Killing Mr. Sunday (Brooks) 25
Dakota Lawman: Last Stand at Sweet Sorrow 24–25 (Brooks)
Dancy, Steve 96–97
dandy 160
Danites 117
D'Annunzio, Gabriele 156
Darwinism 143

213

Index

Daves, Delmer 12, 37, 171n10
Day of the Jackal (Zinnemann) 129
Dead Reckoning (Cromwell) 98
Death Head Crossing (Reasoner) 94
De Carlo, Yvonne 39, 63
Decision at Sundown (Boetticher) 14, 16
"Declaration of Principles" (*Citizen Kane*) 158–59
La Decena Trágica 154–55, 179n39
De Havilland, Olivia 26
Dekker, Albert 48, 65, 101, 140
Delany, Dana 109
DeMille, Cecil B. 32
dentists 52, 110–11
Depression (1929) 56, 65, 83
The Derby Man (McCarthy) 172n19
derelict-professional 8
Des Esseintes (*A rebours*) 153, 159, 179n40
Destry Rides Again (Marshall) 23, 50, 172n26
De Toth, André 26, 34–36
De Troyes, Chrétien 158
Deuces Are Wild (Wheeler) 19, 22–23
Devereaux, Owen (*The Man from Colorado*) 16–17
Dexter, Brad 29
Díaz, Porfirio 33–34, 143, 160–61
Dierkes, John 53
Dieterle, William 170n11
Dietrich, Marlene 153
dime novel 87, 113, 167
Dimsdale, Washington (*Destry Rides Again*) 172n26
Dix, Richard 65
Dmytryk, Edward 17, 85
Doc Denton (*Legion of the Lawless*) 13–14
Dr. No (Young) 178n21
Dodge City 34, 48–49, 97, 109, 117, 175n8
Dodge City (Curtiz) 14, 25–26, 51
Dolworth (*The Professionals*) 138–39
Domergue, Faith 12
Don Quijote 80, 145, 156–58, 160
Doña Bárbara (Gallegos) 152–53, 179n35
Doña Perfecta (Galdós) 80
Doniphon, Tom (*The Man Who Shot Liberty Valance*) 8, 28, 58, 170n16
D'Onofrio, Vincent 138
Doohan, James 40

doppelgänger 49
Doucette, John 47
Douglas, Gordon 26–27
Douglas, Kirk 27, 110–11
Douglas, Paul 21
Dracula 137
Drew, Ellen 16
druggist, pharmacist 59, 80, 101–2, 106
dude (term) 114, 143–44
Duel in the Sun (King Vidor) 33
Duggan, Andrew 15
Dumas, Maurice (*Gunsights*) 92–93
Duryea, Dan 39
Duvall, Robert 104
Dwan, Allan 111

Earps 6, 28, 30, 46, 48, 97, 108–11, 124, 128, 136, 174ch3n14, 174ch4n8, 176n7
East, Easterner 6–10, 16, 18, 23, 28, 33, 36, 41, 43, 48, 50–52, 56–57, 60, 62–63, 65, 78, 92, 94, 96–97, 110, 112–14, 125, 127–29, 132, 145, 171n18, 172n19, 173n34
Eastwood, Clint 6, 70, 79, 87, 119, 129
Edwards, Ethan (*The Searchers*) 44, 100
Edwards, John Newman 55, 133, 172n27, 172n28, 177n5
Ehrengard (*The Professionals*) 138–39
Eickhoff, Randy Lee 117
Eidson, Thomas 125
El Dorado (Hawks) 9
Elliott, Alison 175n7
Ellis, Greg 118, 175n5
En el sendero de las mandrágoras (Ancona Albertos) 153–60, 179n36, 179n37, 179n38, 179n39, 179n40, 179n41, 179n42, 179n43
engineer, engineering 6, 23, 34–35, 39–40, 44, 98, 100, 120
Enright, Ray 48
Erickson, Leif 95
Estleman, Loren D. 111

The Far Country (Mann) 13, 17, 100–1
Fardan, Rico (*The Professionals*) 138–39
farmers 7–8, 18, 29, 41, 65, 73–75, 84, 89–90, 93, 118, 120–21, 134–36, 138
Farrow, John 90
The Fastest Gun Alive (Rouse) 94–96
The Fate (Wheeler) 19–20, 23–24
Feist, Felix 76
Final Girl (horror film motif) 152

Index

The Final Tally (Wheeler) 19, 21–23
Firecreek (McEveety) 102–3
Firefly 40–42
"First Principal" (Guthrie) 57–58
Fitzgerald, Barry 39
5 Card Stud (Hathaway) 66–67, 69, 79
Fix, Paul 9, 47
Flaubert, Gustave 80, 173*n*9
Fleischer, Richard 171*n*5
Fleming, Ian 174*n*5
Fly, C.S. 92–93, 109, 124, 126, 174*n*4
Flynn, Errol 26
Folsom, James K. 62, 72–73, 144
Fonda, Henry 12, 55, 75, 85, 100, 102, 148
Fonda, Jane 148
Fong, Benson 123, 176*n*9
Ford, John 6, 8–10, 16, 28, 31, 38–40, 42–43, 51, 54–55, 58, 60, 63, 78, 86–87, 90, 100, 110, 117, 128, 169*n*2, 170*n*16, 171*n*12, 171*n*14, 176*n*9; *Fort Apache* 75, 100; *The Horse Soldiers* 9–10; *The Man Who Shot Liberty Valance* 6, 8, 28, 31–32, 35, 38, 50, 54, 58, 80, 87, 171*n*12, 172*n*26; *McLintock!* 60, 62–64, 100, 103, 173*n*34; *My Darling Clementine* 6, 14, 78, 110, 128 *Rio Grande* 60; *Stagecoach* 31, 39, 41–43, 51, 63, 73, 86, 90, 117, 171*n*12, 171*n*14; *Young Mr. Lincoln* 55
Forrest, Gen. Nathan Bedford 45, 67
Forsaken (Cassar) 117–19
Fort Apache (Ford) 75, 100
Fort Pillow massacre 45
Fort Worth (Marin) 49
Forty Guns (Fuller) 46, 83, 153
Fox, Edward 129
Foy, Eddie 111, 174*n*7, 175*n*8
Frail, Dr. Joe (*The Hanging Tree*) 37–39, 41, 44, 171*n*10
France, Anatole 154, 179*n*38
Fredericksburg, battle of 84
Freeman, Mona 90
"Friends in San Rosario" 58–60
frontier 7–8, 10, 13–14, 20, 30, 46, 52–54, 56, 58, 62, 65, 72–73, 75–76, 78, 83, 87, 97, 100, 104, 106, 108, 111, 113, 117, 125, 131–32, 140, 144, 146–47, 168, 169Intro*n*1, 169*ch*1*n*5, 170*ch*1*n*13, 170*ch*2*n*1, 171*n*12, 172*n*26, 173*ch*2*n*36, 173*ch*3*n*3, 176*ch*5*n*10, 176*n*13, 176*ch*6*n*2

Frontier Fury (Henry) 75
Frye, Northrop 102, 112
Fuentes, Carlos 147, 150–51, 173*n*31, 178*n*25, 178*n*27, 179*n*32; *Gringo viejo* 28, 128, 147–48, 178*n*25, 178*n*27
Fuller, Samuel 10, 46, 83, 153
Fuqua, Antoine 138, 140
Futterman, Jerem (*The Searchers*) 100, 176*n*9

Galdós, Benito Pérez 80
Gallegos, Rómulo 152–53
gambling 19, 22, 47, 52, 66, 85, 98, 100, 108, 113, 121, 145
Gambon, Michael 104
Ganivet, Ángel 174*n*18
Gannon (*The Far Country*) 17, 100–101
Garcia-Rulfo, Manuel 138
Garrett, Pat 60–61
Garson, Greer 18
Garth, Dr. Julia Winslow (*Strange Lady in Town*) 18–20, 170*n*8
Gatewood (*Stagecoach*) 41, 63
Gautier, Cecille (*Canadian Pacific*) 32–33
Gautier, Théophile 163–64
Geer, Will 67, 121
Geronimo: An American Legend (Hill) 124
El gesticulador (Usigli) 69–70, 162–63, 165–68
Gettysburg, battle of 11, 81
Gilbert and Sullivan 109
Gilda (Charles Vidor) 70
Gilded Age 62, 97
Gillom (*The Shootist*) 25
Gilmore, Virginia 51
Glau, Summer 41
Going, Joanna 109
Goldwater, Sen. Barry 64
Gómez, Juan Vicente 152
Grafton, Sam (*Shane*) 101, 103, 141
The Great Sioux Uprising (Bacon) 11–12
Greeley, Horace 50, 80, 171*n*17
"The Green Moustache" (Bonham) 126–27
Greenleaf, Raymond 16
Gregory, James 46
Grey, Zane 53, 115
Griffith, James 71
Gringo viejo (Fuentes) 28, 128, 147–48, 178*n*25, 178*n*27

215

Index

Gruber, Frank 39, 171n11
Gulager, Clu 122
The Gunfight at Dodge City (Newman) 48
Gunfight at the O.K. Corral (Sturges) 110–11, 175n8
The Gunfighter (King) 106–7
Guns for San Sebastian (Verneuil) 68–69
Guns of the Magnificent Seven (Wendkos) 138, 171n18
Gunsights (Leonard) 92–93
gunsmith 44–47, 96
Gunsmoke 74
Guthrie, A.B., Jr. 57–58, 172n29
Guzmán, Martín Luis 5, 149–53, 179n34
Gyurko, Lanin 149–51, 178n25

Hadleyville (*High Noon*) 95
Hale, Alan, Jr. 74, 77
Hale, Barbara 29
Hale, Richard 76
Hallie (*The Man Who Shot Liberty Valance*) 38
Halloween (Carpenter) 152
Hamilton, John 32
Hampden, Walter 18
The Hanging Tree (Daves) 37–39, 63
Hannasseys, Terrills (*The Big Country*) 113–14
Haraldson, Harald 47
Hardin, John Wesley 118
Harding, Ann 65
Hare, Lumsden 53
Harmon, Mark 89
Harold, Vinnie (*The Fastest Gun Alive*) 95
Harrigan (*The Wild Bunch*) 139–40
Harris, Neal (*The Oregon Trail*) 52–54
Harris, Stacy S. 12
Harrison, Pres. Benjamin 124–25
Haskin, Byron 39, 98; *Silver City* 39; *Warpath* 98–99
Hastings, Morgan (gunsmith) (*The Sons of Katie Elder*) 46–47
Hathaway, Henry 44, 46, 66; *The Sons of Katie Elder* 46–47, 56
Hawke, Mason 77–86, 88, 173n7
Hawke: Ride with the Devil (Vaughan) 81–82, 173n7
Hawke: Showdown at Dead End Canyon (Vaughan) 82–84, 173n7

Hawke: The King Hill War (Vaughan) 84–85, 173n7
Hawke: The Law of a Fast Gun (Vaughan) 77–80, 173n7
Hawke: Vendetta Trail (Vaughan) 78, 173n7
Hawks, Howard 9, 33
Haycox, Ernest 43, 56–57
Hayden, Sterling 77
Hayes, George "Gabby" 54
Heaven with a Gun (Katzin) 70–71, 119–20
Heaven's Gate (Cimino) 93
Heflin, Freddie (*Cop Land*) 14
Heflin, Van 93
Henry, Will 75
Hernandez, Juano 73
Hershey, Barbara 70
Heston, Charlton 113
Heyes, Herbert 26
Heywood, Herbert 13
Hibbs, Jesse 170n1
Hickman, Howard 103
Hickok, Wild Bill 57
High Noon (Zinnemann) 68, 95, 129, 131–32
"High Wind" (Haycox) 56–57
Hill, Walter 124
Hippocratic Oath 21, 25
Hobbes, Halliwell 170n11
Hoffman, Dustin 87
Holden, Pastor Joseph (*Pillars of the Sky*) 75–76
Holden, William 9–10, 16, 41, 139
Holliday, Dr. John "Doc" 8, 43, 52, 92, 108, 110–11, 113, 128, 145, 174n6, 175n9
Holliman, Earl 47
Hollywood 5, 19, 32, 39, 45, 55–56, 89, 100, 120, 133, 172n20, 178n22
Holt, Greyston 71
Homais (*Madame Bovary*) 80, 173n9
Homans, Peter (Western "types") 7–9
Homeier, Skip 36
homesteaders 8, 48, 55, 72, 93, 103–4, 136
Hong, James 120
Hooper, Tobe 152
Hopkins, Bo 140
Hopper, Dennis 47
Hostetler, Dr. (*The Shootist*) 28
Hostiles (Cooper) 124–25

216

Index

Houde, Serge 72
Hour of the Gun (Sturges) 110
Howard, David 103
Howard, Ron 25, 125
Huang Fei-hong (Wong Fei Hung) 148, 178n30
Hubley, Season 122
Huerta, Adolfo de la 149
Huerta, Victoriano 139, 146–47, 153–56, 159, 162
Hughes, Tony 17
Hull, Henry 53, 55, 90
Humberstone, Bruce 36
Hunnicutt, Arthur 73
Hunter, Evan 27
Hunter, Stephen 170n16
Huston, John 29, 175n11
Huysmans, Joris-Karl 153, 179n40; see also À rebours
Hyselman (undertaker) (*The Sons of Katie Elder*) 47

iconography 72–73, 90, 141, 173n4, 177n14, 177n15
Idearium español (Ganivet) 174n18
In Old California (McGann) 101–2
Incident at Fort Keogh (Wheeler) 19–21
Indian agent 62, 100, 170n1
Indians 11–12, 18, 32–33, 44, 50–53, 62, 64, 68, 70, 75, 99–100, 115–16, 120–21, 123–24, 127, 137, 152, 169n3, 170n1, 176n10, 176n12
"El inmortal" (Borges) 176n9
L'Innocente (D'Annunzio) 156
Irish 19–21, 34, 39, 41, 63, 104, 112
Ives, Burl 113

Jaffe, Sam 69
Jagger, Dean 46, 51, 99, 102, 116, 174n16
Jake (*The Professionals*) 82, 138
James, Jesse 55, 90, 104, 124, 133, 138, 140, 172n28
Japan, Japanese 85–86, 121, 134–35, 137, 158, 171n18, 177n8
Jarnac, Marcel (*Cornered*) 98
Jeffords, Tom 12
Jeffreys, Anne 48
Jerome, Arizona 174n2
Jesse James (King) 55
Jesse James films 55, 90, 124, 138, 140, 172n28
Jeter, Michael 104

Jews 62–65, 109, 120, 176n9
John War Eagle 12
Johnny Guitar (Ray) 77–78, 153
Johnson, Ben 103
Johnson, Brad 89
Johnson, Dorothy M. 37, 127
Johnson, July (*Bandolero!*) 67–68
Jones, Carolyn 71
Jones, Dick 50
Jones, Serenity (*Kung Fu*) 121
Jones, Tommy Lee 125
Jory, Victor 17, 32
Judd, Cameron 86–87, 90; *The Quest of Brady Kenton* 90–92; *Sharpshooter: Brimstone* 87–88; *Sharpshooter: Gold Fever* 88; *Sharpshooter: Repentance Creek* 86–87

Kambei (*Seven Samurai*) 136, 177n9
Kamiakin (*Pillars of the Sky*) 75–76
Kane, Joseph 56
Kane, Will (*High Noon*) 95
Kansas Pacific (Nazarro) 32, 140
Karlson, Phil 13
Kasdan, Lawrence 83, 97, 108–9, 111, 174n14, 175n7
Katsu Shintaro 86
Kaylee (*Firefly*) 40, 42
Kazan, Elia 10, 21, 146–47
Keating, Larry 34
Keitel, Harvey 14
Keith, Brian 44
Kellogg, Mark 152, 179n33
Kendall, Cy 103
Kennedy, Arthur 44
Kennedy, George 47, 67
Kennedy, Pres. John Fitzgerald 20–21, 105, 134
Kenton, Brady 90–92
Kikuchiyo (*Seven Samurai*) 136
"The Killing at Triple Tree" (Hunter) 27
Kilmer, Val 110
King, Henry 106, 172n28
King of the Pecos (Kane)
kirisute-gomen, 135
Kitano Takeshi 86
Kitses, Jim 13, 105
Kitty (*Gunsmoke*) 74
"Knight thesis," "Lyon thesis" 30
Krauze, Enrique 178n27
Kruschen, Jack 63–64, 100, 103
Ku Klux Klan 73–75

217

Index

Kuhne, Louis 159
Kung Fu 77, 119–23, 176*n*9, 176*n*11
Kurosawa Akira 134–37, 158, 171*n*18, 175*n*6, 177*n*9

Lacomb, Père 32–33
Ladd, Alan 176*n*10
Lamarr, Hedy 90
Lambert, Jack 73
Lancaster, Burt 39, 105, 132, 138
Landau, Martin 44
Lang, Fritz 50, 52, 55, 63, 70, 153, 169Intro*n*2, 169*ch*1*n*7, 172*n*20, 172*n*21, 172*n*28
Lang, Stephen 124
Lassiter, Karl 37
The Last Frontier (Mann) 76
The Last Manhunt (West) 92, 127–30
Last of the Mohicans 125
Last Stand at Saber River (Lowry) 45–46
Last Train from Gun Hill (Sturges) 27
Latham, Louise 116
Laughlin, Tom 120
Laughton, Charles 66
Lawman (Winner) 31, 105
Leadville, Colorado 77, 91, 108, 177*n*12
LeMat revolver 119
Leonard, Elmore 45, 92–93
Leone, Sergio 102
LeRoy, Mervyn 17
Levi, Primo 138
Levin, Henry 16
Li, Jet 148
Lincoln, Pres. Abraham 20, 55, 99
Lincoln County War 60–61, 83
Lister, Dr. Joseph 18, 20, 22, 170*n*8, 170*n*9, 170*n*11
Little Big Horn (Warren) 75
Little Big Man (Penn) 87
Litvak, Anatole 70
Live and Let Die (Fleming) 174*n*5
Lloyd, Kathleen 122
Lonesome Dove Church (Miles) 71–72
Loomis, Noel M. 33–34, 138
"Lorena" 82
Los de abajo (Azuela) 5, 141, 144–45, 160, 164, 177*n*16, 178*n*19 *see also* Azuela, Mariano
Louvenia (*Forty Guns*) 46
Lowery, Robert 62
Luna, Diego 104

Lyon, Francis D. 28
Lyon, W.H. 30

MacLane, Barton 50
MacMurray, Fred 52
MacRae, Gordon 98
Madame Bovary (Flaubert) 80, 173*n*9
Madero, Francisco 139, 147, 153–55, 159–63
Madigan, Amy 115
Madison, Guy 10
Madsen, Virginia 89
Mafia 78, 173*n*8
The Magnificent Seven (Fuqua, 2016) 138, 140–41, 171*n*18
The Magnificent Seven (Sturges, 1960) 68, 105, 131–32, 134–38, 171*n*18, 177*n*7
Malden, Karl 37, 44
Malone, Dorothy 75–76
Mamakos, Peter 100
The Man Behind the Gun (Feist) 76–77
The Man from Colorado (Levin) 16–17
The Man Who Shot Liberty Valance 6, 8, 28, 31–32, 35, 38, 50, 54, 58, 80, 87, 171*n*12, 172*n*26
Mañach, Jorge 151
Mandan 24
Mangold, James 14
Mann, Anthony 12–13, 17, 26, 38, 100, 133; *The Far Country* 13, 17, 100–1; *The Last Frontier* 76; *The Tin Star* 12–13, 16, 51; *Winchester '73* 13, 100
Mann, Horace 176*n*2
Mapache (*The Wild Bunch*) 69, 139, 177*n*12
Maragon, Julie (*The Big Country*) 113–14
Marcus, Josephine (Sadie, Josie) 109, 111, 124
Marin, Edwin L. 17, 32, 49–50, 171*n*16
"Mark and Bill" (Estleman) 111–12
Marnie (Hitchcock) 116
Marshall, George 75, 172*n*26
Martin, Dean 47, 67
Martin, Strother 62
Martínez Estrada, Ezequiel 151
Marvin, Lee 8, 31, 138
Massey, Raymond 34
Masterson, Ed 97, 174*n*14
Masterson, William "Bat" 48–49, 136
Maté, Rudolph 16
Matthews, Lester 36
Mature, Victor 110, 174*n*5
Maunder, Wayne 120

218

Index

Maupassant, Guy de 42, 154, 173*n*31
Maximilian (Mexico) 133, 167
McCarthy, Gary 172*n*19
McCord, Doc (*The Tin Star*) 12–14, 26, 41
McCrea, Joel 28, 72–73
McEveety, Vincent 102–3
McGann, William 101
McIntire, John 12, 17, 41, 100
McKay, Jim (*The Big Country*) 113–14
McKinnon, Ray 125
McLaglen, Andrew V. 66, 132–33; *Bandolero!* 66–68; *Chisum* 60–62, 64, 101; *The Undefeated* 132–33
McQueen, Steve 44, 136
McSween, Alexander 60–61
McVey, Paul 103
Meek, Donald 42
Meiji Restoration 135
melodrama 35, 39, 91–92, 94, 140
Métis 32–33
Meyer, Emile 93, 103
Mifune Toshiro 136, 158
Miles, Terry 71
Milland, Ray 90
mining 17, 23, 30, 34–37, 39, 65, 72–73, 77, 90–91, 93, 96–97, 100, 102, 108, 120, 126, 140, 172*n*22, 174*n*4
miscegenation 54, 170*n*3
The Missing (Ron Howard) 125–26, 129
Mitchell, Cameron 19
Mitchell, Charles 73
Mitchell, Millard 107
Mitchell, Thomas 39, 41, 51
Mitchum, Robert 66, 79
Mizoguchi Kenji 154
Moffatt, Larkin (mining engineer) (*Silver City*) 39
Monroe Doctrine 133
Mormons 71, 115, 117
Mowbray, Alan 110
Muni, Paul 170*n*11
Munny, Will (*Unforgiven*) 129
Murphy, Audie 72, 170*n*1
musha-shugyō (Zen) 158
My Darling Clementine (Ford) 6, 14, 78, 110, 128

The Narrow Margin (Fleischer) 171*n*5
Nausea (*La nausée*) 159
Neal, Patricia 122
Neilson, James 140

Nevada Smith 44–46, 48, 68, 120
New Deal 49, 65
New Orleans 62, 78, 119, 173*n*8
Nichols, Dudley 40, 54
Nietzsche, Friedrich 153, 162
Night of the Hunter (Laughton) 66
Night Passage (Neilson) 98, 140
Noçon, Peter 125
noir 38–39, 98, 110, 116, 171*n*10, 172*n*20
Norman, Lucille 35
North, Sheree 121
Northfield, MN (James raid) 124, 139
Nyby, Christian 33

O. Henry 58–60, 81
O'Brian, Hugh 28
Obregón, Gen. (and Pres.) Alvaro 147, 149–50, 178*n*23
O'Brien, Dr. Rourke (*Strange Lady in Town*) 18–19
O'Brien, Edmond 31, 39, 50, 87, 98
O'Brien, George 13, 103
Oglala 11, 53
The Oklahoman (Lyon) 28–29
Old Gringo (film) 147–48
Olson, Nancy 32
omissio (rhetorical device) 111
Once Upon a Time in the West (Leone) 102
Only the Valiant (Douglas) 26–27, 75
The Oregon Trail (Fowler) 52–54
Orozco, José Clemente 151
The Outlaw Josey Wales (Eastwood) 79
The Ox-Bow Incident (Wellman) 27
oyabun (boss, yakuza) 86

Paine, Lauran 104
Palance, Jack 83, 138
Pale Rider (Eastwood) 28, 70, 117
Palouses 75–76
pampa 151
Panic in the Streets (Kazan) 10, 21
Panza, Sancho (*Don Quijote*) 145, 157
Parker, Jean 107
Parkman, Francis 52–53, 172*n*24
Parnassian poets 163
Pasteur, Louis 20, 22, 170*n*11
pastoral 6–7, 9
Pate, Michael 29
Pawley, Martin (*The Searchers*) 44
Payton, Barbara 27, 170*n*15
Peabody, Dutton (*The Man Who Shot*

Index

Liberty Valance) 31, 35, 50, 55, 80, 87, 172*n*26
Peck, Gregory 26, 95, 106, 113, 148
Peckinpah, Sam 37, 139
Penn, Arthur 87
Perkins, Anthony 12
Perry Mason 169*n*4, 170*n*14, 171*n*5, 173*n*2, 178*n*22
The Persuader (Ross) 70, 119
The Phenix City Story (Karlson) 13
photographers 92–93, 109, 123–26, 174*n*4, 176*n*13
phrenology 37, 171*n*8
pianists 77–78, 80–81, 83, 85, 121
"The Piano Man" (Vaughan) 80–81
Piazza, Ben 37
picaresque 37, 127
Pillars of the Sky (Marshall) 75
Pinkertons 96–98, 174*n*15
Pleshette, Suzanne 44
Poe, Edgar Allan 163
Polk, Pres. James K. 53, 172*n*23
polygamy 115–16
Powell, Dick 98
Powers, Stefanie 63
Prine, Andrew 60
The Professionals (Brooks) 5–6, 82, 131–32, 137–39, 141
Progressivism 65
Pullman, Bill 97
Pursued (Walsh) 38, 116, 174*n*16
Pye, Douglas 8, 114, 170*n*3

Quade, Sam (*Warpath*) 99–100
Quaid, Dennis 110
Quantrill, William Clarke 67, 78–79, 81
The Quest of Brady Kenton (Judd) 90–92
Quevedo y Zubieta, Salvador 155
Quijano, Alonso (*Don Quijote*) 156, 160
Quinn, Anthony 68, 85, 146

Radiografía de la pampa (Martínez Estrada) 151
railroads 14, 32–36, 41, 49–51, 58, 65, 68, 83, 98, 120, 138–40, 171*n*4, 171*n*7, 177*n*10
Ramos, Samuel 151
ranch, ranchers 5, 12, 15–16, 18, 29, 36, 43, 45, 48–50, 54–56, 59–62, 70–71, 79, 83–85, 87, 89–90, 93–94, 101, 103–5, 113–14, 116, 131, 153, 171*n*11
Rancho Notorious (Lang) 153
Ranown 14–15, 43
Ray, Nicholas 153
Raymond, Guy 67
Raza, Jesus (*The Professionals*) 82, 138–39
Reasoner, James 94
Reconstruction 75, 82, 90
Red Cloud 11–12, 76
Red Sun (Young) 131
regionalist 5, 131, 152
Reid, Carl Benton 10, 169*n*4
"Requiem for Methuselah" (*Star Trek*) 176*n*9
The Return of Frank James (Lang) 55, 63
"Return of the Archons" (*Star Trek*) 116–17
Return of the Magnificent Seven (Kennedy) 69, 171*n*18
Reyes, Toño (*Andrés Pérez, maderista*) 160, 162
Richards, Addison 53
Ride Lonesome (Boetticher) 27
Riders of the Purple Sage (Haid) 73, 115, 117
Riding Shotgun (De Toth) 26, 28
Riel, Louis 32
Rincon Mountain War 92–93
Ringo, Jimmy (*The Gunfighter*) 40, 106–7
Ringo, Johnny (*Tombstone*) 111
Ringo Kid (*Stagecoach*) 40, 42–44, 90
Rio Grande (Ford) 60
Rivera, Diego 151, 179*n*32
Robards, Jason 110
Robinson, Edward G. 16
Rocinante (*Don Quijote*) 157, 160
Rogers, Anthony 9
ronin 134–36, 158, 170*n*42
Roosevelt, Pres. Franklin D. 56, 65, 168
Roosevelt, Pres. Theodore 112
Roquentin (*La nauseé*) 159
Rosas, Juan Manuel 61
Rouse, Russell 94
Rubinek, Saul 87
Rubio, César (*El gesticulador*) 165–67
Russo, James 104
Rutherford, Ann 54
Ryan, Robert 17, 48, 138, 140
Ryker (*Shane*) 8, 84, 93, 101, 103, 169*n*1

Index

saloons 18, 48, 70–71, 73, 77–80, 83, 89–90, 95, 100–101, 103, 107, 113, 119, 121, 141
Samurai, *Seven Samurai* (Kurosawa) 105, 134–36, 154, 158, 171*n*18, 177*n*6, 177*n*7, 177*n*9, 179*n*42
San Francisco 78, 90, 97, 102, 109
Sand, Max (*Nevada Smith*) 44–45
Santa Fe (Pichel) 56
Santis, Joe De 139
Santoni, Reni 138
Santos Luzardo (*Doña Bárbara*) 152–53
Sarmiento, Domingo Faustino 61–62, 131, 176*n*2
Sarsgaard, Peter 140
Sartre, Jean-Paul 159
Saskatchewan (Walsh) 176*n*10
Schaefer, Jack 118, 175*n*6
Schatz, Thomas 131–32
Schell, Maria 37
schoolteachers, schoolmarms 6–8, 12, 18, 25, 38, 74–77, 81, 106–7, 113–14, 176*n*2
Schweig, Eric 126
Scorpion 40
Scott, George C. 38
Scott, Maxwell (*The Man Who Shot Liberty Valance*) 31, 58, 170*n*2
Scott, Randolph
Scott, Sir Walter 113, 175*n*9
Scotty (*Star Trek*) 40
The Searchers (Ford) 44, 82, 89, 100, 170*n*3, 176*n*9
Selleck, Tom 45, 89–90
Sensmeier, Martin 138
Serdán, Aquiles 161–62
Serenity (Whedon) 40–43
Serra, Inara (*Firefly*) 43
Serrano, Gen. Francisco R. 149
Seyrig, Delphine 129
Shakespeare 31–32, 42, 78, 108–11
Shane (Stevens) 8–9, 70, 83–85, 89, 93, 101, 103, 118, 120, 136, 141, 169*n*1, 175*n*6
Shaolin 119–23, 176*n*8, 178*n*30
Sharon, William (*Carson City*) 34–36
Sharpshooter: Brimstone (Judd) 87–88
Sharpshooter: Gold Fever (Judd) 88
Sharpshooter: Repentance Creek (Judd) 86–87
sheepherders 70–71, 84–85
Shelby, Gen. Jo 133, 172*n*28, 177*n*5
Sheriff Cobb (*Firecreek*) 102

Sherman, Vincent 98
Shiloh, battle of 119
Shimura Takashi 136, 177*n*9
Shinbone (*The Man Who Shot Liberty Valance*) 8, 31, 55, 58, 80, 148
Shipman, Nina 53
The Shootist (Siegel) 25, 28, 128
The Shopkeeper (Best) 96–97
Siegel, Don 25, 28
Sierra, Gregory 121
Silver City (Haskin) 39
Silvera, Frank 146, 178*n*22
Silverado (Kasdan) 83
Silverheels, Jay 170*n*10
Simmons, Jean 113
Siodmak, Robert 39
Sioux 11–12, 21, 52–53, 99, 170*n*13
Siqueiros, David Alfaro 151
Slotkin, Richard 14, 33, 133–34, 137–38, 142, 176*n*10, 177*n*7
Solís, Alberto (*Los de abajo*) 142, 145, 164, 166
La sombra del caudillo (Guzmán) 5, 149–53, 179*n*34
The Sons of Katie Elder (Hathaway) 46–47, 56
Soule, John Babsone 171*n*17
South, Southerner 10, 46, 54, 59, 62, 72–73, 75, 78, 81–82, 84, 90, 119, 132, 137, 175*n*9, 177*n*7
Special Forces 134, 137, 177*n*10
spiritism 153, 159
The Spoilers (Enright) 100
Spradlin, G.D. 115
Staite, Jewel 40
Stallone, Sylvester 14
Stand Watie 11
Stanwyck, Barbara 46, 83, 153
Star Trek 40, 116–17, 173*n*2, 176*n*9
Stark, Molly (*The Virginian*) 106, 113
Starretts (*Shane*) 8, 84, 93, 103, 118, 175*n*6
Stars in My Crown (Tourneur) 70, 72
Station West (Lanfield) 98
Steele, Karen 15
Stevens, George 85, 93, 118
Stewart, James 12, 17, 23, 28, 38, 50, 66–67, 98, 100, 102, 172*n*26
Stockwell, Dean 73
Stoddard, Ransom (*The Man Who Shot Liberty Valance*) 8, 13, 28, 31, 38, 58, 148, 172*n*26

221

Index

Stoker, Bram 173*n*31
Stone, Lewis 73
The Story of Louis Pasteur (Dieterle) 170*n*11
Strange Lady in Town (LeRoy) 17–20
Strode, Woody 82, 138
Strong, Leonard 136
Studi, Wes 124
Sturges, John 31, 121, 134–37, 174*n*16, 177*n*7; *Bad Day at Black Rock* 31, 121, 174*n*16; *Gunfight at the O.K. Corral* 110–11, 174*n*8; *Hour of the Gun* 110; *The Magnificent Seven* 68, 105, 131–32, 134–38, 171*n*18, 177*n*7
Sturmabteilung (SA) 49
Suárez, Pino 139, 155, 161
Sullivan, Barry 46, 48, 83, 120
Summerville, Slim 51
Sun Yat-sen 148–49
surveyors 14, 32, 51–52
Sutherland, Donald 117, 175*n*5
Sutherland, Kiefer 117, 175*n*5
Swenson, Karl 37, 47

Tabor, Horace 91
Tada Michitaro 134–135, 171*n*18
Talbott, Gloria 29, 53
Talman, William 119
Tam, Dr. Simon (*Firefly*) 40–42
Tanner, Stephen L. 19
Tarawa (Bloody Beach) 122
Taylor, Vaughn 15
Teal, Ray 11, 15, 49
Tefertiller, Casey 30, 109, 174*n*8
Telotte, J.P. 43
Ten Wanted Men (Humberstone) 36
tenderfoot 23, 50, 60, 96, 113, 172*n*18, 172*n*19
The Texas Chainsaw Massacre (Hooper) 152
Thaxter, Phyllis 49
The Thing from Another World (Nyby) 33
Thompson, Marshall 74
Tierney, Gene 63
The Tin Star (Mann) 12–13, 16, 51
Tokugawa Shogunate 85, 134–35
Toland, Jeff (*Legion of the Lawless*) 13–14
Tombstone (Cosmatos) 78, 108–11, 124
Tombstone, Arizona 30–31, 46, 78, 92–93, 108–11, 124, 136, 170*n*1, 174*n*2, 175*n*8

Tonto (*Stagecoach*) 39, 41–42
Toole, Santiago 19–25
Torrey (*Shane*) 85
"Tough *Hombre*" 33–34
Tourneur, Jacques 70, 72–73
Townes, Harry 71, 173*n*2
Tracy, Spencer 89, 121
Trail Street (Enright) 48
Travers, Henry 25–26
The Treasure of the Sierra Madre (Huston) 175*n*11
Trevor, Claire 40, 48, 65
Trouble in Sundown (Howard) 103–4
Tsui Hark 148–49, 178*n*30
tuberculosis 21–22, 110
Tucker, Forrest 60, 99
Tunstall, John H. 36, 61, 83
Turner, Frederick Jackson 132
Turner, Gentleman Dave (*Forsaken*) 119
Turner Entertainment 45
Twain, Mark 20, 112, 175*n*9
Two Mules for Sister Sara (Eastwood) 68

Ugetsu Monogatari (Mizoguchi) 154
Unamuno, Miguel de 170*n*1
The Undefeated (McLaglen) 132–33
undertakers 25, 47, 81, 121, 128, 137
Unforgiven (Eastwood) 6, 87, 119, 129
The Unforgiven (Huston) 29
Union Pacific (DeMille) 32, 140
Unionism 56, 90, 168
unitarios (Argentina) 31, 61
Urich, Robert 122
Usigli, Rodolfo 69, 162–63, 165–68
Utley, Robert M. 36, 61, 75–76

"The Vacant Chair" 47
Valderrama (*Los de abajo*) 142, 145–46
Vale, Virginia 14
Vallone, Raf 45
Vaughan, Robert 77–85, 173*n*10; *Hawke: Ride with the Devil* 81–82, 173*n*7; *Hawke: The King Hill War* 84–85, 173*n*7; *Hawke: The Law of a Fast Gun* 77–80, 173*n*7
Vera Cruz (Aldrich) 131–33, 137
Verneuil, Henri 68
veterans 15–17, 39, 45, 67, 70, 81–82, 84, 88–90, 98–99, 118, 135, 138
veterinarians 6–7, 11–12
Vidor, Charles 70
Vietnam 45, 68, 120, 131, 134, 137

Index

Villa, Pancho 138–39, 141, 143, 147, 155, 165, 177*n*11, 177*n*13, 177*n*15, 178*n*27
The Violent Men (Maté) 16
The Virginian (Wister) 50, 105–6, 113
Viva Zapata! (Kazan) 146–47; *see also* Zapata, Emiliano

Walesburg (*Stars in My Crown*) 72–73
Walk the Proud Land (Hibbs) 170*n*1
Wallace, Gov. Lew 19, 170*n*10
Wallawallas 75
Waller, Eddy 13
Walsh, Raoul 38, 174*n*16, 176*n*10
Wandering Jew 120, 176*n*9
"The War Shirt" (Johnson) 127
Warpath (Haskin) 98–99
Warren, Charles Marquis 75
Washington, Denzel 138, 140
Waverley (Scott) 170*n*8
Wayne, John 8–9, 28, 31, 40, 47, 54, 56, 60, 62–63, 65, 100–101, 170*n*16, 173*n*33
Wayne, Patrick 63
Welch, Raquel 67
Weldon, Joan 11
Welles, Orson 158–59
Wellman, William A. 27, 65
Wendkos, Paul 138
West, Joseph A. 127
Westbound (Boetticher) 98
Western Union (Lang) 50–52, 172*n*20
Westgate, Dr. Jonathan (*The Great Sioux Uprising*) 11–12
Wharton, Edith 147
Whedon, Joss 40, 43
Wheeler, Richard S. 19–24, 117; *Deuces Are Wild* 19, 22–23; *The Fate* 19–20, 23–24; *The Final Tally* 19, 21–23; *Incident at Fort Keogh* 19–21
Whispering Smith (Fenton) 140
Whitmore, James 10
Whitney, Peter 12, 169*n*7
Whitworth rifle (CSA) 79–80, 173*n*10
Widmark, Richard 21
The Wild Bunch (Peckinpah) 5, 69, 131, 139–40

Wilde, Oscar 77, 91
Wilder, Billy 69
Williams, Bill 17
Willis, Norman 13
Wills, Chill 60
Wilson (*Shane*) 83–85
Wilson, Pres. Woodrow 140
Winchester '73 (Mann) 13, 100
Wincott, Michael 119, 175*n*5
Windsor, Marie 173*n*20
Winner, Michael 31, 105
Winningham, Mare 109
Winslow, Harriet 147–48
Wise, Robert 38
Wiseman, Joseph 146, 178*n*21
Wister, Owen 50, 65, 112–13, 144, 171*n*18
Withers, Grant 100
Wittier (*Firecreek*) 102–3
Wood, Evan Rachel 125
Woods, Harry 54
Wyatt, Jane 32
Wyatt Earp (Kasdan) 97, 108–11, 124, 175*n*7
Wyler, William 113
Wymore, Patrice 76
Wynant, H.M. 15

Yakimas 75
yakuza 85–86
Yaquis 68–69
Yojimbo (Kurosawa) 158, 179*n*42
Young, Carleton 31
Young, Robert 17, 50
Young, Terence 131
Young Mr. Lincoln (Ford) 55

Zahara, Alex 72
Zane, Billy 111
Zapata, Emiliano; Zapatista 146–47, 155, 177*n*11, 178*n*24, 178*n*27; *see also Viva Zapata!*
Zatoichi 85–86
Zen 158, 179*n*42
Zinnemann, Fred 129

www.ingramcontent.com/pod-product-compliance
Lightning Source LLC
Chambersburg PA
CBHW032052300426
44116CB00007B/700